The People's Peace Process in Northern Ireland

The People's Peace Process in Northern Ireland

Colin Irwin
Centre for the Study of Ethnic Conflict
School of Politics
Queen's University Belfast

First published 2002 by
PALGRAVE MACMILLAN
Houndmills, Basingstoke, Hampshire RG21 6XS and
175 Fifth Avenue, New York, N.Y. 10010
Companies and representatives throughout the world

PALGRAVE MACMILLAN is the new global academic imprint of the Palgrave
Macmillan division of St. Martin's Press, LLC and of Palgrave Macmillan Ltd.
Macmillan® is a registered trademark in the United States, United Kingdom and
other countries. Palgrave is a registered trademark in the European Union and
other countries.

ISBN 0–333–96248–6

This book is printed on paper suitable for recycling and made from fully
managed and sustained forest sources.

A catalogue record for this book is available from the British Library.

Library of Congress Cataloging-in-Publication Data

Irwin, Colin, 1946–
   The people's peace process in Northern Ireland/Colin Irwin
      p. cm.
   Includes bibliographical references and index.
   ISBN 0–333–96248–6
      1. Northern Ireland – History. 2. Northern Ireland – Social conditions.
   3. Peace movements – Northern Ireland – Citizen participation. I. Title.

DA990.U45 I79 2002
941.6–dc21   2002025102

10   9   8   7   6   5   4   3   2   1
11   10   09   08   07   06   05   04   03   02

Printed and bound in Great Britain by
Antony Rowe Ltd, Chippenham, Wiltshire

To all the victims of discrimination, exploitation, wilful neglect and violence upon whose suffering the Nunavut Settlement and Belfast Agreement have been built

Contents

List of Figures

List of Tables

Preface

Like so many of my generation of '1960s postwar baby-boomers' I wanted to save the world. This admirable desire is something I should have normally come to terms with, just forgotten about or simply got over, like the, 'flu. But a couple of events encouraged me to persist with this enterprise beyond the years of my youth. Firstly, and this is arguably the foundation upon which the Northern Ireland peace process and the thesis of this book is built, I was confronted with the fact that most people, most of the time, are very nice. They do not want to kill or fight in wars and they do not want to lose their sons or even to see them brutalised by violence, hatred and death. Most people, most of the time, want peace and all the economic and social benefits that flow from it. This reality is something I was exposed to in 1968 in Israel when I was working as a diving instructor at the Red Sea coastal resort of Eilat and, more particularly, when I rode around the country on the buses and had an opportunity to spend some time in Jerusalem. This was just after the 1967 war.

At that time it seemed very plausible to me that all that had to be done was to make this fact known and a rational world would then surely make the appropriate rational decisions to put matters in their correct order and the world would then be 'saved'. With this very simple objective in mind I put an equally simple plan into action. I set sail for the North West Passage, single handed, under the flag of the United Nations.[1] Fortunately for me I was not then encumbered by the disadvantages of a good education particularly with regard to questions of human nature, history, politics and the like.

But in the Arctic I discovered the second truth upon which this book and my work on the Northern Ireland peace process was to be built. I was adopted into an Inuit family and as luck would have it the Inuit were one of the very few peoples in the world who had developed a culture that does not include that most deadly of human behaviours – war.[2] War, it would seem, was not a necessary and inevitable by-product of human existence. The Inuit achieved a state of non-war in many different ways but perhaps the pro-social skill that helped me most in Northern Ireland was learning their techniques of discourse in which the primary objective was to find the common ground at the heart of any dispute and to then build on that with a view to formulating a consensus. Everyone had to agree when difficult decisions had to be made. The life of the community required nothing less.

Perhaps, inevitably, I became increasingly involved in the life and affairs of the Inuit,[3] crossing Arctic North America by dog team in 1973[4] and then working for native organisations involved with land claims settlements. But it was not until I went to university and acquired some academic qualifications in the late 1970s and early 1980s that I was able to do any research that would have a significant impact on their tragic circumstances.[5] My report 'Lords of the Arctic: Wards of the State'[6] did help to precipitate a national debate on the condition of Canada's native peoples[7] but this, again, was as much by luck as judgement. Because the report had to be translated into Inuktitut it necessarily had to be written without recourse to the usual dry academic style of carefully qualified argumentation. The report was therefore widely read, discussed in the popular press and subsequently helped to rekindle the prospects of establishing a regional government for the Inuit – Nunavut. Effective applied social research, I then learned, requires pro-active engagement with the society in question. As a consequence, when I started to work on the Northern Ireland peace process, I paid as much attention to the media as I did to writing for scholarly journals.

With regards to scholarship, when I went to university, it was not to get a degree in any particular discipline but rather to study human conflict and how to resolve it. At that time there were no interdisciplinary programmes available on this topic.[8] So my first degree was a masters in philosophy, religious studies and anthropology with a thesis written on Inuit ethics.[9] But ethics alone certainly could not 'save the world'. Almost everybody, I discovered, knew what was right and wrong; the problem was getting those who were determined to do wrong to change their ways. My second degree, a PhD in social science, focused on the causes and prevention of human conflict from the genetics and sociobiology of human group behaviour through developmental and social psychology to cultural mechanisms of social control as diverse as myth, education and law.[10] Group conflict, it seemed, was endemic to our species[11] and one of the many approaches to its management that then most interested me was education, particularly up to and through puberty.[12]

Perhaps there was nothing especially new in all of this except that the relevant theory was now grounded in what was later to be called evolutionary or Darwinian psychology.[13] With these ideas now in print the Canadian government were willing to fund a comparative study of the systems of education in Israel and Northern Ireland.[14] Needless to say they were segregated, and experimental integrated schools did have a positive impact on children's attitudes and behaviour. But my studies and reports did not have the hoped-for impact on public policy in either of these countries. In Northern Ireland children were being forced to go to segregated schools, even when they and their parents wanted them to be taught together in schools that accepted students from both communities. So I took a series of human rights complaints to UNESCO[15] and the UN.[16] But it did little good. Although the complaints were upheld[17] the British state largely ignored the recommendations of the UN and still require many children to go to segregated schools against their wishes by failing to make adequate provision for integrated education. So, I thought, if questions of ethics and morality, human sociobiology and developmental psychology, education and education policy, the UN and international human rights standards could not resolve the causes of conflict in Northern Ireland, what could? I turned to politics.

This essentially is where this preface ends and the story of this book begins. This book is about how the methods of social science, in particular in-depth interviews and public opinion polls, were used in support of the Northern Ireland peace process. This was done by helping to facilitate a discourse between the different elements of the society, the politicians, civil institutions and the people, with a view to reaching a consensus on how their society should be managed. But before I get into this I would like to end this preface with one last point about theory.

In recent years academic colleagues have sometimes suggested that my applied research is of little interest from a theoretical point of view. I would like to suggest that nothing could be further from the truth. As a theoretician I consider myself to be part of that school of thought that does not view social theories as simple generalisations about this or that part of the human condition but rather that theories should fit together as part of a fabric of explanation[18] that extends from our evolutionary past through our development and acquisition of culture to the social institutions that increasingly look like an emergent world government in the context of globalisation, international law and its application.[19]

From this perspective, when it comes to human conflict and conflict resolution, understandings from all the disciplines of academic enquiry in the humanities and social sciences are relevant to an explanation of the system that gives rise to and shapes human social behaviour.[20] I also hold the view that all theories should be subject to test by experiment so that, for example, if a particular approach to conflict resolution does not work then it follows that the explanation and theory that stands behind that approach is wrong or incomplete. In my experience most approaches, explanations and theories are right but they are nearly always incomplete and that is why they so often fail to produce the hoped-for change.

Systems of human social behaviour are robust. One little adjustment will only rarely produce a significant outcome and is certainly not likely to resolve a conflict. Indeed, because such systems are so robust some social scientists take the view that applied social science is seldom, in practice, possible.[21] Two observations suggest to me that what may be called an 'engaged total systems' approach to conflict resolution can overcome these difficulties.

Firstly, if the applied research deals with a significant majority of the individual elements of the system then the system can be overwhelmed to produce change. Good examples of such radical reform are the Nunavut Settlement[22] for the Inuit of the Canadian Arctic and the Northern Ireland Belfast Agreement[23] dealing, as they do, with a wide range of issues from policing and equality of opportunity to constitutional law and the application of international standards of human rights in what is sometimes referred to as a 'joined-up government' approach to problem solving.

Secondly, when applied research becomes an active and significant part of the system itself it can lever effective change. As well as engaging with as many parts of the system as is possible, from an interdisciplinary point of view, it must also, most critically, engage with those parts of the system that control social change. In the case of Northern Ireland this was the people, the media and the politicians elected to negotiate and implement the Belfast Agreement. This book explains how this was done, although the task is not yet complete. Indeed, it may take several generations. The system of conflict in a deeply divided society like Northern Ireland is robust in the extreme. But the people want change and slowly they will have their way.

Acknowledgements

Thanks must be extended to all those who have helped me along my way. My life of exploration, both physical and intellectual, has been a very great adventure indeed. I can only hope that in some small measure the positive outcomes described in this book justify their kindness, patience and generosity. Of course I cannot list everyone here. Indeed some people who helped me did not even give me their names while others wish to remain anonymous. But I must do my best to list a few from each of the various enterprises that led to my work on the Northern Ireland peace process.

Below and above the seas of Plymouth Sound and the north-west passage: John Heath, Richard Smith, John Goldsworthy, Terry Woodford, Michael Cassidy, Michael Ritchey and George Greenfield. *In the Canadian Arctic*: Karmoyak, Tipana, Napatchikadlak, William Ellis, Ernie Lyall, Kako, Aupudluk, Keith Sharpe, David Aglukark, Jack Anawak, Mike Murphy and Jack Hicks. *In Israel*: Willy Halpert, Louis Guttman, Eliu Katz and Haviva Bar. *At the University of Manitoba*: Klauss Klostermier, Michael Stack, Joan Townsend and Paul Churchland. *At Syracuse University*: Donald Campbell, William Shields, William Starmer, Alexander Rosenberg, Polly Ginsberg and Tom Gamble. *At Dalhousie University*: Jerry Barkow. *At the Queen's University of Belfast*: John Blacking, Reginald Byron, Elisabeth Tonkin, Brian Walker, Fred Boal, Tom Hadden, Steven Livingstone, P.L. de Silva, Adrian Guelke, Mrs Gracey, Anne Langford, Tom Collins and Senator George Mitchell. *At the University of Ulster:* Brice Dickson. *In Northern Ireland more generally*: Terrance Flanagan, Brian Lambkin, Cecilia Linehan, Billy Hutchinson, Dawn Pervis, David Ervine, David Adams, Garey McMichael, Jim Gibney, Gerry ó hEára, Conor Murphy, Mark Durkan, Sean Farran, Alban Maginness, Barbara McCabe, Kate Fearon, Stephen Farry, Hugh Casey, Alan Evans, Peter Weir, Jim Wilson, Graham Gudgion, Ian Paisley Jr., John Cobain, Jeffrey Dudgeon, Edmund Curren, David Neely, Chris Moffat, Graham Gingles, David Pozorski, Bill Nolan, Steven Pittam, David Shutt and Alan Leich.

I must also extend my gratitude to the institutions, agencies and charities who provided me with an academic home in Israel and Northern Ireland, undertook the public opinion poll fieldwork and last, but by no means least, paid all the bills. They were: the Social Science and Humanities Research Council of Canada, the Central Community Relations Unit of the Northern Ireland Office, the Israel Institute of Applied Social Research, Lagan College, Hazlewood College, All Children Together, Market Research Northern Ireland, the Joseph Rowntree Charitable Trust, the Queen's University of Belfast (in particular the Department of Anthropology, School of Law and Institute of Irish Studies) and the Queen's University of Belfast Foundation. Finally I must also thank my close family members who have always supported me in (almost) everything I have tried to do: my mother and father, Lillian and Gerald; my brother and sister, Malcolm and Helen; my daughter and her mother, Melissa and Kunga; and my partner Hae-kyung.

Glossary and Abbreviations

Anglo-Irish Agreement – Signed by the British and Irish governments in November 1985

Articles 2 and 3 – Articles in the 1937 Irish Constitution which laid claim to the six counties of Northern Ireland

Belfast Agreement – Signed by the British and Irish governments in April 1998 and otherwise known as the Good Friday Agreement (GFA)

BBC – British Broadcasting Corporation

DENI – Department of Education, Northern Ireland

Direct Rule – From Westminster over Northern Ireland and introduced in 1972 following the suspension of Stormont

Downing Street Declaration – Proposals for a Northern Ireland settlement published by the British and Irish governments in December 1993

DUP – Democratic Unionist Party

EC/EU – European Community/European Union

ECHR – European Convention on Human Rights

EEC – European Economic Community

FEC – Fair Employment Commission

Framework Document – Proposals for a Northern Ireland settlement published by the British and Irish governments in February 1995

IICD – Independent International Commission on Decommissioning

IRA – Irish Republican Army, also referred to as the Provisional IRA formed after a split with the Official IRA in 1969

LVF – Loyalist Volunteer Force

Mitchell Principles – Six conditions for inclusive political discussions contained in the Mitchell Report of February 1996

NIO – Northern Ireland Office

NIWC – Northern Ireland Women's Coalition

Patten Report – Commission report on reform of the RUC published in 1999

PR – Proportional representation

PUP – Progressive Unionist Party

RUC – Royal Ulster Constabulary

SACHR – [Northern Ireland] Standing Advisory Commission on Human Rights

SDLP – Social Democratic and Labour Party

SF – Sinn Féin

UDA – Ulster Defence Association

UDP – Ulster Democratic Party

UFF – Ulster Freedom Fighters
UKUP – United Kingdom Unionist Party
UUP – Ulster Unionist Party
UVF – Ulster Volunteer Force

Introduction

In the referendum of 22 May 1998 the people of Ireland, North and South, agreed on how they should live together on the island of Ireland in partnership with the peoples of the British Isles. Eighteen months earlier no one would have considered the signing of the historic Belfast Agreement a serious possibility with Sinn Féin/IRA at war and the Unionists vowing never to accept the proposals put on the table by the British and Irish governments. But the negotiations were, in the end, successful. Numerous political and social factors contributed to this outcome: for example, the persistence of the two governments, the determination of the main paramilitary groups to bring an end to the war, the election of 'New Labour' in May 1997 and their overwhelming majority in the House of Commons, the involvement of the American president and the skill of the talks chairman, Senator George Mitchell.[1]

The list could go on but, in part, it was also due to the refinement and extensive use of a new approach to political discourse that involved in-depth interviews with party negotiators, the testing of their proposals by public opinion survey and the publication of the results of these polls in the popular press. This tool added a degree of transparency to the negotiations when it was most needed and allowed the politicians on both sides of the conflict to map out areas of compromise and common ground without running the danger of getting too far ahead of their supporters.[2] Critically the research methods used, the timing of the polls and the final drafts of the questions were all agreed by the parties engaged in the peace process so that the results of the polls could not be dismissed lightly.

This is the first time that public opinion polls have been used, in such a systematic way, with a view to establishing a direct line of communication between the people who want peace and the politicians who must make the peace. By asking a representative sample of the population the right questions at the right time and widely publishing the results of the polls in the popular press the people of Northern Ireland were effectively given a 'seat' at the negotiating table and a 'voice' in 'their' peace process. In the hope that others might learn from this experience and apply any practical lessons of value to their own peace-building activities this book is written to explain the methods used so that they can be replicated, provide sample questions and news reports by way of examples, and review the lessons learned so that successes can be built upon and failures avoided. Finally, within the bounds of restrictions imposed by privilege, every effort is made to provide a party political perspective on this aspect of the Northern Ireland peace process largely undertaken in private interviews.

In an effort to maintain some clarity in all of this the book has been divided into two parts. Part I, 'Public Opinion Polls and Peace Processes', brings together a number of academic chapters that review the political context and impact of each of the eight polls, describes the quantitative and qualitative research methods used and concludes with an analysis of the contribution polling might now make to the resolution of conflicts in general. Part II, 'The Northern Ireland Peace Polls', illustrates how the work was done in Northern Ireland using a 'show and tell' format that includes copies of the newspaper reports bridged with 'links' written to highlight the role the parties had in designing the questions, their intended impact and political outcome. Finally, the book ends with a conclusion and sample questionnaire that could be edited, amended and redrafted for use in other parts of the world.

Perhaps it should also be stressed at this point that the emphasis here is on practical methodologies rather than theories of mediation, negotiation, conflict analysis and the like. Almost every social scientist, these days, does qualitative and quantitative methods and could replicate what has been done here. Most journalists, lawyers, politicians and policy-makers, with the help of a market research company, could also undertake the work and it is to this end that this book has been written. In time, hopefully, with a body of comparative research to hand, a robust theoretical analysis can and will be made by those with particular interests in such matters.

Public opinion polls and peace processes

The first of the academic chapters 'Political Negotiations and Public Opinion Polls'[3] attempts to answer the sceptic's question as to whether or not the polls had any impact on the Northern Ireland peace process at all and if so what that impact was. Beyond the fact that the parties put a considerable effort into the designing and running of the polls, as a collective enterprise, the value of the work manifested itself in many different ways that were not always apparent at the time or had not even been a deliberate act of design or intent. This was particularly true of the early polls. Some things worked and some things didn't, but as the work progressed everyone became more sophisticated in the use of this new instrument of public discourse. In this chapter the role of each poll in the peace process is reviewed and the most critical questions examined. Some of the issues brought to light through this analysis include the value of purely academic research projects; the inclusion and exclusion of political players as part of the polling process; the different roles of small and large parties; maintaining the independence of researchers; questions run as confidence-building measures; when to deal with matters of procedure and substance; pacing the research and timing of publications to complement the process of negotiations; managing preconditions and objections to negotiations; managing sensitive political problems; enhancing the involvement of 'the people' in 'their' peace process; managing the structure of complex agreements and their analysis; testing comprehensive settlements as a 'package'; when to best explore alternatives to a settlement; post-agreement polls and the problems of renegotiation and implementation.

But none of this would have been possible without the development of new methodologies designed to reconcile the conflicting interests of the separate communities in this deeply divided society. The second chapter, 'The Calculus of Agreement',[4] describes and explains all the research methods used so that these new techniques can be applied elsewhere. Subjects dealt with include: working with political parties as informants in a conflict setting; questionnaire design and how to calculate consensus; data analysis and the presentation of results; the role, structure and drafting of complex and simple questions; the ranking of problems and their potential solutions; reports and questions to be avoided; pre-testing instruments; research ethics and working with the media; costs and the importance of independent funding. Many of the topics dealt with in this list are simply concerned with questions of research technique but as the work is applied and as it also involves parties who have associations with groups engaged in acts of violence then both the practical and moral issues raised are the subject of special attention.

Chapter 3, 'The Drafting of Consensus and the Decommissioning Story',[5] focuses on what was arguably the most unique feature of the Northern Ireland peace polls, the direct engagement of the political parties, representing both constitutional and paramilitary groups, with all aspects of the programme of research. This chapter describes the nature of this qualitative work undertaken with the parties through hundreds of 'face-to-face' interviews in which party representatives put forward their own proposals for questions and critiqued the suggestions of others. All this information was anonymously shared between the parties through successive drafts that contained extensive footnotes detailing the changes various parties proposed through each round of the questionnaire design. Polls were not run until all the parties agreed that the issues they wished to raise were fairly dealt with and that other parties' questions were not biased or leading in any partisan way. As a consequence of their participation in this process the parties were able to take ownership and responsibility for the research. Consequently the results of the polls were taken seriously. As one negotiator with paramilitary connections once put it 'their fingerprints are all over them'. This chapter illustrates the methods used through a detailed examination of one of the most difficult issues that had to be dealt with during the negotiations: the decommissioning of paramilitary weapons.

'Polling as Peace Building'[6] is the final chapter in the academic section and is included to highlight and review the positive contribution polling could now make to the resolution of conflicts in general. This chapter is deliberately upbeat. It is written in the hope that others will be encouraged to try the methods described here in the face of what are all too often the most desperate of circumstances. Although public opinion polls certainly cannot achieve peace, they can improve the prospects for a successful outcome by assisting and supporting the many complex social and political processes that must be dealt with. More specifically, issues addressed include: inter-track dialogue; contact group formation; confidential lines of communication; establishing confidence in the peace process; formulating new policies for conflict resolution; agenda setting; prioritising the elements of a conflict and a settlement; defining the parameters of negotiations and an agreement; developing a common language and neutral terminology; defining the 'middle' ground; testing radical proposals and a balanced agreement; scheduling decisions; supporting pro-agreement parties; monitoring implementation; establishing leader, party, public and international confidence in the decisions made and maintaining their ongoing involvement in the peace process.

Of course much that was done in Northern Ireland will not work elsewhere. But then much that was done in Northern Ireland did not work very well there either and it was only through the persistent effort of exploring every possible opportunity for success that progress was made. This chapter is intended to be a catalogue of opportunities to be explored, discarded if necessary, but more hopefully to be built upon and improved.

The Northern Ireland peace polls

Poll by poll the second part of the book describes the Northern Ireland experience and how, when the results of each poll were published, progress was made and the negotiations moved forward. But the old adage that 'the light at the end of the tunnel is another tunnel' was always true and a new set of difficulties then had to be addressed, another poll run and a little more progress made. For so long as the parties were willing this is how it was done. There was no 'quick fix'. Each of the eight polls is the subject of a chapter. However, very briefly, before the role of each poll is reviewed it may be as well to say a little about the Northern Ireland conflict, the parties to the negotiations and their political aspirations.[7]

Following the Irish Civil War of 1919–21 the island of Ireland was partitioned into the independent state of Ireland in the South and the British province of Ulster in the North. Although, in 1990, the secretary of state for Northern Ireland had declared that 'Britain has no selfish, strategic or economic interest in Northern Ireland' this had certainly not been the case during the better part of the past 500 years. But in the context of shared membership of the European Union the British and Irish governments now only wanted to resolve any outstanding questions on the status of Northern Ireland to the satisfaction of the people who lived there. Yet reconciliation between the largely Catholic Nationalist minority who wanted to be part of a united Ireland and the largely Protestant Unionist majority who wanted to remain part of the United Kingdom seemed to be quite unattainable. In the North persistent discrimination against Catholics had led to violent clashes between the local police force and civil rights protesters in 1968. The provincial government lost control of events and in an attempt to restore order British troops were deployed in 1969 but this only led to increased violence, the formation of new paramilitary groups, detention without trial and the imposition of Direct Rule from Westminster in 1972. In the hope of ending what was now a new civil war, referred to as the 'Troubles', various political initiatives were tried but none brought an end to the conflict. In 1993 efforts were made to include all parties in any future negotiations on Northern Ireland including, critically, those who represented paramilitary groups – providing they declared ceasefires. In December of that year the British and Irish governments issued the *Downing Street Declaration* and in 1994 the major paramilitary groups did declare ceasefires. In 1995 the two governments published the *Framework Document*, a proposed outline for a settlement, and in 1996 ten parties were elected to the Northern Ireland Forum for Peace and Reconciliation. Crucially, a system of proportional representation (PR) was used to elect party members to the Forum, thus ensuring participation from all sections of the Northern Ireland community including those with paramilitary connections. Subject to the maintenance of their ceasefires these parties gained the right to nominate representatives to the 'Stormont Talks', the negotiations on the future of Northern Ireland, along with the other 'constitutional' parties and the British and Irish governments all under the chairmanship of Senator George Mitchell of the USA.[8] The ten parties, who also appointed negotiators to work on the public opinion polls, were as follows:

Five mainly Protestant and Unionist parties, two with Loyalist paramilitary connections:

- The Ulster Unionist Party (UUP), with 30 seats in the Forum was the largest Unionist party and was first established in 1886 to oppose Home Rule for Ireland. Its leader was David Trimble and it became one of the 'pro-agreement parties' following the successful negotiation of the Belfast Agreement in April 1998.

- The Democratic Unionist Party (DUP), with 24 seats in the Forum, was established in 1971 to strongly oppose a British 'sell out'. Its leader was the Reverend Ian Paisley and it became the largest party in the Unionist 'anti-agreement camp'.
- The United Kingdom Unionist Party (UKUP), with 3 seats in the Forum, was a small independent Unionist Party. Its leader was Robert McCartney and it became anti-agreement.
- The Progressive Unionist Party (PUP), with 2 seats in the Forum, was the political representative of the Ulster Volunteer Force (UVF) which was first established to oppose Home Rule in 1913 and re-established in 1966 along with the Red Hand Commando (RHC). The leader of the PUP was David Ervine and it became pro-agreement.
- The Ulster Democratic Party (UDP), also with 2 seats in the Forum, was the political representative of the Ulster Defence Association (UDA) and Ulster Freedom Fighters (UFF). The UDA was formed in 1971 to oppose a British 'sell out'. The leader of the UDP was Gary McMichael and it became pro-agreement.

Two mainly Catholic and Nationalist parties, one with Republican paramilitary connections:

- The Social Democratic and Labour Party (SDLP), with 21 seats in the Forum, was the largest Nationalist party and was first established in 1970 to work for a united Ireland through peaceful means. Its leader was John Hume and it became pro-agreement.
- Sinn Féin (SF), with 17 seats in the Forum, was the political wing of the Irish Republican Army (IRA) which had played an active role in the Irish Civil War of 1919–21 and was re-established as the Provisional IRA in 1969. The leader of Sinn Féin was Gerry Adams and it became pro-agreement.

Three cross-community centre parties:

- The Alliance Party of Northern Ireland, with 7 seats in the Forum, was the largest centre party; its political background was Liberal and it was established in 1970 to represent both Catholics and Protestants. Its leader was John, later Lord Alderdice and it became pro-agreement.
- The Northern Ireland Women's Coalition, with 2 seats in the Forum, was a cross-community centre party established to participate in the work of the Forum and bring a women's political agenda to the peace process. Its leader was Monica MacWilliams and it became pro-agreement.
- The Labour Party of Northern Ireland, with 2 seats in the Forum, was a centre socialist party established to participate in the work of the Forum and peace process. Its leader was Malachi Curran and it became pro-agreement.

The first poll, 'Peace Building and Public Policy' was conducted in April and May of 1996 just as the Forum was being established (Chapter 5). The poll was undertaken as a piece of pure research to explore various policy options for improving relations between the two communities in Northern Ireland. As far as the peace process was concerned the poll demonstrated the validity of the methods used, the independence of the research and the value of publication in the popular press. Subsequently the political parties elected to take part in the Stormont talks all agreed to participate in a similar programme of research to address the problems they had to resolve.

The second poll, 'After the Elections' (Chapter 6) and the third poll 'The Stormont Talks' (Chapter 7), conducted in April and September 1997, dealt with various problems of procedure that had to be solved before inclusive negotiations could get underway. Providing the ceasefires were not broken the people of Northern Ireland wanted inclusive talks. The fieldwork for the fourth poll 'In Search of a Settlement' (Chapter 8) was completed in December 1997 and published in January 1998 to assist the parties with all the decisions they had to make on major questions of substance that were part of the final agreement. Negotiations started to make real progress and just before a deal was cut in April the fifth poll 'A Comprehensive Settlement' (Chapter 9) was run to test a settlement package to see if it could win the support of the people of Northern Ireland in a referendum. It could and on 22 May 1998 71 per cent of the population voted in favour of the Belfast Agreement.

However, the Ulster Unionists would not share power with Sinn Féin without a start to decommissioning and the peace process stalled on the 'government and guns' problem. Three polls were commissioned to help address this impasse. The sixth poll, the 'Implementation of the Belfast Agreement' (Chapter 10) led to new negotiations in March 1999. The seventh poll 'The Mitchell Review' (Chapter 11) demonstrated popular support for any reasonable set of arrangements that would solve the 'government and guns' problem and the eighth poll 'The Future of the Peace Process' (Chapter 12), demonstrated Ulster Unionist voter support for new decommissioning proposals that would place 'arms beyond use'. Although an inclusive Executive was established and power was devolved to the new Northern Ireland Assembly the peace process became increasingly unstable in the spring of 2001 when confronted with the necessities of elections. This and other problems of implementation are also dealt with in Chapter 12 by way of a series of articles that analysed the trends through all the polls.

In the 'Conclusion', a review is undertaken of the difficulties encountered in the peace process following the elections, the impact of the events of 11 September 2001 and the effects these had on negotiations and polling. Surveys of public opinion continued to play a critical role in support of political progress. However, changes in political culture, marked by the end of all party negotiations and the establishment of the Executive, greatly effected the use of polls as an aid to collective decision-making. With the benefits of hindsight it was now possible to say how different kinds of polls were used to what effect at different stages in the Northern Ireland peace process. This process still has a very long way to go but a great deal has been achieved and sufficient experience gained to start applying the methods of the peace polls elsewhere. Finally, a sample questionnaire is supplied in the Appendix.

Part I
Public Opinion Polls and Peace Processes

1
Political Negotiations and Public Opinion Polls

Eight surveys of public opinion were conducted in support of the Northern Ireland peace process between April 1996 and May 2000. Critically the questions for seven of these polls were drafted and agreed with the co-operation of party negotiators to enhance the peace process by increasing party inclusiveness, developing issues and language, testing party policies, helping to set deadlines and increase the overall transparency of negotiations through the publication of technical analysis and media reports. This chapter reviews the principal findings of these polls and their role in the political development and implementation of the Belfast Agreement.

Poll 1: Peace building and public policy[1]

This poll was undertaken as a piece of pure research by a group of academics at Queen's University[2] and conducted as a random sample of the population of Northern Ireland in April and May of 1996. Most of the questions dealt with problems of discrimination and segregation as they related to employment, policing, education, Irish language, public parades and housing. The Catholic community, which had been systematically discriminated against in the past, wanted stronger policies than Protestants to deal with this particular problem but Protestants were willing to accept more reforms than were presently in place providing this would also improve the quality of services, fairness and choice. Both communities wanted policies that would reverse the trend towards increased segregation. Other questions also dealt with political arrangements for the future of Northern Ireland. Areas of compromise that were potentially most acceptable to both Irish Nationalists and British Unionists started to be identified. A selection of a few results may help to illustrate these points.

As with most conflicts between peoples, intolerance and discrimination are common threads running through the Northern Ireland problem. When asked 'Should the police make a greater effort to recruit more Catholics and be more acceptable to the Nationalist community by, for example, changing the name and uniform of the Royal Ulster Constabulary?' only 20 per cent of Protestants said 'Yes' compared to 88 per cent of Catholics. With regards to cultural matters only 2 per cent of Catholics were opposed to Irish language schools compared to 39 per cent of Protestants, while only 6 per cent of Catholics would allow all Orange Order parades compared to 42 per cent of Protestants. However, although the Northern Ireland Fair Employment Commission (FEC) had been established to eliminate discrimination, particularly against Catholics, only 28 per cent of Protestants wanted to scrap it while 72 per cent of Protestants and 97 per cent of Catholics wanted to keep the FEC or strengthen it. Clearly some problems were going to be more difficult to deal with than others, as part of a comprehensive settlement.

Another thread running through all conflicts is segregation, in part brought about by questions of personal security. But in Northern Ireland 80 per cent of Protestants would prefer mixed workplaces, 64 per cent mixed neighbourhoods and 63 per cent mixed schools, while 87 per cent of Catholics would prefer mixed workplaces, 68 per cent mixed neighbourhoods and 59 per cent mixed schools. But even if the people of Northern Ireland would prefer to live and work together, could a political agreement be reached that would help to facilitate that ambition?

This was not going to be an easy problem to solve because most Protestants wanted to maintain their ties with the British state while most Catholics wanted strengthened relations with the Irish state. However, when preferences for different potential options were analysed the proposed central feature of the Belfast Agreement – *power sharing with North–South institutions but no joint authority* – was found to be a viable compromise. The possibilities of using public opinion polls as part of the Northern Ireland peace process was clearly demonstrated and this point was not lost on the politicians.

Here are a few practical observations from the experience of the first poll that could be relevant to the running of similar polls elsewhere:

- Cover all major aspects of social and political life effected by public institutions and government departments, since the 'people' and their 'political representatives' often have very different views (and interests) about the nature of the conflict and its resolution.
- Because the work requires many different kinds of expertise, put together an interdisciplinary research team as required.
- Encourage key decision-makers to become involved in drafting the research questions and designing the methodology so that they will take the results more seriously.
- If politicians disagree with the results of the pure research poll – this is welcome – invite them to help design the next survey to their satisfaction.

The state of negotiations in January 1997 and getting started

In January of 1997 the multi-party negotiations for the political future of Northern Ireland had reached an impasse at the Stormont talks. Sinn Féin had broken their ceasefire and were excluded from the talks while the Democratic Unionist Party (DUP) and United Kingdom Unionist Party (UKUP) refused to negotiate before weapons were handed in – the precondition of decommissioning. It was in this context that all ten parties elected to take part in the Stormont talks were invited to participate in a survey to test public opinion on the various issues that were stalling the talks process. Probably because none of the parties wished to appear to be talks-wreckers, all the parties agreed to participate and a series of polls were conducted.

But not all the parties were equally enthusiastic about this new enterprise. Most of them had dismissed the 'Peace Building and Public Policy' poll as irrelevant a year earlier. At that time only the Progressive Unionist Party (PUP) and Sinn Féin (which represented the political interests of the major Loyalist and Republican paramilitary organisations) expressed any interest in a poll designed to explore various public policy options for the improvement of relations between the two communities. But that survey demonstrated both the independence of the work and the validity of the methods used. Additionally the results of the poll were published in the most widely read regional newspaper, the *Belfast Telegraph*,[3] and as a free supplement in a local current affairs magazine, *Fortnight*.[4] The report was also given to all the party members recently elected to the new Northern Ireland Forum established by the government as a vehicle for facilitating the Stormont talks. A number of additional observations are probably worth noting at this point:

- Financial support for the first poll, which critically reviewed public policy in Northern Ireland, had been turned down by the government's Economic and Social Research Council (ESRC) which tends not to fund potentially controversial projects. A grant for the research was, however, forthcoming from the Joseph Rowntree Charitable Trust which actively takes on projects that are potentially controversial and has a special Northern Ireland Programme. They subsequently became the principal sponsors of this work.
- Initially the greatest enthusiasm for running a poll as part of the Northern Ireland peace process came from the smaller centre parties who probably saw it as an opportunity to give their political agenda a more significant public 'voice'. Specifically the Northern Ireland Women's Coalition Party, Alliance Party, Labour Party of Northern Ireland, Progressive Unionist Party (PUP) and Ulster Democratic Party (UDP) all felt their agenda was being sidelined by the dominant Nationalist and Unionist parties.

- The larger parties, particularly the Ulster Unionists (UUP) and Democratic Unionists (DUP), which probably did not have a need for such a public 'vehicle', were, however, willing to participate as the style of questions used allowed each party to test its own policies, against the policies of competitor parties, as a series of options or preferences.
- Sinn Féin, which was presently excluded from the Stormont talks because the IRA had broken its ceasefire, also probably wanted to be included as it provided them with one of only a few opportunities to participate actively in the peace process.

And here are a few practical observations that came out of this experience:

- As politicians may be sceptical about the benefits of public opinion polls, first undertake a programme of pure research to demonstrate the independence and validity of the work.
- Do not exclude any serious parties from the applied research – it is most helpful to test support for mainstream opinion, centre party compromises and radical reforms together.
- If the large established parties do not show willing, try the small centre parties first after which the larger parties may decide they do not wish to be left out.
- Secure independent funding, remembering that those who control the 'purse strings' could have a veto over the continuation of the research.

Poll 2: After the elections ... ?[5]

The first in this series of polls undertaken with the co-operation of the political parties elected to take part in the Stormont talks was conducted in March and published in April 1997 to help set a context for an invigorated talks process after the May elections. Some general problems were dealt with as well as procedural questions about decommissioning and the participation of parties with paramilitary associations. In general the electorate wanted 'all party talks' subject to a minimum of preconditions. But these had to include paramilitary ceasefires which the IRA had broken. Labour was elected to government in May and subsequently allowed Sinn Féin into the talks after the IRA called a second ceasefire in July. Some observations on some specific questions may be helpful here.

The first question was a very general one designed to put the interviewee at ease: *Do you support the principle of a negotiated settlement for the political future of Northern Ireland?* 94 per cent said 'Yes' ranging from a high of 99 per cent for Alliance voters to a low of 90 per cent for DUP supporters. The idea for this question had been borrowed from President De Klerk who, in a 1994 referendum, had asked the white population of South Africa: *Do you support the continuation of the reform process which the state president began on 2 February 1990 and which is aimed at a new constitution through negotiation?*

69 per cent said 'Yes' and with this mandate he was able to complete his historic agreement with Nelson Mandela and the ANC. We hoped for a similar outcome in Northern Ireland. It was a confidence-building question.

A series of questions then dealt with procedural or 'shape of the table' questions that focused on who should be allowed into the talks and when the decommissioning of illegally held weapons should be undertaken. For the most part the Unionist 'No Parties' – the DUP and UKUP – who wanted the talks as they were then conceived to fail wanted as many preconditions as possible while the Nationalists – the SDLP and Sinn Féin – wanted to proceed with as few preconditions as possible. Along with the centre parties and Ulster Unionists these parties became known as the 'Yes' or pro-Agreement parties after the Belfast Agreement was made in April 1998.

The people of Northern Ireland wanted peace. Not at any price, however; they supported all-party talks providing ceasefires were called but were willing to have decommissioning dealt with as a separate issue. Additionally, with regard to procedural matters, people were asked for their opinions on various uses for referendums to replace, advance, advise or endorse a talks settlement. All these options were acceptable. The only one that wasn't was 'no referendum'. The people wanted to have their say.

With regards to substantive issues some first steps were taken in this poll to try to eliminate the extreme political positions of 'die hard' Republicans and Unionists that would never be acceptable to both communities. As well as finding out what people could agree to it was important to underline what was genuinely unacceptable. On the status of Northern Ireland, independence, which was never realistically on offer, was generally unpopular. Protestants solidly wanted to stay in the Union but Catholics were more flexible, except for Sinn Féin supporters who wanted a united Ireland. Not much common ground there except for the elimination of the separate state option. Progress of sorts. Catholics also wanted stronger relations with the Republic through the establishment of North–South institutions. Protestants were not over-enthusiastic about this option but considered the Anglo-Irish Agreement, which had been signed without their consent, even more unacceptable. The North–South bodies, agreed to as part of a negotiated settlement, were the lesser of these two evils as far as the Protestants were concerned and in these terms were a potential settlement winner. With regards to government within Northern Ireland, Protestants wanted a devolved assembly subject to majority rule; Catholics wanted the same but with responsibility or power sharing. No devolution at all or separate institutions for each community were generally unpopular. People were tired of the Northern Ireland Office running their affairs with little public accountability and they didn't want a political divorce in spite of the 'Troubles'. Some form of devolved government was definitely going to be part of the solution.

Here are a few practical observations from the experience of the second poll:

- Start with some simple confidence-building questions about the peace process in general and other confidence-building measures (CBMs) that could easily be implemented.
- Deal with all of the principal procedural or 'shape of the table' issues before getting into too much detail over substantive or 'negotiated settlement' issues.
- In public opinion polls the elimination of extreme positions, those with little cross-community support, is just as important and just as easy as finding compromises and common ground.
- It is worth noting that several questions that had been drafted and agreed in Northern Ireland could not be run in some polls for lack of space. This was not entirely a bad thing as it provided a working foundation for later polls.

Poll 3: The future of the Stormont talks[6]

The DUP and UKUP said they would not stay in the talks with Sinn Féin present and the Ulster Unionist Party (UUP) said they would consult with their 'grass roots' before deciding if they would stay in or not. If they walked away from the talks the negotiations would have collapsed with no significant Unionist participation. This poll, conducted in September 1997, demonstrated public support for the peace process and for continued Unionist participation. The Ulster Unionists subsequently decided to stay in the talks but refused to engage in 'face-to-face' negotiations with Sinn Féin. A few observations on some specific questions may prove helpful again.

The critical question this time was: *In today's circumstances do you want the political party you support to stay in the talks?* 92 per cent of the people of Northern Ireland said 'Yes' ranging from a high of 100 per cent for Sinn Féin voters to a low of 76 per cent for DUP supporters. These results warranted a front-page headline in the *Belfast Telegraph*. Other questions elaborated this simple 'yes/no' option with various Unionist preconditions: on decommissioning before talks; dealing with the Republic's claim on the territory of Northern Ireland before talks; rejecting the two governments, 'Framework Document' as a basis for talks; and finally, rejecting talks altogether. None of these options was acceptable. The people wanted talks.

But a BBC poll run at the same time also asked if the parties they supported should negotiate with Sinn Féin. For most Protestants this was a step too far, so although the Ulster Unionists stayed in the talks they never spoke directly to Sinn Féin and only addressed them through the talks chairman Senator George Mitchell. This lack of direct communication did long-term harm to the peace process as it seriously delayed the development of a normal working relationship so essential for the building of confidence and trust.

A second set of questions dealt with what to do if various parties walked out of the talks or if the talks collapsed. In practice, under the rules of the negotiations, if the largest Unionist party, the UUP, or largest Nationalist party, the SDLP, left the talks then the talks would collapse. The electorate understood and accepted this reality but also accepted the proposition that if Sinn Féin 'walked' then the talks should continue. However, in the event of a collapse, the people of Northern Ireland also wanted the two governments to put a proposed settlement before them in a referendum. Most people, it would seem, welcome opportunities to exercise their democratic franchise, particularly if the politicians they elect to do a certain job fail to undertake or complete that responsibility.

Here are a few practical observations from the experience of the third poll:

- Systematically deal with all preconditions and objections to a peace process – people generally want 'jaw jaw' in preference to 'war war'.
- Do not avoid sensitive issues because others might take on those same questions in a less helpful way that is potentially more damaging to the peace process.
- Give 'the people' every opportunity to answer questions about the exercise of their democratic franchise – they like it – and the results should send a message to their elected politicians.

Poll 4: In search of a settlement[7]

While all these political negotiations were going on and the official talks were stuck on procedural issues all the parties continued to negotiate substantive issues through the public opinion poll process. Thus, in December 1997, a poll was conducted on all the substantive issues and was published in January 1998 in an effort to help move the talks process forward. After increased violence over the Christmas period this effort proved to be successful and most of the parties started to negotiate in earnest, with the exception of Sinn Féin who held firm to a 'non-partitionist' settlement that excluded the possibility of a regional assembly for Northern Ireland.

This questionnaire was the most complex one of them all. It had to deal with all the elements of an agreement for which options had been in the drafting process for nearly a year. In this case the informant had to provide 273 responses on a wide variety of matters. The other polls were conducted as face-to-face interviews but this one was a 24-page take-home booklet (almost an exam!) that had to be filled out. The first important question in this survey asked the interviewee to rate the significance of 19 causes of the Northern Ireland conflict and the second question did the same for 17 steps that could be taken towards a lasting peace. These questions proved to be very useful and informative when analysed for the two main communities to produce separate rankings of their respective concerns and aspirations. Through this objective measure everyone could see what their opponents' constituencies considered to be most important and the two lists were substantially different. For Protestants the number one issue was paramilitary violence and how to deal with it. For Catholics it was questions of equality and police reform. Reform of the institutions of government, the primary focus of the peace process, was much lower on everyone's list. Unfortunately this failure to get the priorities right weakened the effectiveness of the Belfast Agreement and arguably put the peace process at risk in 1999. The second section of the questionnaire contained 29 questions on a Bill of Rights for Northern Ireland and the third section 25 questions on police reform. All these questions were drafted by all the parties but, for the most part, were left out of the agreement to be dealt with at a later date by commissions.

The questionnaire then went on to deal with the major political/institutional elements of the Belfast Agreement with 39 questions on Strand One which covered relationships in Northern Ireland relating to regional government. Fifty-six questions on Strand Two covered relationships within the island of Ireland, notably North–South bodies. Twenty questions on Strand Three covered relationships between the British and Irish governments and dealt with a replacement for the Anglo-Irish Agreement as well as an additional 16 questions on constitutional issues.

By employing a method of analysis based on the voting system used in the talks – a simple majority from both communities – a summary of what an acceptable agreement would look like was produced as follows:

A comprehensive settlement

- A Regional Assembly made up from elected members who share responsibilities in proportion to their representation and employing a voting system with other checks and balances to ensure the fair participation of both communities in government and the prevention of abuse of power.
- North–South bodies strictly controlled by the elected politicians who establish them to deal with a wide range of issues using various functions and powers appropriate to the areas of government policy being managed.
- Replace the Anglo-Irish Agreement with a Council of the Islands to establish a new relationship between London, Dublin, Cardiff, Edinburgh and Belfast appropriate to the needs of the region as a part of Europe.
- Constitutional reform that embraces the principle of consent and other balanced changes required to implement the various agreements made at the Stormont talks.
- A Bill of Rights that deals specifically with the political, social and cultural problems that have aggravated the conflict and a Human Rights Commission with responsibilities and powers to educate, monitor standards and bring cases to court.

- A reformed two-tier police service restructured with a view to recruiting more Catholics and improving community relations under the authority of a new Department of Justice in a Regional Assembly.

This solution proved to be very close to the deal struck on Good Friday and was used as a basis for testing a 'Comprehensive Settlement' package in poll number five.

Here, again, are a few more practical observations derived from this experience:

- Devise questions that can produce a ranking of the major problems in a conflict and their potential solutions.
- Develop questions that include all of the potential elements of a final agreement by way of informing both the negotiators and the general public.
- Do not be put off by complexity. The people living with a conflict often have a very sophisticated understanding of that conflict.
- Use a method of analysis that reflects the voting procedures used in the negotiations proper in terms of both constituencies and levels of support required.

Poll 5: A comprehensive settlement[8]

With the DUP and UKUP outside the talks and Sinn Féin not willing to actively negotiate, a test 'package' – very similar to the one outlined above – was agreed by the remaining seven parties and a survey conducted in March 1998. The poll also included alternatives put forward by the DUP, UKUP and Sinn Féin. This survey of public opinion proved to be critical as it demonstrated the lack of cross-party support for the extreme Unionist and Republican proposals, while the centre ground settlement agreed to by the seven remaining parties could win support if put to the people of Northern Ireland in a referendum. Subsequently, on 22 May 1998 71 per cent of the population voted in favour of the Belfast Agreement.

In this survey two simple questions were asked about the 'package'. Firstly, *If a majority of the political parties elected to take part in the Stormont talks agreed to this settlement would you vote to accept it in a referendum?* Seventy-seven per cent said 'Yes'. But secondly, when asked *If you said 'Yes' would you still accept these terms for a settlement even if the political party you supported was opposed to them?* the 'Yes' vote dropped to 50 per cent. These results were taken very seriously by both the parties and two governments. If the parties could agree a deal they could 'carry the day'. But if they could not agree then it was very unlikely that the two governments would be able to push a deal through against the opposition of a majority of the parties. Everyone needed everyone else. It was a 'united we stand, divided we fall' situation. Unfortunately the pro-Agreement parties did not hold together as well as they might have after the signing of the Belfast

Agreement while the 'no parties' campaigned with a single voice. Percentage points were lost and by the time the Assembly elections took place in June the Unionist vote got 'shredded', leaving David Trimble and the Ulster Unionists with only a narrow working majority.

After the 'package' as a whole was 'voted on' by the person being interviewed they were asked how they felt about each part of the 'package' separately. It is interesting to note that the respective Protestant and Catholic communities remained strongly opposed to some of the individual reforms but were willing to accept them as part of an overall agreed settlement. The whole, it would seem, was greater than the sum of its individual parts. Another important section of this poll included the repetition of Unionist and Republican alternatives to the comprehensive settlement. These proposals, although strongly supported in the separate communities, continued to receive little or no cross-party support. Visiting these issues again, at this critical point in the negotiations, helped to underline the fact that there was no alternative to the carefully worked out compromise.

Here are a few practical observations from the experience of the fifth poll:

- Test comprehensive agreements as a 'package' as many of its problematic elements will be acceptable as part of a balanced settlement.
- 'Underline' the politically unacceptable alternatives to a comprehensive settlement when it is opportune to do so. For example, when radical groups are actively opposing a 'deal'.
- Timing is of the essence. For example the 'comprehensive settlement' poll would have been almost useless if run months before the parties were ready to 'cut a deal' or the day after the talks collapsed!

Poll 6: Implementation of the Belfast Agreement[9]

The details of the new institutions of government were agreed in a vote of the new Northern Ireland Assembly on 16 February 1999 but the Unionists refused to sit in an Executive with Sinn Féin prior to decommissioning. In an effort to overcome these difficulties a poll was conducted in collaboration with the Assembly parties representing the principal paramilitary groups – Sinn Féin and the PUP. The results were published on 3 and 4 March 1999. Over 90 per cent of the people of Northern Ireland wanted the peace process to succeed and were willing to have their political representatives reach an accommodation to achieve this outcome.

It was intended that the referendum of 22 May should have marked the end of this series of public opinion polls. However, in September of 1998 a few parties indicated their desire to continue the work. Decommissioning was still at the top of the Unionists' agenda – but not Sinn Féin's. Some of the parties wanted to tackle this issue again, perhaps in the hope of renegotiating it. By the end of the year it had become apparent that the failure to set up the Executive with the inclusion of Sinn Féin could bring the agreement down. With this very real concern in mind the PUP and Sinn Féin decided to undertake a poll that would explore all the possibilities for resolving this problem but strictly within the terms of the Belfast Agreement as they understood it. It was now January 1999 and the issue had been festering since the elections the previous summer with Sinn Féin and the Ulster Unionists painting themselves ever more tightly into their respective corners. If funds had been made available in September the problem might have been more easily dealt with then. But some of the parties did not consider it to be a serious problem at that time and would not support a poll. Everyone had a veto. It was not until the problem became almost intractable that the veto was lifted and the poll was funded. But this is all said with the wisdom of 20/20 hindsight. If the problem had been fixed everyone would have said 'it was best left to the politicians to resolve'. But they didn't and it hadn't.

The poll turned out to be both effective and interesting. Effective because it demonstrated that the people of Northern Ireland were willing to be pragmatic and wanted their politicians to do what had to be done to make the Belfast Agreement work. The governments and parties got into a new set of talks after the poll was published, almost tripping over each other in a rush to issue invitations. The poll was interesting as responses to some of the questions clearly demonstrated that the reason why progress with implementation was so slow was because Unionists did not trust Republicans and Republicans did not trust Unionists. An agreement, it would seem, is not enough. Trust and confidence are also required and all the important issues that had been left unresolved in the Belfast Agreement still remained at the top of the Protestant and Catholic 'to do' lists – decommissioning and police reform respectively.

The original plan for implementation of the Belfast Agreement envisaged the setting up of a shadow Executive prior to devolution. Given the months of negotiations with Sinn Féin and the Ulster Unionists only addressing each other through the chair this period of time set aside for developing normal working relationships was essential. Unfortunately this process never started to happen until the new round of negotiations got under way following the publication of this poll. But the two governments and the Northern Ireland civil service also had to make adjustments. The Belfast Agreement was far more complex than the simple devolution of powers to Scotland or Wales. Everyone needed a period of time to test relationships, build confidence and establish trust. The peace process needed careful management. Again, with 20/20 hindsight, perhaps the first priority of the two governments should have been to get all the new institutions up and running, where necessary on an advisory basis, with the devolution of real powers undertaken progressively as and when circumstances might have allowed.[10]

Here are a few practical observations from the experience of the sixth poll:

- Try to retain control over funding so that the parties involved with the polls will not be able to exercise a veto if they think the work is not going to go their way.
- Don't use public opinion polls to renegotiate agreements. Regrettably much of the partisan media will do this anyway.
- Don't assume the work is over once the deal is signed, particularly if many of the issues raised in the research are not dealt with in the agreement!

Poll 7: The Mitchell Review[11]

Decommissioning and setting up the executive still proved to be 'a bridge too far'. The negotiations of that summer failed, with the Unionists refusing to take up their ministerial posts in the absence of a hand-over of weapons. Their slogan was 'No guns, no government'. Faced with a political 'stand-off' Seamus Mallon, the Nationalist Deputy First Minister, resigned throwing the peace process into a review. Senator George Mitchell was persuaded to return to take on this unwelcome task and another poll was conducted in support of these negotiations. It did not produce any remarkably new results. The people of Northern Ireland still wanted their politicians to 'cut a deal'. But on this occasion all the pro-Agreement parties were involved, not just the PUP and Sinn Féin. Critically the Ulster Unionists now took the results of the poll seriously and a 'step-by-step' programme for implementation was agreed.

This was the most difficult poll of them all, not because the issues were particularly complex but because, from the outset, neither Sinn Féin or the Ulster Unionist really wanted to negotiate. When the questions for this poll were starting to be drafted neither of these two parties had actually agreed to participate in the Mitchell Review and their first contributions were no more preconditions to setting up the Executive from Sinn Féin and 'no Executive' without decommissioning and an end to all violence from the Ulster Unionists. Fortunately all the centre parties to this disagreement, the PUP, UDP, SDLP, Alliance and Women's Coalition, played an invaluable constructive role by introducing options for compromises and pointing out the dangers to the peace process of running some of the unhelpful questions suggested by other parties.

As was often done in previous polls some confidence-building questions were asked. Eighty-five per cent of the people of Northern Ireland wanted the Mitchell Review to be a success. But this was probably the last best opportunity to get the Belfast Agreement implemented. It could not be lost so a series of questions were included to highlight people's fears on this point. Only 44 per cent of people asked thought the Review would succeed and support for the Belfast Agreement had dropped from 71 per cent in the referendum to 65 per cent with Protestants now split 50/50. If a way forward could not be found now it was not going to be found. It was make or break time for the Agreement and the politicians who had gambled their careers on its success. Only 10 per cent of Sinn Féin supporters trusted the Ulster Unionists 'a lot' or 'a little' while only 5 per cent of them trusted Sinn Féin 'a lot' or 'a little'. In spite of this lack of trust David Trimble agreed to lead his party into the Executive and Gerry Adams persuaded the IRA to appoint a 'go-between' to work with the Independent International Decommissioning Commission. The British government had also published the Patten report on the reform of the RUC at the beginning of the Review. Important steps had been taken but the peace process was far from done.

Here are a few practical observations from the experience of the seventh poll:

- Even when a very difficult decision has to be made try and include all the critical parties to that decision – however difficult that makes the work.
- When key players refuse to negotiate use neutral parties to feed in constructive suggestions.
- When key players introduce questions designed to produce an unhelpful result get neutral parties to critique the value of such questions.
- Design and run 'cold shower' questions when the point of 'do it or lose it' is reached. Public opinion polls are an excellent medium for dealing with 'contextual' issues.

Poll 8: The future of the peace process[12]

The Mitchell Review moved the Northern Ireland peace process forward by creating conditions in which the Executive could be established. Unfortunately, when the Ulster Unionist Council formally accepted the terms of the Mitchell Review for going into government with Sinn Féin they had also added in the condition that IRA decommissioning should begin within a set period of time and they scheduled another meeting of their Council to vote on the matter. From a Republican point of view their 'voluntary act' had now become an 'act of surrender'. Consequently, beyond appointing an IRA representative to work with General de Chastelain and his Commission, little happened on the decommissioning front, the Unionists withdrew their support for the Executive and the new British Secretary of State for Northern Ireland, Peter Mandelson, suspended the institutions of government set up under the terms of the Belfast Agreement. It was 'back to the drawing board' and the two governments undertook what amounted to an informal review in an effort to solve the decommissioning problem yet again. They were successful. The concepts of decommissioning as a 'voluntary act' undertaken, initially, as a 'confidence-building measure' were now accepted by Unionists and, critically, the idea of decommissioning by 'placing arms beyond use' in secure, inspected dumps was accepted by the IRA.

However, on this occasion, some pro-Agreement Ulster Unionists were reluctant to run another poll in case it gave support to their anti-Agreement lobby, while some members of Sinn Féin had misgivings about using the polls to continually prop up the Belfast Agreement in the face of what many considered to be increasing Ulster Unionist indifference to the principle of shared government. If the Ulster Unionists wanted to exercise their veto and bring down the Belfast Agreement perhaps they should be allowed to do so. But other parties, notably the PUP and SDLP, did want to run a poll and at a special meeting of Rowntree Trustees the decision was made to go ahead.

Events proved their judgement to be correct. In addition to repeating all the contextual peace process questions asked in the Mitchell Review poll the eighth poll, 'The Future of the Peace Process', tested the new proposals for managing decommissioning along with police reform and demilitarisation in general. The results were published in the *Belfast Telegraph* on 25 May 2000. Seventy-two per cent of Ulster Unionist supporters wanted their party to go back into government with Sinn Féin and the Ulster Unionist Council agreed to do so at their meeting of 27 May 2000 by a narrow majority of 459 votes to 403.

The Northern Ireland peace process was back on track again but it took several more turns, both good and bad, with blame being passed around on all sides as to who was or was not living up to their obligations to fully implement the Belfast Agreement. On Friday 27 October 2000 the *Belfast Telegraph*[13] published yet another poll in which a majority of UUP supporters still wanted their party to stay in the Executive and again their Council voted to do so one day later. Fortunately the new institutions, particularly the Executive and Assembly, were now beginning to deliver an effective programme of accountable, regional government. This is what the people wanted, this is what they had voted for and a review of all the polls was published in the *Belfast Telegraph*[14] and *Irish Times*[15] in February 2001 to underscore this point.

Unfortunately the general and local government council elections held in the spring of that year had a polarising effect on the politics of Northern Ireland and it was not until they were past that sensitive political issues, such as police reform, could be properly dealt with. Offers were made to the parties to run more public opinion surveys on their behalf but the media were now regularly commissioning their own polls to help David Trimble and his Ulster Unionists through their various political difficulties. Needless to say the people of Northern Ireland continued to support all positive efforts made to move the peace process forward. This included a BBC[16] poll in support of SDLP and UUP membership of the new Policing Board in September 2001 and, following a start to IRA decommissioning in

October, a *Belfast Telegraph*[17] poll in support of the re-election of David Trimble as First Minister in November 2001. Surveys of public opinion, it would seem, were now an almost everyday part of the Northern Ireland peace process.

Finally then, here are a few more practical observations drawn from the experience of the eighth poll:

- Try not to end the research arbitrarily. Let the parties have a say in when to run the last poll as they are ultimately responsible for the success of the peace process.
- When support for running a public opinion poll is 'mixed' consult widely and do not be afraid to temporarily poll against the wishes of some parties.
- Have an experienced board or advisory group at hand to back up difficult polling/ethical decisions.
- As an independent facilitator or mediator it is generally inappropriate to express personal opinions but reviewing the work done and progress made can sometimes be very helpful.

Conclusion

The public opinion polls, although the most visible aspect of this approach to conflict resolution, were not an end in themselves; the process of poll-making was equally important. As a programme of independent research the parties were encouraged to take the drafting of the questions, the timing of the polls and the publication of the results in any direction that they believed would be helpful to the advancement of the peace process. It was a collective enterprise that they could use as they saw fit until the new institutions of government created under the terms of the Belfast Agreement would render such work superfluous to political requirements. Hopefully this has now been done.

But what are the prospects of using similar methods in other conflict settings? Probably better than one might think. Firstly, the problems of literacy and accessibility may not be as serious as generally thought. For example, the 'Lords of the Arctic: Wards of the State' research that fed into the negotiation of the Canadian Nunavut Settlement used public opinion polls to explore the relevant social and cultural issues from an Inuit point of view.[18] The associated reports were published in both Inuktitut and English and again widely discussed in the popular press to considerable effect.[19]

Of course Canada, Britain and Ireland wanted to reach their respective agreements as did the Inuit and pro-Agreement parties. If people just plain do not want to agree there is probably not a lot that can be done about it. But then again most people do want peace and justice and with 'the people' 'on side' a very great deal can be accomplished even when faced with an intransigent politician who, at some point, must meet his or her destiny with the ballot box.

Which perhaps brings us to the first serious limitations to the application of this method. A respectable degree of democracy and a reasonably free press may be a necessary requirement, although it is possible to imagine circumstances where a dictatorial regime might be persuaded to undertake a programme of research similar to the ones carried out in Northern Ireland and Canada if, for example, another state or international agency would muster the appropriate political and/or economic influence (e.g. the USA, Europe, the UN or World Bank). Access to the relevant parties and their electorate is essential as well as the independence of the researchers – without, it should be stressed, being subject to any forms of intimidation – and an independent source of funding, if at all possible, would be welcome. These are probably the main ingredients for a practitioner's 'wish list'. It could ideally be made longer but we do not live in an ideal world.

The work is both difficult and demanding but very rewarding. Anyone trying this for themselves will undoubtedly be confronted with obstacles not reviewed here. Each poll, personality, party and government will create its own unique set of problems. But if parties and pollsters seek only solutions, in good faith, then a way forward will be found.

2
The Calculus of Agreement

Public opinion polls are now an accepted part of the modern political process. They are used by political parties, for example, to monitor the fortunes of popular support for themselves, their leader and party policies in general. But the results of these polls are rarely made public, being undertaken to inform and develop party strategy. In the hands of the media similar polls are undertaken to create news stories. These polls are designed to shape public opinion and/or generate public debate. When undertaken by a partisan news interest they can be manipulative to the point of not publishing results that could do harm to their benefactor. When undertaken by an independent news agency increased circulation and ratings are the primary objectives. In these polls questions are phrased in the simplest possible terms to create digestible sound bites that will generate headlines and provoke adversarial debate. Common ground and compromise are not the end game. Agreement can bring a news story to a conclusion; disagreement can 'give a story legs'.

Entertaining as these polls might be they cannot help to resolve conflict. On the contrary, they often do more harm than good, forcing a wedge of discord between leaders anxious to reach an accommodation and their electorate who want nothing more than peace. But it does not have to be this way. The eight polls of public opinion conducted between April 1996 and May 2000 in support of the Northern Ireland peace process were undertaken with the expressed intention of mapping out the details of a settlement that the politicians and their supporters could live with. In the hope that others might benefit from this experience the relevant details of questionnaire design and mode of analysis are described below so that the methodology can be replicated. The political dynamics of the role that these polls played in the political process were described in Chapter 1.

Informants and conflict resolution

The results of any public opinion poll are only as good as the questions asked and contrary to much popular opinion the politicians engaged in a conflict generally do have a very sophisticated understanding of both their own political agenda and the views of their competitors. As these politicians and their parties must make the peace they are arguably the most worthwhile informants to work with when formulating issues and drafting questions.

In Northern Ireland, in the first instance, contact with the ten political parties elected to participate in the Stormont talks was established through a formal letter to the party leaders. However, very quickly, most parties assigned a designated member of their organisation to work on the public opinion polls. At this juncture the different political cultures of the various parties started to become apparent. For example, the professional middle-class Alliance party assigned a key member of their research staff, the DUP an upcoming politician with family connections, the UUP a young barrister, the leader of the newly formed Woman's Coalition tried to take on the task herself but delegated the responsibility as her work load increased and so on. The important point to be made here is that every effort was made to accommodate the different ways of working within each party, sometimes meeting at Stormont, or at the Forum, sometimes in their party offices and sometimes in their homes. Critically they had to feel comfortable with what was being done; it was important that they felt the research belonged to them and to this end they decided and agreed the methodology, the questions, the time and form of publication. As a consequence they took the results seriously and did not lightly dismiss the findings as just another media attention-grabbing event.

A few additional related points are probably worth noting at this juncture. Firstly, although there are many clear exceptions to this observation, particularly amongst smaller parties, it is better to work with negotiators and analysts rather than with party leaders. The latter tend to stick to party lines whilst the former will be more intellectually adventurous – especially party researchers.

Secondly, take note that qualitative fieldwork of this kind requires considerable patience and also that a peace process can last several years. A considerable degree of endurance is required. On average each of the Northern Ireland questionnaires went through about eight drafts before all the parties agreed the wording. None of the ten parties ever wanted to meet as a group and as a consequence hundreds of questions were discussed, dissected and redrafted through hundreds of separate meetings. But in the end all of the questions were agreed by all of the parties so none of the wording was leading in any partisan, legal or barrister/witness courtroom sense.

Finally, it proved to be essential to project an air of confidence about what was being done and the positive results that would hopefully flow from the research. Even when things were going badly, parties breaking appointments, not returning phone calls, another atrocity, a deadline slipping, it was essential that all doubts were hidden from view. The parties and negotiators had their problems too and they needed every support that they could get. Confidence was very important and it is interesting to note that the British and Irish governments told Senator Mitchell to project a similar air of quiet certainty.[1]

Questionnaire design and the search for consensus

Different types of questions can be drafted to achieve different positive outcomes. They can be used to build confidence in the peace process, prioritise problems and solutions, eliminate extreme positions, map out common ground and areas of compromise and test comprehensive agreements as packages. Some of these questions were very simple requiring just 'Yes/No' answers, while others were very complex because they contained many parts or began with an extensive preamble that was provided to allow the person being interviewed an opportunity to give an informed response. But when this research project was started little of this was known and new techniques had to be developed to accomplish these various objectives. In particular the problem of achieving agreement on contentious issues in a deeply divided society had to be dealt with. Some sort of analytical and/or statistical methodology was required that could calculate consensus.

In this regard a number of voting techniques have been devised that allow an electorate to select or rank a number of candidates or options in their order of preference and then, using various mathematical treatments, determine the most acceptable candidate or option for the greatest number of voters. Peter Emerson has been a strong advocate for the use of such methods in Northern Ireland.[2] He recommends the de Borda method, or his own variant of it.[3] In the de Borda method points are awarded in order of the voter's preference. For example, if eight candidates or options are on offer the voter's first choice will receive eight points, the second seven points and so on to the voter's final eighth choice which receives only one point. All the points are added up for each candidate or option and then a 'level of consensus' calculated which is simply the points gained expressed as a percentage of the potential maximum number of points that could have been awarded.

This method was tested in the first poll,[4] conducted as a piece of pure research, in the hope that if it did produce a clear result then, if the negotiations failed, the governments could possibly use it in a referendum to resolve the Northern Ireland problem. A random sample of the electorate, taken from the Northern Ireland electoral register, were asked to rank the eight options in Table 2.1 in their order of preference. The 'level of consensus' was then calculated for each option and these are given in the first column of values in Table 2.2.

Unfortunately no clear 'winner' emerged from this analysis, with five options falling within the 61–66 per cent range.[5] At best the three least

Table 2.1   Eight options for the political future of Northern Ireland

	Rank 1 to 8
Separate Northern Irish state – The complete separation of Northern Ireland from both the United Kingdom and the Republic of Ireland and the establishment of a separate state within the European Union.	
Full incorporation into the British state – Direct rule from Westminster and local government similar to the rest of the United Kingdom with *no* Northern Ireland Assembly or separate laws for Northern Ireland and *no* Anglo-Irish Agreement.	
Continued direct rule (no change) – The continuation of direct rule from London in consultation with the Irish government under the terms of the Anglo-Irish Agreement.	
Power sharing and the Anglo-Irish Agreement – Government by a Northern Ireland Assembly and power sharing Executive under the authority of the British government but in consultation with the Irish government under the terms of the Anglo-Irish Agreement.	
Power sharing with North–South institutions but no joint authority – Government by a Northern Ireland Assembly, power sharing Executive and a number of joint institutions established with the Republic of Ireland to deal with matters of mutual interest. (But these arrangements will not include joint authority between the British and Irish governments.)	
Joint authority and power sharing – Government by joint authority between the British and Irish governments in association with an elected power sharing Executive and Assembly.	
Separate institutions for the two main communities – Creation of separate structures for the government of each of the two main communities in Northern Ireland, subject to joint authority by the British and Irish governments.	
Full incorporation into the Irish state – Full incorporation of Northern Ireland into the Republic of Ireland to create a single state within the European Union.	

preferred options could be confidently eliminated – a separate state (49 per cent), separate institutions for each community (40 per cent) and an all-Ireland state (39 per cent). However, when a simpler technique for calculating the support for each option was used a stronger result was produced with support ranging from a low of 22 per cent to a high of 73 per cent. This method only required adding up the percentage of support for the first four options chosen without any elaborate system of point scoring. These results are given in the second column of values in Table 2.2 and are represented graphically in Figure 2.1.

As part of this research project numerous options for the development of public policy were also tested in this way and a general rule seemed to emerge: *present the results as an accumulated percentage of half the number of options on offer.* Clearly a value judgement had to be made when analysing

Table 2.2   Percentage of support for the eight Northern Ireland options*

	Level of consensus	First four preferences	'Yes' All	'Yes' Protestants	'Yes' Catholics	'Yes' UUP	'Yes' SDLP	'Yes' SF
Separate Northern Irish state	49	40	43	48	35	48	37	34
Full incorporation into the British state	61	53	61	85	25	92	28	19
Continued direct rule (no change)	64	65	56	62	49	65	59	31
Power sharing and the Anglo-Irish Agreement	66	73	58	40	81	39	87	70
Power sharing with North–South institutions but no joint authority	**64**	**66**	**60**	**48**	**73**	**52**	**83**	**57**
Joint authority and power sharing	61	53	51	28	81	24	88	73
Separate institutions for the two main communities	40	22	45	30	64	41	60	71
Full incorporation into the Irish state	39	28	44	10	90	7	90	98

* Where a strong-to-weak 'Yes' is the accumulated percentage of 'Essential' plus 'Desirable' plus 'Acceptable' and 'Tolerable'. 'No' is the 'Unacceptable' remainder.

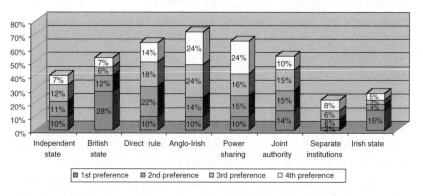

Figure 2.1   Percentage of support for the first four Northern Ireland options chosen

the results from an odd number of options so it might be better to just use even numbers if possible. Additionally this method of analysis and presentation also had the advantage that anyone reading the results did not have to understand anything more complex than a simple percentage. There was no need to explain the intricacies of the de Borda method.

The success of this research was sufficient to persuade the political parties elected to take part in the Stormont talks to get involved in a similar programme of study to explore the issues they wanted answers to. But real peace negotiations require decisions to be made on perhaps hundreds of issues encompassing anything, for example, from police reform and human rights to constitutional reform and who should vote in a referendum. These hundreds of issues in turn require hundreds of answers to hundreds of questions. Practice demonstrated that most people could rank order up to five items without any difficulty, perhaps eight options is a workable maximum, more than eight is too many. The de Borda method and its derivatives had reached their limits. A new method was required.

In consultation with the parties a four-point scale was devised in which the person being interviewed would be asked if a certain option was 'Preferable', 'Acceptable', 'Tolerable' or 'Unacceptable' as part of a settlement. Subsequently 'Essential' and 'Desirable' were substituted for 'Preferable' to make a five-point scale. Working definitions for these terms were agreed by all the parties and were presented to the interviewee as follows:

Most of the remainder of this questionnaire will present you with various options on what could be the different parts of a settlement.

For each option you will be asked to indicate which ones you consider to be 'Essential', 'Desirable', 'Acceptable', 'Tolerable' or 'Unacceptable'.

For the purposes of this poll 'Essential', 'Desirable', 'Acceptable', 'Tolerable' and 'Unacceptable' mean:

'Essential' – *You believe this option is a necessary part of a lasting settlement and should be implemented under any circumstances.*

'Desirable' – *This option is not what you would consider to be 'Essential', but you think this option, or something very similar to it, is a good idea and should be put into practice.*

'Acceptable' – *This option is not what you would consider to be 'Desirable', if you were given a choice, but you could certainly 'live with it'.*

'Tolerable' – *This option is not what you want. But, as part of a lasting settlement for Northern Ireland, you would be willing to put up with it.*

'Unacceptable' – *This option is completely unacceptable under any circumstances. You would not accept it, even as part of a lasting settlement.*

You may use each of the terms 'Essential', 'Desirable', 'Acceptable', 'Tolerable' and 'Unacceptable' as many times as you wish in each question.

In practice the operational style of this type of question was as follows – all the interviewer or informant had to do was tick the appropriate box:

	Essential	Desirable	Acceptable	Tolerable	Unacceptable
Separate Northern Irish state –The complete separation of Northern Ireland from both the United Kingdom and the Republic of Ireland and the establishment of a separate state within the European Union					
And so on...					
And so on...					
As many options as required... And so on...					

This method had several advantages. Firstly, when combined with a political and/or social breakdown, it gave detailed information on how much each section of the community liked or disliked a particular option in the context of a settlement. Secondly, the number of options was unlimited as each one was judged on its own merits although they could still be ranked through a comparative analysis – illustrated later in this chapter. If necessary the results could also be translated into crude 'Yes/No' responses if 'Unacceptable' is considered to be a strong 'No' and if 'Essential', 'Desirable', 'Acceptable' and 'Tolerable' are considered to be a strong to weak 'Yes'. Using this analytical shorthand the results for the eight options for the political future of Northern Ireland given in Table 2.1 are listed in Table 2.2 for 'All' of Northern Ireland for 'Protestants', for 'Catholics' and for the three major Northern Ireland political parties still in the talks. Although the poll for this test was conducted about two years after the first test the results seem to be comparable but analytically far more interesting. When combined with the political breakdown it became clear that the only viable option for peace was 'Power sharing with North–South institutions but no joint authority'. This was the only option acceptable to a majority of Ulster Unionists (52 per cent), Social Democratic and Labour Party supporters (83 per cent) and Sinn Féin voters (57 per cent) – highlighted in **bold**.

Although this 'formula' was the proposed 'political backbone' for an agreement, the detail still had to be 'fleshed out' and other related concerns addressed. This sometimes required drafting questions that dealt with issues that the general public had given little thought to. In these circumstances an explanatory preamble was added. For example the first question in one of the polls that included a section on human rights was written as follows:

Protecting the rights of the people of Northern Ireland

The European Convention on Human Rights

The European Convention on Human Rights protects individuals by guaranteeing each person:

The right...

To life.

Not to be tortured or subjected to inhuman or degrading treatment.

To protection from slavery or forced work.

Not to be unlawfully arrested or detained.

To a fair trial.

To freedom of belief and expression.

To free association.

To privacy and family life.

Not to be discriminated against.

To a remedy for breaches of human rights.

The new Labour government plan to introduce this Convention into the domestic law of the United Kingdom of Great Britain and Northern Ireland. This will allow any complaints regarding failures to meet these minimum standards to be heard by courts in the UK and Northern Ireland. Do you think this is 'Essential', 'Desirable', 'Acceptable', 'Tolerable' or 'Unacceptable'.

	Essential	Desirable	Acceptable	Tolerable	Unacceptable
The European Convention on Human Rights should be part of the domestic law of Northern Ireland.					

An Additional Bill of Rights for Northern Ireland

Some recent negotiated settlements have included a Bill of Rights to deal with many of the special political, social and cultural problems that lay at the heart of their conflict. Please indicate which of these options you consider to be 'Essential', 'Desirable', 'Acceptable', 'Tolerable' or 'Unacceptable'.

	Essential	Desirable	Acceptable	Tolerable	Unacceptable
An additional Bill of Rights to address the special problems of Northern Ireland.					
No additional Bill of Rights, just new laws to address the special problems of Northern Ireland.					

Human rights courts and commissions

How should human rights complaints be dealt with? Please indicate which of these options you consider to be 'Essential', 'Desirable', 'Acceptable', 'Tolerable' or 'Unacceptable'.

	Essential	Desirable	Acceptable	Tolerable	Unacceptable
A special court to hear human rights complaints.					
A commission to monitor, investigate and promote human rights.					
A commission with powers to bring human rights complaints to court.					

This question then went on to explore the issue of human rights in ever-greater detail with 29 options in all (see Appendix).[6]

Analysis and other methodological issues

The analysis of all these questions was done using a variant of the voting system used in the talks themselves. 'Sufficient Consensus' requires that a majority from each community agree the final settlement (50 per cent + one of Nationalists and 50 per cent + one of Unionists). In the poll if more than 50 per cent from each community considered an option 'Essential', 'Desirable', 'Acceptable', or 'Tolerable' then it was a potential 'winner', but if more than 50 per cent considered an option 'Unacceptable' then that

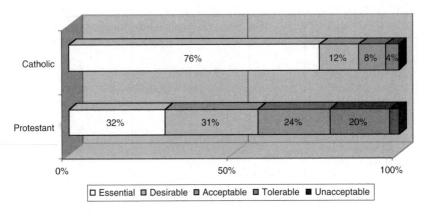

Figure 2.2   Protestant and Catholic support for the option 'The European Convention on Human Rights should be a part of the domestic law of Northern Ireland'

option was considered problematic. It might have to be discarded or 'horse traded' for another 'Unacceptable' option. Thus the results for the above questions on human rights can be presented as illustrated in Figure 2.2 for the option 'The European Convention on Human Rights should be a part of the domestic law of Northern Ireland'.

Human rights were one of the issues where there was considerable agreement between the two communities, although Catholics wanted them strengthened more than Protestants. When analysed and condensed the following result was published in the *Belfast Telegraph* on 10 January 1998 as one section of a comprehensive settlement that, in a similar way, also dealt with a regional assembly, North/South bodies, a Council of the Isles, constitutional issues and police reform (see *A comprehensive settlement* in Chapter 1, p. 18).

• A Bill of Rights that deals specifically with the political, social and cultural problems that have aggravated the conflict and a Human Rights Commission with responsibilities and powers to educate, monitor standards and bring cases to court.

As a provision of the Belfast Agreement signed on 10 April 1998 a new Commission has now been established with these powers and also with the responsibility of drafting a Bill of Rights for Northern Ireland. But not all the questions were drafted to produce this kind of analytical outcome. Some very simple 'Yes/No' questions were also used with the expressed intention of producing a headline in the local press. Although, it should be stressed that these simple questions were always backed up with more sophisticated analysis. For example, with regards to the testing of a comprehensive settlement the following questions were used:

• If a majority of the political parties elected to take part in the Stormont talks agreed to this settlement for the future of Northern Ireland would you vote to accept it in a referendum?
  77 per cent said 'Yes'

• If you said 'Yes' would you still accept these terms for a settlement even if the political party you supported was opposed to them?
  50 per cent said 'Yes'

These two questions followed a preamble that included the 200-word précis of the proposed Comprehensive Settlement given in Chapter 1. Other simple questions included:

• Do you support the principle of a negotiated settlement for the political future of Northern Ireland?
  94 per cent said 'Yes'

• Do you think the current 'Talks' will lead to a settlement?
  74 per cent said 'No'

• The terms of a settlement for the political future of Northern Ireland must receive consent in a referendum. Do you want to be given an opportunity to vote on the terms of a settlement in a referendum?
  94 per cent said 'Yes'

• In today's circumstances do you want the political party you support to stay in the talks?
  92 per cent said 'Yes'

• Do you want the Belfast Agreement to work?
  93 per cent said 'Yes'

This final question was asked in the last three polls and got a headline and front-page story in the *Belfast Telegraph* on 3 March 1999. However, this simple question was preceded by a more complex one that asked the person being interviewed which elements of the Belfast Agreement they considered to be 'Very Important' 'Important', 'Of Some Importance', 'Of Little Importance' or 'Of No Importance' at all. In previous polls people had similarly been asked how 'Significant' they considered various causes of 'The Troubles' to be and how 'Important' they thought various steps were for resolving these problems (see Appendix). Then, by simply taking the percentage response to the first option 'Very Significant' and ranking the results in order of the perceived causes of 'The Troubles', for Protestants and Catholics respectively, Table 2.3 was produced. This methodology presented objectively the major concerns of the two communities that needed

Table 2.3   Protestant and Catholic perceptions of the causes of the 'Troubles'

	Protestant per cent	Very significant	Catholic per cent	Very significant
1st	The Irish Republican Army and their use of violence.	87	The lack of equality and continued discrimination.	71
2nd	All paramilitary groups and their use of violence.	67	The sectarian division of Northern Ireland politics.	66
3rd	The failure of government and the security forces to deal with terrorism.	56	The failure to provide a police service acceptable to all.	62
4th	The Republic's territorial claim on Northern Ireland.	53	The failures of Northern Ireland politicians.	59
5th	The Loyalist paramilitaries and their use of violence.	53	A lack of respect for the people of the 'other' tradition.	57
6th	The Republic of Ireland's involvement in Northern Ireland.	42	The Loyalist paramilitaries and their use of violence.	57
7th	The failures of Northern Ireland politicians.	31	All paramilitary groups and their use of violence.	56
8th	Unaccountable and secretive government.	31	Unaccountable and secretive government.	52
9th	A lack of respect for the people of the 'other' tradition.	30	The continued British presence on the island of Ireland.	51
10th	The sectarian division of Northern Ireland politics.	30	The British Army and their use of violence.	48
11th	The prominent role of the Roman Catholic Church.	29	The Irish Republican Army and their use of violence.	45
12th	Segregated education.	25	The failure of government and the security forces to deal with terrorism.	34
13th	Segregated public housing.	22	Segregated public housing.	33
14th	The lack of equality and continued discrimination.	21	Segregated education.	31
15th	The British government's pursuit of a political settlement.	20	The British government's pursuit of a political settlement.	23
16th	The continued British presence on the island of Ireland.	17	The Republic's territorial claim on Northern Ireland.	21
17th	The 'Established Church' in Britain and the Orange Order.	14	The 'Established Church' in Britain and the Orange Order.	21
18th	The failure to provide a police service acceptable to all.	9	The Republic of Ireland's involvement in Northern Ireland.	16
19th	The British Army and their use of violence.	6	The prominent role of the Roman Catholic Church.	10

to be dealt with if the Belfast Agreement was to translate into a successful peace process. There can be no doubt that a very great deal has been accomplished but, clearly, the Northern Ireland peace process still has quite a long way to go.

A few more points on methodology should be mentioned here. Firstly, in addition to questions that dealt with the peace process it was also necessary to ask a set of demographic questions to make sure that a representative sample of the population was being surveyed. A breakdown of the demographics was regularly compared to census data and the sample parameters of other polls conducted in Northern Ireland. The key variables were gender, age, social class, geographical area, religious affiliation and political support. The parties were particularly interested in the levels of political support and the demographic profile of their own electorate in terms of gender, age, social class and so on. Although the results of any one poll could not be relied upon too much in these matters the trend of all the polls could. In addition to this demographic breakdown detailed reports were also given to the parties, the two governments and the Office of the Independent Chairmen which included tables of results for all questions for each of the main political parties, the Protestant and Catholic communities and Northern Ireland as a whole.

Secondly, in one of the early polls the parties asked people to express their views on who they thought was doing most to advance the peace process. This question did not produce any surprising results and from this point on, although the media thrived on such questions, what could in general be classified as 'beauty contest' questions – for example 'which politician do you think is doing the best job?' – were eliminated from the polls. We tried to stick to the facts and avoid value judgements which would achieve little more than grabbing the occasional headline and confirming the well established prejudices that all those who were negotiating in good faith were endeavouring to overcome.

Finally it should be stressed that all the questions were extensively pre-tested in Protestant and Catholic working-class areas of Belfast 'up the Shankill and down the Falls'. Wording would be changed and explanations or preambles added as required to improve comprehension. The view was taken that we wanted to pitch the questions at what most people could understand most of the time and not at the 'lowest common denominator'. In practice the removal of technical terms and careful structuring of the questionnaire to build comprehension meant most people could handle topics that other media would not attempt with the general public.

Ethics, publication and costs

There are a few practical issues that need to be dealt with if the methods described above are to be successfully replicated. At all times, but perhaps especially when dealing with a divided society, the various political parties that represent its separate communities and a violent conflict that they are trying to overcome, it is essential to be open and clear about questions of research ethics. In addition to agreeing all the questions with the parties involved with each poll, ethics were also dealt with as a matter of consensus with both the relevant parties and the Joseph Rowntree Charitable Trust's Board of Trustees. At the beginning of each questionnaire a statement was read to the person being interviewed clearly stating who was doing the research, who was paying for it, how the results of the research would be publicly disseminated and who would receive copies of the detailed findings. Here is an example from the 'Implementation of the Belfast Agreement' poll:

Good morning/afternoon/evening. My name is ....from MRNI Ltd. We are currently undertaking a survey aimed at discovering how the people of Northern Ireland view the current state of the peace process and the implementation of the Belfast Agreement.

The results of the survey will be analysed and widely published in the local press and in reports that will be sent to all the parties who have been elected to the New Northern Ireland Assembly.

The research is independently funded by the Joseph Rowntree Charitable Trust and is being undertaken by Dr Colin Irwin at the Queen's University of Belfast.

All your answers will be kept completely confidential

The survey involves interviewing one thousand people from across Northern Ireland to complete a representative sample in terms of age, gender, social class, political and religious affiliation and geographical area.

If you would like to take part in the survey I will start by asking you a few questions about your background to see where you fit into our sample.

Needless to say the intentions expressed in the statement were always carried out 'to the letter'. If this had not been the case the parties would have quite justifiably quit working on the project. For this reason all reports were copied to all parties at the same time. With their reports in hand all parties had the results of the surveys available to them so they could freely disagree with and challenge the analysis published in the popular press if they so wished. In this way, as should be the case with all research, everyone kept everyone else honest.

Occasionally a concerned informant would phone the researcher/facilitator at Queen's University about some aspect of a particular public opinion poll. These calls were welcome but one part of the work was not generally made public at the expressed wish of the parties. They wanted the facilitator to take public responsibility for the research so that they would be able to anonymously explore issues that were politically sensitive for them. With this point in mind the only public reference made to their participation was in the *Belfast Telegraph* report accreditations which were drafted and agreed by the parties, the market research company, Queen's University and the Joseph Rowntree Charitable Trust. Here is an example from the 'Comprehensive Settlement' poll published on 31 March 1998[7]:

> About the poll: this research was independently funded by the Joseph Rowntree Charitable Trust and has been undertaken by Dr Colin Irwin of the Institute of Irish Studies at the Queen's University of Belfast in collaboration with representatives of the ten political parties elected to the Stormont talks. The public opinion survey work was conducted by Market Research Northern Ireland between 12–20 March to produce 1000 'face-to-face' interviews that represented a cross-section of the adult population of Northern Ireland in terms of age, gender, social class, religious affiliation and geographical area. In all respects the poll was undertaken within the guidelines set out by the Market Research Society (UK) and in accordance with their code of conduct.

It may be helpful here to say just a little more about some of the other ethical decisions that had to be made. For example, one of the key questions that ran through all the polls was which parties should be included and which excluded from the programme of research. In the first instance the people of Northern Ireland helped to make this decision by electing ten parties to the Northern Ireland Forum for Peace and Reconciliation. Some parties, such as the 'Greens' and 'Socialist Workers' who did not make it into the Forum, may have been disappointed with their exclusion but a cut-off point had to be made and this one had been arrived at by democratic means.

Although Sinn Féin were elected to the Forum they abstained from it and were also not permitted into the Stormont talks when the research work was begun as the IRA were then not holding to a ceasefire. But the drafting of these questions went ahead with their inclusion anyway thus setting a healthy precedent for continuing to work with the UDP when the UFF broke their ceasefire and with the DUP and UKUP when they abstained themselves from the talks. On reflection, then, this question of research ethics was resolved by being as inclusive as possible within the limits of a democratic mandate and not to exclude any party for political reasons.

However, after the terms of the Belfast Agreement were accepted in the referendum of 22 May 1998, only the pro-agreement parties continued to be part of the polling project. The democratic mandate had now changed and it was not considered appropriate to be put in a position where the polls could be used to renegotiate an agreement made by the parties and two governments and endorsed by a significant popular vote. But all the survey reports were still made available to all the parties elected to the new Northern Ireland Assembly whatever their political persuasion.

Some decisions, however, were not quite this simple. For example between the signing of the Belfast Agreement but before it was passed in the May referendum the Rowntree Trust would not permit work to be undertaken with just the pro-agreement parties in support of the 'Yes' campaign. Conversely it was only when the Belfast Agreement appeared to be on the verge of collapse a year later that the Rowntree Trust were willing to relax the normal standards of inclusivity and fund a poll undertaken with just Sinn Féin and the PUP in an effort to get the peace process moving forward again. Having both the moral and financial backing of a responsible and experienced NGO like Rowntree is essential in such circumstances. It was not up to any individual to judge the actions, motives and who was or was not a terrorist or freedom fighter, a democrat or abstainer. If there was a single moral imperative underlying these difficult ethical decisions it was perhaps the popular support of the people of Northern Ireland for the peace process coupled with their overwhelming desire to bring all the harms of the Troubles to an end. If this were not the case the programme of polling research would not have worked.

The parties very much liked seeing the reports published in the *Belfast Telegraph*. At the very least it demonstrated that some progress was being made at the talks in Stormont. But many parties also felt these reports were playing an educative role and in this way represented a genuine contribution to and democratisation of the peace process. The relationship with the *Belfast Telegraph* was fortuitous. It is the most widely read newspaper in Northern Ireland and although it enjoys a good cross-community readership it would generally be regarded as a Unionist paper with a small 'u'. The arrangement with the editor was that they would have a first exclusive on the story so long as they provided the space for its publication, generally one page on each of a two-to-four-day period. The *Belfast Telegraph* has a broadsheet format. These feature stories, written by the author of the research, were not open to editing except for small matters of style but only then with the consent of the author. However, the newspaper retained control of its front page and headlines of which they made much use to everyone's advantage.

If these public opinion poll stories had just been issued as reports to all the local newspapers most of them would have just 'cherry picked' the items that appealed to them. This is what happened to the press releases put out by Queen's University. On two occasions efforts were also made to tie up with the broadcast media. Both attempts were disastrous. The producers' primary interests were the staging of live adversarial debates between representatives of the opposed political parties. They were not interested in exploring compromise and solutions to problems. In the absence of a change of culture within the broadcast media the only answer to this difficulty may be the independent production of documentaries.

Finally the most practical of all matters needs to be addressed, costs. Running a series of public opinion polls like the one undertaken in Northern Ireland is not cheap. But then again violent conflict is always far more expensive. For example, the cost of running the 'Implementation of the Belfast Agreement' poll in Northern Ireland was £11 100 and a quotation from a major international market research company for undertaking a similar poll in Greece was £25 500. However, several steps can be taken to keep costs to a minimum. A sample size of one thousand is generally quite adequate whatever the size of the population being worked with. Quota samples are not only cheaper than random samples, they are also quicker, taking days or weeks to gather as opposed to weeks or months. But if the costs of subcontracting the interviews is simply too much then perhaps this part of the research could be undertaken by, or in collaboration with, the staff and students at a university.

No money was available to run the first public opinion poll when the parties were asked if they would like to participate in such an activity. However, it was difficult to imagine that funds could not be found if all the parties could actually agree a questionnaire. Fortunately the *Belfast Telegraph* offered to cover the costs of the first survey after the paper had embarrassed itself with a rather disastrous phone-in poll. Success tends to breed success and the Rowntree Trust agreed to pay most of the bills after that. But there was no 'blank cheque' and the struggle to secure independent funding acceptable to all the parties, which necessarily excluded British and Irish government sources, continued to be the focus of considerable efforts. Hopefully, some day, the international community will systematically fund these kinds of peace-building activities. They could help to save lives.

3
The Drafting of Consensus and the Decommissioning Story

Perhaps the single most important feature of the polls undertaken in support of the Northern Ireland peace process was the participation of the parties to the Stormont talks in their design and, in particular, their collective agreement to the questions being asked. But this consensus was not arrived at easily. It required the development of both new styles of questions and methods of working with party negotiators through successive drafts that facilitated the anonymous exploration of all possible solutions to problems. The success of the polls was totally dependent on the success of this qualitative dimension of the research. The computer operator's dictum *'garbage in – garbage out'* applies equally to the work undertaken here and its corollary *'carefully phrased and thoughtful question in – relevant and useful solution to problem out'* was the objective that had to be achieved. The value of the public opinion surveys was a direct function of the care and attention given to asking the right questions and it was to this end that the greatest resources were applied. Running a poll would normally take several weeks while the design of the questionnaire would often take as many months.

It would simply not be possible to reproduce all the drafts of all the questions on these pages; however, by focusing on one single issue, decommissioning, it will be possible to illustrate how the drafting was done for one of the polls, the Mitchell Review. But the Mitchell Review was the sixth poll undertaken with the parties and the problem of decommissioning had also been addressed in the previous five polls. The topic had a history and that should be reviewed first to put the problem in its proper context during the negotiations leading up to the Belfast Agreement and during its implementation, or rather lack thereof, after the Agreement was achieved.

Decommissioning before the Belfast Agreement

In the first poll, 'After the Election?', published in the *Belfast Telegraph* on 7 April 1977,[1] the first question to be asked on decommissioning was designed to try and overcome the procedural deadlock created by Unionists who wanted the disarmament of paramilitary groups to be completed before the political parties that represented them were allowed into negotiations on the future of Northern Ireland. Thus the final draft of their preferred option was for a fixed timetable for decommissioning followed by the 'Talks'. Here is a copy of the question with the Unionist[2] option as follows:

The 'Talks' – making progress

Here are some options for making political progress at the 'Talks' and making progress with decommissioning. Please indicate which of the following options you consider to be 'Preferred', 'Acceptable', 'Tolerable' or 'Unacceptable'.

(*Unionist option*) – **Fixed timetable for decommissioning followed by the 'Talks'** – Decommissioning should take place on a fixed timetable that is unrelated to political progress in the 'Talks'. The 'Talks' should take as long as is required to reach a settlement.

Republicans,[3] however, did not trust Unionists to negotiate in good faith once they had given up their arsenal thus their preferred option was as follows:

(*Republican option*) – **Fixed timetable for the 'Talks' followed by decommissioning** – Political progress in the 'Talks' should take place on a fixed timetable. Decommissioning can take place when a settlement is reached.

Two centre party[4] options logically flowed from these positions for two forms of parallel decommissioning based on either a fixed or flexible timetable:

(*First centre party option*) – **Fixed timetable for the 'Talks' and decommissioning** – Political progress in the 'Talks' and decommissioning should take place in parallel in accordance with a fixed timetable that leads to a settlement.

(*Second centre party option*) – **Flexible timetable for both the 'Talks' and decommissioning** – Political progress in the 'Talks' and decommissioning should take place in parallel but no time limits should be set on reaching a political settlement.

Inevitably the options that received the greatest cross-community support were the centre party proposals for some kind of parallel decommissioning. But if decommissioning did not proceed as planned what should happen then? Should the political negotiations on the future of Northern Ireland be allowed to come to a grinding halt? Two options were drafted to deal with this issue: the Unionist option to stop the talks and all the other parties' option of passing the problem onto a subcommittee while negotiations proper went ahead. A copy of the question is given in Table 3.1 as it was asked including the two options and public opinion results for Northern Ireland as a whole. The people wanted talks without too many preconditions.

This issue was visited again by the Unionists in the second poll 'The Future of the Stormont talks' published in the *Belfast Telegraph* on 11 September 1997.[5] Unionists still wanted decommissioning to be completed before political negotiations got under way. Republicans wanted the talks to continue even if the ceasefires broke down and the centre parties were willing to proceed so long as the ceasefires held. A copy of the question is given in Table 3.2 as it was asked with the results for Northern Ireland as a whole copied in where the informant would normally indicate their preference. Again the people were willing to accept talks without decommissioning as a precondition but an end to violence was their 'bottom line'. The ceasefires had to remain firm.

As the first two polls had both dealt with decommissioning in some detail along with other procedural or 'shape of the table' questions the parties agreed that the third poll should only deal with substantive issues. Additionally the British and Irish governments had successfully, for the time being, put the problem of decommissioning to one side by establishing the Independent International Commission on Decommissioning (IICD) to handle the matter. Consequently the only reference to this subject in

Table 3.1   Who should deal with decommissioning

Here are two options for dealing with any major problems that may arise over decommissioning at the 'Talks'. Please indicate which of the following options you consider to be 'Preferred', 'Acceptable', 'Tolerable' or 'Unacceptable'.

Percentage	Preferred	Acceptable	Tolerable	Unacceptable
Stop the 'Talks' until the decommissioning problem is solved – if any major problem arises over decommissioning the 'Talks' should stop until that problem is resolved.	31	15	12	42
Do not stop the 'Talks', let a subcommittee deal with decommissioning problems – if any major problem arises over decommissioning that problem should be delegated to a subcommittee of the 'Talks' so that the principal delegates can continue to move ahead with other business.	69	10	10	11

Table 3.2 Getting to a settlement

Here are some options under which all the parties should be prepared to talk to each other with a view to increasing opportunities for reaching a settlement. Please indicate which ones you consider to be 'Desirable', 'Acceptable', 'Tolerable' or 'Unacceptable'.

All the parties should be prepared to talk to each other ...

Percentage	Desirable	Acceptable	Tolerable	Unacceptable
Even if the ceasefires do not hold	25	19	14	42
So long as the ceasefires hold	34	31	23	12
So long as the ceasefires hold and there is also some decommissioning	27	42	18	13
Only after decommissioning has been completed	33	20	15	32

the third poll, 'In Search of a Settlement', published in the *Belfast Telegraph* on 10 January 1998,[6] was in a general question designed to rank order the steps needed to help secure a lasting peace. The parties formulated seventeen steps and 'Disband all paramilitary groups' came in as the number one priority with 70 per cent of the people of Northern Ireland saying it was 'Essential'.

The fourth poll published in the *Belfast Telegraph* on 1 April 1998[7] tested all the elements of 'A Comprehensive Settlement' against public opinion. Again decommissioning was not given a high priority except for a new proposal to link 'A commitment to the principles of democracy and non-violence' to a 'Duty of Service' for all members of the Executive. This proposal was introduced by Unionists after Republicans and Nationalists[8] had introduced the concept of a 'Duty of Service' linked to 'A commitment to undertake and fulfil the responsibilities of their office'. Unionists were concerned decommissioning by the Irish Republican Army (IRA) just might not happen and Republicans were concerned Unionists would not share power with them. The poll indicated strong support for this concept of a 'Duty of Service' and it became an integral part of the Belfast Agreement. However, subsequent events also proved the concerns of both communities and their respective party leaderships to be well founded. The IRA did not start to decommission and the Unionists did not start to share power. Republicans insisted on 'government before guns' while Unionists required 'guns before government'.

Decommissioning after the Belfast Agreement

The fifth poll 'Implementation of the Belfast Agreement' published in the *Belfast Telegraph* on 3 and 4 March 1999,[9] sought to address this problem but the parties involved with the drafting of the questions now radically changed. In the four previous surveys all ten parties elected to the negotiations had equal access to the polls. But after the Agreement was passed, in the referendum of 22 May 1998, this access was only offered to parties who supported the people's decision. However, some of the pro-agreement parties did not wish to participate in another poll at this time. In particular, the parties with paramilitary connections had very strong reservations about getting involved with a poll in which the Unionists might try to selectively renegotiate the terms of early prisoner releases and the decommissioning of paramilitary weapons.

Additionally the only parties elected to the new Northern Ireland Assembly who could be relied upon not to use the polls in this way were the Progressive Unionist Party (PUP) with ties to the Ulster Volunteer Force (UVF) and Sinn Féin with ties to the IRA. As a consequence of this situation the PUP and Sinn Féin agreed to design a poll together in the hope that the 'government and guns' impasse could be broken and the peace process moved forward. The alternative appeared to be a political vacuum and a return to violence.

Republicans took the view that many parts of the Belfast Agreement, especially those sections important to them, were not being implemented while the public discussion was being focused almost exclusively on the issue of decommissioning. With this point in mind the first question in this poll listed all the different parts of the Belfast Agreement and asked the informant to say which parts were most important to them. For Unionists it was decommissioning but for Republicans it was police reform and questions of equality (Table 3.3).

The second question focused on paramilitary activity and decommissioning in much more detail. Although an end to all paramilitary activity was very important, maintaining the ceasefires was more important than anything else, more important, for example, than an act of 'token' decommissioning (Table 3.4).

These questions were designed to help place the issue of decommissioning back into the broader context of both the Belfast Agreement and the Northern Ireland peace process in general. They did. But, in spite of this, would Unionists and Republicans now be willing to be more flexible about the 'government and guns problem'? Three options were tested on this point in the implementation question as given in Table 3.5.

Option 1, no preconditions, was 'Unacceptable' to a majority of Unionists while option 3, a time limit for decommissioning, was 'Unacceptable' to a majority of Republicans. A workable compromise seemed to be option 2: have the International Commission come up with an acceptable plan. Perhaps the addition of some confidence-building measures, taken as a series of 'steps', could strengthen support for this option. A number of possibilities for these 'steps' were tested in the final question of the poll

Table 3.3 Making the peace process work

On 22 May 1998 a majority of the people of Northern Ireland and of the Republic of Ireland accepted the terms of the Belfast Agreement. The Agreement makes many compromises and contains elements that have been included for one community or the other in the hope that the overall package might eventually lead to peace. From the different parts of the Belfast Agreement listed below please indicate how important you feel each is for the eventual success of the peace process. Please indicate which ones you consider to be 'Very Important', 'Important', 'Of Some Importance', 'Of Little Importance' or 'Of No Importance at all'.

Percentage 'Very Important'	All of NI	Protestant	Catholic	DUP	UUP	PUP	Alliance	SDLP	Sinn Féin
The New Northern Ireland Assembly	47	42	52	30	43	42	81	57	43
North/South bodies	34	21	52	12	14	6	59	55	50
The British/Irish Council	29	20	40	12	13	9	58	41	33
The Equality Commission	40	31	52	17	27	50	66	54	51
The New Human Rights Commission	39	31	52	24	24	49	64	51	53
A Bill of Rights for Northern Ireland	41	36	48	31	30	56	64	46	53
The reform of the police service	32	15	56	13	7	18	39	51	67
The reform of the justice system	33	19	52	16	12	27	38	43	70
The early release of prisoners	23	14	37	7	10	34	31	21	58
The Commission for Victims	39	39	39	40	28	80	69	34	39
Decommissioning of paramilitary weapons	57	69	42	78	67	42	81	49	23
The demilitarisation of Northern Ireland	33	24	46	20	14	10	45	38	59
Changes to the Irish Constitution	32	36	27	35	25	48	49	28	24
Changes to British constitutional law	27	19	38	13	10	14	40	35	41
All parts of the Agreement together	44	38	51	22	32	49	69	55	47

Table 3.4 Paramilitary activity and decommissioning

The Belfast Agreement requires a 'commitment to non-violence and exclusively peaceful and democratic means' and for 'All participants ... to use any influence they have, to achieve the decommissioning of all paramilitary arms within two years ...'. The implementation of these parts of the Agreement can be undertaken in a number of different ways. Please indicate which ones you consider to be 'Very Important', 'Important', 'Of Some Importance', 'Of Little Importance' or 'Of No Importance at all'.

Percentage 'Very Important'	All of NI	Protestant	Catholic	DUP	UUP	PUP	Alliance	SDLP	Sinn Féin
The maintenance of the IRA ceasefire	84	85	79	86	85	89	98	85	70
The maintenance of the UVF ceasefire	83	83	81	85	84	63	98	85	70
An end to all paramilitary beatings and violence	79	84	70	88	88	75	95	83	42
An end to all paramilitary recruiting and targeting	78	83	71	83	87	61	95	82	46
An end to all other paramilitary activity	80	83	73	85	86	55	97	81	53
The start or act of 'token' decommissioning undertaken by the LVF last year	64	70	54	70	69	35	80	62	39
A start or act of 'token' decommissioning by the IRA	72	84	55	91	84	86	85	71	35
A start or act of 'token' decommissioning by the UVF	71	80	57	80	82	35	83	71	38
For Sinn Féin 'to use any influence they have, to achieve the decommissioning of all paramilitary arms within two years'	74	83	60	84	83	85	93	73	39
For the PUP 'to use any influence they have, to achieve the decommissioning of all paramilitary arms within two years'	73	81	60	77	82	49	93	73	39

Table 3.5 Implementation of the Belfast Agreement

I would now like you to consider various options for making progress with the implementation of the Belfast Agreement by indicating which ones you consider to be 'Essential', 'Desirable', 'Acceptable', 'Tolerable' or 'Unacceptable'.

Percentage 'Unacceptable'	All of NI	Protestant	Catholic	DUP	UUP	PUP	Alliance	SDLP	Sinn Féin
(*Option 1*) The Executive of the New Northern Ireland Assembly should be established, including Sinn Féin, without any preconditions and without any further delay	33	54	5	67	58	62	20	8	5
(*Option 2*) The Executive of the New Northern Ireland Assembly should be established, including Sinn Féin, and the problem of establishing a credible decommissioning process should be dealt with by General de Chastelain and his International Commission	19	34	1	54	31	43	7	1	2
(*Option 3*) The Executive of the New Northern Ireland Assembly should be established, including Sinn Féin, but they should not be allowed to stay in government if the IRA do not decommission within the two years allowed for in the Belfast Agreement	24	23	28	38	19	32	5	13	52

Table 3.6 Building trust and confidence

Failure to implement the Belfast Agreement may be due to a lack of trust and confidence between Unionists, Loyalists, Nationalists and Republicans. In an effort to overcome this problem the parties who signed the Belfast Agreement could take a number of different actions or 'steps'. Please indicate which ones you consider to be 'Essential', 'Desirable', 'Acceptable', 'Tolerable' or 'Unacceptable'.

Percentage 'Unacceptable'	All of NI	Protestant	Catholic	DUP	UUP	PUP	Alliance	SDLP	Sinn Féin
Loyalist paramilitary organisations should repeat their apology for the past harms they have done to the Catholic community	18	22	13	38	27	76	2	15	13
Mr Trimble, for the Unionists, should apologise to the Catholic community for the past discriminations they have been subjected to	31	43	15	62	41	78	22	15	14
The IRA should apologise for the past harms they have done to the Protestant community	12	10	15	12	18	4	0	15	13
The British prime minister should apologise to the Irish people for the tragedies of British involvement in Irish affairs	33	48	14	71	44	83	24	15	15
The Taoiseach should apologise for the past religious intolerance permitted by the Irish state towards their Protestant community	25	27	23	25	23	12	24	20	28

The UVF should repeat their promise never to use their weapons in a 'first strike'	4	4	5	7	2	29	0	1	10
Mr Trimble, for the Unionists, should promise to work all the new institutions of government in good faith with Sinn Féin	14	22	5	50	16	43	0	8	3
The IRA should promise never to use their weapons in a 'first strike'	1	1	2	0	1	2	0	1	4
All the new institutions of government should be established, including Sinn Féin	16	27	3	51	22	48	8	6	2
The UVF should make a start on decommissioning	3	2	3	4	1	49	0	1	9
The IRA should make a start on decommissioning	3	1	6	0	1	1	0	1	16

(Table 3.6). Most of the suggestions put forward were acceptable to a majority of the people of Northern Ireland and 91 per cent of the population thought they could form the basis for a 'package' of measures designed to overcome the 'government and guns problem'.

Although the poll undertaken with the co-operation of the PUP and Sinn Féin did not solve the problem of decommissioning it did bring the pro-agreement parties back to the negotiating table with a good deal to talk about. Regrettably these negotiations, chaired by the two governments, failed to produce a positive result twice that summer. Neither the 'Hillsborough Proposal' nor the 'Way Forward Proposal' led to the establishment of the Executive and a start to the process of decommissioning. So Seamus Mallon, the Deputy First Minister of the New Northern Ireland Assembly, resigned, forcing a formal Review of the Belfast Agreement to be undertaken for which Senator George Mitchell agreed to be the facilitator.

Decommissioning and the Mitchell Review

The goodwill created between the pro-agreement parties, through firstly achieving the Agreement and then its ratification, had reached an all time low. For Sinn Féin and the Ulster Unionists it was almost the end of the road. Their supporters had serious doubts about the future direction of the Northern Ireland peace process. It just didn't seem to be working – no power sharing and no end to paramilitary violence. Critically Sinn Féin now agreed to participate in another poll, but this time with the rest of the pro-agreement parties, including the Ulster Unionists, providing the poll did not go outside the terms of the Belfast Agreement or Mitchell Review which was limited to finding a resolution to the 'government and guns' problem.

With these points in mind a preliminary draft of the questionnaire was sent to all the pro-agreement parties in late August which included the following three options for the resolution of the problems of implementation as follows:

Review and implementation of the Belfast Agreement
The Belfast Agreement is presently under review in an effort to resolve the 'sequencing' or 'government and guns' problem. From the options on offer for the implementation of the Belfast Agreement please indicate which ones you consider to be 'Essential', 'Desirable', 'Acceptable', 'Tolerable' or 'Unacceptable'.

(*Option 1*) The Executive of the New Northern Ireland Assembly should be established, including Sinn Féin, without any preconditions and without any further delay.
(*Option 2*) The Executive of the New Northern Ireland Assembly should be established, including Sinn Féin, and the problem of establishing a credible decommissioning process should be dealt with by General de Chastelain and his International Commission.

(*Option 3*) Any other option that Sinn Féin and other parties can agree to that they might like to have tested by public opinion although no such option presently exists.

The first two options were taken from the previous poll and had already been agreed to be within the terms of the Belfast Agreement. The third option made it clear that the failed government proposals of the previous summer were now 'off the table' but it also allowed for the development of fresh proposals providing they did not include any new preconditions for the establishment of the Executive. However, as pointed out in the covering letter that went out to all the pro-agreement parties with this draft: 'suggestions for confidence-building measures would be particularly useful. These could range over a wide range of issues of importance to your party'. Confidence-building measures, or CBMs as they are often known, were acceptable to Republicans as they were considered to be voluntary acts undertaken for mutual support in an effort to strengthen and advance the peace process. CBMs were not regarded as new preconditions or changes to the Belfast Agreement. This distinction may appear to be semantic. Perhaps it is. But it went to the core of Republican sensitivities on this point as they considered themselves to be undefeated peacemakers so CBMs were 'OK' while new preconditions amounted to 'surrender'.

Following a round of interviews with party negotiators the second draft started to list some CBMs in a separate question and the observation was also made that the wording of option 2, which featured the de Chastelain decommissioning process, could be improved upon without moving outside the terms of the Belfast Agreement. This was done in the third draft but it also contained three distinctly Unionist 'No, No, No Executive' options, which, from their point of view, did not go outside the terms of the Belfast Agreement as follows:

(*Improved Option 2*) An inclusive Executive of the New Northern Ireland Assembly should be established and the decommissioning process should be dealt with by General de Chastelain.

(*First Unionist Option*) No Executive without an end to all violence and intimidation.

(*Second Unionist Option*) No Executive without a start on decommissioning.

(*Third Unionist Option*) No Executive without a guarantee that decommissioning will be completed by May 2000.

All these options needed a lot more work. The strengths of the decommissioning process were not yet explicit enough and the three 'No, No, No Executive' options didn't solve any problems. They were just a negotiating position. Additionally, while these questions were being drafted a public debate was taking place concerning the state of the ceasefires. A party with ties to a paramilitary organisation that had broken its ceasefire could be removed from government. Clearly the implications for the peace process were very serious indeed. Along with the three Unionist 'No, No, No Executive' options another question that sought to define what a 'complete and unequivocal ceasefire' was precipitated a series of concerned responses from most of the other pro-agreement parties. This point can best be illustrated by reading through the draft ceasefire question below with all the footnotes provided to the parties, which should also be carefully read in their order of appearance. Footnote (a) is particularly revealing of the concerns then being raised.

What is a ceasefire?[a]

Do you believe the Belfast Agreement requires a 'complete and unequivocal ceasefire' to include:

A cessation of attacks on the security forces? Yes or No

A cessation of attacks on members of the 'other' community? Yes or No

A cessation of attacks on economic targets? Yes or No

An end to the manufacture and use of bombs? Yes or No[b]

An end to the procurement of weapons? Yes or No

An end to the recruitment of new members? Yes or No

An end to so called 'punishment attacks' on members of their own community? Yes or No

An end to the banishment of members of their own community from the Province? Yes or No

An end to so called 'internal policing or housekeeping activities' against members of their own organisations? Yes or No

An end to all paramilitary activities? Yes or No

The disbanding of paramilitary organisations? Yes or No

And...

---

[a] Several parties felt that the 'ceasefire' question as drafted was unhelpful for the purposes of the Review as they felt it attempted to alter the terms of the Agreement by determining the Secretary of State's definition of a ceasefire by way of this public opinion poll. Similarly most parties felt that some of the conditions for setting up the Executive in the 'Implementation' question were outside of the terms of the Agreement and that this poll should not be used to make that determination. However, these issues are central to the success of the Review and therefore need to be addressed in a way that might be considered to be helpful. With this point in mind two approaches are being proposed here. Firstly, following the style of a question in the most recent *Belfast Telegraph* poll (6 September 1999 – Table 3.7), a set of questions are drafted above asking people what they think a ceasefire is and when they believe an Executive should be set up in accordance with their understanding of the Agreement. Secondly, a series of specific options have now been included in the 'Confidence Building Measures' questions and 'Implementation' questions to deal with these problems in what many parties consider to be a more practical and helpful way. Your views on these points, as with all matters, are most welcome.

[b] This option has been added in at the request of a party.

Table 3.7   Copy of question from *Belfast Telegraph* poll published 6 September 1999

Do you believe the Good Friday Agreement requires decommissioning to take place ... ?

Percentage 'Yes'	Total	Protestant	Catholic	DUP	UUP	SDLP	Sinn Féin
Prior to the setting up of the Executive	35	56	13	60	61	14	9
At the same time as the setting up of the Executive	40	34	47	29	32	52	32
After the setting up of the Executive	19	5	34	4	5	29	57
Never	2	3	2	5	2	2	1
Don't know	3	2	3	3	1	4	2

What are the requirements for establishing the Executive?

Do you believe the Belfast Agreement requires:

  No Executive without an end to all violence and intimidation? Yes or No

  No Executive without a simultaneous start on decommissioning? Yes or No[c]

  No Executive without a guarantee that decommissioning will be completed by May 2000? Yes or No

The ceasefire question was subsequently replaced with a number of CBMs and the 'No, No, No Executive' question went through yet another draft, which is also copied below. It includes a new option, taken almost as a quote from the Belfast Agreement and represents the Republican understanding of the pro-agreement parties' decommissioning commitments. The rationale for these changes was detailed to the parties in footnotes d and e below and the new CBMs are included in the results for that question given at the end of this section in Table 3.10.

What are the requirements for establishing the Executive?

Do you believe the Belfast Agreement requires:[d]

  All parties to co-operate with the Independent Commission and use any influence they may have to achieve the decommissioning of all

[c] 'simultaneous' has been added in at the request of the proposer of this question.

[d] This question has been moved here at the request of the proposer. The additional question that dealt with the meaning of a ceasefire has been cut for three reasons. Firstly, a selection of five confidence-building measures have now been included in that question which provide for a number of different approaches to deal with the problems of paramilitary violence in ways that most parties consider to be as effective and as helpful as can be expected at this point in the peace process in the absence of full implementation. Secondly, many parties considered it inappropriate for this poll

(continued)

paramilitary arms by May 2000 in the context of the implementation of the overall settlement? Yes or No[e]
No Executive without an end to all violence and intimidation? Yes or No
No Executive without a simultaneous start on decommissioning? Yes or No
No Executive without a guarantee that decommissioning will be completed by May 2000? Yes or No

In the meantime the drafting of the Implementation question took a new direction with the addition of the proposals put forward by the two governments the previous summer (Table 3.8) and a new 'step by step' approach that would allow for parallel implementation and decommissioning (Table 3.9). Again these options, with the questions and notes, are copied below:

Review of the implementation of the Belfast Agreement

The Belfast Agreement is presently under review in an effort to resolve problems of implementation.[f] From the options listed below[g] please indicate which ones you consider to be 'Essential', 'Desirable', 'Acceptable', 'Tolerable' or 'Unacceptable'.

(*Option 1*) The Executive of the New Northern Ireland Assembly should be established, including Sinn Féin, without any preconditions and without any further delay.
(*Option 2*) An inclusive Executive of the New Northern Ireland Assembly should be established and the decommissioning process should be dealt with by General de Chastelain.[h]
(*Option 3*) An agreement for setting up the Executive should be arrived at by the parties in the Mitchell Review.[i]

to be used to tell the Secretary of State what the definition of a ceasefire might be, particularly when the Secretary of State is not part of this research exercise. Thirdly, this issue is most probably going to be placed before the courts and perhaps that is the proper place for this issue to be resolved. Again it might be considered inappropriate for this poll to be used to influence or challenge the decision of the courts.
[e] This option has been added in at the request of a party.
[f] Several parties felt the phrase 'including the "sequencing" or "government and guns" problem' should be deleted.
[g] This sentence has also been shortened with the removal of the phrase 'to deal with this issue' which seems unnecessary.
[h] All parties considered this redrafting of 'The Executive of the New Northern Ireland Assembly should be established, including Sinn Féin, and the problem of establishing a credible decommissioning process should be dealt with by General de Chastelain and his International Commission' option to be worded very much better.
[i] This option has been added in as a 'lead in' or 'transition' option to the proposals set out below.

Table 3.8 The Way Forward Proposal[j]

I would like you to read this card. It contains the major elements of a possible proposal for the implementation of the Belfast Agreement.

1. The general PRINCIPLES which underpin this stage of the peace process are:
* The establishment of an inclusive Executive exercising devolved power;
* The decommissioning of all paramilitary weapons by May 2000;
* Decommissioning to be carried out in a manner determined by the International Commission on Decommissioning headed by General de Chastelain.

2. A laid out TIMETABLE for this process to be undertaken as follows:
* Within 2 weeks ministers will be nominated to the Executive.
* Within 3 weeks devolution of powers from Westminster will commence.
* As soon as specified by the International Commission, the decommissioning process will begin.
* Within 3 months the International Commission will report on the progress of decommissioning.
* By May 2000 decommissioning will be completed.

3. A built in FAILSAFE if either the commitment to devolved government or decommissioning, within the terms of the Good Friday Agreement, are not met. If triggered under the Agreement's review process the institutions established by the Agreement would be suspended.

Do you consider this proposal for the implementation of the Belfast Agreement to be acceptable?

Yes or No?

If you said 'Yes' would you still accept this proposal even if General de Chastelain required a little more time to complete the process of decommissioning?[k]

Yes or No?

But these draft questions were getting both too specific and complex to deal with the problems that had to be resolved in the negotiations at that time. Probably only one detailed proposal could be tested against public opinion in this way and the parties were not ready to do that yet. The parties wanted to test all of the proposals against each other as well as more clearly bringing out the features of the decommissioning programme that had already been agreed. A new set of options was now drafted to meet these objectives as follows:

Review of the implementation of the Belfast Agreement
The Belfast Agreement is presently under review in an effort to resolve problems of implementation. From the options listed below please indicate which ones you consider to be 'Essential', 'Desirable', 'Acceptable', 'Tolerable' or 'Unacceptable'.

[j] Several parties wanted to include the Way Forward Proposal. I have done this in the style of the 'Comprehensive Settlement' question that we asked in a previous poll.

[k] Several parties wanted to include this possibility in some way.

Table 3.9   Parallel implementation[1]

I would like you to read this card. It contains the major elements of a possible proposal for the implementation of the Belfast Agreement in a number of steps.

	Devolved government	*Decommissioning*	*Date*
Step 1	Shadow Executive and commitment to a plan for government	Commitment to decommission	1 week
Step 2	Establishment of Implementation Committee	Appointment of paramilitary representatives to Commission	
Step 3	Establishment of Civic Forum, Assembly Committees Shadow North/South Council British/Irish Council representation and development of a programme of government	Definition and confirmation of the practical modalities of decommissioning	
Step 4	Programme of government	Programme of decommissioning	3 months
Step 5	Powers of administration	Start to decommissioning	
Step 6	Executive with ministerial powers Powers of legislation Changes to Articles 2 and 3 North/South Council	Continued programme of decommissioning	
Step 7	Review of implementation	Review of decommissioning	
Step 8	Completion of implementation	Completion of decommissioning	May 2000

Do you consider this proposal for the implementation of the Belfast Agreement to be acceptable?

Yes or No?

If you said 'Yes' would you still accept this proposal even if General de Chastelain required a little more time to complete the process of decommissioning?

Yes or No?

---

[1] One party has suggested that a programme that allowed for a process of incremental or parallel implementation could work. It was proposed that the key concept here

(Continued)

(*Option 1*) A programme of decommissioning should be undertaken by General de Chastelain and his Independent Commission in accordance with his plan which includes:

Paramilitary commitments to undertake decommissioning by May 2000

Appointment of paramilitary representatives to the Commission

Confirmation of the practical modalities of decommissioning

Decommissioning with reports made to the two governments

(*Option 2*) An inclusive Executive of the New Northern Ireland Assembly should be established and the decommissioning process should be dealt with by General de Chastelain in accordance with his plan.

(*Option 3*) 'The Way Forward Proposal' should be accepted which requires an inclusive Executive, the de Chastelain programme for decommissioning and an end to devolution if these requirements are not met.

(*Option 4*) 'The Hillsborough Proposal' should be accepted which requires an inclusive Executive, the de Chastelain programme for decommissioning and a day of reconciliation when arms are placed beyond use.

(*Option 5*) A step-by-step implementation of the Belfast Agreement should be undertaken in parallel with the de Chastelain programme for decommissioning.

(*Option 6*) A combination of the best features of these different proposals that can be agreed to by the parties in the Review.

(*Option 7*) Given the delays in establishing an inclusive Executive and starting the decommissioning process General de Chastelain should be given a little more time to complete his programme of work.

The questionnaire was now starting to become quite stable. That is to say, the overall structure and flow was not being changed with parties wishing to introduce radically new questions and alterations to phrasing was being kept to a minimum. At this point in the work it was occasionally necessary, and acceptable, to bring it to the attention of a party that on several previous occasions they had approved the wording of a question and that to request a revision at this stage in the process would be unreasonable. The sixth draft separated the problems of decommissioning and setting up the Executive as indicated below. Again the footnotes detailing the relevant changes to the draft and the parties reasons for them are included just as they were during the negotiations.

is that the 'product' of government should be delivered in step with the 'product' of decommissioning. The first draft of this proposal attempts to put together a number of different ideas suggested by different parties. Clearly this approach to a solution of the problem faced by the Review needs a lot more thought and work. Only the bare bones of the concept have been sketched out in this table. Your suggestions, as always, would be welcome.

Decommissioning under the terms of the Belfast Agreement[m]

In accordance with the terms of the Belfast Agreement[n] General de Chastelain has published his programme for the decommissioning of all paramilitary weapons by his Independent International Commission. From the parts of this programme listed below please indicate which ones you consider to be 'Essential', 'Desirable', 'Acceptable', 'Tolerable' or 'Unacceptable'.

(*Option 1*) Paramilitary commitments to undertake decommissioning by May 2000.[o]
(*Option 2*) Appointment of paramilitary representatives to the Commission.
(*Option 3*) Confirmation of the practical modalities of decommissioning.
(*Option 4*) Decommissioning with reports made to the two governments.
(*Option 5*) All parts of the decommissioning programme together.

Most of the problems around finding a consensus for the questionnaire had now been solved except for the most critical issue of all – 'Guns before Government' or 'Government before Guns'. In an effort to prompt some creative discussion on this point the following suggestion was made in the current draft of the questionnaire as a note to the 'No, No, No Executive' question – which was then question eight:

Note: The current draft of question 8 is not written in the usual style of our questions and I wonder if the proposers of the options in question 8 might like to consider the following two options as an alternative?

(*Option 1*) Although the Belfast Agreement does not require decommissioning to be undertaken before the establishment of an inclusive Executive, the IRA should decommission some weapons as a confidence-building measure when the Executive is formed.
(*Option 2*) As a confidence-building measure Unionists should move to establish an inclusive Executive without any preconditions and without any further delay.

---

[m] One party had strong misgivings about including this issue as an option in the question on setting up the Executive. Neither did they want it added in as a preamble to that question. They also wanted each part of the question dealt with separately as they took the view that it was too difficult to understand in its previous form. This has all been done in this separate drafting of the question above. Finally they thought it would be best if this issue of decommissioning was dealt with after the questions about setting up the Executive. Other parties felt, however, that it would be better to present the information about de Chastelain's programme before reference is made to it in the next question.
[n] One party considered it important to make reference to the Belfast Agreement here.
[o] One party asked if this requirement was part of the de Chastelain report as well as the Belfast Agreement. The answer appears to be 'Yes' as it is referred to in such terms in paragraph 17(a) of the de Chastelain report.

In practice this solution to the 'Government and Guns' problem became the one adopted in both the Mitchell Review as a 'voluntary act' and also in the subsequent informal review undertaken by the two governments as a 'confidence-building measure'. But the parties were not prepared to accept the concept at this point in the negotiations so a new set of questions were drafted for their consideration. Unionists were still holding firm to their three 'No, No, No Executive' options and also very much wanted the Republican option removed so their preferred question was now as follows:

Conditions for establishing the Executive
Under what conditions do you think an Executive should be established? Please indicate which options you consider to be 'Essential', 'Desirable', 'Acceptable', 'Tolerable' or 'Unacceptable'.

(*Option 1*) No Executive without an end to all violence and intimidation.
(*Option 2*) No Executive without a simultaneous start on decommissioning.
(*Option 3*) No Executive without a guarantee that decommissioning will be completed by May 2000.

However, by adding in what could be characterised as three 'Yes, Yes, Yes Executive' options it would be possible to balance out the Unionist preferences and interpretation of the Belfast Agreement with Republican preferences and their understanding of its terms as follows:

Conditions for establishing the Executive
Under what conditions do you think an Executive should be established? Please indicate which options you consider to be 'Essential', 'Desirable', 'Acceptable', 'Tolerable' or 'Unacceptable'.

(*Option 1*) An inclusive Executive should be formed and all parties should do everything they can to bring an end to all paramilitary violence and intimidation.
(*Option 2*) No Executive without an end to all violence and intimidation.
(*Option 3*) An inclusive Executive should be formed and all parties should co-operate with General de Chastelain and his Commission to start the decommissioning process.
(*Option 4*) No Executive without a simultaneous start on decommissioning.
(*Option 5*) An inclusive Executive should be formed and all parties should co-operate with General de Chastelain and his Commission to complete the decommissioning process by May 2000.
(*Option 6*) No Executive without a guarantee that decommissioning will be completed by May 2000.

But some parties had pointed out that the three 'No, No, No Executive' options made no specific reference to Sinn Féin and therefore precluded the possibility of the Unionists forming an Executive with just the SDLP.

Additionally references were made to 'all violence' and decommissioning in general. A strict reading of these options would require Sinn Féin to be removed from the Executive if Loyalist violence persisted or if Loyalists did not decommission. For the sake of accuracy and precision a new draft of the 'No, No, No Executive' options was produced that corrected these errors:

Conditions for establishing the Executive
Under what conditions do you think an Executive should be established? Please indicate which options you consider to be 'Essential', 'Desirable', 'Acceptable', 'Tolerable' or 'Unacceptable'.

(*Option 1*) No Executive including Sinn Féin without an end to all IRA violence and intimidation.
(*Option 2*) No Executive including Sinn Féin without a simultaneous start on decommissioning by the IRA.
(*Option 3*) No Executive including Sinn Féin without a guarantee that IRA decommissioning will be completed by May 2000.

But this draft now did not address Republican concerns that the options were, from their point of view, outside the terms of the Belfast Agreement. Another possible solution to this problem would be to add a preamble to the question that directly addressed this issue as follows:

Conditions for establishing the Executive
Although the Belfast Agreement does not require any preconditions to be imposed for setting up an Executive with Sinn Féin under what conditions do you think an inclusive Executive should be established? Please indicate which options you consider to be 'Essential', 'Desirable', 'Acceptable', 'Tolerable' or 'Unacceptable'.

(*Option 1*) No Executive including Sinn Féin without an end to all IRA violence and intimidation.
(*Option 2*) No Executive including Sinn Féin without a simultaneous start on decommissioning by the IRA.
(*Option 3*) No Executive including Sinn Féin without a guarantee that IRA decommissioning will be completed by May 2000.

But the question, so drafted, was still very negative in character and would likely produce an emotive response by both anti-agreement Unionists who did not want Sinn Féin in government and Republicans who would consider all the options totally 'Unacceptable'. The question, even in this form, was not going to solve any problems. So a series of less emotive and more politically neutral approaches to dealing with the same set of issues were proposed:

Do you think it is realistic to believe ... ?
Loyalist and Republican paramilitary groups can bring an end to all paramilitary violence and intimidation as soon as an Executive is established? Yes or No

Loyalist and Republican paramilitary groups can simultaneously decommission when an Executive is established? Yes or No

Loyalist and Republican paramilitary groups can complete the decommissioning of all their weapons by May 2000? Yes or No

Do you think it is realistic to believe ...?

Sinn Féin can persuade the IRA to bring an end to all paramilitary violence and intimidation as soon as an Executive is established? Yes or No

Sinn Féin can persuade the IRA to simultaneously decommission when an Executive is established? Yes or No

Sinn Féin can persuade the IRA to complete the decommissioning of all their weapons by May 2000? Yes or No

Do you believe IRA decommissioning can be completed without ...?

Sinn Féin in the Executive? Yes or No

An end to Loyalist violence? Yes or No

Implementation of the Patton Report on police reform? Yes or No

Full implementation of all of the other parts of the Belfast Agreement? Yes or No

Do you believe an inclusive Executive can be established without ...?

An end to IRA violence? Yes or No

A start on decommissioning by the IRA? Yes or No

The completion of IRA decommissioning? Yes or No

Full implementation of all of the decommissioning and non-violence parts of the Belfast Agreement? Yes or No

Do you believe ...?

An immediate and unilateral act of decommissioning by the IRA could destabilise dissident Republican groups leading to more splits and violence? Yes or No

Allowing Sinn Féin into the Executive without any immediate prospect of decommissioning could destabilise dissident Unionist groups leading to more splits in their party and the collapse of the New Northern Ireland Assembly? Yes or No

An immediate and unilateral act of decommissioning by the IRA could destabilise dissident Republican groups leading to the replacement of Gerry Adams by a more hard-line leader of Sinn Féin? Yes or No

Allowing Sinn Féin into the Executive without any immediate prospect of decommissioning could destabilise dissident Unionist groups leading to the replacement of David Trimble by a more hard-line leader of the UUP? Yes or No

Decommissioning is being used as a 'stalling tactic' by Unionists? Yes or No

Decommissioning is being used as a 'destabilising tactic' by Republicans? Yes or No

From all these possibilities the 'Do you believe IRA decommissioning can be completed without...?' and 'Do you believe an inclusive Executive can be established without...?' questions were accepted along with two new decommissioning options for the Confidence-Building Measures question:

Building trust and confidence
I would now like you to consider various options for building trust and confidence between the two communities by indicating which ones you consider to be 'Essential', 'Desirable', 'Acceptable', 'Tolerable' or 'Unacceptable'.

(*Option 1*) The mandate of the International Commission on Decommissioning should include all privately held weapons.
(*Option 2*) The British government should publish their paper on the demilitarisation of Northern Ireland.

Yet another line of enquiry was also explored but not taken up as a set of questions. However, several of the options did become part of the deal struck in the Mitchell Review as conditions for setting up the Executive: namely that the IRA should say they will decommission, appoint a representative to work with the de Chastelain Commission and for the General to say the IRA decommissioning process had begun.

When to establish an inclusive Executive
If temporary arrangements are put in place to implement the Belfast Agreement when do you think an Executive, including Sinn Féin, should be established? Please indicate which options you consider to be 'Essential', 'Desirable', 'Acceptable', 'Tolerable' or 'Unacceptable'.

(*Option 1*) When all the parties to the Belfast Agreement start working together to bring about the decommissioning of all paramilitary weapons.
(*Option 2*) When the IRA say they will decommission as part of the peace process.
(*Option 3*) When the IRA appoint a representative to work with General de Chastelain's Commission.
(*Option 4*) When the IRA agree to decommission by May 2000.
(*Option 5*) When General de Chastelain says the IRA decommissioning process has begun.
(*Option 6*) When the IRA says the 'war is over'.
(*Option 7*) When the IRA start decommissioning.
(*Option 8*) When the IRA complete their decommissioning.
(*Option 9*) When the IRA bring an end to all their violence and intimidation.
(*Option 10*) When the IRA disband.

With very minor changes to some wording here and there the draft questionnaire was now pre-tested and run. The full results for the decommissioning and confidence-building measures questions are given below with 'final–final' changes referenced in the footnotes as they were to the parties (Tables 3.10–3.15).

Conclusion

In practice the work undertaken to produce an acceptable draft question-naire went through the following stages:

1. A letter was sent out to all parties inviting them to participate in the design and running of a public opinion poll in support of the peace process.
2. At an initial meeting with party officers a party negotiator would be assigned to the task and issues relating to methods, topics, timing and publication would be discussed.
3. An outline or 'first draft' questionnaire would be sent out to the party contacts for discussion purposes with a covering letter that summarised the views of parties with regards to methods, topics, timing and publica-tion. This letter would also contain a list of the party contacts so that they would be free to discuss any matters arising with each other.
4. The second and subsequent meetings with party representatives would review the draft questionnaire to register party requests for changes and additions.
5. The third and subsequent letter and draft questionnaire noted all requests for changes and additions. For the sake of clarity, footnotes would be removed relating to previous drafts so that all notes referred only to current alterations.
6. When the questionnaire started to 'stabilise' it would be sent out for pre-testing to identify fieldwork difficulties relating to problems of com-prehension and length. The parties were notified that this stage in the work had been reached and that they should identify any final changes they might like as well as indicating which questions could possibly be left out to be dealt with in a later poll if so required.
7. Final changes were made by those running the poll on the evidence of objective fieldwork tests. These changes were noted in the final draft which was sent to all the parties with a covering letter detailing the sur-vey research schedule and publication date.
8. From this point onward parties were not permitted to interfere in any way with the programme of research, analysis of data and publication. However, they did receive full statistical reports and were free to make criticisms of the findings if they so wished.

Frequently the work of drafting questions went down 'blind alleys', became pedantic or even party personal, occasionally leading to frustrations and recriminations. At such times the drafting became more than just an intel-lectual exercise designed to find solutions to social and political problems.

(Cont. on p. 75)

Final draft of Mitchell Review decommissioning questions and results

Published in the *Belfast Telegraph* on 26 and 27 October 1999.[10]

Table 3.10 Building trust and confidence

I would now like you to consider various options for building trust and confidence between the two communities by indicating which ones you consider to be 'Essential', 'Desirable', 'Acceptable', 'Tolerable' or 'Unacceptable'.

Percentage 'Unacceptable'	All of NI	Protestant	Catholic	DUP	UUP	PUP	Alliance	SDLP	Sinn Féin
The Review should establish a relationship-building process between all the parties, in particular Sinn Féin and the Ulster Unionist Party, with a collective public act which marks the beginning of the process of reconciliation.	11	18	1	37	3	12	0	0	0
The 'Yes parties' should establish a special committee to co-ordinate the implementation of the Belfast Agreement in full.	12	20	1	43	7	9	3	0	0
All the parties should accept some responsibility for the conflict and state their determination not to repeat the mistakes of the past.	6	10	1	21	3	0	0	1	0
All the parties should state their absolute commitment to all the provisions in the Good Friday Agreement.	7	11	1	23	2	2	0	0	0
Temporary arrangements should be put in place to get the	12	19	3	37	8	9	7	2	2

Assembly working providing they lead to the implementation of the Belfast Agreement in full.

All the parties should state their recommitment to the Mitchell principles of democracy and non-violence.	4	6	2	10	1	2	0	2	1
The two governments should clearly say what is meant by a 'complete and unequivocal ceasefire'.	1	1	3	2	0	0	0	1	7
Both the IRA and Loyalist paramilitary groups should say 'The war is over'.	3	1	6	0	1	0	0	2	17
Both Loyalist and Republican paramilitary groups should indicate their willingness to disarm as part of the peace process.	2	1	4	0	0	3	0	1	13
Both Loyalist and Republican paramilitary groups should end all so-called 'punishment attacks'.	2	0	6	0	0	0	0	1	16
Both Loyalist and Republican paramilitary groups should co-operate with the New Northern Ireland Police Service to bring an end to all beatings and violence.	7	4	10	10	2	4	0	2	29
Ex-prisoners should be encouraged to make a positive contribution to the establishment of a lasting peace through community work.	14	20	8	25	19	0	5	11	9
Decommissioning should include all privately held weapons.	16	22	10	31	18	9	15	7	15
The British government should publish their paper on the demilitarisation of Northern Ireland.	2	3	1	4	3	0	0	0	1

Table 3.11 Decommissioning under the terms of the Belfast Agreement

In accordance with the terms of the Belfast Agreement General de Chastelain has published his programme for the decommissioning of all paramilitary weapons by his Independent International Commission. From the parts of this programme listed below please indicate which ones you consider to be 'Essential', 'Desirable', 'Acceptable', 'Tolerable' or 'Unacceptable'.

Percentage 'Unacceptable'	All of NI	Protestant	Catholic	DUP	UUP	PUP	Alliance	SDLP	Sinn Féin
Paramilitary commitments to undertake decommissioning by May 2000.	3	2	5	6	1	2	0	1	18
Appointment of paramilitary representatives to the Commission.[p]	17	23	9	39	18	4	15	9	13
Confirmation of how, when and where weapons will be decommissioned.[q]	3	1	6	3	1	3	0	1	21
Decommissioning with reports made to the two governments.	4	3	6	5	2	0	0	1	17
All parts of the decommissioning programme together.	3	1	6	1	1	0	2	1	19

[p] (Note from final report to parties). The results for this option seem to be out of step with the other options. Regrettably some people must have interpreted this option as meaning that representatives from paramilitary groups would actually join the Decommissioning Commission and not just co-operate with it. The results for this option should probably therefore be disregarded.

[q] For clarity and better comprehension 'practical modalities of decommissioning' has been replaced with 'how, when and where weapons will be decommissioned'.

Table 3.12 Review of the implementation of the Belfast Agreement

The Belfast Agreement is presently under review in an effort to resolve problems of implementation. From the options listed below please indicate which ones you consider to be 'Essential', 'Desirable', 'Acceptable', 'Tolerable' or 'Unacceptable'.

Percentage 'Unacceptable'	All of NI	Protestant	Catholic	DUP	UUP	PUP	Alliance	SDLP	Sinn Féin
The Executive of the New Northern Ireland Assembly should be established, including Sinn Féin, without any preconditions and without any further delay.	28	44	4	63	37	21	23	5	0
An inclusive Executive of the New Northern Ireland Assembly should be established and the decommissioning process should be dealt with by General de Chastelain in accordance with his programme.	14	22	2	43	13	7	5	1	1
An inclusive Executive, the de Chastelain programme for decommissioning and a day of reconciliation when arms are placed beyond use.ᵀ	10	15	4	28	6	7	2	0	15
An inclusive Executive, the de Chastelain programme for decommissioning and an end to devolution if these requirements are not met.	14	15	11	25	11	7	6	4	27

Table 3.12 Continued

Percentage 'Unacceptable'	All of NI	Protestant	Catholic	DUP	UUP	PUP	Alliance	SDLP	Sinn Féin
A step-by-step implementation of the Belfast Agreement in parallel with the de Chastelain programme for decommissioning.	11	12	7	26	3	5	2	2	22
A combination of the best features of these different proposals that can be agreed to by the parties in the Review.	11	13	7	26	7	0	3	3	21
Given the delays in establishing an inclusive Executive and starting the decommissioning process General de Chastelain should be given a little more time to complete his programme of work beyond the Belfast Agreement deadline of May 2000.[5]	18	24	7	42	18	16	11	5	9

[r] Reference to 'The Hillsborough Proposal' has been dropped as many people had either not heard of it or were not sure what it was. Some people then wanted to discuss the point at some length. For the same reasons reference to 'The Way Forward Proposal' has been cut.

[s] One party considered it important to make reference to the Belfast Agreement here.

Table 3.13 What do you believe?[t]

Do you believe the Belfast Agreement requires...?

Percentage 'Yes'	All of NI	Protestant	Catholic	DUP	UUP	PUP	Alliance	SDLP	Sinn Féin
All parties to co-operate with the Independent Commission and use any influence they may have to achieve the decommissioning of all paramilitary arms by May 2000 in the context of the implementation of the overall settlement.	92	94	87	92	93	89	91	92	86
No Executive including Sinn Féin without an end to all IRA violence and intimidation.[u]	69	81	52	83	80	71	74	60	28
No Executive including Sinn Féin without a simultaneous start on decommissioning by the IRA.	70	80	57	82	80	68	80	65	28
No Executive including Sinn Féin without a guarantee that IRA decommissioning will be completed by May 2000.	72	79	66	80	77	70	93	71	34

[t] Following further discussions with the two parties who had reservations about the exact wording of this question the following drafts have now been agreed. Additionally, because the questions are quite emotive, they have been placed at the end of the questionnaire so that they will not influence the responses to the more substantive questions asked earlier.
[u] The phrase 'including Sinn Féin' and term 'IRA' have been added in for better clarity and precision.

Table 3.14 Do you believe IRA decommissioning can be completed without …?[v]

Percentage 'Yes'	All of NI	Protestant	Catholic	DUP	UUP	PUP	Alliance	SDLP	Sinn Féin
Sinn Féin in the Executive	23	32	11	36	29	16	16	13	3
An end to Loyalist violence	23	31	16	35	29	18	7	16	15
Implementation of the Patten Report on police reform	37	41	36	36	46	25	38	41	20
Full implementation of all of the other parts of the Belfast Agreement	37	44	32	47	43	32	34	36	28

Table 3.15 Do you believe an inclusive Executive can be established without …?

Percentage 'Yes'	All of NI	Protestant	Catholic	DUP	UUP	PUP	Alliance	SDLP	Sinn Féin
An end to IRA violence	29	21	42	18	22	29	26	29	67
A start on decommissioning by the IRA	61	26	59	22	29	30	20	44	92
The completion of IRA decommissioning by May 2000	58	31	61	25	34	27	23	51	90
Full implementation of all of the decommissioning and non-violence commitments of the Belfast Agreement	59	35	52	35	35	32	29	46	68

[v] This is a new question agreed to by the two parties who wanted to deal with the issues addressed here. I have noticed much talk about Loyalist violence in the last few days on the TV and radio etc. This subject is dealt with in this question. But then so too is IRA violence. I am sorry you did not all have an opportunity to comment on this particular question but I have done my best to achieve a sense of balance and context.

It was also a medium through which all manner of concerns could be raised and commented on, and if the matter could not be resolved privately then the issue could still be tested before the arbiter of public opinion. The footnotes and discarded options from the Mitchell Review have been included here precisely to illustrate these points. But when it was done and everyone had had their say the results were taken seriously and did affect the decision-making process. The questions asked were the ones the parties wanted answers to.

Regrettably many academics, journalists and policy-makers fall into the trap of only listening to a politician's public discourse that is principally designed for the consumption of their own electorate, and then too quickly judging them by that rhetoric. In these circumstances many academics, journalists and policy-makers draw the conclusion that engaging with such politicians in any collaborative exercise would be a total waste of time and effort. They could not be more wrong. For the most part public opinion polls undertaken and published without reference to the real political needs of politicians struggling to find honourable accommodations while still maintaining their party's strength are destined to ask the wrong questions at the wrong time. These failings can be avoided. Academics, journalists, policy-makers and politicians can work together to use public opinion polls as part of an enhanced and more creative decision-making process that increases the prospects for greater social and political success. Every possible care and attention should be given to such questions of process and outcome particularly when running public opinion polls in societies struggling to overcome the burdens of deep community divisions.

4
Polling as Peace Building

Effective peace building requires the re-establishment of all those elements of a society that make it a functioning success. In the first instance an absence of dialogue between the conflicting parties must be replaced with reliable channels of communication that can facilitate an honest discourse on all the issues that lie at the heart of the conflict. Secondly, once the talking has begun in earnest, discussion must lead to real negotiations and decision-making on each element of an agreement that provides remedies for every failed social practice and inoperative political institution. Finally, once the agreement is reached it must be implemented in full, with as much rigour, care and attention to success as the negotiations themselves. Peace building requires both vigilance and patience and in this the support of all of the elements of the society and the international community must be encouraged to play a constructive role if a return to violence and war is to be avoided.

In Northern Ireland public opinion polls were used to enhance all of these essential processes by helping to establish real dialogue and effective communications; explore problems and their solutions; define the critical issues and associated questions; and last, but by no means least, help to keep the peace process on track by facilitating a discourse in which the society as a whole could play a part in the decision-making process. But the emphasis here is on 'enhance' and 'help'. Public opinion polls alone cannot bring about change. They can only assist and facilitate in a process that must, in the end, be done by the people and their elected representatives.

There are also things that public opinion polls should not be used for in peace processes. Regrettably they can be designed to undermine the efforts of peace builders when they are employed by one party to a conflict to advance their own agenda while ignoring the concerns of others. Questions can also be designed to create distrust and even despair by addressing just the problems and not their solutions, or by highlighting the fears and prejudices of each community while ignoring the hopes and aspirations of the society to move beyond the failures of the past. Those who have a vested interest in a continuation of the status quo can also use public opinion polls to undo the good that may have been done by attempting to undermine and/or renegotiate agreements by selectively revisiting the concessions that only one side, their side, has made. Responsible editors and journalists should avoid all of these temptations often embarked upon to grab a head-line and create disagreement in an effort to increase circulation, ratings and sales. But responsible editors and journalists, politicians and academics can do otherwise. They can use public opinion polls to help build peace and, step by step, the successes of the Northern Ireland experience point the way to how this can be done.

Of course the Northern Ireland experience is also littered with failure. Some things worked and some things didn't. But the purpose of this chap-ter is to review, with all the benefits of hindsight, the things that did work in the hope that others can now build on what was learned. In practice the experience that others will have in other conflict settings will be very dif-ferent: different peoples, languages, personalities, institutions, interna-tional relations and so on. But the process of trial and error and hopefully progress being made will not be so very different at all.

Establishing real dialogue and effective communication

Inter-track dialogue and diplomacy

Peace building problem All too often political parties find they have to align themselves with different sections of society and communities to get elected. In deeply divided societies this reality can lead to the increased polarisation of party policies and their associated electorate groups[1] when most people, most of the time, would prefer accommodation, peace and the prosperity that flows from political stability. All too often politicians and political parties (track one) find it difficult, if not impossible, to estab-lish a positive dialogue with all the people (track three) through the media and institutions of civil society (track two) in an effort to define a set of common goals with a view to achieving some common ends.

Northern Ireland experience Public opinion polls were used in Northern Ireland to create a form of inter-track diplomacy through an ongoing process of questionnaire design with the politicians, interviews with their electorate and publication of survey results in the local press. This did not happen 'overnight' by way of some carefully designed diplomatic strategy but over a period of months and years during which time all the elements of this peace building exercise were put into place. Firstly, a programme of pure research was undertaken by a group of academics at the Queen's University of Belfast[2] on different aspects of peace building and public pol-icy that included a public opinion poll survey and the publication of the findings in a series of articles in the *Belfast Telegraph*[3] and as a supplement in a local current affairs magazine, *Fortnight*.[4] This study also included questions that began to explore attitudes towards various political solutions to the Northern Ireland problem. Secondly, the political parties elected to participate in the negotiations on the future of Northern Ireland were invited and agreed to participate in the drafting of a new poll designed to address all the issues presently holding up progress in the Stormont talks. They agreed, providing individuals were not cited as being actively involved in the exercise. A degree of discretion was essential especially when 'old enemies' were co-operating in a common enterprise. Thirdly, funding was secured from an independent sponsor, the Joseph Rowntree Charitable Trust, that all parties accepted as neutral, and agreement was reached with the *Belfast Telegraph* that their paper would publish the reports of the surveys without insisting on editorial control of their content. The political consultations, interviews, analysis, writing and publication were genuinely independent, from beginning to end, across all three tracks of the process. Consequently the parties had confidence in the process and took the results of the research seriously.

Public opinion poll action Get the media, newspapers, political parties, appropriate charities and sponsors, universities and academics involved in a collective enterprise of designing and running a series of public opinion polls as part of a peace process.

The formation of a contact group to help resolve the conflict

Peace building problem Political parties, who are at best electoral competitors and at worst actively engaged in hostilities publicly refuse to enter into negotiations with their 'enemies' without first having them agree to a series of unacceptable preconditions. But without dialogue any possibility of achieving a workable agreement on the preconditions, let alone a settlement of the conflict, is impossible – the ultimate 'chicken and egg' problem.

Northern Ireland experience Although the first purely academic piece of research demonstrated public support for a political compromise on the future of Northern Ireland the politicians disagreed with a lot of what was done in this poll. Many of them thought the questions were biased or were the wrong questions on the wrong issues or even that the most important issues had been ignored. Inevitably different politicians from different parties had very different views on these matters. Some of them also thought that the methodology could be improved in terms of the way the questions were asked, analysed or broken down in terms of community and political groups. These criticisms were all very healthy, welcome and provided for a great deal to talk about and agree upon without running the risk of making political decisions that were irreversible. Through a series of private interviews with representatives of each party, firstly the issues to be dealt with in the next poll were agreed as well as the time when they thought it could most effectively be published. Secondly, the introduction to the polling interview was agreed in which it was clearly stated who was doing the research, who was funding it and who would get the results. Thirdly, successive drafts of the questions were circulated until a consensus was reached in which each party felt their issues were dealt with to their satisfaction and that no other party's issues were put forward unfairly with questions that would be considered leading. In this way, informally, quick progress was made on a wide range of issues that were not necessarily being discussed in the formal negotiations at that time because of procedural and/or agenda problems. When the results of the first poll were published a number of procedural problems were solved and both the negotiations proper and the private polls were able to move on to the next set of issues – the different parts of an agreement.

Public opinion poll action Firstly, run a public opinion poll that demonstrates the desire of the people for an honourable settlement and that the possibility of achieving an agreement is real. Secondly, invite all the serious parties to the conflict to appoint a representative to work with the researchers on designing and agreeing a series of public opinion polls with the expressed objective of assisting the parties with their negotiations.

Establishing confidential lines of communication between the parties to a conflict

Peace building problem A breakdown of communication due to a lack of trust: for example, when parties engaged in hostilities will not give up violence in favour of political negotiations because they do not believe the other parties will negotiate in good faith. Or when, perhaps, one party or the other believes the negotiations and/or the ceasefire is only tactical.

Northern Ireland experience When the negotiations for the first poll were begun in January 1997 the Conservatives were in government in Westminster where they relied on the votes of the Northern Ireland Unionists to keep them in power. In this situation the possibility of meaningful compromises being agreed on the future of the Province were very doubtful and consequently the Irish Republican Army (IRA) had broken their ceasefire and returned to hostilities against the British state. In these circumstances there was a breakdown of effective communications between Sinn Féin (the political wing of the IRA) and the other political parties, the two governments and the Office of the Independent Chairmen because the British were opposed to any negotiations with terrorists at war. When Labour replaced the Conservatives in May 1997 Sinn Féin wanted to reinstate their ceasefire and return to political negotiations but only if they believed that these negotiations would be undertaken in good faith. They wanted to be sure that those responsible for managing the talks would not allow the Unionists, in particular Dr Paisley the leader of the Democratic Unionist Party, to frustrate progress through filibusters and other delaying tactics. In particular they were concerned to know how Senator George Mitchell, the senior talks chairman, might handle such matters. These concerns were addressed to Sinn Féin's satisfaction firstly through the informal channels of communication available to them, which included the public opinion poll contact group, and then formally when the embargo on direct communication with the British government was temporarily lifted during an informal suspension of hostilities. Subsequently the IRA called their second ceasefire, the DUP left the talks, the Ulster Unionists did not block progress and the Belfast Agreement was signed on Good Friday 1998. As an academic at Queen's University the poll facilitator also had free access to other scholars, in particular human rights and constitutional lawyers, who were able to give opinions on specific issues when the facilitator or a party to the negotiations so required.

Public opinion poll action Establish independent, reliable and confidential lines of communication between the parties with points of access to other independent third parties who can provide expert advice as required.

Establishing confidence in the peace process

Peace building problem After years of violence, 'off again – on again' war and numerous failed political initiatives to bring the conflict to an end very few people have any confidence that yet another attempt to conclude an agreement will be any more successful than all the failures of the past.

Northern Ireland experience In addition to all the sophisticated questions designed to map out the structure and elements of a peace agreement, a few simple 'Yes/No' questions were included in each of the Northern Ireland polls with the intention of creating a confidence-building headline in the local press. Consequently on the front page of the *Belfast Telegraph* of 7 April 1997[5] under the banner headline 'YOUR VERDICT' subheadlines from the first poll also read '94% want a negotiated settlement' as well as '69% do not want talks to stop' but also more soberly '74% believe Stormont talks will fail'. In the second poll on 11 September 1997[6] the headline was '92% SAY YES' to the question 'Do you want your party to stay in the talks?' and the editorial leader was entitled '"Yes" to talks'. Additionally 'Put talks package to vote' was the front-page story the following day on 12 September[7] with the observation that 'Less than one in ten – 9% – regard the idea as unacceptable'. The third poll moved on from questions of procedure and started to deal with the substance of a settlement so that on 12 January 1998[8] the front-page story was 'Poll signals backing for new assembly', on 13 January[9] it was 'NORTH SOUTH LINKS VERDICT', and on 14 January[10] the front-page story was 'Poll reveals Ulster yes for islands council'. Before the agreement was signed it was tested in the fourth poll. On 31 March 1998[11] the banner headline was '77% SAY YES' and the deal was finally struck on Good Friday. But that wasn't the end of the matter. Implementation became a problem with Unionists wanting 'guns before government' and Republicans wanting 'government before guns'. On 3 March 1999[12] the front-page story was 'DUP voters want deal to work: poll' and the inside page was '93% SAY: MAKE THE AGREEMENT WORK'. But it didn't work all that summer, so with Senator Mitchell as facilitator everyone tried again. By 26 October[13] the *Belfast Telegraph* front-page headline now read '65% STILL FOR DEAL' – that is to say they would still vote 'Yes' while 85 per cent still wanted the agreement to work. Support was not as strong as it was but as the editorial pointed out on that day it was 'Still the best option'. Confidence was maintained.

Public opinion poll action Although the public opinion polls must deal with all the problems and possible solutions that lie at the heart of a conflict, questions of confidence and continued progress should also be addressed by asking people if they want a political agreement, an end to violence, negotiations to be started, timely decisions to be made, democratic institutions to be re-established, the maintenance of human rights standards and the rule of law, effective policing acceptable to the whole community and economic development in the context of peace and so on. Of course nearly everyone wants all these things and asking such questions, arguably, is a trivial use of the polls. But providing such questions are only included in the context of the more serious issues that must be addressed then giving 'a boost' to the self-confidence of both the politicians and their electorate from time to time can be a very worthwhile thing to do in an effort to provide some encouragement to the war-weary population.

Problems, solutions, questions, issues and language

Formulating the policies needed for conflict resolution

Peace building problem Exploring all the possible elements of compromise and accommodation in public may be seen as weakness and open up a party's negotiating position to attacks from more radical elements and/or political opportunists.

Northern Ireland experience The parties elected to take part in the negotiation of the Belfast Agreement frequently found themselves in a complex of 'Catch 22' traps. If a major Unionist, Loyalist, Nationalist or Republican party suggested a creative and bold compromise they would be attacked as traitors by members of their own community opposed to the peace process. But if they said nothing then they appeared to be doing nothing even if, behind closed doors, secret negotiations were taking place in earnest. Unfortunately such secret negotiations allowed for the creation of mischievous rumours and falsified leaked documents which were generally far more radical in their content than the negotiations proper. Both honest open debate and discreet private discussions opened up a party to political attack. Those opposed to an agreement worked very hard to make sure all possible solutions to the Northern Ireland problem 'spelt disaster' in the public mind before they had a chance of becoming a reality. To deal with this problem the parties developed an unwritten 'code of practice' for running the public opinion polls that involved the following key features:

- All questions and options had to be introduced by a party to the negotiations to ensure both relevance and serious intent.
- The wording had to be agreed by all the parties to the negotiations to remove bias, leading or partisan phrasing.
- Questions and options could not be attributed to a party in public or in private communications. The detailed footnotes that accompanied each draft questionnaire made no reference to party connections, and the notes on attribution that accompanied each newspaper report were agreed with all the parties and were generally vague on this particular point.

Public opinion poll action Test all the possible elements of compromise and accommodation proposed as various options in a public opinion poll without attributing the different options to any particular party.

Setting the agenda and 'getting past go'

Peace building problem Each party to a conflict wants their particular agenda dealt with first, preferably, if at all possible, as a precondition to the negotiations proper. Such rigidity can stall negotiations in the pre-negotiation agenda-setting stage so no one 'gets off first base'.

Northern Ireland experience The Unionists took the view that several of the issues that were part of the agenda for the Stormont talks should not be items for negotiation at all because they were in breach of domestic UK or international European law. In particular, Unionists believed decommissioning of paramilitary weapons, particularly those belonging to the IRA, and the removal of the Irish claim over the territory of Northern Ireland, in Articles 2 and 3 of their constitution, were not matters for negotiation. Rather they felt these issues should be settled to the satisfaction of Unionists before the negotiations proper for a power sharing assembly, North/South bodies, police reform and so on. Republicans and Nationalists accepted none of this. They believed Unionists would negotiate no further once they had got what they wanted on these critical points. The talks were stalled and several questions were written specifically to address these problems. For example, in the poll published in the *Belfast Telegraph* on 11 September 1997,[14] 65 per cent of Protestants considered it 'unacceptable' to stay in the talks with Sinn Féin if their ceasefire broke down while only 12 per cent of Catholics shared this view. On the other hand 52 per cent of Catholics considered it 'unacceptable' to make decommissioning a talks precondition while only 16 per cent of Protestants agreed (Table 4.1). The solution to this apparently intractable dilemma was the establishment of the Independent International Commission on Decommissioning to deal with the problem while the talks were in progress.

Table 4.1 All the parties should be prepared to talk to each other ...

Percentage 'Unacceptable'	Protestant	Catholic
Even if the ceasefires do not hold	65	12
So long as the ceasefires hold	16	8
So long as the ceasefires hold and there is also some decommissioning	10	17
Only after decommissioning has been completed	16	52

Opinions were also split on when to deal with the problem of Articles 2 and 3 of the Irish Constitution. But this issue was not so critical as the question of decommissioning. Only 17 per cent of Protestants and 3 per cent of Catholics considered it 'unacceptable' not to 'keep the talks going' on this occasion and 'let reform of the Republic of Ireland's Constitution be dealt with at the same time as all the other issues that must be part of an overall settlement'. This is what happened.

Public Opinion poll action Test proposals for precondition items against public opinion. When 'we' do not want 'their' issues dealt with before 'ours' and 'they' do not want 'our' issues dealt with before 'theirs' the only option that will gain the widest cross-community support will be for all issues to be dealt with at the same time without any preconditions. However, on many occasions, *both* communities will actually prefer negotiations to go ahead without any preconditions or delays at all, particularly if the issue is not critical to their safety or security.

Prioritising the elements of a conflict

Peace building problem Each party to a conflict will not take the issues and concerns of other parties seriously. In particular they believe that the complaints put forward by other parties – particularly those directed at themselves – are little more than political rhetoric designed to ferment discord and distrust between their respective communities. The issues, concerns and complaints, they believe, are not genuine and therefore do not need to be addressed as part of a negotiated settlement.

Northern Ireland experience The party negotiators were invited to list what they believed to be the most significant causes of the Northern Ireland conflict. In practice when one party raised an issue of concern to their own community in a draft, the next round of consultations stimulated a series of counter-concerns from opposition parties. For example when Republicans proposed 'The British presence on the island of Ireland' as a problem Unionists countered with 'The Republic's involvement in Northern Ireland affairs' and so on. Social issues, like segregated education and housing, tended to be introduced by the smaller centre parties as was 'The failures of Northern Ireland politicians'. The question is given in Table 4.2 listing all

Table 4.2 Reasons for the Northern Ireland conflict

People from different communities often hold very different views about the causes of the conflict in Northern Ireland. Please indicate which ones you consider to be 'Very Significant', 'Significant', 'Of Some Significance', 'Of Little Significance' or 'Of No Significance at all'.

Percentage 'Very Significant'	All of NI	Protestant	Catholic	DUP	UUP	Alliance	SDLP	Sinn Féin
The Irish Republican Army and their use of violence	68	87	45	86	87	80	60	20
All paramilitary groups and their use of violence	61	67	56	52	69	78	68	30
The Loyalist paramilitaries and their use of violence	55	53	57	37	55	77	68	37
The failure of government and the security forces to deal with terrorism	48	56	34	58	67	33	39	24
The sectarian division of Northern Ireland politics	47	30	66	17	32	44	72	59
The failures of Northern Ireland politicians	46	31	59	29	27	57	63	50
The lack of equality and continued discrimination	43	21	71	29	15	25	75	69
A lack of respect for the people of the 'other' tradition	43	30	57	17	33	42	66	43
Unaccountable and secretive government	40	31	52	45	26	25	55	48
The Republic's territorial claim on Northern Ireland	38	53	21	60	57	31	16	24
The continued British presence on the island of Ireland	32	17	51	23	14	27	44	73
The failure to provide a police service acceptable to all	32	9	62	7	9	17	65	70
Segregated education	30	25	31	27	23	33	35	23
The Republic of Ireland's involvement in Northern Ireland	29	42	16	61	41	12	11	18
Segregated public housing	28	23	33	28	18	25	35	25
The British Army and their use of violence	24	6	48	6	5	17	47	52
The British Government's pursuit of a political settlement	22	20	23	20	22	14	22	27
The prominent role of the Roman Catholic Church	21	29	10	40	28	13	7	16
The 'Established Church' in Britain and the Orange Order	18	14	21	17	11	12	19	29

the suggestions and results for Northern Ireland as a whole, Protestants, Catholics and each of the major political parties expressed as a percentage of those who said the 'cause' was 'Very significant'.

Public opinion poll action Get all the parties to a conflict to list the elements of the conflict, as seen from their point of view, in mutually acceptable neutral terms and test them against public opinion to see which issues are genuine concerns of the respective communities and which are not.

Prioritising the elements of a solution

Peace building problem Politicians like to make peace deals. It can help to win elections. But easily made peace agreements that do not deal with the issues at the heart of a conflict are probably 'not worth the paper they are written on' and may well be broken 'before the ink is dry'. Beware of strangers bearing peace deals especially if their popularity is slipping at home.

Northern Ireland experience The party negotiators were now invited to list their solutions for the problems just drafted, but where there had been nineteen problems there were now only seventeen 'steps towards a lasting peace'.[15] Some 'steps' were redundant. As before, Unionists tended to focus on security issues and decommissioning, Republicans and Nationalists on equality issues and reform of the police service. Again the centre parties could be relied upon to deal with social issues that the major parties considered to be less important for an agreement although perhaps essential as part of an effective peace process. Interestingly the general public agreed with the centre parties sometimes placing such matters higher on their list of priorities than 'Reformed and shared government'. The question is given in Table 4.3 listing all the suggestions and results for Northern Ireland as a whole, Protestants, Catholics and each of the major political parties expressed as a percentage of those who said the 'step' was 'Essential'.

Public opinion poll action For every element of the conflict raised as a concern ask the parties to propose a potential solution. Rank these 'solutions' in their order of priority for each community and party to the conflict. Make sure everyone's top priorities are included in the settlement or it will most probably unravel, and try to address all the issues raised as part of an ongoing peace process.

Setting the procedural parameters for a peace process

Peace building problem Before an agreement can be reached, 'shape of the table' decisions have to be made about who is eligible to negotiate, how decisions will be made in the negotiations, who will chair the negotiations, pay for them and where they will be held and last, but by no means least, if there is to be a referendum, who is eligible to vote.

Northern Ireland experience Many of the procedural issues were settled by the British and Irish governments before the polls began. The parties to the

Table 4.3 Steps towards a lasting peace in Northern Ireland

As steps needed to help secure a lasting peace please indicate which of the following options you consider to be 'Essential', 'Desirable', 'Acceptable', 'Tolerable' or 'Unacceptable'?

Percentage 'Essential'	All NI	Protestant	Catholic	DUP	UUP	Alliance	SDLP	Sinn Féin
Disband all paramilitary groups	70	70	66	45	79	76	85	39
Stronger and effective anti-terrorist measures	57	69	39	66	77	61	48	22
A Bill of Rights that guarantees equality for all	54	37	77	17	40	60	82	74
A Bill of Rights that protects the culture of each community	49	36	67	26	40	41	71	63
A right to choose integrated education	43	35	53	26	39	50	59	47
Politics without a sectarian division	43	31	58	17	37	47	62	52
A right to choose integrated housing	39	30	50	18	34	48	52	46
The Republic ends their claim on Northern Ireland	38	63	7	74	68	25	6	14
Completely reform the police service	34	7	70	5	6	8	70	86
Open government and Freedom of Information Act	33	24	47	14	25	23	53	41
Return the army to their barracks	31	8	60	11	7	19	60	77
Separate politics and religion in Northern Ireland	27	31	20	28	28	37	19	19
End the Anglo-Irish Agreement	24	36	10	49	40	6	7	14
Separate politics and religion in the Republic	24	30	15	33	30	30	13	13
Reformed and shared government	21	12	32	4	11	25	39	21
British withdrawal from Northern Ireland	20	1	47	1	1	9	36	70
Integrate Northern Ireland into the UK	20	35	4	44	41	8	3	5

Belfast negotiations held in Stormont Castle were elected on a proportional basis. The first ten got in. This ensured participation by parties with both Loyalist and Republican paramilitary connections. The two governments also favoured the John Hume/SDLP proposal of a referendum in both the North and South of Ireland at the same time, Sinn Féin wanted an all 'island of Ireland' referendum, while Unionists preferred leaving it up to the Northern Ireland electorate alone. On 12 September 1997 the results of a poll exploring these and other related procedural issues were published in the *Belfast Telegraph*.[16] People wanted a referendum, they wanted the Stormont Talks to keep going even if Sinn Féin walked out (they didn't) and they wanted the largest Unionist and Nationalist parties to stay in (they did). The only workable compromise on who should vote in a referendum appeared to be the John Hume/SDLP formula, although Northern Ireland Protestants considered the Republic of Ireland vote to be of little or no relevance. However, by subsequently including changes to the Republic's constitution in that vote, its importance, for everyone, was substantially increased. Northern Ireland Catholics also wanted any deal made to be supported by a majority in both communities. This was done in the system of party voting adopted in the Stormont talks and also in the way the polls were analysed. Unionists favoured a simple majority and this is how the Northern Ireland referendum was calculated. So in a way everyone got a bit of what they wanted. Perhaps the most significant contribution made by the polls at this point in the proceedings was to help bring these technical issues into the public discourse and the fact that the people required far fewer preconditions than their political leaders. The people simply wanted them 'to get on with it'.

Public opinion poll action Use public opinion polls to both test the various options for the design of the political negotiations as well as structuring the sampling, demographics and mode of analysis of the data collected in the polls to mirror the decision-making processes that are adopted.

Setting the substantive parameters for a settlement

Peace building problem Real peace agreements that attempt to address all the major problems at the heart of a conflict are necessarily complex, dealing, as they must, with issues ranging from policing and human rights through electoral and constitutional reform to questions of amnesty and support for victims. Nothing substantive can be left out and the respective electorates have to vote 'yes' for an agreement that is necessarily a compromise and that does not deliver on all the promises made by their respective political leaders.

Northern Ireland experience The drafting of all the detailed questions for the 'In Search of a Settlement' poll took almost a year. While these questions were being agreed two polls were run in the spring and autumn of 1997 dealing with procedural issues. The third December poll of that year, published in the *Belfast Telegraph* on 10,[17] 12,[18] 13[19] and 14[20] January 1998, was timed to give a lift to the Stormont talks after the Christmas break. While most people took a summer recess the negotiators worked on the polls and when they took a New Year holiday this poll was being analysed and prepared for publication. The questionnaire went through about a dozen drafts to produce a 22-page booklet that the interviewee filled out at home. The data produced were enormous, dealing with public opinion on every major aspect of the Belfast Agreement: causes of the conflict and solutions, human rights, policing, an assembly, North/South bodies, East/West bodies, constitutional reform, a referendum, implementation, general preferences for a 'package' and a section on demographics. The general public were now very well informed about all the issues that had to be decided. The parties, governments and chair had detailed reports on public opinion as it related to each aspect of the agreement that they now had to make.[21] No one had a good excuse not to 'do the business' and negotiations got under way in earnest.

Public opinion poll action Never be afraid to include any serious issue raised at the drafting stage. With explanatory preambles and the careful use of non-technical terms most issues can be explored with the public in carefully pre-tested booklet-style take-home questionnaires. Even if a question has to be dropped because it is too esoteric or just plain unhelpful, its inclusion at the drafting stage will have raised the issue with the party negotiators and allowed them to wrestle with it.

Developing a common language and neutral terms for the drafting of a settlement

Peace building problem During a conflict the language of political rhetoric and in particular the names of institutions, events and places develop separately within each community to produce distinctive vocabularies, symbols and meanings that are part of their different identities. But a settlement requires one agreed terminology that transcends the polarised and sometimes inflammatory vocabularies of the various communities and parties to a conflict.

Northern Ireland experience The detailed drafting of the 'In Search of a Settlement' questionnaire did not only facilitate the formulation of issues but also the development of a common language and terms acceptable to all parties. The methodology of requiring all parties to agree the questions demanded nothing less. Both sides had to adjust their rhetoric, at least for the purposes of an agreement. For example, Republicans liked to refer to the Republic of Ireland as the 26 counties, Northern Ireland as the 6 counties and the whole island together as the 32 county Ireland or Eire as none of these terms implied partition. On the other hand, Unionists wanted to use the terms 'Northern Ireland' and 'Republic of Ireland' as they recognised partition. Although these terms tended to be used for international legal reasons most parties also agreed to use the terms 'North of Ireland', 'South of Ireland' or simply 'North' and 'South' as well as 'Island of Ireland' for the both together. Similarly the idea of having a 'Council of the British Isles' had been floated around for some years by Unionists. This Council would comprise representatives from England, Scotland, Wales, Northern Ireland and the Republic of Ireland. But the Republic was not 'British', although many maps referred to this group of islands, off the north-west coast of Continental Europe, as the 'British Isles'. Providing the term 'British' was dropped the concept was acceptable and the 'Council of the Isles' was born and subsequently got drafted into the Belfast Agreement.

Public opinion poll action Draft, draft and redraft the questions to be run in each poll with the political contact group until a consensus is reached with regards to all terminology to be used. Necessarily inflammatory and partisan language will have to be replaced with neutral terms if the answers to the survey questions are not to produce biased results that would prejudice the outcome of the research.

Searching for and mapping out 'middle' and 'common' ground

Peace building problem One man's middle ground is another man's surrender. Inevitably, everyone, except perhaps the talks chairman, views a fair compromise as a sell out to the other side.

Northern Ireland experience Once all the questions are drafted to everyone's satisfaction then each issue should contain a series of options or choices for which the informant can indicate their preference. In the first poll done in this series people were asked to rank order their first, second and third choice and so on. This worked reasonably well up to a maximum of about eight choices but it got progressively more difficult and slow. In the second poll those being interviewed were asked to say which options they considered to be 'Desirable', 'Acceptable', 'Tolerable' or 'Unacceptable' and in subsequent polls 'Essential' was also added in as a first choice. This five-point scale worked very well indeed. It was simple to administer in the field if the same style was used throughout the questionnaire. Adding more options didn't make answering the questions more difficult and analysing the results produced easy to understand information that clearly indicated how much each community wanted or did not like each option. For example, here are the results for the controversial North/South bodies options published in the *Belfast Telegraph* on 13 January 1998.[22] Unionists did not want them at all or with as few powers as possible. Republicans wanted them to have strong powers that would effectively make them a government of Ireland as a whole. The polls indicated that the Protestant community would accept North/South bodies with powers of consultation, co-operation and administration providing these powers did not exceed the authority of the respective governments, North and South, that had set them up. Catholics required these bodies as part of an agreement and they got them within the limitations acceptable to the Protestant community (Figure 4.1).

Figure 4.1   On matters of mutual interest North/South bodies should ...

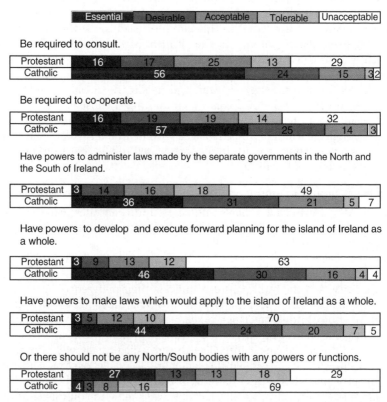

Public opinion poll action Test solutions to problems as a series of graded options that span the issue being raised from the radical position of one party through the centre ground to the radical positions of others. Inevitably the fair compromise, as well as points of agreement, will receive the greatest cross-community support, objectively measured and not subjectively perceived.

Testing the viability of radical proposals against public opinion

Peace building problem Some parties and, at the very least, some members of some parties remain wedded to the radical views of their constituency as the best solution to everyone's problems. They simply will not accept that a compromise with cross-community support is the only viable solution and way forward.

Northern Ireland experience In addition to testing radical proposals as options alongside options for compromise and common ground in all the public opinion poll questions, extreme Republican and extreme Unionist solutions were also tested against the emergent Belfast Agreement shortly before it was made. The Unionist alternative to a comprehensive settlement was published in the *Belfast Telegraph* on Tuesday 31 March 1998.[23] They wanted a devolved government like Scotland or Wales and for Northern Ireland to remain part of the United Kingdom. A simple majority of the population said 'Yes' to this proposal but significantly a higher percentage preferred the Belfast Agreement-style comprehensive settlement from *both* communities and a majority of Catholics did not wish to remain in the UK. The Republican alternative was published the following day, Wednesday 1 April.[24] Although a slim majority of Protestants would accept police reform they would not accept an 'all island of Ireland' body to manage policing. Having the people of Northern Ireland decide their constitutional status was acceptable to both communities but Protestants would not accept having their fate placed before an 'all island of Ireland' vote and almost everyone, except Sinn Féin, wanted a regional assembly. That day the headline read 'Little support for SF agenda'.

Public opinion poll action From time to time test radical proposals against public opinion but be sure to get the radicals involved in the exercise with the questions drafted to their satisfaction. Inevitably such proposals will only receive support from their own constituency and even then that support may not be as strong as they might suppose. Most people can recognise an honourable compromise when they see it – and when they don't.

Testing comprehensive agreements as a set of balanced compromises

Peace building problem Not every part of an agreement can be settled as a search for common ground or even compromise. Some parts, which are very important to one party, will have to be 'horse traded' for other parts, equally important to other parties. The deal, as a whole, will inevitably contain a few victories and disappointments for each side to the conflict. Can the deal be sold?

Northern Ireland experience Yes the deal can be sold. If it is fair and has the potential to deliver peace, with all the benefits that can flow from that, then it will be acceptable. But it does have to be *sold* as the Northern Ireland polls and subsequent referendum campaign clearly demonstrated. The front-page headline of the *Belfast Telegraph* on 31 March 1998[25] read '77% SAY YES'. This result was for Northern Ireland as a whole in response to reading a six-point summary of the proposed settlement and being asked if they would support it if their political party also did. But in a follow-up question this support fell to 50 per cent if the support of their party was withdrawn. Clearly the deal could be done but the two governments would not be able to go over the heads of the parties. They would have to do it together. Two further points are worth noting here. Firstly, the supporters of Loyalist and Republican parties with paramilitary associations had the greatest misgivings about a deal but they trusted their leadership and would follow them. Secondly, when asked about each of the six points of the proposed agreement in turn many people who said 'Yes' to the package as a whole said 'No' to some of the parts of the deal they still did not like. People were willing to compromise, in a big way, for the sake of an honourable settlement.

Public opinion poll action Test the comprehensive agreement to be put to the people in a referendum as a complete set of its major points and then test each element separately. The whole will be greater than the sum of its parts and will probably be 'acceptable' as a comprehensive agreement although individual issues may well remain contentious or even 'unacceptable' in isolation from the total package.

Keeping the peace process 'on tack'

Scheduling the decision-making process

Peace building problem The 'horses have been brought to water' but they simply will not drink. Everyone knows what the compromise is, the shape of the deal is clear, but no one will take the plunge. 'After you sir' – 'No after you'. Without a decision being taken confidence in the peace process starts to fade, a political vacuum forms and violence creeps back on to the streets.

Northern Ireland experience The work with party negotiators to design the first questionnaire began in January of 1997, data collection for the first poll was undertaken between 12 and 22 March and the results were published in the *Belfast Telegraph* on 7, 8 and 9 April. That is about two months for the design of the poll and three weeks for interviews, analysis and writing up. Critically this poll was published to deal with procedural problems holding up the Stormont talks prior to the imminent 1 May general election. A change of government was expected and it was hoped the poll would help to clear the way for a fresh start to the negotiations. In particular, it was intended that the results should stimulate public debate but care was taken not to publish too close to voting day so as to avoid accusations of political interference. From this time on, until the signing of the Belfast Agreement, questionnaire design was ongoing *particularly* when the Stormont talks were in recess. The second poll was published on Thursday 11 and Friday 12 September before an Ulster Unionist Party meeting on Saturday 13 September at which they had to decide if they would go into talks with Sinn Féin on Monday 14 September. If they decided 'No' the talks would collapse. They decided 'Yes'. The third poll, that dealt with all the substantive elements of an agreement, was published on 10, 12, 13 and 14 January to provide 'food for thought' after the Christmas and New Year break (but no holiday for the pollsters!). Deals were made and a 'package' was tested in the fourth poll against public opinion between 12–20 March and published on 31 March. The Belfast Agreement was made on Good Friday, 10 April 1998. The fifth poll published on 3 and 4 March 1999 created an opportunity for new negotiations on the question of decommissioning, and the sixth poll published on 26 and 27 October dealt with issues raised in the Mitchell Review which was brought to a successful conclusion a week later. The seventh poll, like the second poll, was published just days before an Ulster Unionist Party meeting called to decide whether or not to take the party back into the Executive with Sinn Féin. They did.

Public opinion poll action Timing is everything. Arrange with the parties to the negotiations when the results of a poll should be published so that the publication event will precede the decisions to be made in the negotiations by an appropriate period of days or weeks – not longer. Also get the detailed statistical reports to the parties at the same time to both assist them with the decisions they must make and allow them to give informed answers to the press. All of this will help to raise expectations for a conclusion to this part of the peace process. A good talks chairman will seize the moment.

Establishing leader, party, public and international confidence in the decisions to be made

Peace building problem At the moment of decision people start to lose their nerve. Is this a good idea or is it political suicide?

Northern Ireland experience Each poll contained a wide range of questions dealing with issues left over from the previous poll; the beginnings of new questions to be explored in greater depth in future polls; contextual 'how do you feel about' questions; ordering priorities and so on. But each poll also contained a set of questions designed specifically to help resolve particular problems that arose at that point in the peace process. In the first poll the most critical issue to be addressed was decommissioning. People did not want the negotiations to be stopped. If there was a problem they wanted it dealt with by a subcommittee. In the second poll all the objections to negotiations had to be dealt with. Critically Ulster Unionist supporters wanted their party to be in the negotiations with Sinn Féin. The third poll was designed to provide detailed information about public opinion on all the different parts of the agreement that had to be made. The agreement took shape and was tested as a 'package' in the fourth poll. Critically the parties knew before they cut a deal that they could win a referendum. They did. As well as demonstrating continued support for the Belfast Agreement in the three post-agreement polls the first of these polls, the fifth poll, explored various options for overcoming the problem of decommissioning and new negotiations were initiated. The sixth poll dealt with these problems again in the Mitchell Review but also included a lot of questions about how people felt about the failing peace process. People wanted action and the new institutions of government were established. In the seventh poll the concept of 'placing arms beyond use' was tested against public opinion and shown to be generally 'acceptable'. But it was close. Although the Ulster Unionist Council decided to go back into government with Sinn Féin on this basis the vote was only 459 in favour to 403 against.

Public opinion poll action Content is as important as timing. Agree with the parties which questions are going to be run in which poll. The person or team running the poll must have their 'finger on the political pulse' and should know what results are required by paying close attention to people on the street, news reports, radio talk shows, the press and most importantly their private discussions with the party negotiators. Poll results cannot be 'fixed', but they must be relevant and the analysis must draw conclusions appropriate to the needs of the day.

Supporting pro-agreement parties and the people's decision

Peace building problem Those opposed to an agreement, even when it has been endorsed by the people in a referendum, continue to criticise it from their own constituency's point of view as at least unworkable and more probably unfair. Slowly they try to erode support for the agreement in the hope that what they think was lost in the referendum can be reversed in future elections.

Northern Ireland experience All ten parties elected to participate in the negotiation of the Belfast Agreement were treated equally and had the same rights of access to the process of designing and running the public opinion polls as part of the Northern Ireland peace process. However, after the agreement was reached the poll facilitator was asked if he would like to help the pro-agreement 'YES Campaign', but the funders, the Joseph Rowntree Charitable Trust, advised him not to do so as such an action could be considered political and thus might prejudice the independence of future research. However, after the referendum of 22 May 1998, in which a majority voted for the agreement, this restriction was relaxed and he worked with the pro-agreement parties as required although all final reports continued to be made available to both pro- and anti-agreement parties. At this point in the peace process it would have been difficult to work with the anti-agreement parties in good faith as they would have wished to introduce questions with the intention of undermining support for the agreement. Tracking support for the Belfast Agreement also became an essential part of the three post-referendum polls as others were running polls that showed Protestant support to be slipping. Although many people were disappointed with the rate of progress with implementation and had 'second thoughts' about voting for such an agreement again they did want it to work. Some results from the Mitchell Review poll are given in Table 4.4.[26]

Public opinion poll action Periodically run public opinion polls after an agreement is reached to demonstrate continued support for the agreement

Table 4.4 Support for the Belfast Agreement during the Mitchell Review

	All of NI	Protestant	Catholic	DUP	UUP	PUP	Alliance	SDLP	Sinn Féin
How did you vote in the referendum for the Belfast Agreement?									
Yes	74%	64%	89%	32%	82%	85%	90%	96%	89%
No	26%	36%	11%	68%	18%	15%	10%	4%	11%
And if the Referendum was held today how would you vote?									
Yes	65%	49%	88%	31%	56%	56%	79%	95%	90%
No	35%	51%	12%	69%	44%	44%	21%	5%	10%
Do you want the Belfast Agreement to work?									
Yes	83%	72%	98%	50%	87%	91%	98%	98%	97%
No	17%	28%	2%	50%	13%	9%	2%	2%	3%

as both a deal that people would still vote for and more critically as a deal that they would like to see work.

Monitoring the implementation of an agreement

Peace building problem Implementing an agreement can be as difficult, or even more difficult, than reaching the agreement itself, especially when the agreement required significant compromises to be made by all the parties involved. Those opposed to the agreement do all they can to frustrate its implementation by employing the strategy of 'death by a thousand cuts'.

Northern Ireland experience The Belfast Agreement had a two-year transition period built into it designed to allow for all the institutional and social changes required under the terms of the settlement to be implemented. But after thirty years of the 'Troubles' and arguably a civil war that hadn't been properly brought to a close since the 1920s a two-year transition period was just not quite long enough. Everyone started to relax after the deal was cut, most of the people involved with the negotiations were exhausted and the critics of the deal started to 'sharpen their knives'. There were not meant to be any more polls but when it became clear that the agreement was starting to unravel some parties asked for them to be run again. Unlike previous polls these ones included a series of questions that asked people how they felt about the peace process and how satisfied they were with the implementation of the different parts of the agreement. They were worried about a return to violence and specific failures with implementation were clearly identifiable. The politicians got a bit of a 'cold shower' and points requiring urgent action were plainly visible in the statistics. On the one hand, it was hoped that the politicians would have been able to work the agreement through their new institutions without the support of more polls. However, with the benefit of hindsight and four more polls done, it would probably have been best to keep the process going with a poll run about twice a year during the early years of implementation. In this way problems could have been identified better and dealt with before they reached crisis point.

Public opinion poll action Periodically run public opinion polls after an agreement is reached to monitor levels of satisfaction with the implementation of its different parts and the social impact of the peace process in general. Require the relevant parties to take both timely and effective political action to address critical points of discontent and failure.

Providing reports to the public to facilitate their involvement in the peace process

Peace building problem Secret negotiations can leave the public 'in the dark' leading to mischievous speculation about the nature of the agreement or lack of progress in the talks. When an agreement is finally reached it contains quite a few surprises leading to more disinformation and the electorate are unprepared for a referendum when it comes.

Northern Ireland experience Throughout 1996 the poll facilitator published a series of articles on peace building in the *Belfast Telegraph*[27] which were the results of the public opinion survey undertaken by the team of researchers at Queen's University.[28] But in the spring of 1997 the *Belfast Telegraph* ran a rather disastrous phone-in poll in which members of the Orange Order made sure the phone-in vote was 'Yes' for their most controversial march of the year. As a consequence, the editor of the *Belfast Telegraph* came in for much criticism from moderate politicians and he asked the Queen's University team to do a more scientific poll. This was done on the condition that the feature story could not be changed although they would retain editorial control of the front page. All the subsequent polls were published on this basis. The *Belfast Telegraph* had the largest circulation in the province and although it was considered to be a Unionist paper it was widely read in both communities and its editorial policy was pro-agreement. Several attempts were made to work with the broadcast media and other newspapers through a variety of deals and press releases. But all these attempts failed. The press releases were 'cherry picked', the broadcast media only wanted adversarial debates and newspapers from outside the province could not give detailed coverage to complex political issues that only those living in Northern Ireland could properly appreciate. The stories for the *Belfast Telegraph* were delivered a day or two before publication to give the graphic artist time to produce the artwork for the tables of statistics and for the political editors to write their front-page story and occasional leader. The parties looked forward to the publication very much. They felt it helped to keep the grassroots of their constituencies informed and involved in the peace process. On the street, through their letterboxes, in the Maze prison and at Parliament Buildings everyone got the story at the same time.

Public opinion poll action Publish poll results and analysis in the popular press with a view to informing the public on the stage the negotiations have reached, the issues being discussed and the decisions that have to be made. When an agreement is finally reached the public will be ready to vote without the need for any unnecessary delay.

Providing reports to the parties to assist decision-makers with their negotiations

Peace building problem In the 'information age' detailed analysis and access to reliable up-to-date facts about all aspects of public opinion on a conflict are essential if informed decisions are to be made. A failure to provide accurate and timely information can lead to decisions not being made and opportunities lost.

Northern Ireland experience Some large national political parties do have specialist research departments with experts at the ready to analyse, digest and write memoranda on piles of statistical computer print-out. But most of the Northern Ireland parties did not have these facilities available to them so reports were designed and printed to provide them with the key statistics in a way that was unbiased, informative and accessible. This was done by using the questionnaire itself as the basis for the structure of the report. Firstly, the results for Northern Ireland as a whole were reproduced in each question where the informant would usually write in their answer (see Appendix). This would be followed by a community and political breakdown: Protestant, Catholic, Democratic Unionist Party (DUP), Ulster Unionist Party (UUP), Loyalist Parties (Ulster Democratic Party and/or Progressive Unionist Party), Alliance Party, Social Democratic and Labour Party (SDLP) and Sinn Féin. This order was deliberate, flowing from politically more extreme Protestants and Unionists through the centre to politically more extreme Catholics, Nationalists and Republicans. Wherever possible all the results for a particular question were placed on a single page or, for more complex questions, the Northern Ireland, Protestant and Catholic results were placed on one page and the political party results on adjoining pages. The report, like the questionnaire, also contained a demographic section that gave a breakdown of the sample and party support in terms of gender, age and social class (coded from occupation). This section was particularly popular with party electoral strategists. But parties with less than about 5 per cent of the vote were not included in these reports, except for the 'which party do you support' question, as their samples were borderline in terms of statistical significance. Finally, a 'full copy' of the story delivered to the *Belfast Telegraph* was also given to the parties as it nearly always contained a number of analytical tables the newspaper would not have space to publish. The culture of each of the Northern Ireland parties was surprisingly different, and as a result the parties used the statistical reports in different ways and to varying degrees as a research tool for strategy development, negotiating device, public opinion/media resource or for grassroots constituency development and information. Very few compliments were received on the quality of these reports, however, if they were late and not delivered promptly on the day of publication of the *Belfast Telegraph* stories: then numerous complaints could be expected.

Public opinion poll action In addition to reports in the popular press provide detailed statistical reports to all the parties to the negotiations with breakdowns of all questions by both political affiliation and religious, ethnic, racial, linguistic and national group as is appropriate. Be as helpful as possible. For example, demographic analysis of party support is generally also very welcome in terms of age, gender and social class.

Providing reports to the international community to maintain their good offices

Peace building problem The international community are not interested in lending their support to the resolution of the conflict because they have no strategic interest in the area and/or do not believe the conflict can be resolved.

Northern Ireland experience There was a time, perhaps during the Second World War, when Northern Ireland was of strategic interest to the United Kingdom. Indeed, Ireland as a whole was of strategic interest then and Churchill was willing to settle the Northern Ireland problem in the Republic's favour if they were willing to enter the war in opposition to Germany. But world military and economic strategies changed with the advent of nuclear weapons and the creation of the North Atlantic Treaty Organisation and European Union. In this context Ireland, Britain and their close ally America, as well as the European Union, all wanted the Northern Ireland problem solved and all were willing to expend political capital on a successful outcome. The people of Northern Ireland were very lucky, a lot of very influential people and powerful states cared about their situation and were willing to take the risk of getting involved in an apparently intractable conflict. But a successful settlement was the key; nobody wanted to be associated with failure. Although the results of the Northern Ireland polls were rarely reported beyond the pages of the *Belfast Telegraph* the detailed reports given to the parties were also given to the British and Irish governments and to the Office of the Independent Chairmen. Senator George Mitchell, the principal talks chairman and Review facilitator, took a keen interest in the reports and frequently expressed the view in public that an agreement could be reached because that is what the people of Northern Ireland wanted.[29] In this way the polls probably helped to maintain the confidence of the good senator in the peace process and no doubt, through him, the support of the then President of the United States of America, Bill Clinton.

Public opinion poll action Try to publish reports of the polls in the newspapers of any ally who can lend their good offices to the resolution of the conflict and send detailed reports to key decision-makers in the governments of such states. Given the interest in the resolution of the Northern Ireland problem it was not necessary to send reports to other third parties but in many situations it may also be helpful to send detailed reports to both regional and global international organisations (IGOs) and non-governmental organisations (NGOs) in the hope that they too might be willing to lend their support to the achievement of a successful peace process.

Conclusion

In principle it is to be hoped that all of the suggestions made here, for using polls as a tool for peace building, can be applied to assist any society that has fallen victim to a breakdown of constructive democratic dialogue and effective decision-making processes. In practice these methods would be difficult to use where basic rights to freedom of speech and association are not available. But then again there are perhaps tens or even hundreds of situations around the world where the methods used here could be applied with the intention and hope of saving lives[30] and perhaps hundreds or even thousands of situations around the world where less extreme situations could benefit from similar efforts with a view to preventing social harm.[31] Wherever conflicts of interest between groups, communities, peoples and states are not being resolved for a lack of effective dialogue, decision-making and social and political action, perhaps the methods described here should at least be tried. With this point in mind a 'peace polls checklist', derived from the Northern Ireland experience, is given below. It is intended to be a practical place from which to make a start. Hopefully, in time, others will refine and add to it.

Peace polls check list

General research background

- Which universities in the region have strong social science departments?
- Which academics have experience with surveys of public opinion in the region and have an interest in a peace process?
- Which academics could give additional support from departments of politics, law, social geography, languages, media studies and so on?
- Which NGOs and IGOs have an interest in the region and could give financial and research policy support?
- Which market research companies operate in the region and have undertaken polls amongst the relevant communities?
- What polling has been done on a peace process?
- What is the demographic profile of the relevant groups to the conflict in terms of total population, social geography, language, education, age and so on?

- Which newspapers are pro-peace process?
- Which newspapers have a cross-community readership and/or will sometimes publish reports in co-operation with newspapers from other communities?

General research action

- Design, run and publish a public opinion poll on confidence-building measures, the desire of the people for a negotiated settlement and some initial suggestions for an agreement from as wide a range of political perspectives as is possible.

Applied research background

- Which political parties have a democratic mandate?
- Which political parties represent radical, moderate and centre polices?
- Which political parties represent groups in conflict?
- Which political parties are essential to a successful peace process?
- Contact the parties that must make the peace and the parties who are willing to do most to achieve peace and invite them all to participate in a programme of polling research in support of a peace process.

Applied research action

- Agree a programme of polling research with these parties including: topics to be dealt with, methods (sample structure, size, distribution, languages to be used and so on), research ethics, timing and publication.
- In co-operation with the parties test all options for confidence-building measures, problems and solutions, procedural and substantive matters, and contextual concerns of the public in relation to the conflict – all as may be required.
- Publish results in the popular press, on the internet and in detailed reports to the parties and relevant IGOs, NGOs and governments who can, and hopefully will, give political and economic support to a peace process.
- Continue to give support to the parties until the implementation of an agreement is well advanced, the reformed institutions are functioning as planned and most of the more difficult problems identified in the research have been dealt with.

Part II
The Northern Ireland Peace Polls

5
Peace Building and Public Policy

In the deeply divided society of Northern Ireland generations of conflict have created a situation in which all aspects of political, economic, social and cultural life have fallen victim to the ill-effects of discrimination and segregation, distrust, bitterness and violence. Depending largely on an individual's particular intellectual or practical interests the critical solution to such endemic dysfunction can range the spectrum of these activities from the reform of the political institutions of government (top-down) to how children are socialised and educated in school (bottom-up). But where to start? The answer is everywhere and any one place is almost as important as any other. The starting point depends on the individual and what they can do to make a difference.

Events determined the place of starting for this particular programme of research. After the fieldwork for the 'Peace Building and Public Policy' poll was completed, the annual ritual of the Northern Ireland marching season created a timely opportunity for the first of a series of articles to be published in the *Belfast Telegraph*. In terms of conflict resolution this particular starting point focused on the rights of the Orangemen to march, the rights of concerned residents' groups to oppose such marches and the institutions that society could put in place to adjudicate and resolve such conflicts of divergent interests for the benefit of the greater common good.

Belfast Telegraph, Thursday 4 July 1996

The parades question: independent body wins the public's vote of confidence

As the marching season reaches its climax with Drumcree and the Twelfth, a public opinion poll reveals there is wide popular support for an independent body on parades.[1]

On the radio, in the press, and at countless public meetings republicans blame the Orangemen and unionists for failure to compromise on the routing of parades. On the other hand, those who claim a right to march accuse republicans of exploiting all possible opportunities to obstruct their 'sacred rights' for political ends. As with so many things in Northern Ireland there seems to be no middle ground. And even if there were it would only be occupied by the supporters of the Alliance Party. Everyone, it would seem, has resigned themselves to yet another Marching Season dominated by protests with more of the same next year and the year after that.

But it does not have to be this way. The vast majority of people in Northern Ireland will accept compromise and this includes the supporters of Sinn Féin. As part of a Province-wide survey on 'Peace Building and Public Policy' a random sample of the population were asked to place various options for change in their order of preference. If you want to you can try the 'Parades Question' for yourself before you read the results. Just put a tick in the box against your first, second, third and finally least preferred option (Figure 5.1). This is the question as it appeared in the survey:

'Here are some alternative options for the way disputed parades and marches could be handled in Northern Ireland. Please read them carefully and then tick them in your order of preference.'

Figure 5.1   The parades question

	First Preference	Second Preference	Third Preference	Least Preferred Option
Allow all parades – All parades should be allowed to march on all public roads and should be provided with police protection.				
RUC to rule on disputes – The decision to allow parades to march through different areas should be left to the RUC.				
Independent body to rule on disputes – There should be an independent body to rule on all disputes relating to the routing of parades.				
No parades where they are not wanted – No parades should be allowed to march through areas where a majority of the residents do not want them.				

From 715 completed questionnaires the results for Northern Ireland as a whole bring few surprises as most people choose 'Allow all Parades' or 'Let Residents Decide' as their first choice. However, when it comes to their second choice an 'Independent Body' has wide popular support (Table 5.1).

This trend continues to be maintained even when the results are broken down for Catholics and Protestants with a surprising 19 per cent of

Protestants wanting to 'Let residents decide' (Table 5.2). One possibility for decision-making in Northern Ireland is based on the principle that a majority from each of the two main communities must agree to any given proposal before it can be adopted. When it comes to parades this principle would work very well. Of the four options put on offer here an 'Independent body' is the only one that can pass this test. Similarly it may be possible to resolve other politically contentious issues.

If we now take a look at the results of the survey broken down by the electorate from each of the five main political parties the results start to get even more interesting (Table 5.3). Predictably Alliance voters do hold the middle ground with an 'Independent body' being their first choice. The DUP give their support to the 'Right to march' and the RUC. An 'Independent body' is their third choice. The UUP and DUP electorate are in agreement for their first choice but the UUP clearly choose an 'Independent body' as their second choice as do Sinn Féin and the SDLP who both put the rights of residents first.

In public the leaders of these political parties would be expected to give voice to the first choice of their supporters. But everyone knows that nearly everyone wants peace and the establishment of an 'independent body' to rule on disputed parades is the first choice of many and the second choice of most. A majority from each of the two main communities in Northern Ireland would be willing to support this compromise. In this case the objectives of 'peace building' would best be served by abandoning the principle

Table 5.1 All Northern Ireland support for parades options

All of NI per cent	Allow all parades	RUC decides	Independent body decides	Let residents decide
1st preference	25	10	20	45
2nd preference	9	31	50	10

Table 5.2 Catholic and Protestant support for parades options

	Allow all parades	RUC decides	Independent body decides	Let residents decide
Catholics per cent				
1st preference	6	3	17	75
2nd preference	3	16	69	13
Protestants per cent				
1st preference	42	15	24	19
2nd preference	15	43	35	7

Table 5.3   Political support for parades options

	Allow all parades	RUC decides	Independent body decides	Let residents decide
Alliance per cent				
1st preference	16	9	40	34
2nd preference	4	42	35	20
DUP per cent				
1st preference	63	17	13	7
2nd preference	18	49	25	8
UUP per cent				
1st preference	46	15	23	16
2nd preference	13	43	40	4
Sinn Féin per cent				
1st preference	0	0	7	93
2nd preference	9	9	77	6
SDLP per cent				
1st preference	6	3	16	74
2nd preference	4	13	72	11

of 'Nothing is agreed until everything is agreed'. Perhaps the politicians should not be afraid to take a lead in this matter and collectively advocate the setting up of some sort of Parades Commission.

* * *

A Parades Commission was established later that year but it created almost as many problems as it solved. Inevitably each side accused the Commission of making a political decision in favour of the 'other' community when a ruling went against them. This problem of contentious parades had to be visited again, almost every year, when the marching season came around.

In the meantime Loyalist violence brought the Province of Northern Ireland to a standstill in the lead-up to the 1996 Drumcree stand off. For the most part this violence emanated from the Protestant public housing estates and sadly this reality created an opportunity to address the issue of government housing policies that encouraged the segregation of these estates into Catholic and Protestant enclaves.

At the time I had only recently established contacts with the political leaders of the principal Loyalist paramilitary groups and was quite nervous about publishing a story that emphasised the control that such organisations had over these estates. So before taking the story to the *Belfast Telegraph* I had a leading Loyalist read it and asked if there would be any problem for me if I put it into print in the popular press. He assured me there wouldn't be.

On the contrary, he emphasised the importance of public discussion about such issues and encouraged me to continue with my work. The Loyalist leadership, it would seem, was genuinely interested in exploring the possibilities for creating a normal peaceful society in Northern Ireland devoid of paramilitary violence.

Unfortunately the housing question story was one of only three that the *Belfast Telegraph* did not publish. Events moved on very fast and they wanted a positive story on police reform, not a story that emphasised the fact that the writ of the Royal Ulster Constabulary did not run to working-class areas where the summary 'justice' of the paramilitaries prevailed.

Good neighbours (not published)

Boycotts and road blocks, punishment beatings and summary executions, expulsions and 'ethnic cleansing'. These are the 'stock in trade' of the paramilitary organisations and everyone knows that handing in a few guns will not bring an end to their violence and threats. But most people in Northern Ireland just want to be good neighbours. Is there an answer to the housing question and can the processes of intimidation and segregation ever be reversed?

Nearly a thousand families were forced to abandon their homes during the riots that spread across the Province from their epicentre at Drumcree this summer. Slogans were painted on cars, phone lines cut, gangs of masked men shouted abuse, windows were 'put in' and petrol bombs thrown. The local 'Hoods' had their way in spite of frequent pleas from neighbours to leave their friends alone. Each time this happens Northern Ireland comes one step closer to total segregation as it has done, year by year, over the past quarter century. *This is not what people want.*

In the recent Rowntree poll a random sample of the Northern Ireland population were asked to put five options for government housing policies in their order of preference. You can try the question if you wish. It appeared in the questionnaire as follows:

Option A – Separation Establish separate housing authorities and separate housing estates for Catholics and Protestants in public housing in Northern Ireland.

Option B – No change Leave housing allocation policy as it is where people are generally required to choose between a predominantly Catholic or predominantly Protestant estate.

Option C – Guaranteed choice Ask people if they would prefer to live in a Catholic, Protestant or mixed-religion neighbourhood and make sure they are housed according to their wishes by adequately funding mixed housing projects.

Option D – Choice with incentives for mixed housing Ask people if they would prefer to live in a Catholic, Protestant or mixed-religion neighbourhood.

House them according to their wishes, give funding priority to mixed housing projects and provide other incentives such as shorter waiting lists.
Option E – Integration Require persons in public housing in Northern Ireland to live in mixed estates.

Unlike the 'Parades' question (*Belfast Telegraph*, 4 July), which showed up strong differences of opinion, the results for the 'Housing question' clearly indicate a broad consensus for mixed housing policies. Very few people want the government to introduce forced segregation or forced integration (Table 5.4). Home owners would like to see incentives for mixing. Housing executive tenants are more reticent, however, and would prefer to simply have 'Guaranteed choice'. The results are taken from 715 completed questionnaires.

Table 5.4   Support for housing options

All of NI per cent	Segregated housing	No change to housing	Guaranteed choice	Preference for mixing	Integrated housing
1st preference	4	19	32	34	11
2nd preference	4	16	38	33	9

A similar consensus is produced when people are asked if they would personally like to live in a mixed housing area and if they would be willing to accept an equal balance of Catholics and Protestants as neighbours (Table 5.5). Eighty-seven per cent of Alliance voters would like to live amongst people of both religions followed by SDLP supporters at 70 per cent, the UUP at 66 per cent, Sinn Féin at 43 per cent and DUP at 32 per cent.

Table 5.5   Support for mixed housing

Per cent	Alliance	SDLP	Home owners	UUP	All of NI	Housing executive	Sinn Féin	DUP
Yes to mixed housing	87	70	68	66	65	50	43	32
Yes to equal mixing	76	70	66	59	63	56	60	30

Attitudes may have hardened a little since Drumcree but they have probably not changed a lot. Even during the height of the troubles almost a third of all applicants for public housing in the north of Belfast indicated a willingness to live in mixed estates, and before the ceasefires the government's Northern Ireland Social Attitudes survey identified a majority of people in favour of increasing the availability of mixed housing.

So why can't people just be good neighbours? Most academics who have studied 'The Troubles' have looked at the housing question at one time or another and have come up with an exhaustive list of reasons for increased segregation. They range from the economic migration of the better off from city centres to the suburbs; to a lack of housing stock for one community or the other to expand in this or that area; to the building of the 'Peace Lines'; to fear and intimidation – pure and simple.[2]

Segregation is most marked in the public sector where, in the 1970s, Margaret Keane[3] documented 'the total collapse of allocations control in some areas into the hands of unofficial housing allocators, both Protestant and Catholic, who gave priority to political sympathy and ethnic identity'. The paramilitaries continue to bring their influence to bear in the management of public housing today. Some of the estates are the largest in Europe and create economies of scale for the Housing Executive and paramilitaries alike. Keane also notes that if housing policy 'is based on managing conflict through separating groups and partitioning the city into ethnic neighbourhoods it may contain intergroup conflict but it also provides opportunities for the flourishing of extremists whose power has thus been enhanced'.

The RUC, the Northern Ireland Housing Executive, and the Department of the Environment are all, to various degrees, unwilling or unable to deal with these problems. On many housing estates, beyond the boundaries of coloured kerb stones, the government has relinquished much of its authority and accepted limitations to 'the rule of law'.

Next to the political future and governance of the Province we are told that the most important item for discussion at the Peace Talks is decommissioning. But is decommissioning enough? Will simply taking the guns out of politics also remove the spectre of organised crime from this deeply divided society? The necessities of peace building require that in addition to decommissioning, the disengagement of paramilitary organisations from all aspects of civil life should be on the Peace Talks agenda. Disbanding has been mentioned. Assuming a successful outcome, then, and perhaps only then might people be able to realise their most modest of aspirations to just be good neighbours.

Policies for integrated schools were passed into law in 1977 and again in 1989. The Department of the Environment and the Housing Executive would do well to follow this lead by becoming more proactive. At the very least they should put some plans before the people of the Province. How, in practice, will mixing be achieved for those who desire it? How can their rights of freedom of association and expression of political opinion be met? If the dream can be imagined, and if it is attractive, the politicians just might do what has to be done to turn it into a reality. In the meantime the dream will only continue to find expression in the statistics of public opinion polls while the youth of the Province seek new dreams in other lands.

* * *

So called 'peace lines' – walls of brick, concrete and steel – continued to be built across the urban landscape of Belfast. It is relatively easy to do so, it only requires the efforts of planners and civil engineers. Building peace is far more difficult. That requires the co-operation of politicians and a bureaucracy willing to take risks.

As for the 1996 'Drumcree Two' parade, that was also a total disaster. The police could not contain the Loyalist violence and made the decision to allow the Orangemen down their traditional route past the Catholic estates when it seemed clear to them that the only alternative available was the use of troops with live ammunition. Northern Ireland had more than enough willing martyrs. Making more served no one's best interests.

Policing issues lie at the centre of many conflicts when such forces are thought to be acting on behalf of one community against another. In such circumstances they become the shock troops of street politics that must bear the brunt of the failed institutions they are asked to serve and the questioned legitimacy of the state. They are in a no-win situation.

As far as Catholics were concerned the reform of the Royal Ulster Constabulary was always a number one priority as part of a successful peace process.

Belfast Telegraph, Friday 2 August 1996

Changing the force of habit: can we accept changes to the structures of policing in Northern Ireland, and if so, how much?

While members of the Police Authority are forced to resign, threaten to resign or consider asking the Chief Constable to resign, the people of Northern Ireland express their views on the policing question in the search for an acceptable compromise.[4]

The announcement by government that they will look into the management of contentious parades is welcome. But nearly all commentators are agreed that it is too little and too late. This initiative should have been taken a year ago after the first Drumcree stand-off.

On the other hand, when it comes to the issue of policing, one authoritative report follows hard on the heels of another. Everyone has something to say, the Centre for the Study of Conflict at Coleraine, the Northern Ireland Police Authority, the Government in a White Paper and the Standing Advisory Commission on Human Rights (SACHR).

So why do we still have a policing problem? Why does Cardinal Daly find it necessary to ask for an independent inquiry into the role of the RUC at Drumcree? The reason is quite simple. No one is willing to grasp the nettle and say what really has to be done in fear of alienating the Nationalists or Unionists or, worse still, both, by proposing some sort of compromise. 'Leave it to the politicians at The Talks' is the wise consensus. Everyone, it would seem, is playing 'Pass the Parcel'. Perhaps the people of Northern Ireland can shed some light on this thorny issue.

In the Rowntree survey on 'Peace Building and Public Policy' a random sample of the population were asked to put a range of five different policing options in their order of preference. You can try the question if you wish. It appeared in the questionnaire as follows:

Option A – No change Leave current policing structures as they are while attempting to recruit more Catholics.

Option B – Create new community policing units within the RUC Create new policing units to deal with domestic, community and non-violent sectarian problems at a local level as part of the RUC.

Option C – Create new community policing units outside the RUC Create a number of new police forces at the local level to deal with less serious crimes leaving the RUC to deal with more serious crimes for Northern Ireland as a whole.

Option D – Create a new single police force Disband the RUC and create a new single police force with fair representation from both communities.

Option E – Create a number of regional and city police forces Disband the RUC and create a number of new regional and city police forces in, for example, Belfast, (London)Derry and East and West of the River Bann.

From 715 completed questionnaires the results show how deeply divided the two main communities are on the policing question (Table 5.6). As a matter of first choice Protestants are clearly in favour of keeping the RUC much as they are while most Catholics would like to see the RUC disbanded and replaced with a single new service. Even when the 13 per cent who did not declare themselves as being either Catholic or Protestant are included in the results the outcome does not change significantly as these

Table 5.6 Support for RUC reforms

	No reform of RUC	New units as part of RUC	New units outside RUC	One new police force	Several new police forces
Protestants per cent					
1st preference	62	27	7	3	2
2nd preference	21	58	10	7	4
3rd preference	7	8	69	7	9
Catholics per cent					
1st preference	18	7	7	56	11
2nd preference	9	22	13	14	43
3rd preference	9	24	54	5	8

'Others' are also split on the question of policing. Given this deep division of opinion it is only when we go to the third choice of each community that a consensus can be reached with a majority of both Catholics and Protestants willing to accept a new service outside the RUC.

The recent Police Authority survey also found a majority of both Catholics and Protestants in favour of a 'functional splitting of the force'. So some sort of two-tier police service may be an acceptable compromise. The Police Authority also came to the conclusion that most people were happy to keep the culture of the RUC much as it is without radical changes to name, symbols and uniform. However, when these issues are put in the context of making the police force more acceptable to the Nationalist community the Rowntree survey produced a more positive response with 50 per cent of the population in favour of reforms (Table 5.7).

Table 5.7   Support for changes to RUC name and uniform

Question: 'Whatever the future structure of the police force might be do you think it should make a greater effort to recruit more Catholics and be more acceptable to the Nationalist community by, for example, changing the name and uniform of the RUC?'

Per cent	All of NI	Alliance	DUP	UUP	SF	SDLP
Yes	50	50	3	21	78	92
No	39	43	90	75	10	2
Don't know	11	7	7	4	12	6

Fifty per cent of Alliance party voters were also in favour of reforms, with the DUP at only 3 per cent, the UUP at 21 per cent, Sinn Féin at 78 per cent and the SDLP at 92 per cent. The Sinn Féin electorate were probably less in favour of reforms than the SDLP as most Sinn Féin supporters would not believe the RUC capable of implementing effective change. After Drumcree SDLP support for reforms may now have slipped for similar reasons.

But the people of Northern Ireland are not in disagreement over everything that relates to the improvement of the police service. Nearly everyone wants a more effective complaints procedure (Table 5.8).

Table 5.8   Support for independent complaints agency

Question: 'At the present time complaints against the RUC are investigated by the police and supervised by an independent commission. Are you in favour of establishing a completely independent agency to investigate complaints against the RUC?'

Per cent	All of NI	Alliance	DUP	UUP	SF	SDLP
Yes	69	77	39	56	93	91
No	20	18	55	35	0	3
Don't know	11	5	6	9	7	6

So where do all these questions and statistics get us? Most people want a new complaints procedure, most people will accept a two-tier police force and most people would prefer a single force to a number of regional and city forces. Protestants are reticent when it comes to reform. Catholics require reform. So the only basis for a compromise seems to be some sort of two-tier service with as many reforms implemented as can possibly be managed.

Such a suggestion may well give offence to both Unionists and Nationalists. Hopefully, the offence is equal. But the bottom line is this. Policing is being used as a bargaining chip at the Talks while policing policies that are found to be wanting by one community or the other have already brought business to a close at the Forum and are threatening the Peace Process.

Many are sceptical about the prospects for establishing an independent body to rule on contentious parades. However, if the problems of policing can be solved then the prospects of successfully dealing with the parades issue will be greatly increased. The necessities of Peace Building require that parades and policing should not be dealt with in isolation of each other. Similarly, SACHR has advised the NIO 'that the piece-meal way in which reform of policing has been approached is not helpful and is potentially dangerous as such compartmentalisation may well mislead'.[5] The time has come to stop playing 'Pass the Parcel'.

* * *

In Northern Ireland the end of the summer's marching season marks the beginning of the autumn transition to the chilly discourse of community politics apparently frozen in time. Children go back to school, political parties hold their annual conferences and the politicians elected to sort out the problems of the Province get back to blaming each other for all the failures that surround them. Holidays are over, the weather becomes less temperate and street politics gives way to the season of political recrimination.

On 12 September the first article was published in the *Belfast Telegraph* with the deliberate intention of trying to eliminate some of the more radical political futures from the range of available possibilities by trying to focus in on the solutions that could gain the widest support from across both communities. Would the politicians be persuaded to take the hint?

Belfast Telegraph, Thursday 12 September 1996

The battle for the middle ground: voters give their views on what is necessary for a political settlement

Northern Ireland is arguably the 'Graveyard' of political deals and compromises. But what are the options on offer to resolve the constitutional question and could the parties represented at the Talks reach agreement on the future governance of the Province?

In the recent Rowntree poll on 'Peace Building and Public Policy in Northern Ireland' a random sample of the population was asked to put eight options for the future political development of the Province in their order of preference.

When the results from the 715 completed questionnaires are analysed for each of the five main political parties Alliance voters, predictably, favour the middle-ground compromises as their first choice. SDLP and UUP supporters reach this same point of agreement with their third choice while DUP and Sinn Féin voters find these proposals most difficult to accept reaching them only as a fourth preference (Table 5.9).

Clearly the best prospects for a negotiated settlement at the Peace Talks rests with the SDLP and UUP as they would be able to carry the majority of the Catholic/Nationalist and Protestant/Unionist communities with them at a referendum.

Such an agreement could also be expected to receive the support of the Alliance Party and probably some of the other smaller parties represented at the Talks. The SDLP and UUP would appear to have an electoral mandate to shape the terms and conditions for the future governance of the Province. But this summer's marching season has shaken everyone's confidence to the core. At this critical time in the peace process the results of the public opinion survey suggest several opportunities for significant advances to be made by focusing on what is possible.

Firstly, the elimination of political arrangements unacceptable to all parties – an independent state and separate institutions for the management of a segregated society. Secondly, the elimination of political arrangements that are completely unacceptable to one community or the other – full incorporation into either the British or Irish state with no other political arrangements.

Finally, some DUP and Sinn Féin supporters will find it very difficult to reach the middle ground, others will find it easier, but the numbers clearly indicate a few are there already. These people require special consideration and every encouragement to be politically bold.

THE DECISION IS YOURS

You can try the question if you wish. It appeared in the questionnaire as follows:

> 'Here are some alternative options for the future political development of Northern Ireland. Please read them carefully and then tick them in your order of preference below.'

Option A – Separate Northern Irish state The complete separation of Northern Ireland from both the United Kingdom and the Republic of Ireland and the establishment of a separate state within the European Union.

Option B – Full incorporation into the British state Direct rule from Westminster and local government similar to the rest of the United Kingdom with *no*

Table 5.9 Political support for a settlement of the Northern Ireland 'question'

	Independent state	British state	Direct rule	Anglo-Irish Agreement	North/ South institutions	Joint authority	Separate institutions	Irish state
DUP per cent								
1st choice	17	62	13	1	1	1	4	0
2nd choice	35	23	29	2	8	0	2	0
3rd choice	21	4	34	19	6	6	9	0
4th choice	5	0	11	45	26	5	8	0
UUP per cent								
1st choice	6	58	11	9	12	2	2	0
2nd choice	11	17	48	11	10	3	0	1
3rd choice	23	7	24	25	13	7	0	0
4th choice	14	12	8	27	28	6	4	1
Alliance per cent								
1st choice	9	20	10	19	25	9	1	7
2nd choice	5	15	18	29	21	10	3	0
3rd choice	7	7	26	20	24	15	0	0
4th choice	2	12	27	21	12	17	6	4
SDLP per cent								
1st choice	8	2	6	14	13	27	1	29
2nd choice	8	5	7	17	21	23	10	10
3rd choice	3	3	11	23	19	21	11	8
4th choice	4	6	18	20	22	12	11	6
Sinn Féin per cent								
1st choice	8	0	0	5	3	10	5	69
2nd choice	8	3	3	5	5	46	24	5
3rd choice	9	0	3	17	26	29	11	6
4th choice	3	3	9	18	39	9	12	6

Northern Ireland Assembly or separate laws for Northern Ireland and *no* Anglo-Irish Agreement.

Option C – Continued direct rule (no change) The continuation of direct rule from London in consultation with the Irish government under the terms of the Anglo-Irish Agreement.

Option D – Power sharing and the Anglo-Irish Agreement Government by a Northern Ireland Assembly and power sharing Executive under the authority of the British government but in consultation with the Irish government under the terms of the Anglo-Irish Agreement.

Option E – Power sharing with North–South institutions but no joint authority Government by a Northern Ireland Assembly, power sharing Executive and a number of joint institutions established with the Republic of Ireland to deal with matters of mutual interest. (But these arrangements will not include joint authority between the British and Irish governments.)

Option F – Joint authority and power sharing Government by joint authority between the British and Irish governments in association with an elected power sharing Executive and Assembly.

Option G – Separate institutions for the two main communities Creation of separate structures for the government of each of the two main communities in Northern Ireland, subject to joint authority by the British and Irish governments.

Option H – Full incorporation into the Irish state Full incorporation of Northern Ireland into the Republic of Ireland to create a single state within the European Union.

* * *

When a war is over and peace is made prisoners are generally set free. As far as the Irish Republican Army were concerned there was no reason why the civil war between Ireland and the British state in Northern Ireland should be an exception to this rule. And if the Republican prisoners were going to be set free as part of a settlement then the Loyalists would certainly expect nothing less for their incarcerated heroes.

This subject was tackled for the first and last time in this poll. Although most Catholics had some sympathy for an amnesty as part of a political agreement most Protestants did not consider the activities of the fighters from either side to have any legitimacy at all. As far as they were concerned terrorists should be locked up and they would not mind too much if the authorities 'threw away the key'.

This subject came up again as the peace process developed and the questionnaires went through their various drafts. On most occasions it was raised by Republicans who thought the public opinion polls could be used to keep what was an important issue for them in the public eye. But the Loyalists thought better of it. They understood the Protestant establishment very well and knew that there was very little support for their cause amongst the Protestant middle class.

Everyone knew that the early release of prisoners was going to have to be part of a settlement but it was rarely discussed in public until it appeared in the final agreement. Given all the difficulties this issue raised over the coming years of implementation a more open and honest approach to prisoner releases might have been more helpful. As part of a constructive debate it might have been possible to relate amnesty to firmer commitments to bring an end to all paramilitary intimidation and violence. Perhaps an opportunity was missed.

Belfast Telegraph, Monday 30 September 1996

Ulster amnesty rejected

All the political indicators suggest that a majority of the people of Northern Ireland could live with a political settlement negotiated by the SDLP and Ulster Unionists. But would such an agreement deliver peace? What about public attitudes towards questions of amnesty and emergency legislation, and is making deals with paramilitary organisations a real possibility?

Over 3000 people have been killed as a result of the Troubles. More often than not the paramilitaries regard the deaths as 'regrettable' but apologies are quite rare as is condemnation directed against the activities of their own organisations.

When the Loyalists called their ceasefire they did apologise but out of deference to their victims they did not seek or expect forgiveness. The IRA have found similar statements more difficult to make but so too have the British government with regard to deaths in (London) Derry on Bloody Sunday.

More frequently relatives ask for no retaliation, understanding fully the tragic consequences of 'tit for tat' killings. Sometimes, but not often, parents do forgive the murderers of their son or daughter. Senator Wilson comes to mind.

But the paramilitaries want their prisoners released from jail. When and under what circumstances might the people of Northern Ireland give thought to such a proposition?

In the recent Rowntree poll on 'Peace Building and Public Policy in Northern Ireland' a random sample of the population were asked to put three government policies with reference to the peace process, remission of sentences and amnesty in their order of preference. You can try the question if you wish.

Option A – Prosecution and standard remission Prosecute all crimes committed by members of paramilitary groups and the security forces to the full extent of the law. Sentence those found guilty in accordance with standards of practice found in the rest of the United Kingdom.

Option B – Prosecution and amnesty Prosecute all crimes committed by members of paramilitary groups and the security forces but allow those serving sentences to be freed subject to terms negotiated as part of a political settlement.

Option C – Public admission of guilt and immunity from prosecution Allow members of paramilitary groups and the security forces to confess their crimes to a public 'Truth Commission' in return for immunity from prosecution and allow those serving sentences for such crimes to be freed.

Of the 715 completed questionnaires 74 per cent of respondents selected option A – prosecution and standard remission, as their first choice; 21 per cent preferred option B – amnesty, and only 5 per cent were in favour of option C – immunity. However, when these results are broken down for Protestants and Catholics and the five main political parties the statistics become more interesting. Those in favour of some sort of special arrangement as part of a peace settlement (option B plus option C) are – Protestants 10 per cent, Catholics 49 per cent, Sinn Féin 77 per cent, SDLP 47 per cent, Alliance 19 per cent, UUP 8 per cent and DUP 3 per cent (Table 5.10).

Table 5.10   Support for paramilitary amnesty or immunity

Per cent	All of NI	Protestants	Catholics	Sinn Féin	SDLP	Alliance	UUP	DUP
Yes to amnesty or immunity as part of a peace settlement	26	10	49	77	47	19	8	3

Clearly the two main communities are divided on this matter with many Catholics, Nationalists and Republicans willing to accept some sort of amnesty while most Protestants and Unionists find such suggestions quite unacceptable.

A similar result is achieved when people are asked to put four options on emergency legislation in their order of preference. In general most Protestants would like to see these laws kept in place with 54 per cent selecting option D as their first choice. Only 13 per cent of Catholics share this view. The choices were as follows:

Option A – Repeal emergency legislation now Immediately repeal emergency legislation brought in to deal with terrorism.
Option B – Repeal emergency legislation when 'Mitchell' is accepted Repeal emergency legislation brought in to deal with terrorism when all the political parties and paramilitary organisations accept the Mitchell recommendations for decommissioning and the peace process.
Option C – Repeal emergency legislation when a political settlement is reached Repeal emergency legislation brought in to deal with terrorism when all the political parties and paramilitary organisations accept the terms of a negotiated political settlement for the future of Northern Ireland.
Option D – Keep emergency legislation Keep emergency legislation 'on the books' so that the police and courts will always have the powers of search, seizure and internment of suspected terrorists at their disposal.

However, finding an acceptable compromise on the question of emergency legislation may not be too difficult. Catholics prefer option C and most Protestants who did not accept option C as their first choice did choose it as their second choice. The policy of repealing these laws as part of a peace settlement seems to have the widest popular support (Table 5.11).

But what about the prisoners? A 'Truth Commission' and immunity has very little support. Amnesty as part of a peace settlement is more acceptable, but most people (particularly Protestants) would prefer to see the law run its full course. Perhaps substantial increases in remission could become part of a negotiated agreement. But if the paramilitaries want this, or some kind of amnesty, then they would appear to have a long way to go in persuading the people of Northern Ireland in the merits of their case. Realistic

Table 5.11 Support for repeal of emergency legislation

	Repeal now	Repeal with Mitchell	Repeal with settlement	Keep emergency law
Protestant per cent				
1st choice	8	10	27	54
2nd choice	8	32	46	13
Catholic per cent				
1st choice	22	26	39	13
2nd choice	11	52	31	5

proposals that would bring an end to all forms of intimidation and violence would be welcome. The ball is in their court.

* * *

Top-down approaches to conflict resolution makes for all the headlines involving, as it does, the political leaders and military commanders who must bring hostilities to an end. Bottom-up approaches get far less attention but, in the long term, are no less important for sustaining a lasting peace.

I first came to Northern Ireland in the late 1980s to do research on the subject of integrated education and published on the social merits of this approach to improving community relations in the early 1990s.[6] Regrettably this work, like many other studies,[7] did not produce the hoped-for changes in government policies. So, with the support of those who pioneered integrated education in Northern Ireland, Lagan College and All Children Together, a number of human rights complaints were taken to UNESCO in Paris[8] and the UN Committees on Economic, Social and Cultural Rights and the Rights of the Child in Geneva.[9]

International human rights standards, agreed to by the British state, are very clear on a number of points: integrated education should be actively encouraged although parents should still be allowed to educate their children in accordance with their wishes; children should not be required to go to segregated schools if that is not what they or their parents want; the educational facilities in the integrated sector should be as every bit as good as the segregated sector; and finally, government policies must be designed to effectively deliver these rights. On this last point, in 1997, the United Nations Committee on Economic Social and Cultural Rights found British government policies severely wanting:[10]

18. The Committee expresses its concern that the educational structure in Northern Ireland is heavily segregated with most Protestants attending Protestant schools and most Catholics attending Catholic schools

and only approximately 2 per cent of the school population attending integrated schools. The Committee is of the view that current government policy, which appears to consist of a willingness to consider the conversion of existing Protestant or Catholic schools into integrated schools if it is the wish of the majority in a given school, is ineffective and likely to preserve the status quo. This situation is particularly deplorable given that it has been reported that approximately 30 per cent of parents in Northern Ireland would prefer to send their children to integrated schools.

29. The Committee recommends that appropriate measures be considered in Northern Ireland to facilitate the establishment of additional integrated schools in areas where a significant number of parents have indicated their desire to have their children enrol in such schools.

Belfast Telegraph, Tuesday 22 October 1996

Hitting a brick wall

The people of Northern Ireland want the government to support integrated schools. They always have done. In today's report from the 'Peace Building and Public Policy Poll' the education question is explored and whether DENI's new policies for 'transformation' can deliver real parental choice.

On Thursday 22 October 1968 a *Belfast Telegraph* headline read 'Clear Call for End to Religious Separation in Schools'. The paper reported that their National Opinion Polls survey found 65 per cent of young people between seventeen and twenty-four years of age in favour of integration at the primary school level while 70 per cent supported integration at the secondary level. Today, 28 years later, only 2 per cent of children in Northern Ireland are in integrated schools. Why did all these people change their minds? Or did they?

In the recent Rowntree poll a random sample of the Northern Ireland population were asked if they would like to send their children to a single or a mixed religion school. From 715 completed questionnaires 61 per cent chose mixed. That's no significant difference from 1968. They were also given four options for government education policies with reference to integrated schools. These are schools which strive to maintain an equal balance of students, staff and governors from each community. You can try the question if you wish. Assume that the academic quality of all the schools is the same, and then put the options in your order of preference.

Option A – Separation Establish separate education authorities to manage separate schools for Catholic and Protestant children in Northern Ireland with no state-funded integrated schools.
Option B – No change Leave education policy as it is where parents generally have to choose between sending their child to a Catholic or Protestant school.

Option C – Guaranteed choice Ask parents if they would prefer to send their child to a single religion school or to an integrated school and make sure their wishes are met by adequately funding integrated schools.
Option D – Integration Establish a single education authority to manage integrated schools for Catholic and Protestant children in Northern Ireland with no state-funded Catholic and Protestant schools.

Forty four per cent chose 'Guaranteed choice' as their first preference and 25 per cent chose 'Integration' with no government support for single religion schools. This 25 per cent must be very serious about integrated education indeed (Table 5.12). So why are only 2 per cent of children in integrated schools? Perhaps the integration movement has failed because they are all from just one community? Not so. Fifty-nine per cent of Catholics and 63 per cent of Protestants said 'yes' to mixed religion schools and a majority of the electorate from the two largest political parties also said 'yes' with the UUP at 68 per cent and SDLP at 61 per cent. The Alliance party were at 87 per cent with Sinn Féin at 37 per cent and the DUP at 28 per cent (Table 5.13). So what is the problem?

Table 5.12 Support for different integrated education policies

Per cent	Separation	No change	Guaranteed choice	Integration
1st preference	5	30	40	25
2nd preference	7	33	40	20

Table 5.13 Support for mixed schools

Per cent	Alliance	UUP	Protestants	All of NI	SDLP	Catholics	Sinn Féin	DUP
Yes to mixed schools	87	68	63	61	61	59	37	28

The fact is children are being turned away from integrated schools for lack of places. This is a breach of their Human Rights. In 1995 the UN Committee on the Rights of the Child told the British government to make greater provision for integrated schools and DENI have now come up with a plan called 'Framework for Transformation'. But the plan is both fundamentally flawed and compromised by spending cuts. It is proposed that Transforming schools will be able to get started with only 1 per cent of their students from the minority community. This policy could put children at risk.

Common sense, personal experience and educational research all tell us that placing a very small group of students from one community in a school dominated by the other community has the potential to do more harm than good. Instead of learning, playing and making friends in a balanced social environment that naturally promotes mutual respect these children can become the targets and victims of sectarian abuse. In these circumstances the abusers are also harmed as they are provided with opportunities to perfect their skills as both bigots and bullies.

Parents who are interested in truly integrated education should be wary of 'Transforming' integrated schools unless they have an 'integrated' philosophy and ethos and are making real efforts to recruit governors, staff and pupils from the other community in significant numbers. Government must set adequate standards for these schools. Education and Library Boards must make sure those standards are met. Finally, the wishes of parents must be paramount. They must be allowed to choose a Catholic, Protestant or Integrated school for their child. That is what the people of Northern Ireland want and it should be their right by law.

Trying to create more integrated schools on the cheap may impress a few foreign dignitaries who fly in on a whistle stop tour. It may also get the UN Committee on the Rights of the Child off the government's back for a few more years. But cutting corners with integrated education is positively dangerous. No one ever said real peace building was easy – or cheap. It isn't. Conflict is easy – it is also far more expensive.

* * *

If forced segregation is one of the cornerstones of continued conflict in a deeply divided society discrimination is the other. Catholics have been discriminated against. There is no doubt about that. But changes in the world economic order, the decline of old industries and the rise of new ones, have all served to confuse both the realities and perceptions of discrimination in Northern Ireland. Stronger legislation will not, in and of itself, put matters right.

Belfast Telegraph, Wednesday 20 November 1996

The FEC ... fair to meddling? Ulster verdict on jobs body

A Protestant has won a record £77,000 in damages for religious and political discrimination. But what do the Northern Ireland public think of the Fair Employment Commission and what future direction should Fair Employment legislation take?[11]

The British government like to make the point that they believe Fair Employment legislation in Northern Ireland to be the best in all of Europe. Many Americans, however, do not think the laws go far enough and would like strong affirmative action programmes for Catholics in line with the 'McBride Principles'. One thing is for sure, discrimination laws are here to stay, they are changing the patterns of employment and these laws are controversial. So what direction should the future of Fair Employment legislation take and who wants to keep the FEC?

In the recent Rowntree poll a random sample of the Northern Ireland population were asked to put five options for fair employment policies in their order of preference. You can try the question if you wish. It appeared in the questionnaire as follows:

Option A – Stop fair employment activities Repeal fair employment legislation, scrap the Fair Employment Commission and allow employers to give jobs to whom they wish.

Option B – No change Leave current fair employment legislation and policies as they are. Don't cut them back but don't extend their powers either.

Option C – Preference to under-represented community Allow employers to give a job to a candidate from the under-represented community when two candidates (one a Catholic and one a Protestant) are equally qualified for the same job.

Option D – Active selection from the under-represented community **Require** employers to select qualified candidates from the under-represented community until a balance is achieved in their workforce that reflects the balance of the two communities in the area.

Option E – Special relief for areas of high unemployment **Allow** employers in areas of high unemployment to recruit from one community only leaving it up to government to ensure an overall balance of employment between the two communities in Northern Ireland as a whole.

From 715 completed questionnaires 28 per cent of Protestants wanted to scrap the FEC while only 3 per cent of Catholics thought it should go (Table 5.14). The largest group of people, 42 per cent of Catholics and 47 per cent of Protestants, wanted to keep it as it is. Everyone else, 55 per cent of Catholics and 25 per cent of Protestants, wanted the powers of the FEC to be strengthened. The clear consensus seems to be to keep the FEC but with some modest improvements. There was also a clear consensus on sharing. Eighty-two per cent would prefer a mixed religion workplace and only 12 per cent wanted to work with people from just their own religion – 6 per cent didn't know.

Table 5.14 Catholic and Protestant support for fair employment policies

Per cent	Stop FEC	Keep FEC	Allow preference	Require active selection	Special relief
Catholics' 1st choice	3	42	20	23	12
Protestants' 1st choice	28	47	10	8	7

It comes as no surprise that Catholics strongly support the principles of Fair Employment. But the result that will be most welcome at the FEC is the fact that a significant majority of Protestants are willing to accept laws to prevent discrimination in the workplace. Caution, however, is required as some of the results are strangely ambiguous.

While 28 per cent of Protestants said no to the FEC and 47 per cent said keep it, another 25 per cent said strengthen it. The DUP are most clearly split on this issue with 37 per cent of their voters choosing 'Stop the FEC' as their *first* choice and an almost equal number, 35 per cent, selecting 'Stop the FEC' as their *last* choice! UUP supporters recorded 25 per cent and 33 per cent respectively for this question. So many Protestants strongly support Fair Employment laws while a significant minority clearly feel very hurt by them. Who are these people and what, if anything, can the government and FEC do to put matters right?

The facts are these – those Protestants who strongly support the FEC are younger, they are better educated and most of them have jobs. Those Protestants who want to see an end to the FEC are older, more likely to be men than women, suffer from higher rates of unemployment and have often reached the age of retirement.

Both groups seem to be evenly spread across the Province. So it doesn't seem to be just some kind of (London) Derry or 'West of the Bann' majority/minority sort of thing. Social class doesn't seem to be much of an influencing factor either.

Finally, 40 per cent of those who wanted to scrap the FEC thought Catholics were treated much better than Protestants and 30 per cent of them would prefer to be in a single religion workplace. On the other hand only 14 per cent of Protestants who supported the FEC thought Catholics were treated much better than themselves and only 9 per cent of them would prefer a single religion workplace.

So, in general, Northern Ireland attitudes towards sharing out the benefits of employment seem to be very healthy indeed. However, when it comes to the Protestant community there seems to be a very real generation gap. Perhaps we do not have to look too far for an explanation.

The world, Europe and Northern Ireland have changed. Older industries have given way to 'hi-tech'. Many have lost their jobs and sometimes find it convenient to blame the Japanese, Koreans or East Europeans. But in Northern Ireland it is also possible to blame the Catholics. The FEC clearly needs to do more to put their message across to those who have fallen victim to the new economic order. But those who have suffered most are family men with grown-up children and these sons and daughters must now look to the new 'hi-tech' jobs for their future.

Most people are able to understand the problem. Coming to terms with its hard realities is, of course, more difficult. Fortunately nearly everyone is agreed on the solution – peace and the prosperity that will hopefully come with it.

* * *

The United Nations and the Universal Declaration of Human Rights were established and agreed to by the peoples of the world at the end of the Second World War in an effort to bring an end to all wars. The former was meant to resolve dangerous political disagreements as they arose while the latter – through the creation of social justice – was meant to prevent such situations arising. But this strategy for conflict resolution can only work when human rights are effectively applied and most ruling majorities in most societies prefer to ignore them when it is to their advantage to do so. The Protestant majority of Northern Ireland were no exception to this rule, so for them human rights were popularly seen as a Catholic 'MOPE' agenda for those who saw themselves as the 'Most Oppressed People Ever'.

As a small 'u' Unionist paper the *Belfast Telegraph* did not consider human rights to be a top priority for their readership so an article on minority rights was the second story that they did not publish. But, with only one more exception, they subsequently took everything that was written for them and did deal with human rights when the subject came up again in the talks.

What is interesting about this story is that each side saw the other's rights as being of little significance while still wishing to advocate and defend their own rights when it suited them. A Bill of Rights for Northern Ireland, that everyone had a hand in writing and that everyone could therefore give allegiance to, was the answer.

It should be stressed how very important this whole matter is for the ultimate success of the Northern Ireland peace process. In the course of my research on integrated education I was frequently told that the establishment of integrated schools could only be regarded as incidental to the resolution of the conflict in Northern Ireland and that the only viable solution to the social problems there was a political agreement.

But when the agreement came it did not bring about all the social changes that many hoped for. In a deeply divided society like Northern Ireland, peace building, it is now clear, must be worked at in each and every aspect of economic, social and cultural life at the same time. The new Northern Ireland Commission for Human Rights, set up under the terms of the Belfast Agreement, has a central role to play in this enterprise.

No winners please – this is Northern Ireland (not published)

Approximately 70 children go to Irish language schools without any financial assistance from the government. So what? Who cares? Today's report from the 'Peace Building and Public Policy Poll' explores the Irish language question and asks if supporting minority rights could improve community relations.[12]

Every year, as part of their Social Attitude Survey, the government asks the people of Northern Ireland if they think government should be doing more to improve community relations. Surprise, surprise – most people say 'Yes'. But how far are people really willing to go to achieve better under-standing between the two communities? It isn't always their first choice, but most people in Northern Ireland, both Catholic and Protestant, are willing to support the 'Independent Review for Parades and Marches' ('Independent body wins the public's vote of confidence' – *Belfast Telegraph*, 4 July 1996). How much further will they go?

In the recent Rowntree poll a random sample of the Northern Ireland population were asked to put three options for the support of single com-munity programmes in their order of preference. You can try the question if you wish. It appeared in the questionnaire as follows:

Option A – Stop supporting single community programmes Stop funding all sport, language and other cultural activities associated with Unionism and Nationalism and leave the support of these activities entirely in the hands of their respective communities.

Option B – Fund single community programmes equally Fund the sport, language and cultural activities of each community with equal levels of resources.

Option C – Priority funding of programmes linked to good community relations Give priority funding to sport, language and cultural programmes where cross-community committees are established to maintain good community relations over contentious issues (for example, Nationalist and Orange marches and Sunday opening).

From 715 completed questionnaires 53 per cent chose Option C, 'Priority funding of programmes linked to good community relations', as their first choice and 34 per cent chose Option B, 'Fund single community pro-grammes equally', while only 13 per cent chose Option A, 'Stop supporting single community programmes'. So most people want fairness and are willing to make grants conditional (Table 5.15).

Table 5.15   Support for community programmes

All of NI per cent	No support	Equal support	Support linked to good community relations
1st preference	13	34	53

This may be all well and good as a principle but will this support be maintained when people are confronted with a real issue? In the Rowntree poll people were also asked to put four options for the support of Irish language education in their order of preference. Again, you can try the question if you wish. It appeared in the questionnaire as follows:

Option A – No provision for the Irish language Stop using public funds to pay for the provision of Irish language education in any form.

Option B – Provision subject to demand (no change) Provide different forms of Irish language education subject to demand and availability of resources (a mixture of classes, streams and schools).

Option C – Guaranteed provision of Irish as a second language Allow parents, if they so wish, to choose Irish language classes as an optional second language for their children in existing schools where the primary language of education is English.

Option D – Guaranteed provision of Irish medium education Allow parents, if they so wish, to choose Irish medium education (in which the main language of instruction is Irish) for their children either in Irish medium schools or in separate Irish medium streams in existing schools as appropriate.

Twenty-two per cent chose 'No provision for the Irish language' as their first preference. Thirty-one per cent were happy to leave things as they are while 34 per cent wanted more support for Irish education as a second language and another 14 per cent wanted funds made available for Irish medium schools and streams (Table 5.16).

This result isn't quite so good. 'No support' has increased from 13 per cent to 22 per cent when confronted with the reality of provision for Irish language education. However, that still leaves a majority of 79 per cent wanting to maintain current levels of funding or even increased funding. So why are 70 children in Irish language schools not receiving any government support? Who objects to this modest expenditure?

A political breakdown of those who oppose the funding of Irish language education proves to be most revealing. Seventy-six per cent of DUP voters are against it while absolutely zero per cent of Sinn Féin supporters selected this option as their first choice. Everyone else falls in between these two

Table 5.16 Support for Irish language programmes

All of NI per cent	No Irish education	Same provision for Irish	More Irish language	More Irish schools
1st preference	22	31	34	14

extremes with the UUP at 37 per cent, Alliance at 10 per cent and the SDLP at 2 per cent.

Although some Protestants clearly don't care much for the Irish language, many of them do care strongly about the right to march. Sixty-three per cent of DUP voters thought all parades should be allowed to march on all public roads and should be provided with police protection. Conversely, Sinn Féin voters have little time for Orange marches. Zero per cent chose 'Allow all parades' as their first preference (*Belfast Telegraph*, 4 July). Again, everyone else fell in between with the UUP at 46 per cent, Alliance at 16 per cent and the SDLP at 6 per cent (Table 5.17).

So those who want to march don't want provision made for the Irish language – 'I win and you lose'. On the other hand those who oppose marching want provision for the Irish language most of all – 'You lose and I win'. The necessary outcome of all of this is that everyone is a loser. The extremists have their way at any cost. 'I lose and you lose' and everyone else who is willing to compromise has to lose.

John Hume looks forward to the day when the Apprentice Boys parade in (London)Derry will be a festive occasion to be enjoyed by both communities with, he suggests 'a carnival atmosphere'. Most people would share this point of view and are also quite content to let those who wish to learn and speak Irish do so.

Many would consider the preservation of an ancient language in this region of Europe to be part of our common heritage and that it should not be held hostage to the fortunes of political division. In Scotland the government will spend £10 million on Gaelic broadcasting this year. In Northern Ireland we have spent £10 million on policing contentious parades.

But these issues shouldn't simply be viewed as trading one community's aspirations against the other's either. There is a better way and South Africa have found it. Their new constitution is built on a foundation of comprehensive 'Rights'. Fortunately, all the political parties here are agreed on the necessity of a Bill of Rights for Northern Ireland.

Rights are for everyone. They can take us away from an 'I lose and you lose' confrontation and bring us to an 'I win and you win' outcome. This is what the vast majority of the people of Northern Ireland want. If this

Table 5.17   Support for Irish language and parades compared

Per cent	DUP	Protestants	UUP	All of NI	Alliance	SDLP	Catholics	Sinn Féin
'No' to Irish language	76	39	37	22	10	2	2	0
'Yes' to all parades	63	42	46	25	16	6	6	0

research has demonstrated anything it is the breadth and depth of that consensus on many social and cultural issues. A Bill of Rights could go a long way to sorting out many of our problems. Why does government wait? The people are ready now.

* * *

Meanwhile, in the talks, very little was happening and the spectre of failure seemed very real indeed. What would happen if the politicians elected to agree the political future of Northern Ireland could not get the business done? At this juncture some new ideas would not go amiss at all. Perhaps, in partnership with the people of Northern Ireland, public opinion polls could now be used to help move the peace process forward?

The results for the 'constitutional question' were analysed again, but this time by Catholic and Protestant community instead of political party affiliation and it was concluded that the polls could be used in this way. This point was made very clearly, on the pages of the *Belfast Telegraph*, in the hope that some gentle prodding just might galvanise the politicians into actions that would make such polling superfluous to their needs.

It wasn't, and with the co-operation of the parties the Belfast Agreement was signed four polls later and the new institutions of government were up and running another three polls after that.

Belfast Telegraph, Tuesday 3 December 1996

Ulster people could decide way forward

Sinn Féin and the SDLP have withdrawn themselves from the activities of the Forum. Sinn Féin are excluded from the Talks and the Loyalist ceasefire is at breaking point. Perhaps the Talks are at breaking point also. What are the options for the constitutional question and could the people of Northern Ireland give shape to their own political destiny?

Let's get straight to the point. If the current talks process fails could the people of the Province decide their own political future? Some may view such a suggestion with a certain degree of horror. Indeed, some may have an interest in not finding a quick solution, in not putting the matter before the people and insisting that the people can not possibly choose between the various complex options. No one should assume that the issues are easy and require little thought. On the other hand no one should assume that the people of Northern Ireland are politically unsophisticated and unable to deal with such matters until they have at least had an opportunity to try.

In the recent Rowntree poll a random sample of the Northern Ireland population were asked to put eight options for the future political development of Northern Ireland in their order of preference as follows:

Option A – Separate Northern Irish state The complete separation of Northern Ireland from both the United Kingdom and the Republic of Ireland and the establishment of a separate state within the European Union.

Option B – Full incorporation into the British state Direct rule from Westminster and local government similar to the rest of the United Kingdom with *no* Northern Ireland Assembly or separate laws for Northern Ireland and *no* Anglo-Irish Agreement.

Option C – Continued direct rule (no change) The continuation of direct rule from London in consultation with the Irish government under the terms of the Anglo-Irish Agreement.

Option D – Power sharing and the Anglo-Irish Agreement Government by a Northern Ireland Assembly and power sharing Executive under the authority of the British government but in consultation with the Irish government under the terms of the Anglo-Irish Agreement.

Option E – Power sharing with North–South institutions but no joint authority Government by a Northern Ireland Assembly, power sharing Executive and a number of joint institutions established with the Republic of Ireland to deal with matters of mutual interest. (But these arrangements will not include joint authority between the British and Irish governments.)

Option F – Joint authority and power sharing Government by joint authority between the British and Irish governments in association with an elected power sharing Executive and Assembly.

Option G – Separate institutions for the two main communities Creation of separate structures for the government of each of the two main communities in Northern Ireland, subject to joint authority by the British and Irish governments.

Option H – Full incorporation into the Irish state Full incorporation of Northern Ireland into the Republic of Ireland to create a single state within the European Union.

Of the 715 who completed the questionnaire almost everyone was able to identify their first choice and most people were able to list all eight options without too much difficulty. As so many choices were offered it may help to start by eliminating the options that are most definitely not acceptable to one community or the other – or both. Very few people from either community want an independent state or separate institutions for the management of a segregated society (Table 5.18). Most Catholics do not want full incorporation into the British state and most Protestants do not want full incorporation into the Irish state (Table 5.20). So these four options can be taken out of the equation as non-starters for a political compromise.

This process of elimination leaves four options available from which to develop new constitutional arrangements for Northern Ireland: continued

Table 5.18 Little support for 'separate institutions' or single 'Irish state'

All of NI per cent	Independent state	British state	Direct rule	Anglo-Irish Agreement	North/ South institutions	Joint authority	Separate institutions	Irish state
8th choice	19	14	5	4	4	5	10	39
7th choice	13	15	10	4	2	9	36	10

Table 5.19 Northern Ireland support for political settlement options

All of NI per cent	Independent state	British state	Direct rule	Anglo-Irish Agreement	North/ South institutions	Joint authority	Separate institutions	Irish state
1st choice	10	28	10	10	10	14	2	15
2nd choice	11	12	22	14	15	15	6	4
3rd choice	12	6	18	24	16	15	6	3
4th choice	7	7	14	24	24	10	8	5

direct rule; power sharing and the Anglo-Irish Agreement; power sharing with North–South institutions; and joint authority and power sharing (Table 5.19).

Of these options Catholics would prefer joint authority and would like to see an end to direct rule. Conversely Protestants would prefer direct rule and would find joint authority very difficult to accept. The only acceptable compromise for both communities would seem to be the establishment of an Assembly with a power sharing Executive in combination with either the Anglo-Irish Agreement or North–South institutions (Table 5.20).

Table 5.20 Catholic and Protestant support for political settlement options

	Independent state	British state	Direct rule	Anglo-Irish Agreement	North/ South institutions	Joint authority	Separate institutions	Irish state
Catholics per cent								
1st choice	8	3	6	14	11	24	2	32
2nd choice	9	5	9	17	16	26	9	9
3rd choice	2	4	10	21	22	23	11	6
4th choice	4	4	18	21	23	11	12	6
Protestants per cent								
1st choice	10	49	14	7	10	6	2	2
2nd choice	14	19	34	13	13	3	2	1
3rd choice	19	8	26	25	11	7	2	1
4th choice	10	9	11	28	26	9	4	2

With the least favoured options removed and a little more flesh put on the bones of the middle ground compromises the poll could now be run again in an effort to better define the wishes of the people. For example, different kinds of North–South institutions could be proposed ranging from something like the Anglo-Irish Agreement to the creation of a body with executive powers. People could also be asked to pick and choose the areas of policy that they think such a body should deal with: the environment, tourism, agriculture, fisheries, representation in Europe and so on.

With the experience of the polls established, the people of Northern Ireland would be well-prepared to make their choice known through some kind of referendum. Acceptance by both communities would be required. The issues would have to be presented in simpler terms than those used here and perhaps in stages that progressively eliminated unacceptable options. Finally the politicians could be asked to work out the detail and put the will of the people into practice.

So, if the Talks fail, the people of Northern Ireland can help to decide the political future of the Province. They can express their views through public opinion polls and referendums. They can move the peace process forward by 'breaking the logjam'.

6
After the Elections

All the articles produced for the *Belfast Telegraph* were now rewritten in a more academic style and published with my colleagues on the 'Peace Building and Public Policy' project, Tom Hadden and Fred Boal. Tom had an interest in the local current affairs magazine *Fortnight*. So, with a grant from Rowntree, we were able to include a free booklet with the December issue developing a theme of Tom's 'Separation or Sharing'.

The IRA ceasefire had broken down, the Stormont talks were stalled and an early end to the war was nowhere in sight. Without a lasting settlement the prospects for building peace through the range of public policies we proposed seemed very remote indeed. All parts of the peace process had to be worked on at the same time and that included 'top-down' politics. The time had come to engage with the politicians. So I wrote to the leader of each of the parties elected to participate in the negotiations and invited them to join in a collaborative project to run a public opinion poll on all of the issues holding up the talks that were of particular concern to them. This was in January of 1997.

To be absolutely honest about it I had not expected both Sinn Féin and Ian Paisley's Democratic Unionist Party to agree. I thought if one of them chose to participate then inevitably the other would decline. But this did not happen and providing I didn't make a 'big thing' of the fact that everyone had to agree the drafts of the questions to be used then everyone was willing to have their ideas tested alongside the proposals of their political competitors. So while the talks proper excluded Sinn Féin and continued to be stuck on decommissioning, our unofficial exercise was fully inclusive and started to move beyond the procedural issues of who should be in the talks and under what conditions to substantive issues concerning the political future of Northern Ireland.

But the people of Northern Ireland had lost confidence in the political process, so the first thing that had to be done was to try and establish some sense of real hope for a successful outcome by tapping into the desire of the people for an honourable peace. This unquenchable desire for a negotiated settlement was the foundation upon which all the polls were built and an agreement eventually mapped out. Eight polls, times one thousand people interviewed, times one hundred-plus options or questions in each poll amounts to nearly one million answers freely given, recorded and analysed. One answer for almost every person with a right to vote in Northern Ireland. This was truly 'the people's peace process'.

Belfast Telegraph, Monday 7 April 1997

Few believe peace is at hand

An overwhelming majority of the people of Northern Ireland are in favour of a negotiated settlement – but only a small percentage believe the Stormont talks will lead to an agreement.

In a question: *'Do you support the principle of a negotiated settlement for the political future of Northern Ireland?'* 94 per cent said 'Yes' ranging from a high of 99 per cent for Alliance voters to a low of 90 per cent for DUP supporters (Table 6.1) – not very low!

Table 6.1   Support for a negotiated settlement

Per cent	All of NI	Protestant	Catholic	DUP	UUP	Alliance	SDLP	Sinn Féin
Yes	94	93	97	90	97	99	97	96
No	6	7	3	10	3	1	3	4

In 1994 President De Klerk asked the white population of South Africa – 'Do you support the continuation of the reform process which the State President began on 2 February 1990 and which is aimed at a new constitution through negotiation?' With only a 69 per cent positive response he was able to complete his historic agreement with Nelson Mandela and the ANC. Why then don't we have an agreement here? The answer to that question is very difficult to answer but unlike De Klerk the people of Northern Ireland have reached this point in their journey many times before. About every ten years or so some sort of 'negotiations', 'agreement' or 'talks' fail to deliver a lasting peace. So when the people here are asked *'Do you think the current "talks" will lead to a settlement?'* only 26 per cent said 'Yes' ranging from a pessimistic low of 12 per cent for Sinn Féin supporters to a high of 31 per cent for SDLP voters (Table 6.2) – not very high!

Table 6.2   Believe there will be a settlement

Per cent	All of NI	Protestant	Catholic	DUP	UUP	Alliance	SDLP	Sinn Féin
Yes	26	25	28	24	24	27	31	12
No	74	75	72	76	76	74	69	88

* * * *

Over the course of the polls the percentage of those wanting a deal fell off a little as people slowly came to realise that a settlement required compromise. But this welcome sense of realism also translated into a greater proportion of people believing a deal was actually possible. This realism translated into pragmatism when it came to doing business and overcoming the problems of inclusive talks and decommissioning.

Belfast Telegraph, Monday 7 April 1997

Truce holds key: sharp divisions on how talks replace the guns

After the general election a new government in Westminster will have an opportunity to make a fresh start at the Stormont talks. With 94 per cent of the people of Northern Ireland willing to lend their support to negotiations is there anything a new government can do to give hope to the 74 per cent of the population who do not think the talks can deliver a settlement?

Some of the political parties at the talks seem to be caught, like two bus drivers facing each other down some deserted country road, neither willing to give way for fear of showing weakness in front of their passengers. But what do the people of Northern Ireland really think? Do they want their political leaders to move closer to some sort of accommodation and compromise on the key issues that have been holding up the talks? Will they continue to support their leaders on such a quest or will they abandon them? This critically important question was asked in the *Belfast Telegraph/* Queen's Survey by presenting a range of policy options to a representative sample of the public and inviting them to say which policies they consider to be 'Preferred', 'Acceptable', 'Tolerable' or 'Unacceptable'. For the purposes of the poll these terms mean:

'Preferred' – This may not be exactly what you want but this option, or something very similar to it, would be your first choice.
'Acceptable' – This option is not what you would prefer if you were given a choice but you could certainly 'live with it'.
'Tolerable' – This option is not what you want. But, as part of a lasting peace settlement for Northern Ireland, you would be willing to put up with it.
'Unacceptable' – This option is completely unacceptable under any circumstances. You would not accept it, even as part of a peace settlement.

Question 1
Here are some options for the different conditions under which political parties with an electoral mandate and perceived association with paramilitary organisations could be allowed into the 'talks'. Please indicate which of the following options you consider to be 'Preferred', 'Acceptable', 'Tolerable' or 'Unacceptable'.

• *Immediate all-party 'talks'* – All parties, including those associated with paramilitary organisations, should be allowed into the 'talks' now without any preconditions.

• *All-party 'talks' after a ceasefire* – All parties, including those associated with paramilitary organisations, should be allowed into the 'talks' as soon as a ceasefire is called and the 'Mitchell' principles are agreed to.

• *All-party 'talks' after a ceasefire and other preconditions* – All parties, including those associated with paramilitary organisations, should be allowed into the 'talks' when a ceasefire is called, the 'Mitchell' principles are agreed to and a number of other preconditions, such as a period of 'Probation' and a start on decommissioning, are satisfied.

• *No to parties with paramilitary connections* – The 'talks' should continue but political parties who have any association with paramilitary organisations should not be allowed to remain in the 'talks'.

Table 6.3   Protestant and Catholic support for all-party talks options

	Preferred	Acceptable	Tolerable	Unacceptable
Protestant per cent				
Immediate all-party 'talks'	17	9	15	59
All-party 'talks' after a ceasefire	40	32	20	9
All-party 'talks' after a ceasefire and other preconditions	34	37	16	13
No to parties with paramilitary connections	18	19	19	45
Catholic per cent				
Immediate all-party 'talks'	65	15	11	9
All-party 'talks' after a ceasefire	27	44	16	13
All-party 'talks' after a ceasefire and other preconditions	9	37	22	32
No to parties with paramilitary connections	6	17	15	61

Protestants at 40 per cent and DUP supporters at 43 per cent marginally prefer the option of 'All-party "talks" after a ceasefire' over the option of 'All-party "talks" after a ceasefire *and* other preconditions' which is the first choice of UUP supporters at 44 per cent. On the other hand Catholics clearly prefer 'Immediate all-party "talks"' at 65 per cent with the SDLP coming in at 62 per cent and Sinn Féin at 87 per cent. But 59 per cent of Protestants find this option 'Unacceptable', so an immediate ceasefire followed by 'All-party "talks"' as soon as possible would seem to be the people's most acceptable choice (Table 6.3).

Apart from who should be at the talks one of the most difficult obstacles on the road to real talks would seem to be decommissioning.

Question 2
Here are some options for making political progress at the 'talks' and making progress with decommissioning. Please indicate which of the following options you consider to be 'Preferred', 'Acceptable', 'Tolerable' or 'Unacceptable'.

• *Fixed timetable for the 'talks' followed by decommissioning* – Political progress in the 'talks' should take place on a fixed timetable. Decommissioning can take place when a settlement is reached.

• *Fixed timetable for the 'talks' and simultaneous decommissioning* – Political progress in the 'talks' and decommissioning should take place in parallel in accordance with a fixed timetable that leads to a settlement.

• *Flexible timetable for both the 'talks' and simultaneous decommissioning* – Political progress in the 'talks' and decommissioning should take place in parallel but no time limits should be set on reaching a political settlement.

• *Fixed timetable for decommissioning followed by the 'talks'* – Decommissioning should take place on a fixed timetable that is unrelated to political progress in the 'talks'. The 'talks' should take as long as is required to reach a settlement.

Table 6.4 Protestant and Catholic support for talks and decommissioning options

	Preferred	Acceptable	Tolerable	Unacceptable
Protestant per cent				
Fixed timetable for the 'talks' followed by decommissioning	20	18	23	40
Fixed timetable for the 'talks' and simultaneous decommissioning	22	34	27	18
Flexible timetable for the 'talks' and simultaneous decommissioning	15	36	33	16
Fixed timetable for decommissioning followed by the 'talks'	50	22	17	11
Catholic per cent				
Fixed timetable for the 'talks' followed by decommissioning	52	22	15	10
Fixed timetable for the 'talks' and simultaneous decommissioning	21	37	29	14
Flexible timetable for the 'talks' and simultaneous decommissioning	22	32	27	19
Fixed timetable for decommissioning followed by the 'talks'	14	23	24	39

Senator George Mitchell is clearly faced with a formidable task when confronted with the problem of trying to persuade the parties to reach a compromise on decommissioning. Fifty-two per cent of Catholics want a fixed timetable for the 'talks' followed by decommissioning while an almost equal percentage of Protestants (50 per cent) want the opposite – a fixed timetable for decommissioning followed by the 'talks'. But only a small percentage of Catholics and Protestants (about 17 per cent) find the compromise options of simultaneous 'talks' and decommissioning 'Unacceptable'. The level of 'Unacceptability' for these compromises rises from a low of about 6 per cent for Alliance voters to 8 per cent for the SDLP, 10 per cent for the UUP, 20 per cent for the DUP and 34 per cent for Sinn Féin (Table 6.4).

The British and Irish governments have now passed legislation to set up an international body to deal with the day-to-day practicalities of decommissioning. But even with this legislation in place and a compromise found on simultaneous 'talks' and decommissioning the parties have not, as yet, reached agreement on how to deal with decommissioning problems.

Question 3
Here are two options for dealing with any major problems that may arise over decommissioning at the 'talks'. Please indicate which of the following options you consider to be 'Preferred', 'Acceptable', 'Tolerable' or 'Unacceptable'.

• *Stop the 'talks' until the decommissioning problem is solved* – If any major problem arises over decommissioning the 'talks' should stop until that problem is resolved.

• *Do not stop the 'talks', let a subcommittee deal with decommissioning problems* – If any major problem arises over decommissioning that problem should be delegated to a subcommittee of the 'talks' so that the principal delegates can continue to move ahead with other business.

Table 6.5 Support for separating decommissioning problems from the main talks

All of NI per cent	Preferred	Acceptable	Tolerable	Unacceptable
Stop the 'talks' until the decommissioning problem is solved	31	15	12	42
Do not stop the 'talks', let a subcommittee deal with decommissioning problems	69	10	10	12

The results leave little margin for any doubt about the people's preference (Table 6.5). Sixty-nine per cent of the adult population of Northern Ireland do *not* want the 'talks' to stop with only 12 per cent finding this option 'Unacceptable'. Perhaps the answers to all these questions can be combined into a package that has the potential to clear the way to real talks. It would have to include a ceasefire followed by a reasonably short period of probation combined with the establishment of an international body and a talks subcommittee to deal with decommissioning problems.

* * *

Newspapers, and the *Belfast Telegraph* was no exception to this particular rule, like to run political 'beauty contest' questions in their public opinion polls. But this can all too often end up with a lot of very unhelpful 'finger pointing', and although it may make for good copy it very rarely serves the necessities of conflict resolution well. But how an electorate think their own party is performing in the peace-making stakes is a slightly different matter. As far as the two governments were concerned the view could be taken that it was their job to make peace. So a little 'finger pointing' in that direction would do no harm at all as the two governments seldom missed an opportunity to blame the Northern Ireland politicians for all the political failures. Five, ten or even fifteen years of the 'Troubles' is a tragedy – twenty-five years is arguably bad parenting.

Belfast Telegraph, Monday 7 April 1997

Voters query parties' push: SDLP tops the league table in peace efforts

How do the voters rate their own political parties, when it comes to peace building, and for that matter the performance of the British and Irish governments?

Nationalists and Republicans probably don't think Unionists and Loyalists are doing very much to advance the Northern Ireland peace process. The feeling is probably mutual. So there isn't much point in asking DUP supporters what they think of Sinn Féin or how they in turn rate the actions and policies of the DUP.

So everyone interviewed for the survey was asked *How much do you think the Northern Ireland party you support is doing to* – firstly – *try and reach a political settlement at the Stormont talks?* – secondly – *resolve the issue of contentious parades?* – and thirdly – *build confidence between the two main communities in Northern Ireland?* Do you think they are doing *'A lot'*, *'A little'*, *'Not very much'*, *'Nothing at all'* or perhaps you have *'No strong views'* on the matter?

Everyone interviewed for the poll was also asked *'How much is the British government doing to* – *try and reach a political settlement at the Stormont talks?* – *resolve the issue of contentious parades? and build confidence between the two main communities in Northern Ireland?'*

Finally everyone interviewed was asked *'How much is the Irish government doing to* – *try and reach a political settlement at the Stormont talks?* – *resolve the issue of contentious parades? and build confidence between the two main communities in Northern Ireland?'*

Table 6.6   How much is your party doing to ...?

'A lot' per cent	All of NI	Protestant	Catholic	DUP	UUP	Alliance	SDLP	SF
Try and reach a political settlement at the Stormont talks	42	41	47	39	45	41	65	26
Resolve the issue of contentious parades	40	39	45	50	38	33	51	62
Build confidence between the two main communities in Northern Ireland	39	34	48	36	32	51	60	39

Table 6.7   How much is the British government doing to ...?

'A lot' per cent	All of NI	Protestant	Catholic	DUP	UUP	Alliance	SDLP	SF
Try and reach a political settlement at the Stormont talks	10	14	5	11	16	15	5	1
Resolve the issue of contentious parades	10	15	2	22	10	12	2	0
Build confidence between the two main communities in Northern Ireland	11	18	3	25	12	13	3	1

Table 6.8   How much is the Irish government doing to ...?

'A lot' per cent	All of NI	Protestant	Catholic	DUP	UUP	Alliance	SDLP	SF
Try and reach a political settlement at the Stormont talks	12	7	18	2	6	13	19	30
Resolve the issue of contentious parades	11	13	9	18	6	13	10	8
Build confidence between the two main communities in Northern Ireland	13	14	14	18	8	13	16	22

Of all the Northern Ireland political parties the SDLP seems to have the highest approval rating for their performance (Table 6.6). Sixty-five per cent of their electorate think they are doing 'a lot' to try and reach a political settlement at the Stormont talks compared with the UUP at 45 per cent, Alliance at 41 per cent, DUP at 39 per cent and Sinn Féin at 26 per cent. Sixty per cent of SDLP supporters also believe they are doing 'a lot' to build confidence between the two main communities in Northern Ireland compared to the UUP at 32 per cent, Alliance at 51 per cent, DUP at 36 per cent and Sinn Féin at 39 per cent. The DUP get their highest approval rating for trying to resolve the issue of contentious parades. Fifty per cent of their voters think they are doing 'a lot' but Sinn Féin supporters think their party is doing even more with an approval rating of 62 per cent for this issue.

On average about 40 per cent of those asked thought their party was doing 'a lot' to resolve all these problems. However, only about 10 per cent thought the British government were also doing 'a lot' and the Irish government didn't do much better with an average 12 per cent approval rating (Tables 6.7 and 6.8). Clearly people here take the view that new governments in both London and Dublin have plenty of room for improvement when it comes to the development of their policies for Northern Ireland.

* * *

It was spring again in Northern Ireland. The 'Marching Season' and 'Drumcree Three' were just a few months away. But there was still no Parades Commission in place with statutory powers to deal with the inevitable problems of the summer. Not wishing to upset the Unionists and their slim majority in the House of Commons the Conservative government of John Major chose only to undertake a review of the issue and leave any action until after the May general election. At that time the problem could be in the hands of a new Labour Secretary of State. It was. But whatever happened in Westminster the problem still had to be faced up to by the politicians in Northern Ireland and now they had a chance to test public opinion on this critical issue. What were the people's views of the government's report and proposed Parades Commission?

Belfast Telegraph, Tuesday 8 April 1997

Drumcree three: rule of law is what people of Northern Ireland want

In the second day of the poll the focus is on the seemingly intractable issue of parades. But the people of Northern Ireland see a way forward by recourse to law and a Bill of Rights.

No one can afford a Drumcree Three. But with the marching season now under way and no agreement in place that will guarantee a peaceful summer, what solutions do the people of Northern Ireland offer to resolve the problem of contentious parades? The establishment of the Parades Commission may not be enough. In addition to mediation the survey has identified two more solutions that are acceptable – the rule of law and a Bill of Rights.

The bill for last year's disturbances was at least £30 m. Compensation for criminal damage has reached £20 m, policing costs another £10 m and the losses to the tourism industry and inward investment are still being counted. But these are just the direct costs – the education budget has been cut to meet the demands of an escalating security bill. And then there are also the social costs. The poll offered a range of alternatives for dealing with the North Report.

Solution No. 1 – The rule of law
The 'North Report' contains a number of distinct elements. First and foremost it recommends establishing a 'Parades Commission' to monitor traditional parades in Northern Ireland, set standards of behaviour and provide mediation between those who want to march and residents who do not want them to pass through their area. This Commission is now in place and is inviting all the interested parties to take advantage of their services.

But objections have already been raised against the appointment of a prominent member of the SDLP, Berna McIvor. If the rest of the North Report's recommendations are passed into law and the Commission is given statutory powers to rule on contentious parades then these mild-mannered objections have all the potential to escalate into a Drumcree Three if the new laws do not have the support of the vast majority of the people.

In the shadow of a general election mediation seems to be working better than it ever has before. But professional mediators and a climate of 'goodwill' may not always be enough. What laws are acceptable to paraders and residents alike? In the survey the different options were put before a representative sample of the adult population. This important question was asked in the survey by presenting a range of policy options to the public and inviting them to say which policies they considered to be 'Preferred', 'Acceptable', 'Tolerable' or 'Unacceptable'. For the purposes of the poll these terms have the following specific meanings:

'Preferred' – This may not be exactly what you want but this option, or something very similar to it, would be your first choice.
'Acceptable' – This option is not what you would prefer if you were given a choice but you could certainly 'live with it'.
'Tolerable' – This option is not what you want. But, as part of a lasting peace settlement for Northern Ireland, you would be willing to put up with it.
'Unacceptable' – This option is completely unacceptable under any circumstances. You would not accept it, even as part of a peace settlement.

Question
Here are some options for dealing with the 'North Report' which recommends establishing an independent body to oversee both the mediation and legal control of contentious parades. Please indicate which of the following options you consider to be 'Preferred', 'Acceptable', 'Tolerable' or 'Unacceptable'.

• *Completely reject the 'North Report'* – The 'North Report' should be rejected in full. Decisions on contentious parades should continue to be made by the police.

• *Modify 'North Report' to give stronger right to parade* – All parades 'customarily held along a particular route' should be allowed to take place.

• *Modify 'North Report' to ensure that all parades and public demonstrations are treated equally before the law* – The legal control of all marches, parades and public demonstrations should be the same for everyone and disputes should be settled as a matter of law by tribunals and courts.

• *Accept the 'North Report' in full without delay* – The 'North Report' should be accepted in full by everyone in Northern Ireland and introduced into law without delay.

• *Modify 'North Report' to place stronger restrictions on parades* – Residents should have a legal right to decide which parades can go through their area.

The bad news for an incoming government is that only 9 per cent of Protestants and 25 per cent of Catholics are willing to accept the 'North Report' in full (Table 6.9). Thirty-one per cent of Catholics would like to have stronger restrictions placed on parades and an almost equal proportion of Protestants (32 per cent) would like a stronger right to parade. But the good news is very good. An almost equal majority of both Protestants (36 per cent) and Catholics (37 per cent) agree that the 'North Report' should be modified to ensure that all parades and public demonstrations are treated equally before the law. Forty-six per cent of Alliance voters select this option as their first choice as do 39 per cent of UUP supporters and 37 per cent of the SDLP electorate (Table 6.10). Fifty-seven per cent of Sinn Féin voters selected 'stronger restrictions on parades' as their 'Preferred' option but only 5 per cent of them find the 'equal treatment before the law' option 'Unacceptable'. Similarly 40 per cent of DUP voters chose a 'stronger right to parade' as their 'Preferred' option but only 16 per cent consider 'equal treatment before the law' to be 'Unacceptable'.

This broad consensus to accept The 'rule of law' and place the adjudication of contentious parades before tribunals and courts is not unexpected as many Protestants do not believe the Parades Commission will always be able to rise above the influence of political pressures.

Decisions taken by tribunals and courts are open to appeal and laws that treat everyone equally should be able to hold up to a challenge in the European Court of Human Rights. In Canada, under their Bill of Rights, the government is willing to pay the costs of bringing important cases before

Table 6.9   Support for parades options

	Preferred	Acceptable	Tolerable	Unacceptable
Protestant per cent				
Completely reject the 'North Report'	25	11	17	48
Modify 'North Report' to give stronger right to parade	32	29	22	17
Modify 'North Report' to ensure that all parades and public demonstrations are treated equally before the law	36	23	30	11
Accept the 'North Report' in full without delay	9	18	22	51
Modify 'North Report' to place stronger restrictions on parades	8	13	17	63
Catholic per cent				
Completely reject the 'North Report'	8	5	13	74
Modify 'North Report' to give stronger right to parade	9	13	17	61
Modify 'North Report' to ensure that all parades and public demonstrations are treated equally before the law	37	37	19	7
Accept the 'North Report' in full without delay	25	32	25	18
Modify 'North Report' to place stronger restrictions on parades	31	36	19	14

Table 6.10   Political support for parades 'rule of law' option

Modify 'North Report' to ensure that all parades and public demonstrations are treated equally before the law – per cent	Preferred	Acceptable	Tolerable	Unacceptable
DUP	20	24	40	16
UUP	39	29	23	8
Alliance	46	33	18	4
SDLP	37	37	18	8
Sinn Féin	24	47	23	5

the courts. The British and Irish governments might like to follow this approach by offering to support any group wishing to appeal decisions taken under a new regime of legal controls. Those who *always* insist on the right to parade and those who *always* insist on the right of residents to 'say no' should be given every opportunity to take their protests off the streets of Northern Ireland and into the international courts. This is what the people of Northern Ireland want – The 'rule of law'.

* * *

As it happened the preferred option of The 'rule of law' never did get implemented as – so rumour has it – the judiciary in Northern Ireland refused to take on the responsibility of making decisions about contentious parades. But if special laws to deal with such problems could be part of a peace settlement then that might be a different proposition. Perhaps a Bill of Rights was the answer?

Belfast Telegraph, Tuesday 8 April 1997

Wide support for bill of rights

If the people of Northern Ireland could reach agreement on a 'Bill of Rights' then it is entirely possible that questions, like the right to parade, could be settled without the necessity of making appeals to European Courts. With the blessing of a new government in Westminster the people of Northern Ireland could try and find their own solutions to their own problems.

Some negotiated settlements, for example South Africa, have included a 'Bill of Rights' to deal with many of their political, social and cultural problems by giving special protection to the individuals and different communities that make up their society. In Northern Ireland these laws could include, for example, parades and language rights, education and questions of 'parity of esteem'. What do the people of Northern Ireland think of this idea?

Question

Here are some options for the management of individual and community rights in Northern Ireland. Please indicate which of the following options you consider to be 'Preferred', 'Acceptable', 'Tolerable' or 'Unacceptable'.

• *A government 'Bill of Rights' for Northern Ireland* – The government should provide a 'Bill of Rights' for Northern Ireland whatever happens at the 'talks'.

• *A 'Bill of Rights' for Northern Ireland negotiated at the 'talks'* – The parties at the 'talks' should negotiate a 'Bill of Rights' for Northern Ireland.

• *A 'Bill of Rights' for the United Kingdom* – A single 'Bill of Rights' for the whole of the United Kingdom with no special provision for Northern Ireland.

• *A 'Bill of Rights' for the island of Ireland* – A single 'Bill of Rights' for the island of Ireland with special protection for both the Unionist and Nationalist communities.

Overall the option that is most 'Preferred' by of the people of Northern Ireland is for the government to provide a 'Bill of Rights' (Table 6.11). But most people – 74 per cent – also don't think the Stormont talks will ever produce a negotiated settlement and perhaps that is why only 25 per cent think the politicians at the talks should be involved with the negotiation of such a bill.

Table 6.11   Support for a bill of rights

All of NI per cent	Preferred	Acceptable	Tolerable	Unacceptable
A government 'Bill of Rights' for Northern Ireland	33	36	19	12
A 'Bill of Rights' for Northern Ireland negotiated at the 'talks'	25	43	22	10
A 'Bill of Rights' for the United Kingdom	25	36	21	18
A 'Bill of Rights' for the island of Ireland	23	20	22	35

Forty-two per cent of Catholics (Table 6.12) would prefer a 'Bill of Rights' for the island of Ireland (SDLP 41 per cent and Sinn Féin 58 per cent) while 32 per cent of Protestants would prefer a Bill of Rights for the United Kingdom as a whole (DUP 29 per cent and UUP 34 per cent). However, when the two options for a Northern Ireland 'Bill of Rights' are added together 52 per cent of Catholics and 62 per cent of Protestants would welcome such a bill while only about 11 per cent of the adult population would find this option 'Unacceptable'. On the other hand 55 per cent of Protestants find an island of Ireland bill 'Unacceptable' (DUP 59 per cent and UUP 56 per cent). Similarly 27 per cent of Catholics are also not willing to accept a UK bill (SDLP 21 per cent and Sinn Féin 55 per cent).

Clearly a Bill of Rights for Northern Ireland is the most acceptable way forward. If the politicians at the talks want an opportunity, or some might

Table 6.12   Protestant and Catholic support for a bill of rights

	Preferred	Acceptable	Tolerable	Unacceptable
Protestant per cent				
A government 'Bill of Rights' for Northern Ireland	37	38	15	11
A 'Bill of Rights' for Northern Ireland negotiated at the 'talks'	25	40	26	9
A 'Bill of Rights' for the United Kingdom	32	40	18	10
A 'Bill of Rights' for the island of Ireland	10	11	25	55
Catholic per cent				
A government 'Bill of Rights' for Northern Ireland	27	35	25	14
A 'Bill of Rights' for Northern Ireland negotiated at the 'talks'	25	48	17	10
A 'Bill of Rights' for the United Kingdom	15	31	26	27
A 'Bill of Rights' for the island of Ireland	42	29	20	9

say privilege, of negotiating such an important piece of legislation, then they are going to have to persuade the people who voted for them that they are able to handle the task.

* * *

But a Bill of Rights could only ever be a prelude or conclusion to a comprehensive settlement. The central constitutional questions, the political future of Northern Ireland, had to be settled and the Stormont talks hadn't even decided who should be allowed into the negotiations yet! But in the poll all the parties were able to take their first steps together on these central issues and test their ideas against public opinion to see which ones had the greatest cross-community support.

Belfast Telegraph, Wednesday 9 April 1997

Still polls apart: people longing for real talks to start

The final part of the survey covers the key constitutional issues and there is strong public support for referendums to move the Stormont talks forward.

Even if there is a ceasefire and even if the problems of decommissioning can be resolved could the leading parties in Northern Ireland ever find some basis for agreement on the political future of Northern Ireland? The results from the survey suggest it is going to be very difficult to put certain parts of the constitutional puzzle together. Protestants want to stay in the Union and have an end to the Anglo-Irish Agreement. Catholics want North–South institutions and 'responsibility sharing'. Can these different views and aspirations be reconciled?

Many of the parties at the Stormont talks have approached the problem of a negotiated settlement on the principle of 'Nothing is agreed until everything is agreed'. No one can say this strategy has worked. Perhaps it is time to try something new. Why don't the parties agree to attempt to settle those matters where there is a basis for some sort of consensus, do that first, gain some confidence, and then move on to the more difficult tasks? With this strategy in mind the political future of Northern Ireland was split up into a number of component parts for the purposes of the *Belfast Telegraph*/Queen's Survey that dealt with:

- The status of Northern Ireland;
- The relationships between Northern Ireland, the United Kingdom and the Republic of Ireland;
- Regional government within Northern Ireland.

The public were given a range of options and invited to say which ones they considered to be 'Preferred', 'Acceptable', 'Tolerable' or 'Unacceptable'. For the purposes of the poll these terms have the following specific meanings:

'Preferred' – This may not be exactly what you want but this option, or something very similar to it, would be your first choice.

'*Acceptable*' – This option is not what you would prefer if you were given a choice but you could certainly 'live with it'.
'*Tolerable*' – This option is not what you want. But, as part of a lasting peace settlement for Northern Ireland, you would be willing to put up with it.
'*Unacceptable*' – This option is completely unacceptable under any circumstances. You would not accept it, even as part of a peace settlement.

Question 1
With regard to the status of Northern Ireland please indicate which of the following options you consider to be 'Preferred', 'Acceptable', 'Tolerable' or 'Unacceptable'?

• *Separate Northern Irish state* – The complete separation of Northern Ireland from both the United Kingdom and the Republic of Ireland and the establishment of a separate state.

• *Part of the United Kingdom* – No change in the sovereignty of Northern Ireland as part of the United Kingdom.

• *A new all Ireland state* – A united single state comprised of the whole of Ireland.

• *Joint authority* – Joint authority between the British and Irish governments.

Table 6.13   Support for status of Northern Ireland options

	Preferred	Acceptable	Tolerable	Unacceptable
Protestant per cent				
Separate Northern Irish state	11	23	16	51
Part of the United Kingdom	85	10	4	1
A new all Ireland state	3	5	9	83
Joint authority	4	9	24	64
Catholic per cent				
Separate Northern Irish state	15	12	21	52
Part of the United Kingdom	28	18	29	25
A new all Ireland state	39	24	18	19
Joint authority	23	42	19	17

For Protestants the constitutional status of 'The Union' is not something that is open to a great deal of negotiation (Table 6.13). Eighty-five per cent prefer this option while an almost equal number, 83 per cent, consider 'A new all Ireland state' to be 'Unacceptable'. By way of contrast only 39 per cent of Catholics want a united Ireland followed by 28 per cent wishing to remain part of the UK and 23 per cent in favour of 'Joint authority'. However, this apparent flexibility is largely due to the influence of SDLP supporters. Seventy-eight per cent of Sinn Féin voters prefer 'A new all Ireland state' and 60 per cent of them consider remaining part of the United Kingdom to be 'Unacceptable'.

Clearly the options presented here, while providing some possibilities for constitutional accommodation, still have major obstacles to overcome. These difficult issues will probably have to be visited again.

Question 2

With regard to relationships between Northern Ireland, the United Kingdom and the Republic of Ireland, please indicate which of the following options you consider to be 'Preferred', 'Acceptable', 'Tolerable' or 'Unacceptable'?

• *No special relationships* – No special arrangements need to be established for the government of Northern Ireland beyond those presently agreed to in international law as part of the international community and as partners in the European Union.

• *Anglo-Irish Agreement* – Government in consultation with the Irish government under the terms of the Anglo-Irish Agreement.

• *North–South institutions* – The establishment of a number of joint institutions between Northern Ireland and the Republic of Ireland to deal with matters of mutual interest.

• *East–West institutions* – The establishment of a number of joint institutions between the United Kingdom and the Republic of Ireland to deal with matters of mutual interest.

Table 6.14 Support for relations between states options

	Preferred	Acceptable	Tolerable	Unacceptable
Protestant per cent				
No special relationships	59	10	10	20
Anglo-Irish Agreement	10	9	24	57
North–South institutions	17	21	26	37
East–West institutions	12	26	30	32
Catholic per cent				
No special relationships	20	13	23	44
Anglo-Irish Agreement	29	37	22	13
North–South institutions	46	31	16	7
East–West institutions	9	41	39	11

Catholics clearly prefer 'North–South institutions' with 46 per cent of their number selecting this option as 'Preferred' (Table 6.14). Although 59 per cent of Protestants do not want any special relationships to be established with the Republic of Ireland 17 per cent do want 'North–South institutions', 21 per cent consider such institutions 'Acceptable' and a further 26 per cent are willing to tolerate them as part of a lasting peace settlement. One thing Protestants do not want is the continuation of the Anglo-Irish Agreement. Fifty-seven per cent consider that option to be 'Unacceptable'.

So Catholics want 'North–South institutions' and Protestants consider them to be the 'lesser of current evils' and may be willing to accept them as part of a negotiated settlement. The DUP would be most resistant to such an agreement. Fifty-three per cent of their supporters consider such institutions to be 'Unacceptable' while only 29 per cent of UUP voters share the same objections.

But what are North–South institutions? They can be almost anything from consultative and co-operative bodies that consider agricultural issues, such as what to do about BSE and Foul Pest, to Executive bodies that could co-ordinate economic development. Clearly what kinds of institutions have what powers over what areas of public policy are all matters for clarification and much discussion.

Question 3
With regards to regional government within Northern Ireland please indicate which of the following options you consider to be 'Preferred', 'Acceptable', 'Tolerable' or 'Unacceptable'?

• *Devolved majority rule* – Government by an elected Northern Ireland Assembly that operates on a basis of simple majority rule.

• *Devolved responsibility sharing* – Elective government that operates on a basis of sharing responsibilities and powers.

• *No special regional government (UK)* – Integration into the *British* state and no separate Northern Ireland laws.

• *No special regional government (Ireland)* – Integration into the *Irish* state and no separate Northern Ireland laws.

• *Separate institutions for the two main communities* – Creation of separate structures for the government of each of the two main communities in Northern Ireland.

'Devolved responsibility sharing' is the clear preference of 53 per cent of Catholics with only 7 per cent strongly opposed to this option (Table 6.15). Forty-three per cent of Protestants would prefer 'Majority rule' but 26 per cent also prefer 'Responsibility sharing' with a further 21 per cent considering this

Table 6.15   Support for devolved government options

	Preferred	Acceptable	Tolerable	Unacceptable
Protestant per cent				
Devolved majority rule	43	20	21	16
Devolved responsibility sharing	26	21	29	24
No special regional government (UK)	26	23	23	29
No special regional government (Ireland)	5	17	17	62
Separate institutions for the two main communities	10	13	19	58
Catholic per cent				
Devolved majority rule	13	10	23	55
Devolved responsibility sharing	53	23	17	7
No special regional government (UK)	13	20	32	35
No special regional government (Ireland)	24	23	32	21
Separate institutions for the two main communities	10	19	22	49

option to be 'Acceptable' and another 29 per cent willing to tolerate it as part of a lasting peace settlement.

As with 'North–South institutions' the concept of 'Devolved responsibility sharing' will mean many different things to different people, or for that matter different parties. Perhaps the local politicians can be persuaded to use the opportunity presented by the general election to elaborate on their preferred models for regional government with a view to debating these issues if and when real talks start in earnest.

* * *

Sifting through the possible futures of Northern Ireland by way of public opinion poll is one thing but turning such analysis into political realities is quite another. Democracy and political legitimacy require that the people, directly or through their elected representatives and agreed institutions, make the final decision. But when the legitimacy of those institutions is in question and some of the elected representatives refuse to talk to each other let alone negotiate, what then?

Belfast Telegraph, Wednesday 9 April 1997

Referendums could bypass politicians

The political vacuum created by the frustrations of little or no progress at the Stormont talks has very nearly plunged Northern Ireland back into the Troubles at their bloodiest and most violent. Intransigence and its companion dangers cannot be risked again. When all else fails do the people of Northern Ireland want to be consulted and given an opportunity to play their part in referendums?

The *Northern Ireland (Entry into Negotiations) Act* allows the Secretary of State 'from time to time [to] direct the holding of a referendum for the purpose of obtaining the views of the people of Northern Ireland on any matter relating to Northern Ireland'. How do 'the people' want this power to be exercised on their behalf? In the *Belfast Telegraph*/Queen's Survey this question was addressed as follows:

Here are some options for the use of referendums in Northern Ireland. Please indicate which of the following options you consider to be 'Preferred', 'Acceptable', 'Tolerable' or 'Unacceptable'?

• *A referendum to replace the 'talks'* – The 'talks' process should be abandoned and the people of Northern Ireland should decide their own political future through a series of referendums.

• *A referendum to advance the 'talks'* – If the 'talks' become 'stalled' by serious difficulties a few key issues could be placed before the people in a referendum.

• *A referendum to advise the 'talks'* – The issues under discussion at the 'talks' should be placed before the people so that they can advise the politicians on the best way forward.

• *A referendum to endorse a 'talks' settlement* – A referendum should only be used to ascertain the will of the people when a final settlement has been agreed to at the 'talks'.

• *No referendums* – Only elected politicians should decide the political future of Northern Ireland.

Table 6.16   Support for referendum options

All of NI per cent	Preferred	Acceptable	Tolerable	Unacceptable
A referendum to replace the 'talks'	26	13	19	42
A referendum to advance the 'talks'	31	36	22	11
A referendum to advise the 'talks'	21	46	22	12
A referendum to endorse a 'talks' settlement	20	39	25	16
No referendums	12	6	12	70

There is little difference in the responses to this question by way of political affiliation or religious denomination (Table 6.16). Everyone in Northern Ireland seems to be of a single mind. Only 12 per cent of the population want to leave the future of Northern Ireland entirely in the hands of politicians. Seventy per cent find this option 'Unacceptable'. But

42 per cent also find the option of replacing the talks by a referendum 'Unacceptable'.

Referendums to endorse, advise or advance the talks appear to be the most acceptable option. And of these the most popular overall is a referendum to advance the talks. This proposal is very clear and to the point – 'if the "talks" become "stalled" by serious difficulties a few key issues could be placed before the people in a referendum'.

The politicians have now been fairly warned. If they cannot decide the outstanding matters that prevent the establishment of real talks, the people of Northern Ireland will be very pleased to do it for them. It should be remembered that 69 per cent of the people surveyed for this poll were willing to have decommissioning problems dealt with by a subcommittee so that the main business of the talks cannot be held up.

A full 94 per cent also want a negotiated settlement. Armed now with both the legal powers and public support to use a referendum, to resolve 'a few key issues', there is surely no reason why that most modest of aspirations, a lasting peace, should continue to be denied.

7
The Future of the Stormont Talks

The first poll undertaken with the parties had been published on 7, 8 and 9 of April 1997, a few weeks before the general election of 1 May 1997, with the deliberate intention that the results might stimulate a public debate on the political future of Northern Ireland. It didn't. Although 94 per cent of the people wanted a negotiated settlement the parties remained caught up in questions of procedure. Who would negotiate with whom and under what conditions?

On 1 May Labour won an overwhelming majority in the Westminster elections and unlike the Conservatives they now replaced they did not need the support of the Ulster Unionists to press forward with their programme of government. The new prime minister, Tony Blair, announced that the talks would go ahead, that the 'peace train was going to leave the station' and that 'all the parties should get onboard'. With serious negotiations on substantive issues now a very real possibility the IRA announced a new ceasefire on 19 July starting 20 July 1997. The DUP and UKUP said they would not go into talks with Sinn Féin while the IRA still held on to their guns but Mr Trimble, the leader of the Ulster Unionists, said his party would consult with their 'grassroots' before coming to a decision.

In this context the second poll was quickly drafted with the parties to address all possible outstanding preconditions to inclusive talks before they were destined to get under way on Monday, 15 September 1997. Some issues were being dealt with for a second time. But it had to be done. The people of Northern Ireland were given another opportunity to make their views known on what was now increasingly becoming their peace process.

Belfast Telegraph, Thursday 11 September 1997

Yes vote for talks

Here are the findings of an in-depth opinion poll undertaken on the eve of Monday's crucial Stormont talks.

Question 1: Should your party stay in the talks?

Ninety-two per cent of the people of Northern Ireland want the party they support to stay in the talks. But, as might be expected, Protestants are less enthusiastic than Catholics on this point. Between 99 and 100 per cent of Alliance, SDLP and Sinn Féin supporters said 'Yes' (Table 7.1). This almost unanimous vote of confidence in their parties' policy on this point does not carry over into the Unionist camp. Although 93 per cent of Ulster Unionist supporters want their party to stay at the talks only 76 per cent of Democratic Unionists share this view. Clearly Unionists, and in particular the Rev Paisley's electorate, harbour some reservations about the peace process that may not be shared by the other sections of Northern Ireland's society.

Question – 'In today's circumstances do you want the political party you support to stay in the talks?'

Table 7.1   Should your party stay in the talks?

Per cent	Yes	No
All of NI	92	8
Protestant	86	14
Catholic	98	2
DUP	76	24
UUP	93	7
Alliance	99	1
SDLP	99	1
Sinn Féin	100	0

Question 2: Is the peace process biased?

Although each of the two main communities believe the 'other' community is being treated better than themselves Protestants feel this apparent injustice more strongly than their Catholic counterparts (Table 7.2). Fifty-eight per cent of Protestants think Republicans are favoured 'A lot' by the peace process. Nine per cent of Catholics share this view. On the other hand only 21 per cent of Catholics think Loyalists are being favoured 'A lot' while only 2 per cent of Protestants would agree. The statistics break down in a similar way for all the groups and political parties much as might be expected. Protestants clearly feel hard done by and a smaller but significant percentage of Catholics would seem to have some sympathy for their plight.

Question – 'How much do you think the handling of the peace process by the current government favours the Republicans, Nationalists, Unionists,

Loyalists and political party you support?' The options were: 'A lot', 'A little', 'No strong views', 'Not very much' or 'Not at all'.

Table 7.2   Who does the peace process favour 'a lot'?

Per cent	Protestants A lot	Catholics A lot	DUP A lot	UUP A lot	Alliance A lot	SDLP A lot	Sinn Féin A lot
Republicans	58	9	66	60	19	9	8
Nationalists	53	8	60	52	13	9	7
Unionists	3	24	1	4	7	16	48
Loyalists	2	21	1	4	4	13	45
Party you support	1	6	1	1	2	7	9

Question 3: How important is decommissioning?

Similar questions were asked in the poll published in the *Belfast Telegraph* on 7 May. Although the wording and results have changed a little the conclusions to be drawn remain the same (Table 7.3). A majority of Catholics, 52 per cent, find prior decommissioning unacceptable while a majority of Protestants, 65 per cent, find talks without a ceasefire unacceptable. As before, the only possible compromise seems to be some sort of parallel decommissioning.

The poll run earlier in the year also demonstrated clear public support for the problem of decommissioning to be handed over to a subcommittee so that the talks could not be held up. The need for the Independent International Decommissioning Commission, as proposed by the British and Irish governments, probably can not be overstated. For many Unionists the road to successful talks may well depend on their active participation in and the successful working of this key institution.

With regard to talks, ceasefires and decommissioning everyone polled was presented with four options and asked which ones they considered to be 'Desirable', 'Acceptable', 'Tolerable' as part of a lasting settlement or 'Unacceptable' under any circumstances. (The same options apply to the remainder of the questions in this poll.)

Question – All the parties should be prepared to talk to each other …
• Even if the ceasefires do not hold
• So long as the ceasefires hold
• So long as the ceasefires hold and there is also some decommissioning
• Only after decommissioning has been completed

Question 4: Is the Irish Constitution an obstacle?

What other problems stand in the way of all-party talks? The Constitution of the Republic of Ireland makes a claim on the territory of Northern Ireland in Articles 2 and 3. The Republic of Ireland have said they are willing to introduce and support appropriate changes to their constitution to

Table 7.3   Protestant and Catholic support for ceasefire/talks options

	Desirable	Acceptable	Tolerable	Unacceptable
Protestant per cent				
Even if the ceasefires do not hold	11	13	11	65
So long as the ceasefires hold	25	30	29	16
So long as the ceasefires hold and there is also some decommissioning	25	46	19	10
Only after decommissioning has been completed	46	24	14	16
Catholic per cent				
Even if the ceasefires do not hold	45	26	17	12
So long as the ceasefires hold	44	33	15	8
So long as the ceasefires hold and there is also some decommissioning	27	40	16	17
Only after decommissioning has been completed	16	16	16	52

address this issue as part of an agreement reached at the Stormont talks. Some Unionists would like this done before talks start. The vast majority of people in Northern Ireland want to 'Keep the talks going', 77 per cent considered this option 'Desirable' or 'Acceptable' while only 10 per cent found it 'Unacceptable'. Even Protestants favoured this option over the alternative of delaying the talks (Table 7.4). Two options were put on offer in the poll:

Keep the talks going – Do not delay the talks, let reform of the Republic of Ireland's Constitution be dealt with at the same time as all the other issues that must be part of an over all settlement.

Delay the talks – Until the reform of the Republic of Ireland's Constitution has been dealt with.

Table 7.4   Support for Irish constitutional reform and delaying the talks

	Desirable	Acceptable	Tolerable	Unacceptable
All of NI per cent				
Keep the talks going	48	29	13	10
Delay the talks	11	14	20	55
Protestant per cent				
Keep the talks going	36	29	18	17
Delay the talks	18	19	19	44
Catholic per cent				
Keep the talks going	63	28	6	3
Delay the talks	3	6	20	71

Question 5: Is the Framework Document acceptable?

Even if the Unionists do enter the talks some take the view that the Framework Document should not be used as a basis for a final settlement. By far the most popular option is for all the parties to negotiate the Framework Document and try to reach an agreement on what they want to keep, change or add (Table 7.5). The second most popular option is to accept it. Even Protestants favour this over outright rejection. The poll included three options on this issue:

• *Accept the Framework Document* – as a basis for a final settlement on the future of Northern Ireland.

• *Negotiate the Framework Document* – all the parties should negotiate the Framework Document and try to reach an agreement on what they want to keep, change or add.

• *Reject the Framework Document* – as a basis for a final settlement on the future of Northern Ireland.

Table 7.5   Support for the Framework Document as a basis for negotiations

	Desirable	Acceptable	Tolerable	Unacceptable
All of NI per cent				
Accept the Framework Document	17	29	27	27
Negotiate the Framework Document	31	31	25	13
Reject the Framework Document	9	12	22	57
Protestant per cent				
Accept the Framework Document	14	21	25	40
Negotiate the Framework Document	30	28	26	16
Reject the Framework Document	14	17	21	48
Catholic per cent				
Accept the Framework Document	20	39	29	12
Negotiate the Framework Document	32	36	22	10
Reject the Framework Document	4	6	21	69

Question 6: Is there an alternative to the talks?

Some Unionists (and some political commentators) take the view that the talks process has a destabilising influence on the Province. There may be some truth in this observation but how do the people of Northern Ireland regard alternatives to the talks? Only 12 per cent of the people of Northern Ireland considered either of these options to be 'Desirable'. Most Catholics, about 65 per cent, found the options 'Unacceptable' and a smaller but significant percentage of Protestants shared their views (Table 7.6). These alternatives to the talks just do not seem to command a great deal of support. The options were:

• *Stop all negotiations and govern* – The British government should bring an end to the current talks process and simply try to govern Northern Ireland.

• *Stop all negotiations and introduce devolution* – The British government should bring an end to the current talks process and introduce devolved government to Northern Ireland similar to the proposals for Scotland and Wales.

Table 7.6 Support for stopping the talks

	Desirable	Acceptable	Tolerable	Unacceptable
All of NI per cent				
Stop all negotiations and govern	12	23	17	48
Stop all negotiations and introduce devolution	12	15	18	55
Protestant per cent				
Stop all negotiations and govern	18	30	16	36
Stop all negotiations and introduce devolution	18	18	17	47
Catholic per cent				
Stop all negotiations and govern	6	14	15	65
Stop all negotiations and introduce devolution	5	11	18	66

Summary

Ninety-eight per cent of Catholics want the political parties that represent them to stay in the talks. The SDLP and Sinn Féin have decided to do so. Eighty-six per cent of Protestants want the political parties that represent them to stay in the talks. The Loyalists and Unionist parties have difficult decisions to make.

Whatever their reservations, or however unfairly they may feel they have been treated, a significant majority of Unionist voters seem to have decided that they still want their elected politicians to represent their interests at the Stormont talks. How the leaders of these parties can best feel they are able to do this is, of course, a matter for them. But one thing seems to be quite clear. Their electorate desire them to find a way.

* * *

As far as the people of Northern Ireland were concerned there was no alternative to the talks. There never was. But all the agreements made since the resumption of the Troubles had failed because, at some point, someone or some party had walked away from the deal on the table. The politics of Northern Ireland were a testament to the veto by abstention. So what did the people of Northern Ireland want to be done if the politicians they had elected to negotiate a settlement on their behalf didn't show up on the appointed day? When and under what circumstances would the people of Northern Ireland want the British and Irish governments to go over the heads of the politicians and bring matters to a close with a referendum? 'Plan A', a negotiated settlement, was always going to be the best option. But a 'plan B', hopefully never to be used, was not a totally bad idea.

Belfast Telegraph, Friday 12 September 1997

The people's vote

Day two of the findings of an in-depth opinion poll undertaken on the eve of Monday's crucial Stormont talks.

Question 1: Should walkouts stop the talks?

Although 92 per cent of the people of Northern Ireland want their party to stay in the talks some parties have already left and others could take their leave at almost any time. What then, do those who are remaining do their best to take matters forward?

If any of the remaining Unionists leave (presumably the UUP) then 59 per cent of Protestants would consider it to be unacceptable to continue with the talks (Table 7.7). Only 33 per cent of Catholics and 18 per cent of Protestants would have a serious problem with Sinn Féin leaving, and as for any of the other main parties leaving (presumably the SDLP) a majority of Catholics, 51 per cent, could not entertain the talks going ahead. The reality at the talks, under the current rules, is that if either the UUP or SDLP walk out then the talks will be brought to an end. In some way that reality seems to be both understood and accepted by the Unionist and Nationalist communities respectively.

Four options on this issue were put forward as questions in the poll and everyone interviewed was asked which ones they considered to be Desirable', 'Acceptable', 'Tolerable' as part of a lasting settlement or 'Unacceptable' under any circumstances.

- *If any parties leave the talks* – The remaining parties, whoever they are, should continue with their negotiations and try to conclude a settlement that can be placed before the people of Northern Ireland in a referendum.

- *If Sinn Féin leave the talks* – The remaining parties, whoever they are, should continue with their negotiations and try to conclude a settlement that can be placed before the people of Northern Ireland in a referendum.

• *If the remaining Unionists leave the talks* – The other remaining parties, whoever they are, should continue with their negotiations and try to conclude a settlement that can be placed before the people of Northern Ireland in a referendum.

• *If any of the main parties leave the talks* – Then the talks should be stopped.

Table 7.7 Support for the talks continuing even when parties 'walk out'

	Desirable	Acceptable	Tolerable	Unacceptable
All of NI per cent				
If any parties leave the talks	23	28	22	27
If Sinn Féin leave the talks	30	26	19	25
If the remaining Unionists leave the talks	15	18	20	47
If any of the main parties leave the talks	20	16	19	45
Protestant per cent				
If any parties leave the talks	19	25	25	31
If Sinn Féin leave the talks	39	27	16	18
If the remaining Unionists leave the talks	12	12	17	59
If any of the main parties leave the talks	23	15	22	40
Catholic per cent				
If any parties leave the talks	28	32	19	21
If Sinn Féin leave the talks	20	25	22	33
If the remaining Unionists leave the talks	20	27	22	31
If any of the main parties leave the talks	17	18	14	51

Question 2: A referendum if talks fail?

And if a settlement cannot be agreed or if the UUP or SDLP leave, what then? The views of both Catholics and Protestants are very similar on this issue (Table 7.8). A referendum either next May if a settlement has not been reached or a referendum if the talks collapse is quite acceptable with rates of unacceptability ranging between just 9 and 13 per cent. Conversely an imposed settlement or 'No referendum' is hardly acceptable at all. In these cases rates of unacceptability range between 47 and 65 per cent for Catholics and between 66 and 67 per cent for Protestants. The four options that dealt with this problem were as follows:

• *Referendum next May* – If the talks do not produce an agreement by the end of next May the two governments should place a settlement package before the people of Northern Ireland in a referendum.

- *Referendum if talks collapse* – In the event of the talks collapsing the two governments should place a settlement package before the people of Northern Ireland in a referendum.

- *Impose settlement if talks collapse* – In the event of the talks collapsing the two governments should impose a settlement package on the people of Northern Ireland.

- *No referendum* – In the event of the talks collapsing the British government should not hold a referendum but should simply try to govern Northern Ireland.

Table 7.8   Support for a referendum if the talks collapse

	Desirable	Acceptable	Tolerable	Unacceptable
All of NI per cent				
Referendum next May	33	41	17	9
Referendum if talks collapse	22	46	20	12
Impose settlement if talks collapse	4	12	25	59
No referendum	6	9	19	66
Protestant per cent				
Referendum next May	37	36	17	10
Referendum if talks collapse	26	44	17	13
Impose settlement if talks collapse	3	9	22	66
No referendum	8	11	14	67
Catholic per cent				
Referendum next May	28	47	16	9
Referendum if talks collapse	17	51	21	11
Impose settlement if talks collapse	7	16	30	47
No referendum	4	7	24	65

Question 3: Do you want to have a say in Ulster's future?

More specifically, when offered a simple 'Yes' or 'No' response to the question: 'Do you want to be given an opportunity to vote on the terms of a settlement in a referendum?' 94 per cent of the people of Northern Ireland said 'Yes' (Table 7.9).

Table 7.9   Support for a referendum on the terms of a settlement

Per cent	Yes	No
All of NI	94	6
Protestant	94	6
Catholic	93	7
DUP	93	7
UUP	97	3
Alliance	94	6
SDLP	90	10
Sinn Féin	97	3

Question 4: A referendum North and South?

But voting on the terms of a settlement may mean very different things to different people, when it comes to who should vote, or rather where the vote should take place. The most popular option overall was 'Only Northern Ireland' with 92 per cent of Protestants considering such a referendum 'Desirable' or 'Acceptable' with 44 per cent of Catholics holding similar views (Table 7.10). However 32 per cent of Catholics also considered this option unacceptable. Catholics would prefer separate referendums in the 'North' and 'South' or in the island of Ireland as a whole. But this latter option is unacceptable to 86 per cent of Protestants. So separate votes in the 'North' and 'South' is probably the only acceptable compromise and even then most Protestants may well consider the vote in the South to be irrelevant. The four options put on offer were:

- *Only Northern Ireland* – A referendum in Northern Ireland only.

- *Both North and South* – Separate but concurrent referendums in both Northern Ireland and the Republic of Ireland.

- *Island of Ireland* – A single referendum in the island of Ireland as a whole.

- *UK GB and NI* – A single referendum in the United Kingdom of Great Britain and Northern Ireland as a whole.

Table 7.10 Support for who should vote in a referendum

	Desirable	Acceptable	Tolerable	Unacceptable
All of NI per cent				
Only Northern Ireland	52	20	12	16
Both North and South	13	26	13	48
Island of Ireland	16	16	12	56
UK GB and NI	10	19	22	49
Protestant per cent				
Only Northern Ireland	74	18	5	3
Both North and South	4	11	14	71
Island of Ireland	2	5	7	86
UK GB and NI	14	19	15	52
Catholic per cent				
Only Northern Ireland	24	24	20	32
Both North and South	24	45	13	18
Island of Ireland	34	30	16	20
UK GB and NI	7	18	31	44

Question 5: What percentage passes a referendum?

What kind of vote is acceptable to both communities in Northern Ireland? Of the three options put on offer, Protestants would prefer a referendum based on a simple majority; only 9 per cent find this option unacceptable (Table 7.11). On the other hand, most Catholics would prefer a referendum that required a separate majority from each of the two main communities. A weighted majority is the second choice option for both Catholics and Protestants.

In practice this compromise may turn out to be the only viable option as separate votes from each community may require some sort of community registration. Other problems not dealt with here include determining what is an acceptable level of turn-out, how should abstentionism be dealt with and should people be required to vote as a matter of law.

And if these problems weren't enough to be getting on with what about votes on different aspects of a settlement that clearly deal with changes to the constitutional status of Northern Ireland, on the one hand, and aspects of a settlement that have nothing to do with the constitutional status of Northern Ireland on the other hand. Should these issues be treated differently? The three options on offer were:

- *Simple majority* – A simple majority of the people of Northern Ireland – more than 50 per cent.

- *Weighted majority* – A larger majority of the people of Northern Ireland – approximately 70 per cent.

- *A majority from both communities* – A separate majority of the people from each of the two main communities in Northern Ireland – more than 50 per cent from each community.

Table 7.11   Support for what counts as an acceptable referendum majority

	Desirable	Acceptable	Tolerable	Unacceptable
All of NI per cent				
Simple majority	29	32	21	18
Weighted majority	18	31	30	21
A majority from both communities	29	29	17	25
Protestant per cent				
Simple majority	42	34	15	9
Weighted majority	21	34	26	19
A majority from both communities	15	29	21	35
Catholic per cent				
Simple majority	13	29	29	29
Weighted majority	13	30	34	23
A majority from both communities	48	29	12	11

Summary

Ninety-four per cent of the people of Northern Ireland want a referendum that will give them an opportunity to vote on the terms of a settlement. But when, how and under what circumstances do the people want to exercise this right of consent? All these issues need to be opened up to the widest possible debate over the coming months. In the meantime it should not be forgotten that all these problems could melt away to almost nothing if all the parties elected to the Stormont talks could reach an agreement on a negotiated settlement and commend that settlement to the people. Perhaps the people of Northern Ireland understand this and perhaps that is why, on Monday, they want their parties to be at the talks.

8
In Search of a Settlement

The drafting of the questionnaire for this poll had been nearly a year in the making. Some issues, such as police reform, were meant to have been included in the March/April 1997 poll but were left out for lack of space. All the questions had been worked on through the election period of the spring and the summer break. Even when the talks were in recess the drafting and refining of the various options went ahead with the designated group of party negotiators.

Although the DUP and UKUP would not go into the formal talks with Sinn Féin they both continued to work on the polls so that all the issues that had to be dealt with would be fairly tested against public opinion from the widest possible range of political perspectives. No one abstained themselves from the programme of research.

In addition to being more inclusive than the talks proper, the issues dealt with were also broader than the talks agenda agreed to with the two governments. Any serious matter of relevance to a settlement and the wider peace process could be raised. The only items not dealt with in this poll were the procedural questions so exhaustively tested against public opinion in the previous two polls. All the parties agreed it was time to move on to matters of substance.

The fieldwork for the poll was completed between 4 and 22 December 1997 using a booklet-style questionnaire (see Appendix). The results were analysed over the Christmas holidays with the results being published in the *Belfast Telegraph* on 10, 12, 13 and 14 January 1998. Not to be outdone, the two governments also published their 'Propositions on Heads of Agreement' document on 12 January but it was little more than a pale copy of the very comprehensive piece of research undertaken by the parties. The results of that collective enterprise are given below from the broadest of peace building concerns to the detail of the institutional and constitutional reforms that would be required if the Northern Ireland peace process was going to be a success.

Belfast Telegraph, Saturday 10 January 1998

Steps we need to take to win peace

Today the *Belfast Telegraph* publishes the first of a four-part series from an opinion poll – 'In search of a settlement: the people's choice' – on the future of Northern Ireland. The Stormont talks start up again on Monday but have the governments and parties got their priorities right? What are the steps that have to be taken to secure a lasting peace? Is social justice or an end to partition the number one priority for Catholics, and what do Protestants want out of a settlement?

People from different communities often hold very different views about the causes of the conflict in Northern Ireland. Additionally, perhaps the two governments who set up the Stormont talks and the politicians elected to take part in the talks are not focusing on the problems that are of the greatest importance to their respective constituencies. With these points in mind people were asked to indicate which issues they considered to be 'Very Significant' 'Significant', 'Of Some Significance', 'Of Little Significance' or 'Of No Significance at all'.

Catholics put a lack of equality and discrimination first (71 per cent said it is 'very significant') followed by sectarian politics at 66 per cent, the failures of the police service at 62 per cent and then Loyalist violence at 57 per cent (Table 2.3). Protestants place Republican violence at the top of their list at 87 per cent, followed by more security issues and then the Republic's territorial claim in fourth place at 53 per cent. Both Catholics and Protestants place 'unaccountable and secretive government' eighth on their lists. Could it be that the Stormont talks, with their emphasis on reforming the political institutions of government, have got it wrong? Even if these reforms can be agreed, can they deliver the peace that everyone wants or are they simply a means to that end?

What then are the steps that have to be taken in an effort to secure a lasting peace? With this point in mind people were asked to indicate which options they considered to be 'Essential', 'Desirable', 'Acceptable', 'Tolerable' or 'Unacceptable' as part of a lasting settlement.

Catholics placed a Bill of Rights first (78 per cent said it was 'Essential'), police reform second at 70 per cent followed by security issues (Table 8.1). For Protestants security issues were their first and second priority followed by an end to the Republic's territorial claim. 'Integration of Northern Ireland into the UK' was their seventh choice while Catholics ranked 'British withdrawal from Northern Ireland' as their ninth option. Both Catholics and Protestants placed, for example, 'A right to choose integrated education' (7th and 11th choice respectively) before 'Reformed and shared government' (12th and 14th choice respectively).

Clearly the Stormont talks with their the primary focus on the reform of the institutions of government have got it wrong or, at the very best, these

Table 8.1   Protestant and Catholic priorities for peace in Northern Ireland

	Protestant per cent	*Essential*	*Catholic per cent*	*Essential*
1st	Disband all paramilitary groups	70	A Bill of Rights that guarantees equality for all	78
2nd	Stronger and effective anti-terrorist measures	70	Completely reform the police service	70
3rd	The Republic ends their claim on Northern Ireland	62	A Bill of Rights that protects the culture of each community	67
4th	A Bill of Rights that guarantees equality for all	37	Disband all paramilitary groups	67
5th	End the Anglo-Irish Agreement	36	Return the army to their barracks	61
6th	A Bill of Rights that protects the culture of each community	36	Politics without a sectarian division	59
7th	Integrate Northern Ireland into the UK	35	A right to choose integrated education	53
8th	A right to choose integrated education	35	A right to choose integrated housing	51
9th	Politics without a sectarian division	32	British withdrawal from Northern Ireland	46
10th	Separate politics and religion in Northern Ireland	31	Open government and Freedom of Information Act	46
11th	A right to choose integrated housing	30	Stronger and effective anti-terrorist measures	40
12th	Separate politics and religion in the Republic	30	Reformed and shared government	32
13th	Open government and Freedom of Information Act	24	Separate politics and religion in Northern Ireland	20
14th	Reformed and shared government	12	Separate politics and religion in the Republic	15
15th	Return the army to their barracks	8	End the Anglo-Irish Agreement	10
16th	Completely reform the police service	7	The Republic ends their claim on Northern Ireland	7
17th	British withdrawal from Northern Ireland	1	Integrate Northern Ireland into the UK	4

reforms must be seen as a means to an end and not as an end in themselves.

Having first prioritised the causes of the conflict and their potential solutions the next problem that has to be tackled is searching out the areas of policy and reform where agreement can be found. At the Stormont talks such agreement is based on the principle of 'Sufficient Consent' which requires a simple majority (more than 50 per cent) from each of the two main traditions. If this same principle is applied to the results of the public opinion poll then it is possible to say what parts of a settlement are 'Essential', 'Desirable', 'Acceptable' or 'Tolerable' when total responses pass the 50 per cent mark for both communities. These responses are highlighted in **bold** (Table 8.2).

Both Catholics and Protestants consider a Bill of Rights to be 'Desirable', so making progress on this issue, which is the number one priority for most Nationalists, should not be a problem at the talks. On the other hand, complete reform of the police service, the second priority for Nationalists, is not acceptable to a majority of Protestants. But complete reform doesn't mean no reform. What reforms, then, are acceptable? To explore this question, and many others, all the issues dealt with here must now be examined in greater detail.

Protecting the rights of the people

The European Convention on Human Rights protects individuals by guaranteeing each person the right to life; not to be tortured or subjected to inhuman or degrading treatment; to protection from slavery or forced work; not to be unlawfully arrested or detained; to a fair trial; to freedom of belief and expression; to free association; to privacy and family life; not to be discriminated against; to a remedy for breaches of human rights.

The new Labour government plan to introduce this Convention into the domestic law of the United Kingdom of Great Britain and Northern Ireland. This will allow any complaints regarding failures to meet these minimum standards to be heard by courts in the UK and Northern Ireland. Both communities consider this option to be 'Desirable' (Table 8.3).

Table 8.3   Support for European Convention on Human Rights

Accumulated percentage	Religion	Essential	Plus desirable	Plus acceptable	Plus tolerable
The European Convention on Human Rights should be part of the domestic law of Northern Ireland	Protestant	32	63	87	97
	Catholic	76	**88**	96	**100**

Some recent negotiated settlements have included a Bill of Rights to deal with many of the special political, social and cultural problems that lay at the heart of their conflict. Again, both communities consider this option to be 'Desirable' (Table 8.4). With regard to the application and enforcement

Table 8.2   Protestant and Catholic support for peace process reforms

Accumulated percentage	Religion	Essential	Plus desirable	Plus acceptable	Plus tolerable
British withdrawal from	Protestant	1	7	15	27
Northern Ireland	Catholic	46	69	86	94
End the Anglo-Irish	Protestant	36	56	76	93
Agreement	Catholic	10	21	40	63
Integrate Northern Ireland	Protestant	35	57	82	90
into the UK	Catholic	4	6	19	35
The Republic ends their	Protestant	62	81	89	94
claim on Northern Ireland	Catholic	7	12	25	41
Reformed and shared	Protestant	12	22	53	73
government	Catholic	32	50	73	90
Open government and	Protestant	24	52	76	91
Freedom of	Catholic	46	69	91	97
Information Act					
A Bill of Rights that	Protestant	37	65	88	98
guarantees equality for all	Catholic	78	91	99	100
A right to choose	Protestant	35	60	91	97
integrated education	Catholic	53	74	96	99
A right to choose	Protestant	30	54	88	96
integrated housing	Catholic	51	73	95	99
A Bill of Rights that	Protestant	36	62	92	99
protects the culture of each	Catholic	67	86	97	98
community					
Politics without a sectarian	Protestant	32	63	88	97
division	Catholic	59	86	96	98
Separate politics and	Protestant	30	53	80	92
religion in the Republic	Catholic	15	36	62	80
Separate politics and	Protestant	31	57	82	93
religion in Northern Ireland	Catholic	20	46	74	84
Disband all paramilitary	Protestant	70	81	91	95
groups	Catholic	67	82	91	96
Return the army to their	Protestant	8	21	42	59
barracks	Catholic	61	77	95	98
Completely reform the	Protestant	7	15	30	47
police service	Catholic	70	83	94	97
Stronger and effective	Protestant	70	89	97	99
anti-terrorist measures	Catholic	40	58	79	88

of Human Rights Catholics consider the establishment of a commission with powers to monitor, investigate and bring complaints to court to be 'Desirable'. Protestants consider these options to be 'Acceptable' (Table 8.5).

Table 8.4 Support for a special Northern Ireland Bill of Rights

Accumulated percentage	Religion	Essential	Plus desirable	Plus acceptable	Plus tolerable
An additional Bill of Rights to address the special problems of Northern Ireland	Protestant	27	58	83	94
	Catholic	54	83	92	98
No additional Bill of Rights, just new laws to address the special problems of Northern Ireland	Protestant	10	25	66	85
	Catholic	16	33	59	72

Table 8.5 Support for the enforcement of Human Rights

Accumulated percentage	Religion	Essential	Plus desirable	Plus acceptable	Plus tolerable
A special court to hear Human Rights complaints	Protestant	21	41	82	93
	Catholic	51	79	95	98
A commission to monitor, investigate and promote Human Rights	Protestant	13	36	74	91
	Catholic	41	74	94	98
A commission with powers to bring Human Rights complaints to court	Protestant	21	41	80	91
	Catholic	50	80	96	99

In addition to the European Convention on Human Rights other international conventions include the right to food, clothing and shelter; health; education; work; safe and fair conditions of work; social security; and cultural expression. Including these economic, social and cultural rights in a Northern Ireland Bill of Rights is also thought to be 'Desirable' by a majority in both communities (Table 8.6).

Table 8.6 Support for economic, social and cultural rights

Accumulated percentage	Religion	Essential	Plus desirable	Plus acceptable	Plus tolerable
Economic, social and cultural rights should be part of a Northern Ireland Bill	Protestant	41	67	93	98
	Catholic	72	93	99	100

Some international conventions also include collective rights of peoples and members of minorities. Both communities consider the right to self-determination, parity of esteem and not to be treated as a member of a community against their will to be 'Desirable'. Similarly religious, language, cultural, educational and democratic group rights are all 'Acceptable' and these rights should be introduced into Northern Ireland law as part of a Bill of Rights (Table 8.7).

It may also be necessary to include some rights that deal specifically with some of the political, social and cultural problems that are distinctive features of the Northern Ireland conflict. Both communities consider the right to peaceful demonstrations and parades, freedom of worship and religious

Table 8.7   Support for collective rights

Accumulated percentage	*Religion*	*Essential*	*Plus desirable*	*Plus acceptable*	*Plus tolerable*
The right…					
To self-determination	Protestant	32	**62**	**87**	**95**
	Catholic	63	**86**	**95**	**96**
To practise their religion,	Protestant	30	49	77	**94**
use their language and	Catholic	80	94	98	**99**
enjoy their culture					
To be taught or educated	Protestant	11	24	**54**	**83**
in their distinctive	Catholic	55	78	**98**	**99**
language					
To participate effectively in	Protestant	23	43	**80**	**92**
government on matters	Catholic	61	84	**96**	**99**
affecting them					
To parity of treatment	Protestant	26	**51**	**78**	**93**
and esteem	Catholic	68	**88**	**97**	**99**
Not to be treated as	Protestant	32	**56**	**82**	**91**
members of a distinct	Catholic	76	**90**	**96**	**98**
community against					
their will					
and…					
A Bill of Rights that	Protestant	17	40	74	**89**
includes collective	Catholic	61	**86**	**96**	**99**
and minority rights					
A British and Irish	Protestant	10	18	46	**65**
Treaty to protect	Catholic	46	74	88	**98**
minority rights					
No Bill of Rights or	Protestant	9	24	56	**76**
Treaty to protect	Catholic	13	22	43	**57**
minorities, just new					
policies and laws					

expression, freedom from intimidation or incitement to hatred to be 'Essential' and freedom of political expression 'Desirable'. The right to choose integrated or single religion housing is 'Acceptable' as is the right to choose Catholic, Protestant or integrated education, and although Catholics consider the right to use and be educated in the Irish language to be 'Essential', a majority of Protestants are willing to tolerate these rights as part of a lasting settlement (Table 8.8).

Various British governments have taken several important steps in an effort to meet these demands for rights appropriate to the needs of Northern Ireland. For example, the establishment of the Fair Employment Commission (FEC), the Standing Advisory Commission on Human Rights (SACHR) and now the incorporation of the European Convention into domestic UK law.

Table 8.8 Support for rights and freedoms of expression and association

Accumulated percentage	Religion	Essential	Plus desirable	Plus acceptable	Plus tolerable
The right to ...					
Freedom of political	Protestant	47	69	97	100
expression	Catholic	70	89	97	99
Freedom of religious	Protestant	53	74	97	100
expression	Catholic	76	91	98	100
Freedom from	Protestant	57	80	96	97
incitement to hatred	Catholic	82	89	95	96
Freedom of worship	Protestant	65	85	100	100
	Catholic	84	96	100	100
Freedom from	Protestant	73	87	99	100
intimidation	Catholic	88	94	98	99
Peaceful demonstrations	Protestant	53	77	93	99
and parades	Catholic	54	72	84	96
The right to use the	Protestant	8	20	47	81
Irish language	Catholic	63	84	98	100
Education in Irish	Protestant	7	15	42	78
language schools	Catholic	57	81	98	99
Education in Integrated	Protestant	23	48	76	96
schools	Catholic	55	83	97	99
Education in Catholic	Protestant	13	28	69	92
schools	Catholic	56	81	96	99
Education in Protestant	Protestant	22	46	87	98
schools	Catholic	54	75	94	98
Choose single religion	Protestant	13	23	53	77
public housing	Catholic	32	43	66	79
Choose mixed religion	Protestant	22	47	79	92
public housing	Catholic	47	73	92	97

But still a very great deal more is required, by both Catholics and Protestants, as part of a lasting settlement. Perhaps the British government should instruct their staff to produce a provisional draft of the appropriate legislation with a view to placing it before the parties for their consideration.

However, the results of this section of the poll also present a challenge to the Irish government. If they do wish to satisfy local Nationalist aspirations in these matters they will have to make an effort to meet these reforms, measure for measure, in their own domestic law. Additionally any failure in these matters may well be met with cries of 'double standard' and 'hypocrisy' from Unionists who value these rights and want both communities to enjoy their benefits in the North.

Reforming RUC quite 'acceptable'

In a report commissioned by the government Dr Maurice Hayes has recommended the establishment of a completely independent agency to deal with all aspects of investigations into complaints against the RUC. Both communities consider this proposal to be quite 'Acceptable' (Table 8.9), as is the recruitment of more Catholics. Special training in community relations and human rights, the rigorous monitoring of policing standards and the establishment of a policing charter are all considered to be 'Desirable' by a majority in both communities (Table 8.10). However, the recent changes to the oath of allegiance is only 'Tolerable' for Protestants while other reforms targeted at the culture and character of the police force, such as a change of name and uniform, are not acceptable to a majority of Protestants although Catholics consider these reforms to be 'Essential'.

At the present time the Royal Ulster Constabulary is a single force that has responsibility for providing all policing duties throughout the whole of Northern Ireland. Between the options of disbanding the RUC and creating

Table 8.9 Support for independent investigation of complaints against the RUC

Accumulated percentage	Religion	Essential	Plus desirable	Plus acceptable	Plus tolerable
Give the existing commission more scope to initiate and supervise complaints but maintain the role of the RUC in the investigation	Protestant	22	44	83	**94**
	Catholic	12	19	34	**51**
Establish a completely independent agency to deal with all aspects of investigations into complaints against the RUC	Protestant	13	37	69	**83**
	Catholic	75	90	**95**	**98**

Table 8.10 Support for RUC reforms

Accumulated percentage	Religion	Essential	Plus desirable	Plus acceptable	Plus tolerable
Special training in community relations and human rights	Protestant	30	**64**	**98**	**100**
	Catholic	65	**87**	**98**	**100**
A policing charter to set duties and responsibilities in law	Protestant	24	**55**	**90**	**98**
	Catholic	52	**78**	**95**	**99**
Monitor policing standards and publish reports	Protestant	23	**58**	**90**	**99**
	Catholic	61	**84**	**94**	**99**
Recruit more Catholics	Protestant	19	42	72	**91**
	Catholic	72	86	97	**99**
A new name for the RUC more acceptable across the whole community	Protestant	3	10	25	41
	Catholic	59	77	92	96
New emblems and symbols more acceptable across the whole community	Protestant	3	11	25	43
	Catholic	58	76	91	96
Require police to declare their membership of Loyal orders	Protestant	9	18	28	46
	Catholic	71	83	90	95
Do not allow police to be members of Loyal orders	Protestant	5	13	22	31
	Catholic	69	81	88	95
Make the Oath of Allegiance more acceptable across the whole community	Protestant	9	24	38	**53**
	Catholic	57	73	84	**89**
The police should not normally be armed	Protestant	5	17	30	38
	Catholic	34	65	82	91
Leave the police service as it is	Protestant	28	54	77	90
	Catholic	2	3	9	21

a new force on the one hand and no change on the other the most acceptable reform for both Catholics and Protestants is the creation of a two-tier service that includes new community policing units (Table 8.11). Perhaps this new service could benefit from a change of name and uniform as well as being disarmed so that their community role and duties can be seen to be very different from the established force.

Present responsibility for policing in Northern Ireland is divided between the Secretary of State, the Chief Constable and the Police Authority of Northern Ireland. Community Police Liaison Committees, established by

Table 8.11   Support for changes to the structure of the RUC

Accumulated percentage	Religion	Essential	Plus desirable	Plus acceptable	Plus tolerable
Create new community policing units as part of the RUC	Protestant	12	40	**76**	**88**
	Catholic	23	46	**63**	**73**
Create new community policing units separate to the RUC	Protestant	3	9	33	**52**
	Catholic	20	42	67	**80**
Disband the RUC and create a new single police force	Protestant	1	3	9	18
	Catholic	47	68	85	94
Disband the RUC and create a number of regional and city forces	Protestant	1	3	10	17
	Catholic	24	49	78	89
Leave current policing structures as they are	Protestant	30	54	81	91
	Catholic	3	4	12	25

Table 8.12   Support for responsibility for policing options

Give more responsibility for the management of the police services to…	Religion	Essential	Plus desirable	Plus acceptable	Plus tolerable
The Secretary of State	Protestant	8	16	39	**62**
	Catholic	11	23	53	**73**
A new Department of Justice and Northern Ireland Assembly	Protestant	5	22	**51**	**74**
	Catholic	25	52	**76**	**87**
The Chief Constable	Protestant	23	49	81	**94**
	Catholic	5	11	35	**54**
The Police Authority of Northern Ireland	Protestant	17	40	78	**90**
	Catholic	5	10	34	**54**
A number of regional and city police authorities	Protestant	3	9	37	**66**
	Catholic	11	32	64	**83**
Community Liaison Committees	Protestant	4	14	40	**61**
	Catholic	22	49	77	**90**
Or no change – leave the responsibility for the police service as it is	Protestant	22	48	77	**88**
	Catholic	2	3	8	**23**

District Councils, also have a consultation role. Reform of these responsibilities could include giving more powers to any of these bodies or persons. However, the option that has the greatest cross-community support is for a new Department of Justice in a new Regional Assembly to manage the provision of all policing services in Northern Ireland (Table 8.12).

The drafting of a policing charter and the appropriate legislation needed for the implementation of these reforms would be welcomed by Nationalists and provide an acceptable basis for discussion by Unionists. Clearly setting up a Department of Justice cannot proceed in the absence of an overall settlement but perhaps some of the proposals reviewed here could be implemented as confidence-building measures before the coming marching season.

Belfast Telegraph, Monday 12 January 1998

Why Ulster now wants to have new assembly: wide cross-section quizzed for views on regional organisations

Today the political parties returned to the Stormont talks after a stormy, political recess. The first item on their agenda was strand one, which deals with regional government. In other words who wants an assembly and in what form would it be acceptable to both Unionists and Nationalists.

Table 8.13   Support for the different powers of a devolved assembly

Establish a Northern Ireland Regional Assembly with ...	Religion	Essential	Plus desirable	Plus acceptable	Plus tolerable
An elected assembly	Protestant	24	48	86	94
	Catholic	25	50	80	91
An appointed second chamber or senate	Protestant	3	17	57	79
	Catholic	7	25	62	81
Powers of administration	Protestant	17	35	70	86
	Catholic	26	49	80	91
Powers to initiate and develop new policies	Protestant	18	39	77	91
	Catholic	15	39	81	92
Powers to make new laws	Protestant	16	40	75	90
	Catholic	24	46	79	91
Powers to alter taxes	Protestant	15	36	68	84
	Catholic	24	46	75	87
Committees that shadow and monitor the departments of the Northern Ireland Office	Protestant	10	23	56	75
	Catholic	16	32	68	82
Or no assembly – Northern Ireland should *not* have a regional assembly	Protestant	6	15	29	52
	Catholic	7	19	34	57

At the present time Northern Ireland is governed under Direct Rule from Westminster with many important decisions being made by the Northern Ireland Office. Most of these decisions could be made by a democratically elected assembly. Approximately 50 per cent of both Catholics and Protestants consider this option to be 'Desirable' (Table 8.13). An appointed second chamber, powers to administer, initiate and develop new policies, powers to make new laws and alter taxes and the establishment of committees that shadow and monitor the departments of the Northern Ireland Office are all 'Acceptable'. But how can an assembly be structured so that these powers will be used for the benefit of everyone and avoid the dangers of majoritarianism or what Nationalists call 'A return to Stormont'?

Executive to be only from parties committed to non-violence

Catholics would prefer for the appointments in an assembly to be assigned equally between the two main traditions and for voting by weighted majority or 'Sufficient Consensus' – which requires a majority from both of the main

Table 8.14   Support for committee appointments and cross-community voting

Accumulated percentage	Religion	Essential	Plus desirable	Plus acceptable	Plus tolerable
Chairpersons and the membership of committees are assigned ...					
In proportion to the representation of each party in the assembly	Protestant	27	50	78	92
	Catholic	18	38	63	83
Equally between the two main traditions	Protestant	13	26	42	69
	Catholic	52	77	88	95
Voting in the Assembly is by ...					
Simple majority for all business	Protestant	24	49	85	91
	Catholic	7	22	46	61
'Weighted' majority to ensure the support of both of the main traditions for *all* business	Protestant	9	21	52	75
	Catholic	27	52	80	89
'Weighted' majority for *contentious* business only	Protestant	3	11	40	69
	Catholic	9	24	55	76
'Sufficient Consensus' which requires a majority from *both* of the main traditions for *all* business	Protestant	6	20	49	74
	Catholic	27	59	85	93
'Sufficient Consensus' for *contentious* business only	Protestant	2	11	40	70
	Catholic	13	26	63	82

traditions (Table 8.14). Protestants would prefer for appointments to be made in proportion to the representation of each party in the assembly and for voting to be by simple majority. The clear compromise on these points is for appointments to the executive, the chairs and membership of committees to be proportional to the representation of each party in the assembly and for voting to be by weighted majority or 'Sufficient Consensus'.

Additionally a majority from both communities believe the members of the executive should only come from parties committed to principles of democracy and non-violence and that they should be voted in by the members of the assembly (Table 8.15). With regards to the leadership in an assembly a majority of both Catholics and Protestants find it quite 'Acceptable' that there should be a leader and deputy leader representing the two main traditions and they also consider it 'Desirable' to be able to directly vote for these leaders.

Table 8.15   Support for leader, deputy leader, executive and their appointment

Accumulated percentage	*Religion*	*Essential*	*Plus desirable*	*Plus acceptable*	*Plus tolerable*
Members of the Executive are appointed …					
Equally between the two	Protestant	11	23	47	71
main traditions	Catholic	60	82	92	95
In proportion to the	Protestant	21	45	74	90
representation of each party in the assembly	Catholic	16	38	67	86
From the party or coalition	Protestant	6	20	52	77
that can form a majority	Catholic	5	14	33	51
Only from parties	Protestant	64	82	92	97
committed to principles of democracy and non-violence	Catholic	34	55	72	82
And the Executive in the Assembly is …					
Appointed by the	Protestant	5	13	40	59
Secretary of State	Catholic	7	17	41	69
Nominated by the	Protestant	5	20	52	76
Secretary of State for approval by the assembly	Catholic	8	29	57	81
Voted in by the	Protestant	20	46	80	92
members of the assembly	Catholic	18	41	75	91

Table 8.15   Continued

Accumulated percentage	Religion	Essential	Plus desirable	Plus acceptable	Plus tolerable
Made up from the Chairpersons of each committee in the assembly	Protestant	4	17	61	85
	Catholic	11	30	68	87
Or no executive – all the business of government is conducted by the various committees	Protestant	2	8	30	60
	Catholic	4	17	42	72
The Assembly should have ...					
A leader and deputy leader representing the two main traditions	Protestant	15	39	64	83
	Catholic	28	61	86	92
A 'panel' of three prominent politicians sharing power	Protestant	7	18	54	75
	Catholic	13	30	65	84
And they should be ...					
Appointed by the Secretary of State	Protestant	5	11	35	56
	Catholic	10	19	43	68
Nominated by the Secretary of State for approval by the assembly	Protestant	8	17	46	72
	Catholic	9	25	58	81
Voted in by the members of the assembly	Protestant	16	35	73	88
	Catholic	15	36	75	91
Voted for directly by the people of Northern Ireland	Protestant	49	70	86	93
	Catholic	38	57	84	94
Or no leader, deputy leader or 'panel'					
All the business of government is conducted by the executive and/or committees	Protestant	3	13	41	72
	Catholic	12	25	62	88

The reform of local bodies is favoured by both traditions

When it comes to local government reform a majority of both Catholics and Protestants find such a prospect quite 'Acceptable' and would be willing to have a new assembly decide how this should be done. For example, there could be fewer councils with more powers. But reforms could go further (Table 8.16). A majority from both communities are willing to accept the introduction of new laws to ensure that the views of representatives from

Table 8.16   Support for reform of local government

More powers and responsibilities should be given to local government...	Religion	Essential	Plus desirable	Plus acceptable	Plus tolerable
Even if there is no Northern Ireland Assembly	Protestant	15	39	**74**	**89**
	Catholic	17	37	**70**	**87**
But a new Northern Ireland Assembly should decide how this is done	Protestant	13	34	**79**	**91**
	Catholic	14	37	**78**	**88**
To replace the work presently undertaken by various boards	Protestant	7	30	**70**	**87**
	Catholic	10	34	**80**	**92**
And combine some of the smaller 26 District Councils to create larger units of local government	Protestant	5	24	**58**	**81**
	Catholic	12	32	**68**	**84**

Table 8.17   Support for measures to prevent abuse of power

All levels of government in Northern Ireland should be protected by laws that ensure...	Religion	Essential	Plus desirable	Plus acceptable	Plus tolerable
The views of representatives from the whole community are taken into account	Protestant	34	**63**	**87**	**93**
	Catholic	75	**94**	**100**	**100**
Political and administrative responsibilities are shared	Protestant	18	**45**	**78**	**90**
	Catholic	65	**85**	**97**	**98**
Power cannot be abused by one group over another	Protestant	47	**71**	**96**	**98**
	Catholic	81	**92**	**98**	**99**
And independent committees or courts of arbitrators should be established to resolve problems that become intractable	Protestant	24	**51**	**82**	**92**
	Catholic	61	**82**	**96**	**100**

the whole community are taken into account, that political and administrative responsibilities are shared, that power cannot be abused by one group over another, and that independent committees or courts of arbitrators are established to resolve problems that become intractable (Table 8.17). Indeed most of these reforms are considered to be 'Desirable' by both Protestants and Catholics.

Surprise in the latest findings: Conclusion

Given the reservations Nationalist politicians have about 'A return to Stormont' and the strong desire on the part of Unionist politicians for a new regional assembly, the results of this part of the survey are slightly surprising. Perhaps Protestants are not as enthusiastic about the prospects of establishing another layer of government as their political leaders seem to think and perhaps Catholics' desire for accountable government is stronger than their political leaders have judged to be the case. Providing adequate safeguards can be put in place to prevent abuse of power then an assembly could be a welcome part of an overall settlement package in both communities.

Belfast Telegraph, Tuesday 13 January 1998

Feasibility and reality of North–South bodies: Fisheries Commission seen as acceptable role model

Today, the focus from the opinion poll is on North–South relationships, the bodies that should be set up to deal with them, their responsibilities and powers. North–South bodies are contentious – while Nationalists consider them to be an essential part of an overall settlement, Unionists do not want them to develop into an 'unofficial' all-Ireland government. How can these aspirations and concerns be reconciled?

The Stormont talks have been divided into three parts called strands. Strand two covers relationships within the island of Ireland and deals with North/South bodies. For example the Foyle Fisheries Commission has been established as a 'North/South Body' between the former Northern Ireland parliament at Stormont and the Republic of Ireland to jointly manage the waters of the Foyle estuary. Similar bodies, or a single body, could be established to deal with other matters of mutual concern.

These bodies could be set up to deal with various aspects of government policy with different powers or functions. Responsibilities to consult and co-operate on matters of mutual interest are 'Acceptable' to a majority in both communities and powers to administer laws made by the separate governments in the North and the South of Ireland are 'Tolerable' (Table 8.18). Stronger powers to develop plans and laws for the island of Ireland as a whole are not acceptable to Protestants.

Areas where action could be taken

Apart from managing the waters of the Foyle estuary, what other areas of common concern could become candidates for co-operation in North–South bodies?

Catholics would like 'matters of mutual interest' to apply to all areas of government policy but Protestants would like to restrict the mandate of North/South bodies to exclude taxation, local government and planning, policing and security, defence and foreign policy (Table 8.19). All the other

Table 8.18   Support for powers of North/South bodies

On matters of mutual interest North/South bodies should ...	Religion	Essential	Plus desirable	Plus acceptable	Plus tolerable
Be required to consult	Protestant	16	33	**58**	**71**
	Catholic	56	80	**95**	**98**
Be required to co-operate	Protestant	16	35	**54**	**68**
	Catholic	57	82	**96**	**99**
Have powers to administer laws made by the separate governments in the North and the South of Ireland	Protestant	3	17	33	**51**
	Catholic	36	67	88	**93**
Have powers to develop and execute forward planning for the island of Ireland as a whole	Protestant	3	12	25	37
	Catholic	46	76	92	96
Have powers to make laws which would apply to the island of Ireland as a whole	Protestant	3	8	20	30
	Catholic	44	68	88	95
Or there should not be any North/South bodies with any powers or functions	Protestant	27	40	53	71
	Catholic	4	7	15	31

Table 8.19   Support for functions of North/South bodies

And what areas of government policy should North/South bodies deal with?	Religion	Essential	Plus desirable	Plus acceptable	Plus tolerable
The environment	Protestant	24	42	**65**	**79**
	Catholic	63	86	**96**	**100**
Agriculture	Protestant	22	40	**61**	**74**
	Catholic	66	87	**96**	**99**
Fisheries	Protestant	21	40	**63**	**77**
	Catholic	62	86	**96**	**99**
Tourism	Protestant	26	43	**65**	**77**
	Catholic	71	91	**97**	**99**
Medical care and research	Protestant	23	39	**58**	**70**
	Catholic	57	81	**95**	**98**
Roads and public transport	Protestant	17	32	**56**	**69**
	Catholic	60	83	**95**	**98**
Water, gas and electric	Protestant	14	30	**53**	**65**
	Catholic	53	82	**94**	**99**

Table 8.19   Continued

And what areas of government policy should North/South bodies deal with?	Religion	Essential	Plus desirable	Plus acceptable	Plus tolerable
Communications	Protestant	15	32	56	68
	Catholic	57	83	97	100
Industrial development boards	Protestant	12	25	47	65
	Catholic	54	83	97	100
Financial institutions	Protestant	7	17	41	59
	Catholic	50	76	94	99
Economic development in general	Protestant	11	25	49	66
	Catholic	57	85	95	100
Training and employment	Protestant	11	27	47	61
	Catholic	55	81	95	98
Joint representation in Europe	Protestant	11	23	42	61
	Catholic	61	85	97	99
Trade	Protestant	13	27	50	66
	Catholic	62	84	96	98
Taxation	Protestant	6	13	29	44
	Catholic	43	62	82	95
Broadcasting and film	Protestant	7	20	43	66
	Catholic	43	69	92	100
Minority languages	Protestant	6	13	34	60
	Catholic	52	76	94	100
Culture and sport	Protestant	9	23	50	68
	Catholic	59	82	96	99
Local government and planning	Protestant	8	14	30	45
	Catholic	49	72	91	97
Social services	Protestant	9	16	34	51
	Catholic	49	72	87	95
Human rights	Protestant	18	31	45	60
	Catholic	75	89	97	99
Education	Protestant	13	20	38	52
	Catholic	58	78	90	98
Policing and security	Protestant	14	20	31	40
	Catholic	61	83	92	96
Defence	Protestant	12	18	30	40
	Catholic	58	79	93	97
Foreign policy	Protestant	9	16	30	46
	Catholic	53	79	91	98

'matters of mutual interest' are either 'Acceptable' or 'Tolerable'. In the survey this covered twenty areas of policy where action could be taken.

The 'Acceptable' areas of policy were the environment, agriculture, fisheries, tourism, medical care and research, roads and public transport, water, gas and electricity, communications, trade and culture and sports.

The 'Tolerable' areas were industrial development boards, the regulation of financial institutions, economic development in general, training and employment, joint representation in Europe, broadcasting and film, minority languages, social services, human rights and education.

Reform of constitution needed to put down a foundation

Just as Catholics do not want a regional assembly to be 'A return to Stormont' and majoritarian politics, Protestants do not want North/South bodies to be a 'backdoor' to an all-Ireland government. With this point in mind no one should be surprised to discover that Protestants would prefer a North/South body for each issue and for these bodies to be established (or dissolved) and controlled by elected politicians from the Northern Ireland Assembly, Dublin and Westminster (Table 8.20).

Additionally while dealing with all aspects of government business is just 'Tolerable' for a majority from both communities (50 per cent for Protestants

Table 8.20 Support for who should control North/South bodies

Accumulated percentage	Religion	Essential	Plus desirable	Plus acceptable	Plus tolerable
Matters of mutual interest should be dealt with by ...					
One North/South body for	Protestant	4	11	28	45
everything	Catholic	32	59	84	95
A separate North/South	Protestant	8	26	49	66
body for each issue	Catholic	12	31	64	80
Powers to establish and dissolve North/South bodies should be given to ...					
A Northern Ireland Assembly	Protestant	5	11	28	46
and the Irish Dail	Catholic	26	51	80	92
(Parliament)					
Westminster and Dublin	Protestant	1	5	17	32
	Catholic	6	25	57	79
Westminster, Dublin and a	Protestant	9	21	40	59
Northern Ireland Assembly	Catholic	19	44	77	88
North/South bodies should be ...					
Able to act independently	Protestant	9	19	37	55
	Catholic	18	47	79	88

Table 8.20 Continued

Accumulated percentage	Religion	Essential	Plus desirable	Plus acceptable	Plus tolerable
Controlled by and responsible to the respective governments, parliamentary bodies and NI Assembly who establish them	Protestant Catholic	15 21	30 46	**51** **78**	69 92

The management of North/South bodies should be undertaken by …

	Religion	Essential	Plus desirable	Plus acceptable	Plus tolerable
Elected politicians	Protestant Catholic	14 24	27 41	**56** **77**	75 91
Civil servants	Protestant Catholic	2 7	7 18	32 43	53 68
Both elected politicians and civil servants	Protestant Catholic	3 9	15 29	43 69	66 86
Representatives of business, trade unions, local government etc. as and when required	Protestant Catholic	8 24	25 52	48 82	69 **94**

Table 8.21 Support for control options for North/South bodies

Accumulated percentage	Religion	Essential	Plus desirable	Plus acceptable	Plus tolerable
North/South bodies should …					
Only deal with specific projects agreed to by the politicians who set up the bodies	Protestant Catholic	12 10	23 23	**49** **62**	72 86
Only deal with policies agreed to by the politicians who set up the bodies	Protestant Catholic	7 8	15 25	41 62	68 85
'Harmonise' their actions, policies and laws in the areas of policy they are responsible for	Protestant Catholic	3 23	16 50	46 84	69 98
Only deal with policies the European Union is responsible for	Protestant Catholic	1 3	10 12	35 42	61 70
Only do business with the European Union	Protestant Catholic	1 3	8 10	30 33	**54** **60**

Table 8.21 Continued

Accumulated percentage	Religion	Essential	Plus desirable	Plus acceptable	Plus tolerable
Deal with all aspects of	Protestant	4	11	30	50
government business	Catholic	31	56	82	96
Appointments to a North/South body should be made …					
In proportion to the	Protestant	17	34	60	77
representation of each	Catholic	12	31	59	81
party in the Northern					
Ireland Assembly					
Equally between the two	Protestant	6	17	39	63
main traditions in	Catholic	39	66	87	96
the North					
Equally between	Protestant	5	13	29	48
Northern Ireland and	Catholic	39	62	88	97
the Republic of Ireland					
Voting on business in a North/South body requires …					
A simple majority only	Protestant	10	25	47	64
	Catholic	6	20	48	67
A weighted majority	Protestant	5	16	42	64
	Catholic	9	30	64	79
A majority from *both* of the	Protestant	9	19	47	71
main traditions in the North	Catholic	29	56	82	91
A majority from *both*	Protestant	8	19	34	53
Northern Ireland and the	Catholic	31	58	86	93
Republic of Ireland					
Unanimity – everyone has	Protestant	21	39	53	66
to agree	Catholic	22	45	67	81

and 96 per cent for Catholics), Protestants are more willing to accept specific projects and policies selected for action by their politicians (Table 8.21). Protestants would also like appointments to North/South bodies to be made in proportion to the representation of each party in the Northern Ireland Assembly. Finally a majority of both communities are willing to accept the restriction that business in a North/South body must be passed unanimously – everyone has to agree.

Without North/South bodies it is difficult to see how any settlement package can receive the support of the Nationalist community. However, with all the safeguards proposed here in place Unionist politicians should have little to fear providing all of this is done in good faith. But good faith alone is not the stuff that good law is made of. For Unionists and Nationalists constitutional reform and an acceptable replacement for the Anglo-Irish Agreement are required to provide the bedrock and context in which all the other reforms can be seen to be and are made safe.

Belfast Telegraph, **Wednesday 14 January 1998**

What hope for Council of the Isles?

Is a Council of the Islands or Isles an acceptable replacement for the Anglo-Irish Agreement? In the fourth and final article from the poll this question is examined and the need for constitutional reform.

Prime Minister Tony Blair at the weekend put forward his proposals for a Council of the Isles in a bid to move the talks process forward. For most people in Northern Ireland, it is probably the first time that they heard the phrase, but is the idea workable and what support would such a body command?

Over the years a number of different institutions have been mooted, including a Council of Ireland, a Council of the British Isles, a British-Irish Council, a Council of the Islands and now a Council of the Isles. However, the only body that ever saw the light of day was the Anglo-Irish Agreement and Secretariat. Could a Council of the Islands or Isles be the replacement for the Anglo-Irish Agreement that is needed to establish a new east–west relationship in strand three of the Stormont talks?

Most international treaties are based on a number of principles and the Anglo-Irish Agreement is no exception to this rule. Which of these principles, if any, could be a basis for a new treaty? With this question in mind people were asked to indicate which principles they considered to be 'Essential', 'Desirable', 'Acceptable', 'Tolerable' or 'Unacceptable' as part of a lasting settlement. All of the principles, ranging from the promotion of peace, stability and equality in Northern Ireland to a recognition of its constitutional status were considered 'Acceptable', Desirable' or 'Essential' by a majority from both communities (Table 8.22).

In contrast to the principles that underpin the workings of the Anglo-Irish Agreement, the institutions of government that it created, the Anglo-Irish Secretariat and their offices in Belfast, did not fair so well (Table 8.23). Although most Catholics considered them to be 'Acceptable' or even 'Desirable' most Protestants only found them 'Tolerable' and even a proposal to extend these facilities to include London and Dublin did not receive any better support.

Fortunately one new proposal was 'Acceptable' to a majority from both communities: the establishment of a regional 'Council of the Islands' that would facilitate co-operation between Scotland, Wales, England, Northern Ireland and the Republic of Ireland. This proposal could not have even

Table 8.22 Support for the principles of a new Anglo-Irish Treaty

Accumulated percentage	Religion	Essential	Plus desirable	Plus acceptable	Plus tolerable
Co-operation in Europe	Protestant	16	40	73	92
	Catholic	40	72	94	98
Peace and stability in Northern Ireland	Protestant	55	81	94	96
	Catholic	79	91	99	100
Equal rights of the two major traditions	Protestant	31	53	79	91
	Catholic	76	90	99	100
Rejection of violence for political objectives	Protestant	65	81	95	97
	Catholic	68	85	97	100
Reconciliation between Unionists and Nationalists	Protestant	33	57	81	89
	Catholic	60	85	96	98
Respecting the identities of the two communities	Protestant	34	61	84	91
	Catholic	74	88	96	98
A society free from discrimination and intolerance	Protestant	50	79	95	96
	Catholic	83	93	98	99
Both communities to participate fully in the structures and processes of government	Protestant	33	56	78	88
	Catholic	71	89	96	98
The consent of *a majority* of the people of Northern Ireland is required for any change in its status	Protestant	68	82	93	96
	Catholic	27	49	73	85
The recognition of the present status and wishes of the majority of the people of Northern Ireland	Protestant	66	84	93	95
	Catholic	21	41	66	84
The right of *a majority* of the people of Northern Ireland to establish a united Ireland in the future	Protestant	29	38	57	77
	Catholic	45	66	85	93

been given serious consideration under the previous Conservative government. It is a clear break with the Framework Document and it is only with the creation of a Scottish Parliament and Welsh Assembly by the Labour government that such an option can come into play. It is imaginative and bold. It could mark the beginning of a new relationship for everyone on these islands, British and Irish, into the next millennium, a relationship

Table 8.23   Support for the institutions of a new Anglo-Irish Treaty

As part of a new treaty that replaces the Anglo-Irish Agreement the British and Irish governments should establish ...	Religion	Essential	Plus desirable	Plus acceptable	Plus tolerable
A special organisation for consultation between the two governments on Northern Ireland issues only	Protestant Catholic	5 17	17 49	44 81	61 93
Offices in Belfast for consultation between the two governments on Northern Ireland issues only	Protestant Catholic	4 16	16 41	45 80	63 93
A special organisation for consultation between the two governments on any issues of mutual interest	Protestant Catholic	4 19	13 51	44 86	65 96
Offices in London, Dublin and Belfast for consultation between the two governments on any issues of mutual interest	Protestant Catholic	4 22	18 54	43 86	68 96
An inter-parliamentary body to promote good relations between Dublin and Westminster	Protestant Catholic	3 23	17 52	40 85	70 97
An inter-parliamentary body responsible for all agreements made between London and Dublin	Protestant Catholic	3 21	11 43	32 81	58 94
A regional 'Council of the Islands' that facilitates co-operation between Scotland, Wales, England, Northern Ireland and the Republic of Ireland	Protestant Catholic	6 14	25 33	52 72	75 89
Or the Anglo-Irish Agreement should be brought to an end and should not be replaced	Protestant Catholic	31 5	45 12	61 29	75 47
However the Republic of Ireland should rejoin the Commonwealth	Protestant Catholic	9 6	19 10	52 31	75 50

built on consent as a region in Europe that attempts to put aside the past failures of borders, partition and competing nation-states. The 'ball' is now clearly in the courts of the London and Dublin governments.

Constitutional issues

In an effort to meet the concerns of the different communities in Northern Ireland several possibilities are available for the modification of the constitutional relationships that exist between the Republic of Ireland, Northern Ireland and the United Kingdom. This can be done by modifying the Constitution of the Republic of Ireland and the various Acts of Parliament in Westminster that establish the constitutional status of Northern Ireland (Table 8.24).

The complete deletion of the Republic of Ireland's constitutional claim over Northern Ireland is considered to be 'Essential' by 63 per cent of

Table 8.24   Support for various constitutional reforms

Accumulated percentage	Religion	Essential	Plus desirable	Plus acceptable	Plus tolerable
The Republic of Ireland's constitutional claim over Northern Ireland should ...					
Be completely deleted	Protestant	63	83	91	95
	Catholic	5	9	18	30
Be modified to only allow for a united Ireland with the consent of a majority of the people of Northern Ireland	Protestant	22	37	**56**	**72**
	Catholic	19	37	**59**	**77**
Be replaced with an 'aspiration' for a united Ireland	Protestant	1	5	16	35
	Catholic	8	26	57	78
Be replaced with a responsibility for the well being of the Nationalist community in Northern Ireland	Protestant	3	7	25	**51**
	Catholic	13	25	54	**74**
Be amended to reflect any new agreements reached at the Stormont talks	Protestant	4	15	36	**64**
	Catholic	7	27	59	**81**
Be replaced with full and guaranteed rights of Irish citizenship for all members of the Nationalist community in Northern Ireland	Protestant	5	10	27	**50**
	Catholic	27	43	67	**81**

Table 8.24   Continued

Accumulated percentage	Religion	Essential	Plus desirable	Plus acceptable	Plus tolerable
Or the Republic of Ireland's Constitution should not be changed at all	Protestant	4	6	12	28
	Catholic	25	40	61	78
The constitutional status of Northern Ireland as part of the United Kingdom should ...					
Be completely removed	Protestant	2	4	11	16
	Catholic	44	66	77	89
Only allow for a united Ireland with the consent of a majority of the people of Northern Ireland (no change)	Protestant	42	60	73	86
	Catholic	14	31	54	74
Be replaced with an 'aspiration' for a single state comprising the whole of the British Isles and Ireland	Protestant	2	8	26	43
	Catholic	2	17	34	53
Be replaced with a responsibility for the Well-being of the Unionist community in Northern Ireland	Protestant	10	18	38	60
	Catholic	6	19	46	71
Be amended to reflect any new agreements reached at the Stormont talks	Protestant	7	16	41	63
	Catholic	9	28	63	83
Be replaced with full and guaranteed rights of British citizenship for all members of the Unionist community on the island of Ireland	Protestant	21	33	51	62
	Catholic	9	25	57	75
Or the constitutional status and boundaries of Northern Ireland should not be changed at all	Protestant	51	70	84	90
	Catholic	5	8	21	38
Alternatively both governments could provide for Joint Authority, or Repartition					
Shared authority and sovereignty of Northern Ireland with the Republic of Ireland	Protestant	2	5	15	25
	Catholic	20	48	78	88

Table 8.24   Continued

Accumulated percentage	Religion	Essential	Plus desirable	Plus acceptable	Plus tolerable
Redefine the boundaries of Northern Ireland so that a maximum of Unionists are in the 'North' and a maximum of Nationalists are in the 'South'	Protestant	2	7	18	32
	Catholic	2	8	18	31

Protestants while 70 per cent of Catholics consider such a deletion to be 'Unacceptable' as part of a lasting settlement. Is this where the Stormont talks founder or can a compromise be found? Fortunately the answer to this apparently intractable problem is a very strong 'yes'.

A majority of both Catholics and Protestants find it quite 'Acceptable' for both the Republic of Ireland's constitution to be modified to only allow for a united Ireland with the consent of a majority of the people of Northern Ireland and for the constitutional status of Northern Ireland as part of the United Kingdom to be subject to the same principle of consent – which it presently is. And if this were not good news enough, both the British and Irish governments jointly agreed to these principles of consent when they signed the Anglo-Irish Agreement.

Additionally, as part of any balanced constitutional reform, it should also be noted that a majority of both Catholics and Protestants are willing to accept or tolerate both the British and Irish governments having a responsibility for the well-being of their citizens in both Northern Ireland and on the island of Ireland as a whole and that all their rights of British or Irish citizenship should be guaranteed. Perhaps these rights should be extended to Irish citizens in England, Scotland and Wales – but this question was not asked.

Finally, although a majority of Catholics considered joint authority to be 'Acceptable' this option was 'Unacceptable' to Protestants and neither community wanted to consider repartition as the way forward.

Many Nationalists and Unionists also find the language used in section 75 of the British 1920 Government of Ireland Act and the 1937 Constitution of the Republic of Ireland to be a little outdated. While introducing balanced reforms that fully embrace the principle of consent any other redrafted sections and articles should pay close attention to the use of modern phrases and terms that avoid giving offence. Many of the new agreements reached at the Stormont talks will provide opportunities for this kind of legal 'housekeeping'. If the two governments can get it right then they will be able to cast the foundation upon which a lasting settlement can be built. Their citizens, both British and Irish, eagerly await the outcome of their constitutional labours.

A comprehensive settlement

In broad terms the major elements of a lasting settlement that seem to emerge from this opinion poll can be summarised as follows:

- A Regional Assembly made up from elected members who share responsibilities in proportion to their representation and employing a voting system with other checks and balances to ensure the fair participation of both communities in government and the prevention of abuse of power.
- North/South bodies strictly controlled by the elected politicians who establish them to deal with a wide range of issues using various functions and powers appropriate to the areas of government policy being managed.
- Replace the Anglo-Irish Agreement with a Council of the Islands to establish a new relationship between London, Dublin, Cardiff, Edinburgh and Belfast appropriate to the needs of the region as a part of Europe.
- Constitutional reform that embraces the principle of consent and other balanced changes required to implement the various agreements made at the Stormont talks.
- A Bill of Rights that deals specifically with the political, social and cultural problems that have aggravated the conflict and a Human Rights Commission with responsibilities and powers to educate, monitor standards and bring cases to court.
- A reformed two-tier police service restructured with a view to recruiting more Catholics and improving community relations under the authority of a new Department of Justice in a Regional Assembly.

Perhaps the parties and governments can improve on this 'package', particularly the detail. But any radical departure from these basic arrangements will require sound reasons if it is to be acceptable to a majority from both communities. Certainly these proposals should be more widely acceptable than the Framework Document.

Implementation

A comprehensive settlement has to deal with many changes to political life. These reforms could be introduced all at once, or gradually over a period of time, perhaps as a final or interim agreement that may be subject to periodic review. Although Protestants would prefer the settlement to be final, all these options are 'Acceptable' to them while Catholics consider an interim agreement that can be reviewed after a set period of time to be their most 'Acceptable' choice (Table 8.25).

Even if an overall settlement can be agreed and does receive consent, intractable disputes may arise or parts of the settlement may need to be radically reformed at some time in the future. Of the two proposed mechanisms that could be put into place to deal with such eventualities the establishment of an international court with the responsibility of ruling on disputes is 'Acceptable' to a majority from both communities, while allowing voters to initiate a change after a minimum period of ten years is less 'Acceptable' to Catholics and only 'Tolerable' for Protestants (Table 8.26).

Table 8.25 Support for implementation options

Accumulated percentage	Religion	Essential	Plus desirable	Plus acceptable	Plus tolerable
The settlement should be final with no more changes allowed	Protestant	17	37	58	72
	Catholic	8	19	36	53
The settlement should be final but changes could be introduced over an agreed transitional period	Protestant	3	17	54	79
	Catholic	11	32	67	86
Allow for an interim agreement that can be reviewed after a set period of time	Protestant	5	15	51	78
	Catholic	14	39	79	96
Introduce reforms slowly subject to periodic assessment and review	Protestant	8	23	51	77
	Catholic	15	39	68	90

Table 8.26 Support for mechanisms to manage disputes

As part of a settlement ...	Religion	Essential	Plus desirable	Plus acceptable	Plus tolerable
An international court should be established with the responsibility of ruling on disputes	Protestant	6	21	56	73
	Catholic	38	62	90	97
A mechanism should be put in place that will allow voters to change the terms of the settlement after a minimum period of 10 years	Protestant	2	17	46	69
	Catholic	18	37	69	91

Balancing the needs for future political stability and the very real fears of both communities faced with radical political change is not going to be easy. But a lasting settlement seems to be what is really important. Providing the parties at the Stormont talks can reach an agreement, then both communities appear to be willing to accept whatever arrangements have to be made to make it work.

9
A Comprehensive Settlement

Following the publication of the results of the 'In Search of a Settlement' poll the eight parties still in the talks started to negotiate the details of an agreement in earnest. Some parties even requested electronic copies of the statistics so that they would be able to undertake further analysis. All the major elements of a comprehensive settlement, and public attitudes towards them, were now plainly visible for everyone to see.

But the individual parts of an agreement are not the same thing as a balanced set of compromises taken as a whole. How would the public react to an overall package? Would they vote for it in a referendum and would they continue to support their political leaders if they made such a deal? There really was no reason why the parties should not now reach an agreement if they had a mind to do so and that, essentially, was the final question that had to be addressed. Did the parties have the political will to see it through? Or, put another way, from a public opinion perspective, would the public stick with the parties and the difficult decisions they had to make or would the public desert their leaders if they accepted the deal now on the table?

An outline of a final agreement was drafted and circulated to all the parties with a view to testing it, as a comprehensive settlement 'package', against public opinion. But it proved to be quite impossible to get all the parties to reach an agreement on a single text on this occasion. The DUP and UKUP (who remained outside the talks) wanted too many changes, particularly to power sharing and North/South bodies, while Sinn Féin (who were still in the talks) would not put their name to a partitionist settlement that recognised the division of the island of Ireland into the North and South. So a 'package', very similar to the one drawn up from the previous poll, was agreed and tested by the seven remaining parties while the DUP, UKUP and Sinn Féin were given an opportunity to test their own alternative proposals against this carefully thought out compromise.

Belfast Telegraph, Tuesday 31 March 1998

Majority say 'yes' to the search for settlement

Today, the *Belfast Telegraph* publishes the first of a two-part opinion poll on the key issues of a referendum package. The majority of people in Northern Ireland are behind the politicians at the talks in their search for a comprehensive settlement, according to the survey. The poll reveals that if the parties can agree a settlement, then a strong vote of support from the people seems to be assured. But, if that agreement cannot be reached and the backing of the major parties is lost, the yes vote drops to 50 per cent from 77 per cent.

Nearly a year ago, just before the general election, in the first public opinion poll in this series, the people of the Province were asked 'Do you support the principle of a negotiated settlement for the political future of Northern Ireland?' 94 per cent said 'Yes' ranging from a high of 99 per cent for Alliance voters to a low of 90 per cent for DUP supporters.

But anyone could read what they wanted to into this question – for themselves or their own community. It did not test what could be a real comprehensive settlement. Now, a year later, that has been done and it includes a regional assembly, North/South bodies, a 'Council of the Isles', constitutional reform, a Bill of Rights and reform of the RUC, all the major elements of what the people of Northern Ireland might be asked to vote on in a referendum on 22 May – see 'A comprehensive settlement' below.

This was the question that was asked: 'If a majority of the political parties elected to take part in the Stormont talks agreed to this settlement would you vote to accept it in a referendum?' (Table 9.1). Seventy-seven per cent said 'Yes' ranging from a high of 96 per cent for Alliance voters to a low of 50 per cent for DUP supporters.

But some of the parties elected to take part in the Stormont talks may oppose a comprehensive settlement so a second question was also asked: 'If you said "Yes" would you still accept these terms for a settlement even if the political party you supported was opposed to them?' (Table 9.2). This time the 'Yes' vote fell to 50 per cent ranging from a high of 87 per cent for Alliance voters to a low of 22 per cent for Sinn Féin supporters.

Clearly, if the government tries to go over the heads of *all* the political parties at the Stormont talks then the possibilities of securing a 'Yes' vote in a referendum would be very close indeed. However, the support of the

Table 9.1 Support for a comprehensive settlement with party approval

Per cent	All of NI	Protestant	Catholic	DUP	PUP+ UDP	UUP	Alliance	SDLP	Sinn Féin
Yes	77	74	81	50	68	83	96	95	61
No	23	26	19	50	32	17	4	5	39

Table 9.2 Support for a comprehensive settlement with party opposition

Per cent	All of NI	Protestant	Catholic	DUP	PUP+ UDP	UUP	Alliance	SDLP	Sinn Féin
Yes	50	46	53	24	24	50	87	70	22
No	50	54	47	76	76	50	13	30	78

major centre parties, the UUP, Alliance and SDLP, should ensure a positive outcome.

The DUP seem to have arrived at a crossroads with 50 per cent saying 'Yes' and 50 per cent saying 'No'. Evidently the leadership of this party is in a position to take their electorate in either direction but their current 'No' campaign would appear to have the potential to reduce their party's support for a comprehensive settlement to 24 per cent.

The Loyalists seem to be in a somewhat similar situation with PUP and UDP support for a 'Yes' vote also falling to 24 per cent if the endorsement of their parties are withdrawn. However, quite unlike the DUP, their 'Yes' vote rises to 68 per cent if the Loyalist leadership are willing to support a comprehensive settlement. Similarly, the Sinn Féin 'Yes' vote falls from a high of 61 per cent to a low of 22 per cent when the backing of their party is removed.

Apparently Republicans and Loyalists have something in common. Although their electorate may have deep misgivings about a comprehensive settlement they seem willing to place their trust in the leadership of their parties and, for the most part, will vote 'Yes' if encouraged to do so.

A comprehensive settlement

- A REGIONAL ASSEMBLY made up from elected members who share responsibilities in proportion to their representation and employing a voting system, with other checks and balances, to ensure the fair participation of the whole community in government and the prevention of abuse of power.
- NORTH/SOUTH BODIES strictly controlled by the elected politicians who establish them to deal with a wide range of issues using various functions and powers appropriate to the areas of government policy being managed.
- Replace the Anglo-Irish Agreement and establish a COUNCIL OF THE ISLES to create a new relationship between London, Dublin, Cardiff, Edinburgh and Belfast appropriate to the needs of the region as a part of Europe.
- CONSTITUTIONAL REFORM that embraces the principle of consent of a majority of the people of Northern Ireland to keep or change its status, guaranteed rights of British and/or Irish citizenship, and any other balanced

changes required to implement the various agreements made at the Stormont talks.

- A BILL OF RIGHTS that deals specifically with the political, social and cultural problems that have aggravated the conflict and a Human Rights Commission with responsibilities and powers to educate, monitor standards and bring cases to court.
- REFORM THE RUC to create community policing units as part of a two-tier service restructured with a view to recruiting more Catholics and improving community relations under the authority of a new Department of Justice in a Regional Assembly.

Compromise or common ground?

Some recent commentators have suggested that this comprehensive settlement represents a three-all draw with a regional assembly, Council of the Isles and changes to Articles 2 and 3 a win for Unionists and North/South bodies, a Bill of Rights and police reform a win for Nationalists. The 'spin doctors' may see it this way but what is the reality on the ground? To measure public opinion on this issue everyone interviewed was asked to say which parts of a comprehensive settlement they considered to be 'Essential', 'Desirable', 'Acceptable', 'Tolerable' or 'Unacceptable' (Table 9.3).

A regional assembly is almost equally acceptable in both communities with only 11 per cent of Protestants and 15 per cent of Catholics considering this part of an overall package to be 'Unacceptable'. North/South bodies are 'Essential' for 33 per cent of Catholics and 'Unacceptable' for 40 per cent of Protestants while a 'Council of the Isles' gets only a warm response from Protestants and is 'Unacceptable' to 30 per cent of Catholics.

Table 9.3   Protestant and Catholic support for the different parts of a comprehensive settlement

Per cent	Religion	Essential	Desirable	Acceptable	Tolerable	Unacceptable
A Regional	Protestant	19	16	40	14	11
Assembly	Catholic	13	16	36	20	15
North/South	Protestant	3	10	19	28	40
bodies	Catholic	33	26	23	10	8
Council of the	Protestant	4	20	38	21	17
Isles	Catholic	6	12	30	22	30
Constitutional	Protestant	36	18	27	12	7
reform	Catholic	20	25	33	13	9
A Bill of Rights	Protestant	12	23	36	20	9
	Catholic	48	23	20	6	3
Reform the	Protestant	3	8	19	22	48
RUC	Catholic	40	21	21	9	9

Constitutional reform has the highest support from both communities with 36 per cent of Protestants and 20 per cent of Catholics saying it is 'Essential' and only 7 per cent and 9 per cent respectively saying it is 'Unacceptable'. A Bill of Rights is also equally acceptable in both communities, although a high 48 per cent of Catholics consider it to be 'Essential'. Finally, reform of the RUC is 'Essential' for 40 per cent of Catholics and 'Unacceptable' for 48 per cent of Protestants.

In all of this there seems to be as much common ground as there is compromise. The reality is not a simple three-three draw. Additionally, the levels of 'Unacceptable', which can be considered to be equivalent to a 'No' vote, rise to 30 per cent for Catholics and 48 per cent for Protestants on some issues. But, with the agreement of a majority of the parties at the talks, only 19 per cent of Catholics and 26 per cent of Protestants said 'No' to the total package as a comprehensive settlement. A negotiated settlement seems to be what is really important and many of those who said 'Yes' were willing to do so while considering many parts of the package to be 'Unacceptable' from their point of view. Under the right circumstances the whole can become more significant than the sum of its constituent parts.

Alternatives to a comprehensive settlement

Some Unionists do not want a comprehensive settlement along the lines of the one reviewed here. Some of them do not want devolution either but some of them do. With this point in mind everyone polled was asked: 'Do you want Northern Ireland to have a devolved parliament similar to those planned for Scotland and Wales?' Fifty-eight per cent said 'Yes' ranging from a high of 78 per cent for UUP voters to a low of 23 per cent for Sinn Féin supporters (Table 9.4).

In an effort to mirror the recent Scottish referendum everyone who said 'Yes' to a devolved parliament was also asked: 'Do you want a Northern Ireland parliament to have powers to alter taxes?' Only 38 per cent said 'Yes' ranging from a high of 51 per cent for UUP voters to a low of 15 per cent for Sinn Féin supporters (Table 9.5).

The Scottish 'Yes – Yes' campaign was very well organised with all the major political parties speaking with one voice. If the same were done here perhaps a 'Yes – Yes' campaign for devolution in Northern Ireland could succeed. But it is very unlikely that the SDLP, let alone Sinn Féin, would

Table 9.4 Support for devolution similar to Scotland and Wales

Per cent	All of NI	Protestant	Catholic	DUP	PUP+ UDP	UUP	Alliance	SDLP	Sinn Féin
Yes	58	74	41	66	61	78	76	51	23
No	42	26	59	34	39	22	24	49	77

Table 9.5   Support for local powers to alter taxes

Per cent	All of NI	Protestant	Catholic	DUP	PUP+ UDP	UUP	Alliance	SDLP	Sinn Féin
Yes	38	49	27	44	40	51	50	34	15
No	62	51	73	56	60	49	50	66	85

Table 9.6   Support for maintaining the Union with Britain

Per cent	All of NI	Protestant	Catholic	DUP	PUP+ UDP	UUP	Alliance	SDLP	Sinn Féin
Yes	69	97	33	99	100	98	93	41	7
No	31	3	67	1	0	2	7	59	93

Table 9.7   Support for a united Ireland

Per cent	All of NI	Protestant	Catholic	DUP	PUP+ UDP	UUP	Alliance	SDLP	Sinn Féin
Yes	32	2	70	0	0	1	11	63	90
No	68	98	30	100	100	99	89	37	10

support such a vote. It should also be noted that the 'Yes' vote for a devolved parliament is only 58 per cent while the support for a Northern Ireland Assembly as part of a comprehensive settlement is 77 per cent. Clearly a settlement is the way forward in this matter.

Some Unionists would also like to have a 'Border Poll'. With this point in mind everyone interviewed was asked: 'Do you want Northern Ireland to be part of the United Kingdom?' 97 per cent of Protestants and 33 per cent of Catholics said 'Yes', to give a total of 69 per cent for Northern Ireland as a whole (Table 9.6).

And just to be double sure the same question was asked the other way around: 'Do you want Northern Ireland to be part of the Republic of Ireland?' Two per cent of Protestants and 70 per cent of Catholics said 'Yes' to give a total of 32 per cent for Northern Ireland as a whole (Table 9.7).

Although nearly a third of the Catholic population (mostly SDLP voters) are presently willing to lend their support to the continuation of the Union it should not be forgotten that most of these Catholics also support a comprehensive settlement. Undoubtedly any failure to reach a settlement, or a concerted effort designed to undermine a settlement, will alienate these Catholics and their present goodwill for the constitutional status quo of the Province as a part of the United Kingdom.

Belfast Telegraph, Wednesday 1 April 1998

Little support for SF agenda

The final part of the opinion poll on a referendum package deals with outstanding issues to be resolved during the last nine days of negotiations. The survey shows a lack of cross-community support for Sinn Féin's non-partitionist agenda of no local assembly, completely independent North–South bodies, no Council of the Isles, consent on an all-Ireland basis and replacing the RUC. But everyone wants a Bill of Rights and there is an overwhelming desire, from all sections of the community, for responsible government institutions that can make a settlement work.

In part one of the survey published yesterday, 77 per cent of those polled said they would vote yes for a comprehensive settlement agreed to at the talks. But this support for a referendum package fell to 50 per cent when backing of the political parties was removed. Today each of the six parts of the settlement is tested to see how it stands up against proposed alternatives. And a range of other issues, for fine-tuning an agreement, is examined. This was done by asking everyone interviewed to say which options they considered to be 'Essential', 'Desirable', 'Acceptable', 'Tolerable', or 'Unacceptable.'

- A REGIONAL ASSEMBLY made up from elected members who share responsibilities in proportion to their representation and employing a voting system, with other checks and balances, to ensure the fair participation of the whole community in government and the prevention of abuse of power.

The 'non-partitionist' option of not having a regional assembly at all is not very popular in either the Catholic or Protestant communities (Table 9.8). A majority of both Catholics and Protestants consider an assembly with powers to monitor and administer the Northern Ireland Office, make new laws and alter taxes to be 'Acceptable' (Table 9.9). Similarly the options of having a second chamber with legislative powers or responsibilities to provide expert advice and reports on all aspects of business undertaken by the assembly, or a special committee to do this work, are all 'Acceptable'.

Table 9.8 Support for proposed regional assembly or no assembly

Per cent	Religion	Essential	Desirable	Acceptable	Tolerable	Unacceptable
A REGIONAL	Protestant	19	16	40	14	11
ASSEMBLY	Catholic	13	16	36	20	15
Northern Ireland	Protestant	3	8	20	21	48
should not have a	Catholic	10	9	23	23	35
Regional Assembly						

Table 9.9   Support for different assembly powers and structures

Accumulated percentage	Religion	Essential	Plus desirable	Plus acceptable	Plus tolerable
Powers to monitor and	Protestant	19	41	78	90
administer the NIO	Catholic	10	32	66	84
Powers to make	Protestant	7	28	66	81
new laws	Catholic	6	24	59	76
Powers to alter taxes	Protestant	4	15	51	72
	Catholic	5	20	52	70
A legislative second	Protestant	3	14	53	77
chamber	Catholic	6	23	63	83
A consultative second	Protestant	3	14	58	79
chamber	Catholic	8	26	65	84
A special committee	Protestant	4	19	62	85
	Catholic	11	34	70	85
No assembly	Protestant	3	11	31	52
	Catholic	10	19	42	65

Clearly the politicians at the Stormont talks are free to choose between these various options for an assembly without prejudicing the proposal.

- NORTH/SOUTH BODIES strictly controlled by the elected politicians who establish them to deal with a wide range of issues using various functions and powers appropriate to the areas of government policy being managed.

Although 40 per cent of Protestants consider this proposal for North/South bodies to be 'Unacceptable' by itself (Table 9.10), 74 per cent of Protestants are willing to accept it as part of a comprehensive settlement. Protestants consider the 'non-partitionist' option of a directly elected 'Council of Ministers' to be 'Tolerable' but they would like a Northern Ireland Assembly to have the final responsibility for decisions taken by North–South bodies (Table 9.11). Catholics would prefer to have the final responsibility for decisions given to both the Northern Ireland Assembly and Irish Dail, or the 'Council of Ministers', or the North/South bodies when given permission to act independently. A majority of Protestants consider all these options to be 'Tolerable' but will not accept North/South bodies acting independently at all times. This seems to be the 'bottom line' on this issue and possibly defines the limits of executive powers from a Unionist point of view.

Table 9.10 Support for proposed North/South bodies and a Council of Ministers

Per cent	Religion	Essential	Desirable	Acceptable	Tolerable	Unacceptable
NORTH/SOUTH BODIES	Protestant	3	10	19	28	40
	Catholic	33	26	23	10	8
A 'Council of	Protestant	3	6	16	23	52
Ministers' appointed	Catholic	14	24	39	13	10
from the Executive						
of the Northern						
Ireland Assembly						
and Irish Dail						
A 'Council of	Protestant	3	7	19	23	48
Ministers' directly	Catholic	21	25	38	9	7
elected by propor-						
tional representation						
North and South						

Table 9.11 Protestant and Catholic views on responsibility for North/South bodies

Accumulated percentage	Religion	Essential	Plus desirable	Plus acceptable	Plus tolerable
The Northern Ireland	Protestant	19	36	69	81
Assembly	Catholic	4	14	42	62
The Irish Dail	Protestant	1	1	7	16
	Catholic	3	9	34	59
Both the N.I. Assembly	Protestant	3	8	24	52
and Irish Dail	Catholic	13	38	82	94
The 'Council of Ministers'	Protestant	1	6	33	58
	Catholic	3	22	71	88
The North/South body with	Protestant	0	5	29	51
permission	Catholic	5	34	77	90
The North/South body	Protestant	3	9	25	44
at all times	Catholic	6	29	66	85
Civil Servants from the	Protestant	0	3	15	50
North and South	Catholic	2	10	42	70

- Replace the Anglo-Irish Agreement and establish a COUNCIL OF THE ISLES to create a new relationship between London, Dublin, Cardiff, Edinburgh and Belfast appropriate to the needs of the region as a part of Europe.

While 30 per cent of Catholics consider this proposal for a 'Council of the Isles' to be 'Unacceptable' by itself, 81 per cent of Catholics are willing

Table 9.12　Support for proposed Council of the Isles and its alternative

Per cent	Religion	Essential	Desirable	Acceptable	Tolerable	Unacceptable
COUNCIL OF THE ISLES	Protestant	4	20	38	21	17
	Catholic	6	12	30	22	30
No 'Council of the Isles' – the Anglo-Irish parliamentary body as it now exists should assume responsibility for issues of common interest throughout the two islands	Protestant	3	4	13	27	53
	Catholic	5	15	30	17	33

Table 9.13　Support for status of the Council of the Isles

Accumulated percentage	Religion	Essential	Plus desirable	Plus acceptable	Plus tolerable
North/South bodies subordinate to 'Council of Isles'	Protestant	10	19	38	60
	Catholic	1	3	23	41
North/South bodies and 'Council of Isles' alongside each other	Protestant	4	16	46	**69**
	Catholic	10	32	68	**82**
'Council of Isles' subordinate to North/South bodies	Protestant	1	4	22	43
	Catholic	10	21	53	68
No 'Council of Isles' just Anglo-Irish parliamentary body	Protestant	3	7	20	47
	Catholic	5	20	50	67

to accept it as part of a comprehensive settlement. The 'non-partitionist' option of limiting the responsibility for East/West relationships to the existing Anglo-Irish parliamentary body is 'Unacceptable' to 53 per cent of Protestants (Table 9.12). Catholics do not seem to have any strong views on this matter, one way or the other, so establishing a 'Council of the Isles' should not present any serious difficulties, at least, for the people of Northern Ireland.

When it comes to the relationship between a 'Council of the Isles' and North/South bodies *both* Catholics and Protestants would prefer for them to work alongside each other and for neither of them to be subordinate to the other (Table 9.13). Hopefully this clear consensus will help to resolve this issue.

- CONSTITUTIONAL REFORM that embraces the principle of consent of a majority of the people of Northern Ireland to keep or change its status, guaranteed rights of British and/or Irish citizenship, and any other balanced changes required to implement the various agreements made at the Stormont talks.

A majority of both Catholics and Protestants consider this proposal for dealing with constitutional reform to be 'Acceptable' (Table 9.14). The balance between the principle of consent, on the one hand, and guaranteed rights of citizenship, on the other hand, seems to have been struck just right. The 'non-partitionist' option of extending the principle of consent to the island of Ireland as a whole is more acceptable to Catholics but 84 per cent of Protestants consider this option to be 'Unacceptable'. Clearly this proposal, if accepted, could undermine the viability of a comprehensive settlement.

Table 9.14 Support for proposed constitutional reform and its alternative

Per cent	Religion	Essential	Desirable	Acceptable	Tolerable	Unacceptable
CONSTITUTIONAL	Protestant	36	18	27	12	7
REFORM	Catholic	20	25	33	13	9
The people of the	Protestant	1	2	4	9	84
island of Ireland as	Catholic	31	24	23	11	11
a whole should decide						
the status of Northern						
Ireland						

- A BILL OF RIGHTS that deals specifically with the political, social and cultural problems that have aggravated the conflict and a Human Rights Commission with responsibilities and powers to educate, monitor standards and bring cases to court.

A Bill of Rights is broadly accepted as one of the strongest areas of 'common ground' by the politicians at the Stormont talks (Table 9.15). Quite a few technical/legal issues will have to be resolved but given the goodwill of both the Protestant and Catholic communities for a Bill of Rights its development will undoubtedly be a welcome addition to a comprehensive settlement.

Table 9.15 Support for proposed Bill of Rights

Per cent	Religion	Essential	Desirable	Acceptable	Tolerable	Unacceptable
A BILL OF RIGHTS	Protestant	12	23	36	20	9
	Catholic	48	23	20	6	3

- REFORM THE RUC to create community policing units as part of a two-tier service restructured with a view to recruiting more Catholics and improving community relations under the authority of a new Department of Justice in a Regional Assembly.

While 40 per cent of Catholics consider reform of the RUC to be 'Essential', 48 per cent of Protestants consider these same proposals to be 'Unacceptable' (Table 9.16). But it should be stressed again that, as part of a comprehensive settlement agreed at the talks, these reforms are acceptable to 74 per cent of Protestants. The 'non-partitionist' proposal for 'a new policing service reflective of the community as a whole and accountable to an all-island body' does not receive significantly more support from the Catholic community than the proposal on offer so there seems to be little to be gained from pursuing this option as it is 'Unacceptable' to 77 per cent of Protestants.

Table 9.16   Support for proposed RUC reform and its alternative

Per cent	Religion	Essential	Desirable	Acceptable	Tolerable	Unacceptable
REFORM THE	Protestant	3	8	19	22	48
RUC	Catholic	40	21	21	9	9
A new policing	Protestant	1	1	10	11	77
service reflective	Catholic	41	19	22	10	8
of the community						
as a whole and						
accountable to						
an all-island body						

Making the settlement work

All of these political reforms will have to deal with many different issues and it is entirely possible that some of the new institutions created as part of a comprehensive settlement will not deliver the hoped-for changes. Several proposals were put forward to deal with this problem. Firstly, it was suggested that all the executive members of a Northern Ireland Assembly, 'Council of Ministers', North/South bodies or 'Council of the Isles' should agree to a 'Duty of Service' that includes 'a commitment to undertake and fulfil the responsibilities of their office' (Table 9.17). A majority of both Protestants and Catholics considered this option to be 'Desirable' and they also took the view that 'a commitment to the principles of democracy and non-violence' was 'Essential'. This strong positive vote sends a clear message to the politicians. The people of Northern Ireland are not only weary of the violence but they are also fed up with party antics, wrecking tactics and abstentionism.

Table 9.17 Support for commitments to a 'Duty of Service' and non-violence

Accumulated percentage	Religion	Essential	Plus desirable	Plus acceptable	Plus tolerable
A commitment to	Protestant	36	58	84	95
their office	Catholic	46	74	94	99
A commitment to	Protestant	56	70	89	97
non-violence	Catholic	63	84	96	99

Table 9.18 Support for enforcement options for a 'Duty of Service'

Accumulated percentage	Religion	Essential	Plus desirable	Plus acceptable	Plus tolerable
An Ethics Committee	Protestant	11	31	64	82
of a NI Assembly	Catholic	6	18	52	72
The Secretary of State	Protestant	4	15	46	73
	Catholic	1	6	32	60
The British and Irish	Protestant	3	10	30	63
governments	Catholic	7	24	69	90
An all-Ireland 'Council	Protestant	1	4	18	43
of Ministers'	Catholic	7	33	81	92
The 'Council of	Protestant	2	13	45	72
the Isles'	Catholic	2	9	41	60
A court of law	Protestant	8	26	67	87
	Catholic	8	22	59	78
A special	Protestant	11	22	56	82
constitutional court	Catholic	14	24	60	80
A special international	Protestant	4	13	38	69
court	Catholic	20	39	74	89
The voters at an election	Protestant	16	35	66	85
	Catholic	13	32	61	83

With regard to any failure to comply with this 'Duty of Service' a majority of both Protestants and Catholics considered it 'Acceptable' for complaints and appeals to be dealt with by an Ethics Committee of a Northern Ireland Assembly, a court of law, a special constitutional court or the voters at an election (Table 9.18). By way of contrast, having the Secretary of State or British and Irish governments make decisions on these matters was only 'Tolerable'. Legal and democratic procedures, it would seem, are to be preferred over mechanisms that invite political intervention.

But will proportionality, responsibility sharing and a 'Duty of Service' backed up with appropriate legal sanctions lead to good governance and the smooth working of these new institutions. Sinn Féin have their doubts and perhaps that is why they cling so tenaciously to their 'non-partitionist' agenda and seek bilateral negotiations with Unionists. But even negotiations are not a substitute for goodwill. Perhaps what is really needed are assurances made in good faith – on both sides. Without that, all of this may be worth nothing at all.

* * *

The fieldwork for the poll was conducted between 12–22 March and published on Thursday 31 March and Friday 1 April. The results were a great encouragement to the parties in the talks as it was now clear that they could 'win the day'. Even Sinn Féin, who had little support for their own proposals outside their own constituency, were pleased with the results. But the DUP and UKUP were not at all pleased, prompting complaints to both myself and the *Belfast Telegraph*. There was also much mischief-making going on with leaked documents from the Northern Ireland Office suggesting that I and the *Belfast Telegraph* might somehow be working for the British government establishment.

Fortunately I had been in this sort of situation before. My report 'Lords of the Arctic: Wards of the State' had helped to set a context for an honourable land claims settlement between the Inuit of Canada's Northwest Territories and the Federal Government of Canada in Ottawa. But the Premier of the Northwest Territories, who was opposed to the deal, viciously attacked me and my research in the Canadian press and in letters to the Federal Minister of Health and Welfare who had commissioned the work. The Premier lost his rearguard action and his territory was split in two to create a new regional government for the Inuit called 'Nunavut'. At the time I was very upset by the Premier's personal attack but a journalist who supported my efforts defended me with a 'Guest Opinion' in the *News of the North* entitled 'Real premiers don't shoot the messenger'.

So on this occasion I had the presence of mind to speak up for myself with a rebuttal published in the *Belfast Telegraph* on 8 April 1998. Fortunately all the mischief-making and complaints of the DUP and UKUP were in vain. They had absented themselves from the talks and the Agreement was made in Belfast two days later on Good Friday, 10 April 1998.

Belfast Telegraph, Wednesday 8 April 1998

Attacks bring hope of change

Both Robert McCartney and Ian Paisley Jr. have openly attacked the *Belfast Telegraph* when they have not liked the results of my public opinion surveys or the way in which they were presented. Last Friday, I got a phone call from a party complaining that I had not published the results of their questions in last week's articles. Perhaps they thought I was following government instructions as outlined in the recently leaked Northern Ireland Office document:

'It will be important to ensure that not all of the results of opinion polls etc. will be in the public domain. It would be open to us to encourage some degree of public opinion polling... where we believe the results are likely to be supportive.'

Before anyone is interviewed for one of my polls they are told that: 'The results of the survey will be analysed and widely published in the local press and in reports that will be sent to all ten parties who have been elected to take part in the Stormont talks.'

Of course I cannot publish all the statistics in the *Belfast Telegraph*, there are simply too many, and I must edit them down to the essential few that illustrate the issues under examination. But all the parties, including the one that phoned me, have all the results to do with as they wish. The theme of the last opinion poll was a comprehensive settlement and its alternatives. The question and results, which the party who phoned me wanted to see in print, are as follows:

'If any of the main paramilitary organisations breaches their cease-fire would you support the government introducing new legal measures to suppress terrorism?' (Table 9.19)

Table 9.19 Support for new legal measures to suppress terrorism

Per cent	All of NI	Protestant	Catholic	DUP	PUP+ UDP	UUP	Alliance	SDLP	Sinn Féin
Yes	74	88	59	81	71	94	87	81	20
No	26	12	41	19	29	6	13	19	80

When I was at Stormont last Wednesday to give the parties their reports I had to tell Sinn Féin that the stories to be published that day could be a bitter pill for them. There was little support for the non-partitionist Sinn Féin agenda. A member of their delegation said: 'That's OK Colin we have been there before'. I am sorry Robert McCartney and Ian Paisley Jr. are unable to take the occasional hard knock with such good grace.

The leaked government document went on to say: 'We have now commissioned... to have both quantitative and qualitative research carried out, without it being seen to be Government inspired...'

I am not a part of this conspiracy. The NIO has had grave misgivings about me since I successfully brought a series of Human Rights complaints against the British state for forcing children to go to segregated schools against their wishes.

I had hoped to meet with Dr Mo Mowlan when she took office with a view to improving relations between myself and her Civil Service. We have much in common, we are both social anthropologists with an interest in the affairs of Northern Ireland. But her Civil Service have always kept me from her door.

Because I am so single-minded and outspoken I am, in government circles, considered to be a loose cannon. Let me tell you now that I am not a loose cannon at all. I am tightly lashed down to the deck of my own small vessel of which I am master and I use my ammunition with great care. I do not sail on the ship of state.

You might ask me if I get discouraged or upset when politicians attack the bearer of what they consider to be bad news. My answer is 'No I don't'. On the contrary such attacks lift my spirits and fill my heart with hope because experience tells me change is at hand.

10
Implementation of the Belfast Agreement

For those directly involved in the talks the signing of the Belfast Agreement was met with not only feelings of pure joy but also with the physical realities of mental and emotional exhaustion. The people of Northern Ireland had been at war with themselves and their neighbours for a quarter of a century but now there was a very real hope that that tragedy would come to an end. An end to the killing, a pact between old enemies, was it really possible?

Although nearly everyone wanted the deal to work it seemed to be necessary to deny that it actually could. No one dared, it would seem, to put their new-found gods of good fortune to the test just in case they woke up to find the Agreement gone leaving only the same old city of Belfast. There were no celebrations, only a sort of quiet waiting. People were a little nervous, perhaps even scared. The prospects of peace brought new uncertainties.

Old habits and distrust born of years of fear and violence created an opportunity for those opposed to the Agreement to work their way into the hearts and minds of the most vulnerable: those who felt themselves to be insecure with change, any change, even change for the better. It was in this context that the anti-agreement parties, the DUP and UKUP, combined their forces in the hope of defeating the Agreement in the referendum. Unfortunately the pro-agreement parties failed to co-ordinate their actions and speak with a single voice. Instead they attempted to sell the settlement to their separate communities as two apparently different sets of arrangements for the political future of the Province. Support for the Agreement slipped but a spirited 'Yes' campaign prevented the referendum vote from falling by more than six percentage points below the 77 per cent recorded in the last poll.

But another hurdle had to be crossed on 25 June 1998: elections to the New Northern Ireland Assembly. Again the anti-agreement Unionists co-ordinated their efforts, this time fielding as many candidates as they could to 'shred' the Unionist pro-agreement vote. They were very successful. The Loyalist UDP got no seats at all and the PUP just two seats, while the UUP lost out to new anti-agreement independents affiliated to the 'No' campaign Paisley camp. With only a slim majority in the Assembly the pro-agreement Unionists led by David Trimble moved very slowly, too slowly, to establish the new institutions of government with Sinn Féin and the SDLP. This situation created serious problems for Republicans who now saw Unionists apparently exercising a veto to keep them out of the Executive so they exercised their veto and hung on to their weapons.

The Agreement, it seemed, had brought no real changes at all and then came the worst atrocity of the Troubles. Dissident Republicans killed twenty-nine people with a bomb in Omagh on 15 August 1998. For a brief few weeks public opinion was so firmly behind the peace process one sensed that if only the Unionists would have then set up the Executive and shared power with the Nationalists and Republicans the IRA would have found themselves so morally isolated, even by their own constituency, they would have then been obliged to make a move on decommissioning. But none of this happened and perhaps one of the best opportunities was lost to significantly move the peace process forward.

On 16 October it was announced that David Trimble and John Hume were to be the joint winners of the 1998 Nobel Peace Prize and I was invited to go to Oslo and give a seminar on the use of public opinion polls as part of the negotiations for the Belfast Agreement. On 10 December David Trimble and John Hume received their prize but again an opportunity was missed to set up the power-sharing Executive in a spirit of magnanimity that can be brought about on such occasions. Republican attitudes hardened. The peace process was now in very serious trouble and members of the PUP, fearing a breakdown of the ceasefires and a return to war, asked me if I could undertake another public opinion poll in an effort to get the peace process back on track. Sinn Féin shared these concerns and early in 1999 we started to draft a questionnaire that would hopefully move things forward.

Sinn Féin, with links to the Irish Republican Army (IRA), and the PUP, with links to the Loyalist Ulster Volunteer Force (UVF) and Red Hand Commando (RHC), were the only parties involved in this particular exercise. The UDP, with links to the Loyalist Ulster Defence Association (UDA) and Ulster Freedom Fighters (UFF), had failed to be elected to the new Northern Ireland Assembly so they were not now as actively a part of the peace process as many would have liked. So they chose not to participate while some of the other pro-agreement parties were not invited to become a part of this exercise as they may have wished to try to use the poll to re-negotiate sections of the Agreement that they alone had problems with. Restrictive as it was this was the only acceptable basis upon which the work could go ahead.

In addition to the parties involved many of the subjects dealt with in this poll were also very different to those dealt with before. The objectives of this poll were very different. We wanted to get the pro-agreement parties and two governments back to the negotiating table to make the decisions now urgently required to implement the Belfast Agreement in full. So people were asked how they felt about the Agreement and its various parts. Were they satisfied with the progress made? Were they fearful if progress were not made? Was the problem a matter of trust and, if so, what could be done to establish confidence in the peace process and move it forward? In addition to matters of procedure and substance dealt with in the earlier polls we now started to introduce questions about the social and political context in which actions had to be taken. We wanted people to face up to the very real possibility of failure and in so doing find solutions to the problems at hand.

Belfast Telegraph, Wednesday 3 March 1999

93 per cent say: make the Agreement work

With 19 March set as the date for devolution, and the process deadlocked over decommissioning, *the Belfast Telegraph* publishes the first of a two-part opinion poll on the implementation of the Belfast Agreement.

Before the Belfast Agreement was signed by the parties at the Stormont talks a group of them tested a possible 'Comprehensive Settlement' in this series of public opinion polls. On 31 March 1998 the result was published in the *Belfast Telegraph*. 77 per cent of the people of Northern Ireland said 'Yes'. For many different reasons the politicians who brokered the Agreement did not back the 'Yes' campaign as rigorously as they could have with a united campaign. The 'No' campaign, however, was well co-ordinated and effective. Subsequently, on 22 May 1998, 71 per cent of the people of Northern Ireland voted 'Yes' in the referendum and in the Republic 94 per cent of the electorate gave their support to the Agreement.

In the latest poll in this series 93 per cent of the people of Northern Ireland said 'Yes' when asked if they wanted the Belfast Agreement to work (Table 10.1) ranging from a high of 98 per cent for Alliance and SDLP voters to 96 per cent for Sinn Féin, 94 per cent for the UUP, 84 per cent for the PUP and 73 per cent for the DUP. By now everyone knows what the Belfast Agreement is and the people interviewed for this poll were reminded what the major elements were before they were asked this question. These results

Table 10.1 Do you want the Belfast Agreement to work?

Per cent	All of NI	Protestant	Catholic	DUP	UUP	PUP	Alliance	SDLP	Sinn Féin
Yes	93	89	97	73	94	84	98	98	96
No	7	11	3	27	6	16	2	2	4

should therefore be taken seriously and the conclusion to be drawn is that the people of Northern Ireland want their political leaders to do what is necessary to achieve a successful outcome.

With this principle as a guide all the elements of the Belfast Agreement will be explored over the coming days. What do people consider to be most important, what will they accept and what will they not accept under any circumstances? Finally, every effort will be made to try to find a way through the difficult problem of decommissioning and setting up the executive.

But who wants what?

Although 93 per cent of the people of Northern Ireland want the Agreement to work it is important to remember that the Agreement makes many compromises and contains elements that have been included for one community or the other in the hope that the overall package might eventually lead to peace.

In the poll published in the *Belfast Telegraph* on Saturday, 10 January 1998 seventeen 'steps' that the parties wanted in the Agreement were listed in their order of priority for both Catholics and Protestants. In the poll published today the elements of the Belfast Agreement are similarly ordered (Table 10.2). This time people were asked to indicate which ones they considered to be 'Very important', 'Important', 'Of some importance', 'Of little importance' or 'Of No Importance at all'.

The table of priorities needs little explanation. However, it is important to note that the 'Decommissioning of paramilitary weapons' remains the number one concern for Protestants while police reform, equality and rights issues continue to be the top priorities for Catholics. Decommissioning is tenth on their list. Clearly all the parties to the Agreement would do well to remember these facts and try to understand where the other parties are coming from as they approach the problem of setting up the Executive.

Education, health and jobs

'The New Northern Ireland Assembly' is the second item on the Protestant list of priorities and joint second on the Catholic list. Again this enthusiasm for the devolution of powers to Northern Ireland is nothing new. It was reported in this series of polls in the *Belfast Telegraph* on 12 January 1998, 'Why Ulster now wants to have new assembly'. But it has now been decided what the devolved departments are going to be so it was possible to ask the people of Northern Ireland how important they considered each one to be (Table 10.3).

Education and Health are the number one priorities. Fifty-nine per cent said these departments were 'very important'. The department of 'Enterprise, trade and investment' came in third at 52 per cent. DUP supporters took

Table 10.2 Protestant and Catholic views of the Belfast Agreement

	Protestant per cent	Very Important	Catholic per cent	Very Important
1st	Decommissioning of paramilitary weapons	69	The reform of the police service	56
2nd	The New Northern Ireland Assembly	42	The Equality Commission	52
3rd	The Commission for Victims	39	The New Human Rights Commission	52
4th	All parts of the Agreement together	38	The New Northern Ireland Assembly	52
5th	A Bill of Rights for Northern Ireland	36	North/South bodies	52
6th	Changes to the Irish Constitution	36	The reform of the justice system	52
7th	The Equality Commission	31	All parts of the Agreement together	51
8th	The New Human Rights Commission	31	A Bill of Rights for Northern Ireland	48
9th	The demilitarisation of Northern Ireland	24	The demilitarisation of Northern Ireland	46
10th	North/South bodies	21	Decommissioning of paramilitary weapons	42
11th	The British/Irish Council	20	The British/Irish Council	40
12th	The reform of the justice system	19	The Commission for Victims	39
13th	Changes to British constitutional law	19	Changes to British constitutional law	38
14th	The reform of the police service	15	The early release of prisoners	37
15th	The early release of prisoners	14	Changes to the Irish Constitution	27

more interest in the departments of 'Agriculture and rural development' and 'Environment' than their counterparts in the UUP, SDLP and Sinn Féin, while the Sinn Féin electorate expressed the most interest in the department of 'Culture, arts and leisure'.

In the New Northern Ireland Assembly the Office of the First Minister and Deputy First Minister will have special responsibility for equality. But some parties wanted a separate ministry to deal with this issue. With this point in mind everyone interviewed for this poll was asked if they thought it would be better if the New Northern Ireland Assembly had a separate 'Department of equality'? Sixty-two per cent said 'Yes' ranging from a high of 78 per cent for Sinn Féin supporters to a low of 48 per cent for Alliance

Table 10.3   Support for new Northern Ireland departments

Per cent 'Very Important'	All of NI	DUP	UUP	SDLP	Sinn Féin
Agriculture and rural development	41	43	36	37	37
Environment	42	41	38	40	39
Regional development	44	42	36	44	40
Social development	44	40	37	47	42
Education	59	55	55	65	47
Higher and further education, training and Employment	59	54	56	62	48
Enterprise, trade and investment	52	47	49	52	51
Culture, arts and leisure	33	31	24	32	38
Health, social services and public safety	59	57	55	61	54
Finance and personal	43	39	40	42	41

Table 10.4   Support for a 'Department of Equality'

Per cent	All of NI	Protestant	Catholic	DUP	UUP	PUP	Alliance	SDLP	Sinn Féin
Yes	62	56	68	58	52	65	48	70	78
No	38	44	32	42	48	35	52	30	22

voters (Table 10.4). Perhaps they take the view that the establishment of such a department is potentially contentious.

The changing political landscape

'North/South bodies' is the tenth item on the Protestant list of priorities and again the joint second choice of Catholics. But attitudes seem to be changing. Only 13 per cent of Protestants considered them to be 'Of No Importance at all' (see *Belfast Telegraph*, 13 January 1998, 'Feasibility and reality of North–South bodies'). But it is now known what the North/South bodies will be and what powers they will have. Under the terms of the Belfast Agreement it has been decided that six implementation bodies will be established to manage projects in the North and South of Ireland (Table 10.5) as well as six additional areas for more general co-operation between the Republic and Northern Ireland (Table 10.6). Again people were asked how important they considered each one to be.

With just one exception a majority of Protestants considered all these new institutions of government to be 'Very Important' or 'Important' ranging from a high of 84 per cent for co-operation on 'Transport' to a low of

Table 10.5 Support for North/South implementation bodies: which jointly develop policies on matters of mutual benefit and implement them

Per cent 'Very Important or Important'	Protestant	Catholic
Inland waterways	58	71
Food safety	80	87
Trade and business development	78	87
Special EU programmes	70	85
Language (Irish and Ulster Scots)	36	72
Aquaculture and marine matters	54	71

Table 10.6 Support for North/South areas of co-operation: which jointly develop policies on matters of mutual benefit but with separate implementation

Per cent 'Very Important or Important'	Protestant	Catholic
Transport	84	85
Agriculture	80	85
Education	84	89
Health	84	90
Environment	81	85
Tourism	81	89

54 per cent for implementation of 'Aquaculture and marine matters'. A minority, only 36 per cent, thought the implementation body for Language (Irish and Ulster Scots) was 'Very Important' or 'Important'. Between 71 per cent and 90 per cent of Catholics thought all these bodies were 'Very Important' or 'Important'.

The SDLP and Sinn Féin would like these bodies to have more powers and responsibilities. With this point in mind people were asked to indicate which areas of general co-operation they thought should eventually become matters for implementation in both the North and the South (Table 10.7). Catholics said 'Yes' to every possibility ranging from a high of 83 per cent for 'Tourism' to a low of 66 per cent for 'Health'. Protestants were not nearly so enthusiastic about such developments, ranging from a high of 47 per cent for 'Tourism' to a low of 19 per cent for 'Education'. Given the importance the people of Northern Ireland place on the need to create new jobs perhaps 'Tourism' will eventually become a matter for both co-operation and implementation along with 'Trade and Business Development'.

But whatever the details of these statistics might be, one thing is clear. Protestant resistance to the establishment of North/South bodies as part of

Table 10.7 Support for further implementation North and South

Per cent 'Yes'	Protestant	Catholic
Transport	34	78
Agriculture	34	81
Education	19	69
Health	20	66
Environment	36	81
Tourism	47	83

the Belfast Agreement is no longer a serious problem. Indeed most Protestants think they are 'Very Important' or 'Important'. The political landscape of Northern Ireland has changed.

Ceasefires, paramilitary activity and decommissioning

The Belfast Agreement requires a 'commitment to non-violence and exclusively peaceful and democratic means' and for 'All participants ... to use any influence they have, to achieve the decommissioning of all paramilitary arms within two years ...'

The implementation of these parts of the Agreement can be undertaken in a number of different ways. In practice it means maintaining ceasefires, bringing paramilitary activities under control and decommissioning. Which is more important? And, more particularly, how do the Ulster Unionists, Progressive Unionists and Sinn Féin supporters regard these critical matters?

Generally speaking the people of Northern Ireland consider the ceasefires to be most important with 84 per cent saying the IRA's was 'Very Important' and 83 per cent for the UVF's (Table 10.8). Second came an end to paramilitary beatings and violence (79 per cent), recruiting and targeting (78 per cent) and all other paramilitary activities (80 per cent). The efforts of Sinn Féin 'to use any influence they have, to achieve the decommissioning of all paramilitary arms within two years' came next at 74 per cent and then the efforts of the PUP at 73 per cent followed closely by a start to IRA decommissioning at 72 per cent and UVF decommissioning at 71 per cent. Finally 64 per cent of those interviewed considered the LVF start to decommissioning to be 'Very Important'.

With the exception of the efforts of the LVF to decommission, the Ulster Unionists considered all of these issues to be almost equally important with an end to paramilitary beatings and violence at the top of their list at 88 per cent 'Very Important'. The Progressive Unionists ranked the IRA ceasefire as their first priority at 89 per cent 'Very Important' followed by a start to IRA decommissioning at 84 per cent which stood in contrast to LVF efforts to decommission at only 35 per cent. Sinn Féin supporters considered both ceasefires to be equally important (70 per cent 'Very Important')

Table 10.8 The importance of ceasefires, no paramilitary activity and decommissioning

Per cent 'Very Important'	All of NI	UUP	PUP	Sinn Féin
The maintenance of the IRA ceasefire	84	85	89	70
The maintenance of the UVF ceasefire	83	84	63	70
An end to all paramilitary beatings and violence	79	88	75	42
An end to all paramilitary recruiting and targeting	78	87	61	46
An end to all other paramilitary activity	80	86	55	53
The start or act of 'token' decommissioning undertaken by the LVF last year	64	69	35	39
A start or act of 'token' decommissioning by the IRA	72	84	86	35
A start or act of 'token' decommissioning by the UVF	71	82	35	38
For Sinn Féin 'to use any influence they have, to achieve the decommissioning of all paramilitary arms within two years'	74	83	85	39
For the PUP 'to use any influence they have, to achieve the decommissioning of all paramilitary arms within two years'	73	82	49	39

followed by an end to various paramilitary activity – between 42 per cent and 53 per cent 'Very Important'. For them the various aspects of decommissioning were least important – between 35 per cent and 39 per cent 'Very Important'.

For most of the people of Northern Ireland the decommissioning of paramilitary weapons is undoubtedly very important indeed. But not quite as important, it would seem, as the silence of their guns.

British security arrangements and policing

With regards to policing the Patten Commission is to make recommendations for the establishment of a new 'police service that can enjoy widespread support from, and is seen as an integral part of, the community as a whole'.

Catholics continue to put police reform at the top of their list of priorities (Table 10.9). When the question was asked again here 56 per cent still considered this provision of the Belfast Agreement to be 'Very Important'. This percentage dropped to 31 per cent for Alliance voters, 17 per cent for Ulster Unionists, 16 per cent for Protestants as a whole, 12 per cent for DUP supporters and 7 per cent for Progressive Unionists. The SDLP and Sinn Féin came in at 55 per cent and 56 per cent respectively.

'Consistent with the level of threat' the Belfast Agreement also requires the British government to deal with security arrangements in a number of different ways. They are:

- the reduction of the numbers and role of the Armed Forces deployed in Northern Ireland to levels compatible with a normal peaceful society;
- the removal of security installations;
- the removal of emergency powers in Northern Ireland; and
- other measures appropriate to and compatible with a normal peaceful society.

On average 64 per cent of Sinn Féin supporters considered this part of the Belfast Agreement to be 'Very Important' (Table 10.10). For Catholics as a whole it was 56 per cent again, 49 per cent for SDLP supporters, 22 per cent for Alliance, 12 per cent for Ulster Unionists, 10 per cent for the Democratic Unionists and 5 per cent for Progressive Unionists.

Perhaps the important point to be noted here, when it comes to dealing with the problem of decommissioning, is the fact that Sinn Féin supporters put the maintenance of the ceasefires at the top of their list at 70 per cent 'Very Important' followed by a rundown of British security arrangements at 64 per cent, then the policing question at 56 per cent followed by an end to paramilitary activities and finally decommissioning. With the exception of a need to maintain the ceasefires, this is not what Unionists want at all, but it is these realities that have to be confronted and dealt with – the separate priorities, concerns and fears of the two communities.

Table 10.9   Support for police reform as per cent 'Very Important'

Per cent	All of NI	Protestant	Catholic	DUP	UUP	PUP	Alliance	SDLP	Sinn Féin
V. Important	33	16	56	12	17	7	31	55	56

Table 10.10   Support for demilitarisation as per cent 'Very Important'

Per cent	All of NI	Protestant	Catholic	DUP	UUP	PUP	Alliance	SDLP	Sinn Féin
V. Important	30	11	56	10	12	5	22	49	64

Belfast Telegraph, Thursday 4 March 1999

Why the peace package is important

Today, the *Belfast Telegraph* publishes the second of a two-part opinion poll on the implementation of the Belfast Agreement. There is overwhelming support for a 'peace package'.

The Unionists want decommissioning before Sinn Féin enter the Executive and Sinn Féin insist that these new institutions of government be established first – including themselves. The SDLP want something in between. They want a compromise and they may get their way. In today's poll the major elements of a possible 'peace package' were tested against public opinion and 91 per cent of the people of Northern Ireland said 'Yes'.

In this question people were asked if they thought it would be a good idea for the parties who signed the Belfast Agreement to undertake a series of actions or 'steps', similar to those outlined here, in an effort to build confidence and trust between the two communities and move the peace process forward (Table 10.11).

Table 10.11   Support for a 'package' to move the peace process forward

Per cent	All of NI	Protestant	Catholic	DUP	UUP	PUP	Alliance	SDLP	Sinn Féin
Yes	91	87	96	79	91	59	97	97	92
No	9	13	4	21	9	41	3	3	8

From a high of 97 per cent for Alliance and SDLP voters support for the package by political party was 92 per cent for Sinn Féin, 91 per cent for the UUP, 79 per cent for the DUP and 59 per cent for the Progressive Unionists. Eighty-seven per cent of Protestants said 'Yes' as did 96 per cent of Catholics. Unlike decommissioning by itself – before, during or after setting up the Executive – the package tries to deal with the reasons why decommissioning is so important – either to be undertaken or delayed – it is designed to build confidence and trust.

What are the fears of failure?

Under the terms of the Belfast Agreement it has been agreed that an Executive will be established in the New Northern Ireland Assembly comprised of the First Minister, Deputy First Minister, three UUP Ministers, three SDLP Ministers, two DUP Ministers and two Sinn Féin Ministers.

This Executive is essential for the successful working of all the new institutions of government created under the terms of the Agreement. But what will happen if the Executive is not established or if Sinn Féin are excluded from it? On this point everyone interviewed was presented with a series of possible outcomes and asked to say which ones they considered to be 'Very Probable', 'Probable', 'Not Sure' about, 'Improbable' or 'Very Improbable' (Table 10.12).

What are the people's greatest fears if the peace process starts to unravel and who will blame whom for the failure? Seventy-four per cent of Protestants believe it is 'Very Probable' or 'Probable' that dissident Republican paramilitary groups will become more active and 69 per cent believe the IRA will go back to war because the Republicans will not work the Belfast Agreement in good faith. On the other hand 68 per cent of Catholics believe it is 'Very Probable' or 'Probable' that dissident Loyalist paramilitary groups will become more active because the Unionists will not work the Belfast Agreement in good faith.

Critically the supporters of the political parties associated with paramilitary organisations express these fears most strongly. Eighty-six per cent of Progressive Unionists believe Republicans will not work the Belfast Agreement in good faith and that the IRA will return to war while 83 per cent of Sinn Féin supporters believe Unionists will collapse the Agreement. In these circumstances a majority of the members of these two parties also believe that the British and Irish governments will impose the terms of the Belfast Agreement through Joint Authority. Ulster Unionists are not nearly so fearful of these potential outcomes. Are they right or wrong? Would it be better

Table 10.12   If the Executive is not established or if Sinn Féin are excluded ...

Per cent 'Very Probable or Probable'	Protestant	Catholic	UUP	PUP	Sinn Féin
The Belfast Agreement and peace process will collapse because Unionists will not work the Agreement in good faith	35	60	23	34	83
The Belfast Agreement and peace process will collapse because Republicans will not work the Agreement in good faith	59	40	49	86	44
Dissident Republican paramilitary groups will become more active	74	63	69	89	72
The IRA and other Republican groups will break their ceasefires and return to war	69	41	66	86	39
Dissident Loyalist paramilitary groups will become more active	68	68	65	34	81
The UVF and other Loyalist groups will break their ceasefires and return to war	58	49	57	20	61
The British and Irish governments will impose the terms of the Belfast Agreement through Joint Authority	50	47	41	64	62

to exclude Sinn Féin from the Executive in the absence of prior decommissioning or try and deal with the very real concerns of the two communities in some other way in the hope that decommissioning will follow?

Implementation of the Belfast Agreement

Towards the end of the interview people were asked to consider various options for making progress with the implementation of the Belfast Agreement by indicating which ones they considered to be 'Essential', 'Desirable', 'Acceptable', 'Tolerable' or 'Unacceptable' as part of a successful peace process (Table 10.13). It is not possible to publish all the results here (they will be sent to all the political parties in the New Assembly). But if 'Unacceptable' is considered to be a strong 'No' and 'Essential', 'Desirable', 'Acceptable' or 'Tolerable' to be a strong to weak 'Yes' then it won't be too difficult to find a way through these statistics.

Table 10.13 Support for options to implement the Belfast Agreement

Per cent 'No' and Per cent 'Yes'	Protestant	Catholic	UUP	PUP	Sinn Féin
OPTION 1 – The Executive of the New Northern Ireland Assembly should be established, including Sinn Féin, without any preconditions and without any further delay	54 No 46 Yes	5 No 95 Yes	58 No 42 Yes	62 No 38 Yes	5 No 95 Yes
OPTION 2 – The Executive of the New Northern Ireland Assembly should be established, including Sinn Féin, and the problem of establishing a credible decommissioning process should be dealt with by General de Chastelain and his International Commission	34 No 66 Yes	1 No 99 Yes	31 No 69 Yes	43 No 57 Yes	2 No 98 Yes
OPTION 3 – The Executive of the New Northern Ireland Assembly should be established, including Sinn Féin, but they should not be allowed to stay in government if the IRA do not decommission within the two years allowed for in the Belfast Agreement	23 No 77 Yes	28 No 72 Yes	19 No 81 Yes	32 No 68 Yes	52 No 48 Yes
OPTION 4 – Republicans should co-operate with the RUC with a view to bringing an end to all paramilitary beatings and violence	3 No 97 Yes	19 No 81 Yes	3 No 97 Yes	3 No 97 Yes	47 No 53 Yes

Table 10.13   Continued

Per cent 'No' and Per cent 'Yes'	Protestant	Catholic	UUP	PUP	Sinn Féin
OPTION 5 – Loyalists should co-operate with the RUC with a view to bringing an end to all paramilitary beatings and violence	3 No 97 Yes	10 No 90 Yes	3 No 97 Yes	4 No 96 Yes	29 No 71 Yes
OPTION 6 – Everyone should co-operate with a new agreed police service with a view to bringing an end to all paramilitary beatings and violence	9 No 91 Yes	3 No 97 Yes	10 No 90 Yes	5 No 95 Yes	9 No 91 Yes
OPTION 7 – The Belfast Agreement signed and accepted by the two governments, parties at the Stormont talks and people of Ireland North and South should be fully implemented without any further delay	30 No 70 Yes	0 No 100 Yes	25 No 75 Yes	63 No 37 Yes	2 No 98 Yes
OPTION 8 – Contrary to the terms of the Belfast Agreement – which does not link decommissioning to the early release of paramilitary prisoners – no more prisoners should be released until their organisations have made a start on decommissioning	7 No 93 Yes	33 No 67 Yes	5 No 95 Yes	25 No 75 Yes	59 No 41 Yes

Option 1 – Allowing Sinn Féin into the Executive without any preconditions should be acceptable under a strict reading of the Belfast Agreement.
But 54 per cent of Protestants are strongly opposed to this option rising to
58 per cent for the UUP and 62 per cent for the PUP. Although 95 per cent
of Catholics support this option it seems to be politically problematic by
itself. Something more is needed.

Option 2 – The foundation for a successful solution to the decommissioning problem may well be this option and have General de Chastelain establish a credible decommissioning process. Only 31 per cent of Ulster
Unionists oppose this option which is acceptable to 98 per cent of Sinn
Féin supporters.

Option 3 – A proposal to have Sinn Féin removed from the Executive if
they do not decommission within two years is even more acceptable to
Ulster Unionists. Only 19 per cent said No. But this time 52 per cent of
Sinn Féin supporters also said No so this option, which some would argue
is in breach of the Belfast Agreement, and would create political problems

for them. If Sinn Féin can handle this difficulty, all well and good, if not it might be possible to bring some other options into play.

Options 4, 5 and 6 – With regards to policing, Republicans clearly have a problem co-operating with the RUC, 47 per cent said No. Loyalists do not seem to share this difficulty but a significant majority from all political groups are willing to have everyone co-operate with 'a new agreed police service'. This option is undoubtedly a critical part of the peace process but its value is more long term and must be seen that way.

Option 7 – All Catholics want full implementation of the Belfast Agreement now but 30 per cent of Protestants are more reticent. Perhaps other steps can be taken to help change their minds.

Option 8 – Finally, 93 per cent of Protestants and 67 per cent of Catholics would like prisoner releases stopped until a start is made on decommissioning. Twenty-five per cent of Progressive Unionists and 59 per cent of Sinn Féin supporters are opposed to this option which is a clear breach of the Belfast Agreement.

Failure to implement the Belfast Agreement is in large part due to a lack of trust and confidence between Unionists, Loyalists, Nationalists and Republicans. In an effort to overcome this problem the parties who signed the Belfast Agreement could take a number of different actions or 'steps' (Table 10.14). Again people were asked to indicate which ones they considered to be 'Essential', 'Desirable', 'Acceptable', 'Tolerable' or 'Unacceptable' and the results have similarly been recorded here in terms of 'Yes' and 'No' responses.

Step 1 – Everyone, except the Progressive Unionists, thought it would be a good idea for Loyalist paramilitaries to repeat their apology – 76 per cent of them said No.

Step 2 – Only 41 per cent of Ulster Unionists objected to Mr Trimble apologising for past discriminations against Catholics. Eighty-five per cent of Catholics thought this was a good idea.

Step 3 – Everyone wanted the IRA to make their apologies known including 87 per cent of Sinn Féin voters and 96 per cent of Progressive Unionists. Clearly they think it is time their own apology was reciprocated.

Step 4 – Protestants were split on the idea of having the British prime minister apologise for the tragedies of British involvement in Irish affairs. But 86 per cent of Catholics thought it was a good idea.

Step 5 – Most Catholics, 77 per cent, and Protestants, 73 per cent, also thought the Taoiseach should apologise for the religious intolerance to be found in his own state. Progressive Unionists were most enthusiastic on this point, 88 per cent said Yes, but then again 83 per cent of them did not want the British prime minister to make his apology!

Table 10.14   Support for 'steps' to move the peace process forward

Per cent 'No' and Per cent 'Yes'	Protestant	Catholic	UUP	PUP	Sinn Féin
STEP 1 – Loyalist paramilitary organisations should repeat their apology for the past harms they have done to the Catholic community	22 No 78 Yes	13 No 87 Yes	27 No 73 Yes	76 No 24 Yes	13 No 87 Yes
STEP 2 – Mr Trimble, for the Unionists, should apologise to the Catholic community for the past discriminations they have been subjected to	43 No 57 Yes	15 No 85 Yes	41 No 59 Yes	78 No 22 Yes	14 No 86 Yes
STEP 3 – The IRA should apologise for the past harms they have done to the Protestant community	10 No 90 Yes	15 No 85 Yes	18 No 82 Yes	4 No 96 Yes	13 No 87 Yes
STEP 4 – The British prime minister should apologise to the Irish people for the tragedies of British involvement in Irish affairs	48 No 52 Yes	14 No 86 Yes	44 No 56 Yes	83 No 17 Yes	15 No 85 Yes
STEP 5 – The Taoiseach should apologise for the past religious intolerance permitted by the Irish state towards their Protestant community	27 No 73 Yes	23 No 77 Yes	23 No 77 Yes	12 No 88 Yes	28 No 72 Yes
STEP 6 – The UVF should repeat their promise never to use their weapons in a 'first strike'	4 No 96 Yes	5 No 95 Yes	2 No 98 Yes	29 No 71 Yes	10 No 90 Yes
STEP 7 – Mr Trimble, for the Unionists, should promise to work all the new institutions of government in good faith with Sinn Féin	22 No 78 Yes	5 No 95 Yes	16 No 84 Yes	43 No 57 Yes	3 No 97 Yes
STEP 8 – The IRA should promise never to use their weapons in a 'first strike'	1 No 99 Yes	2 No 98 Yes	1 No 99 Yes	2 No 98 Yes	4 No 96 Yes
STEP 9 – All the new institutions of government should be established, including Sinn Féin	27 No 73 Yes	3 No 97 Yes	22 No 78 Yes	48 No 52 Yes	2 No 98 Yes
STEP 10 – The UVF should make a start on decommissioning	2 No 98 Yes	3 No 97 Yes	1 No 99 Yes	49 No 51 Yes	9 No 91 Yes
STEP 11 – The IRA should make a start on decommissioning	1 No 99 Yes	6 No 94 Yes	1 No 99 Yes	1 No 99 Yes	16 No 84 Yes

Step 6 – Everyone wanted the UVF to repeat their promise never to use their weapons in a 'first strike'. Even 71 per cent of PUP supporters could accept this option.

Step 7 – Everyone also thought it would be a good idea for Mr Trimble to promise to work in government in good faith with Sinn Féin. Only 16 per cent of Ulster Unionists said No.

Step 8 – The most positively received option was for the IRA to promise never to use their weapons in a 'first strike'. Only 4 per cent of Sinn Féin supporters objected to this proposal. A much welcome development.

Step 9 – This time, and we have not quite got to decommissioning yet, only 22 per cent of Ulster Unionists objected to a government being formed that included Sinn Féin. Apologies and promises, it would seem, do count for something.

Step 10 – The UVF should make a start on decommissioning. Everyone thought this was a very good idea except for PUP supporters who were evenly split on the issue.

Step 11 – Finally, the IRA should make a start on decommissioning. Again this option was widely welcome although 16 per cent of Sinn Féin voters said No. Perhaps, in time, many of them can be won over.

If all the options and steps that are acceptable are put together as a package then 91 per cent of the people of Northern Ireland will support a decision to implement it as part of a strengthened peace process that has the potential to deliver decommissioning. Of course the precise wording, timing and sequencing need to be worked out. But 93 per cent of the people of Northern Ireland also want the Belfast Agreement to work. They want – and therefore might reasonably expect – their political leaders to sort this problem out.

* * *

Sinn Féin, the Ulster Unionists and the Secretary of State for Northern Ireland all invited each other to talks within days of the poll being published and although they had plenty to talk about they did not, unfortunately, 'sort this problem out'. The Hillsborough Declaration, published by the British and Irish Governments on 1 April 1999, required for some arms to be 'put beyond use' at the same time as powers were devolved to the Executive, not, as indicated in the poll, *after* the Executive was established. The proposals of the two governments were therefore, not surprisingly, rejected by Sinn Féin and consequently also by the Loyalists. Unionists, for their part, would not accept anything less. A lack of trust was threatening to bring the whole peace process down so following some suggestions put forward by the *Belfast Telegraph* on 12 May I added my own views to the debate.

Belfast Telegraph, Wednesday 17 May 1999

A better way to implement the Belfast Agreement

The proposal put forward by the *Belfast Telegraph* on 12 May for the progressive devolution of powers to Northern Ireland may be much more than simply a way of 'breaking the deadlock'. It may be a better way of implementing the Belfast Agreement.

The original plan for implementation envisaged the setting up of a shadow Executive prior to devolution. Given the months of negotiations with Sinn Féin and the Ulster Unionists only addressing each other through the chair this period of time set aside for developing normal working relationships was essential. Unfortunately this process never started to happen until the most recent round of negotiations got under way in March.

But the two governments and Northern Ireland civil service also have to make adjustments. The Belfast Agreement is far more complex than the simple devolution of powers to Scotland or Wales. Everyone needs a period of time to test relationships, build confidence and establish trust.

Canada is the expert at this kind of nation-building and we could learn much from her example. When I first went to the Arctic the Northwest Territories were administered by a Commissioner in Ottawa. He moved his offices to Yellowknife in the Northwest Territories in the 1970s and then set up an elected Assembly to advise his various departments. These departments were eventually replaced by ministries with powers to make and implement policy. However, the Commissioner could still overrule them if he thought it necessary. Finally, when this veto is removed a territory becomes a province.

Some very able and talented politicians have been elected to the New Northern Ireland Assembly. But they are not superhuman. A period of learning to work all the new institutions of government is needed.

This point will not be lost on General John de Chastelain, the Canadian chairman of the Independent International Commission on Decommissioning. He wants to get his job done but that requires building trust and confidence between Unionists and Republicans which in turn requires the development of new political relationships. Not an easy task. But he also knows that transforming a territory into a province cannot be done with the simple stroke of a pen. It requires slow careful nation-building.

I recall a member of Sinn Féin once remarking to me that the Progressive Unionists were lucky because they didn't have seats on the Executive so they weren't under the same pressure to decommission. When he said this he may have noticed a slight smile cross my face because I then remembered an Inuk in the Canadian Arctic once telling me that he wished his land did not have any oil and gas because then the white man would leave him alone. That Inuk is now a minister in his own territorial government. It took years to establish that government. People need time.

Decommissioning is the number one priority for Protestants. For Catholics it is police reform. Time can help to sort out that problem too. In the poll published in the *Belfast Telegraph* on 4 March only 9 per cent of Protestants considered it unacceptable for everyone to co-operate with a 'new agreed police service' with a view to bringing an end to all paramilitary beatings and violence. If Sinn Féin and the Unionists can co-operate in this enterprise then the problem of police reform can be resolved.

Any attempt to renegotiate the terms of the Belfast Agreement would inevitably fail. Once broken the pieces could not be put back together again. But if one thing and one thing only could be changed, the pace of change itself, then much might be accomplished that has so far proven impossible.

The peace process needs careful management. In combination with suitable statements from Loyalists, Republicans and General John de Chastelain the two governments should now get all the new institutions up and running, devolving powers as circumstances allow.

11
The Mitchell Review

The Hillsborough proposals for a simultaneous act of decommissioning and the devolution of powers to a new inclusive government in Northern Ireland were not acceptable to Republicans because it carried with it an implication of precondition and therefore surrender. It also followed that if Republicans would not accept the deal and decommission, Loyalists would not either. The proposals for a more managed and gradual approach to implementation proposed by the *Belfast Telegraph*, myself and others were also not acceptable to Republicans and Nationalists because they simply did not trust Unionists and the British government to see such a pro-gramme of implementation through to a conclusion once started. So a new proposal was published by the two governments on 2 July 1999 in their 'Way Forward Statement' that allowed for the establishment of all of the new institutions of government without any preconditions but that these arrangements would be suspended if decommissioning did not start within a set period of time. This was essentially the solution tested against public opinion in the previous poll undertaken with the PUP and Sinn Féin but with the addition of a 'failsafe' clause. Unfortunately, even with this built-in guarantee, these new proposals were not acceptable to the Ulster Unionists. The two governments could delay no longer. On 15 July, when powers were eventually devolved to the New Northern Ireland Assembly the Ulster Unionist Party boycotted the formation of the Executive, the Deputy First Minister, Seamus Mallon, felt it necessary to resign and the Belfast Agreement was plunged into a formal review.

The peace process had now been brought to a grinding halt but Senator George Mitchell agreed to be the facilitator for the review providing it was limited to resolving what had now become known as the 'government and guns' problem. Within these parameters Sinn Féin were also willing to undertake another poll with the participation of all the pro-agreement parties providing no preconditions were attached to the formation of the Executive. The Ulster Unionists also agreed to participate providing that there were such preconditions! Reconciling these two apparently irreconcilable demands proved to be the most difficult of all the negotiations that had to be undertaken as part of the preparations for one of the peace polls. The details of this process will not be repeated again here; it was described in Chapter 4, 'The Drafting of Consensus and the Decommissioning Story', with all the relevant notes to the parties.

The work for the Mitchell Review poll started in August 1999, the formal review began on 6 September, the public opinion poll survey interviews were conducted between 8–15 October and the results were to be published in the *Belfast Telegraph* on 26–27 October 1999. But the outcome of the negotiations proper seemed to have been more in the balance on this occasion than they ever had been in the past. Fearing the collapse of the review, which it was hoped would not take more than a month, some of the members of the negotiating teams asked me to write to all the pro-agreement parties outlining the major results of the poll before they were published. This was done on 22 October as follows:

The 'Yes Parties'
See attached list for 'contacts'

The Mitchell Review

Embargo Wednesday 27 October 12 Noon

Dear...

This is just a short note to let you know that I now have the computer print out results of our poll in and will be writing up the stories over the next few days for delivery to the *Belfast Telegraph* at 9 a.m. on Monday morning. Publication will take place over two days, Tuesday the 26th and Wednesday the 27th.

The results are stronger than I expected and some parties, who have taken a keen interest in them, have also taken the view that sharing the main features of the results with you at this time could be helpful to the peace process. The principal conclusions that can be drawn are as follows:

1. Although Protestant support for the Agreement has slipped a bit from the Referendum result of 22 May 1998 (as many polls have shown) support is still strong, particularly for 'Making the Agreement Work'. Support is holding up and any shift to 'No' is a protest vote.

2. Fears about what will happen if the Review fails are now much stronger than they were when these issues were addressed in the Sinn Féin/PUP poll of last March. People want the Review to succeed as much as they want the Agreement to work.

3. Support for the de Chastelain programme, setting up the Executive, and our equivalents of the Hillsborough and Way Forward proposals have all strengthened. In particular *both* Sinn Féin and UUP resistance to these kinds of proposals has diminished since the March poll. The fear of failure seems to be having an effect across both communities.

4. All the other results are as might be expected with regards to a lack of trust between Sinn Féin and the UUP, for example, and general support for the 'Confidence Building Measures' with some degree of community and political variation. Predictably support for Joint Authority, Direct Rule and the like do not receive cross-community support which leaves only the Belfast Agreement – one way or another.

I have not quite decided how I will end my stories for the 'Tele' but I am sure that given the strength of these results the people of Northern Ireland will be very pleased to support almost any solution you can come up with to make the Review a success.

Your reports should be ready early next week and I will get them to you as soon as I have completed my work with the *Belfast Telegraph*. See you next week and good luck.

Best wishes,
Dr Colin Irwin.

As with the previous 'Implementation of the Belfast Agreement' poll, undertaken with Sinn Féin and the PUP, this new poll also dealt with a number of contextual issues relating to how the people of Northern Ireland felt about the peace process. It also contained an extended series of confidence-building measures (CBMs) that the pro-agreement parties and two governments could implement in an effort to put the political failures of the previous summer behind them. The results of the two polls were not all that different. Significantly, however, the people of Northern Ireland were now more concerned about the prospects of failure, all the pro-agreement parties were involved in the peace polls process so they all took the results seriously and Senator Mitchell, as an independent facilitator, was at hand to assist the parties and two governments achieve a positive conclusion to their deliberations. This was done a couple of weeks later on 15 November 1999.

Belfast Telegraph, Tuesday 26 October 1999

Guns, trust and the Agreement

EXCLUSIVE, today the *Belfast Telegraph* publishes the first of a two-part Queen's University/Rowntree Trust opinion poll on the crisis ridden peace process.

The state of the peace process

In the referendum of 22 May 1998 the people of Ireland, North and South, agreed on how they should live together on the island of Ireland in partnership with the peoples of the British Isles. Eighteen months later the implementation of that Agreement continues to move from one crisis to the next with no guarantee of success clearly in view.

The people of Northern Ireland who voted for the Agreement could not be blamed for losing all hope. Remarkably they have not done so. On the contrary, if the Agreement could be made to work many people who voted against it would be persuaded to give it their support. But dashed hopes, false expectations, distrust and fear of failure have all combined to unsettle the implementation of the Belfast Agreement and very nearly destroy it.

Support for the Belfast Agreement

In last year's referendum 71 per cent of the people of Northern Ireland voted Yes for the Belfast Agreement. In the poll 74 per cent said they voted Yes which is just inside the 'margin of error' for this kind of research (Table 11.1). However, when asked how they would vote if the referendum was held today support dropped to 65 per cent Yes (Table 11.2). There was almost no change in the Catholic vote from 89 per cent Yes down to 88 per cent but the Protestant vote fell from 64 per cent to 49 per cent ranging from a current low of 31 per cent for DUP supporters to a high of 56 per cent for the UUP electorate.

Table 11.1 How did you vote in the referendum for the Belfast Agreement?

Per cent	All of NI	Protestant	Catholic	DUP	UUP	PUP	Alliance	SDLP	Sinn Féin
Yes	74	64	89	32	82	85	90	96	89
No	26	36	11	68	18	15	10	4	11

Table 11.2 And if the referendum was held today how would you vote?

Per cent	All of NI	Protestant	Catholic	DUP	UUP	PUP	Alliance	SDLP	Sinn Féin
Yes	65	49	88	31	56	56	79	95	90
No	35	51	12	69	44	44	21	5	10

But when people are asked 'Do you want the Belfast Agreement to work?' 83 per cent said Yes (Table 11.3) down from 93 per cent when this same question was asked last March before the political failures of the Hillsborough and Way Forward proposals (Table 11.4). Catholic support is holding up, rising from 97 per cent to 98 per cent while Protestant support has fallen from 89 per cent to 72 per cent. DUP support is now split 50/50, it was 73 per cent. But UUP support has only fallen from 94 per cent to 87 per cent. Mr Trimble's voters still want the Agreement to work so most of the shift to 'No' must be seen as a protest vote – a 'midterm' expression of frustration with the implementation of the Belfast Agreement.

Table 11.3   Do you want the Belfast Agreement to work? – October 1999

Per cent	All of NI	Protestant	Catholic	DUP	UUP	PUP	Alliance	SDLP	Sinn Féin
Yes	83	72	98	50	87	91	98	98	97
No	17	28	2	50	13	9	2	2	3

Table 11.4   Do you want the Belfast Agreement to work? – March 1999

Per cent	All of NI	Protestant	Catholic	DUP	UUP	PUP	Alliance	SDLP	Sinn Féin
Yes	93	89	97	73	94	84	98	98	96
No	7	11	3	27	6	16	2	2	4

When it comes to apportioning blame for the political failures of the summer 73 per cent of the people of Northern Ireland thought the political parties were not doing enough, ranging from a high of 89 per cent for Sinn Féin voters to 74 per cent for the SDLP and Alliance, 73 per cent UUP, 70 per cent PUP and 64 per cent DUP (Table 11.5). Similarly 56 per cent of the people of Northern Ireland did not think the two governments were doing enough, ranging from a high of 69 per cent for Sinn Féin and DUP voters down to 55 per cent for the UUP, 54 per cent PUP, 47 per cent Alliance and 40 per cent SDLP (Table 11.6). Everyone, it would seem, should be trying harder.

Table 11.5   Do you think the political parties are doing enough to implement the Belfast Agreement?

Per cent	All of NI	Protestant	Catholic	DUP	UUP	PUP	Alliance	SDLP	Sinn Féin
Yes	27	26	26	36	27	30	26	26	11
No	73	74	74	64	73	70	74	74	89

Table 11.6   Do you think the two governments are doing enough to implement the Belfast Agreement?

Per cent	All of NI	Protestant	Catholic	DUP	UUP	PUP	Alliance	SDLP	Sinn Féin
Yes	44	39	52	31	45	46	53	60	31
No	56	61	48	69	55	54	47	40	69

Dashed hopes

Although 83 per cent of the people of Northern Ireland still want the Agreement to work it is important to remember that the Agreement makes many compromises and contains elements that have been included for one community or the other in the hope that the overall package might eventually lead to peace. In today's poll people were asked how important they thought each part of the Agreement was and how satisfied they were with its implementation (Table 11.7).

As with polls published in the *Belfast Telegraph* on Saturday, 10 January 1998 and Wednesday, 3 March 1999 decommissioning is still the number one priority for Protestants – it is the 12th priority for Catholics. But reform of the RUC has slipped to number two for Catholics topped now by 'Commitments to non-violence, peace and democracy'. Significantly this element of the Agreement comes in at number two for Protestants.

The clear conclusion to be drawn from this result is that if the persistent focus on the issue of decommissioning were shifted to give more emphasis to the 'Mitchell Principles of Democracy and Non-violence' then perhaps a consensus might more easily be attainable where there is presently only disagreement.

'Support for victims of the Troubles' is the third priority for both Catholics and Protestants followed by the new Human Rights Commission, the Assembly and Executive for Catholics and the Principle of Consent and present status of Northern Ireland as part of the UK for Protestants.

Levels of satisfaction with the implementation of the Agreement are not good. Both Protestants and Catholics are most disappointed with the lack of progress on decommissioning at 88 per cent and 63 per cent respectively. Catholics are then least satisfied with the reform of the RUC with 61 per cent saying they are 'Not satisfied' or 'Not satisfied at all'. For obviously very different reasons Protestants are even more dissatisfied with progress on RUC reform with 69 per cent saying they are 'Not satisfied' or 'Not satisfied at all'. Clearly the implementation of the Belfast Agreement is going to be subject to many difficulties and disappointments over the coming years until such time as the parties can learn to better appreciate and understand the priorities and concerns of the 'other' community. The new Secretary of State, Peter Mandelson, does not have an easy task ahead of him.

False expectations

At the heart of the failure to get an Executive up and running is a very different set of expectations about decommissioning (Table 11.8). Although 90 per cent of Ulster Unionists and 86 per cent of Sinn Féin voters believe the Belfast Agreement requires *'All parties to co-operate with the Independent Commission and use any influence they may have to achieve the decommissioning of all paramilitary arms by May 2000 in the context of the implementation of the overall settlement'*, it is right there that the similarity ends. Eighty

Table 11.7 Importance of and satisfaction with the Belfast Agreement

	Protestant per cent	Very Important	Not* satisfied		Catholic per cent	Very Important	Not* satisfied
1	Decommissioning of paramilitary weapons	60	88	1	Commitments to non-violence, peace and democracy	50	52
2	Commitments to non-violence, peace and democracy	54	74	2	The reform of the RUC	45	61
3	Support for victims of the 'Troubles'	49	74	3	Support for victims of the 'Troubles'	43	48
4	The Principle of Consent of the people of Northern Ireland to decide their status	45	53	4	The new Human Rights Commission	42	45
5	The present status of Northern Ireland as part of the UK	44	43	5	The New Northern Ireland Assembly	41	49
6	Demilitarisation – Security arrangements compatible with a normal peaceful society	38	66	6	The Northern Ireland Executive	40	57
7	The full implementation of all parts of the Agreement together	30	63	7	Cultural and language rights	40	50
8	The New Northern Ireland Assembly	30	54	8	The reform of the criminal justice system	39	56
9	Changes to Articles 2 and 3 of the Irish Constitution	29	62	9	The full implementation of all parts of the Agreement together	39	56
10	The Northern Ireland Executive	28	58	10	The Equality Commission	39	45
11	The reform of the criminal justice system	25	65	11	Demilitarisation–Security arrangements compatible with a normal peaceful society	38	59
12	A Bill of Rights for Northern Ireland	24	50	12	Decommissioning of paramilitary weapons	36	63

13	The new Human Rights Commission	21	47
14	The reform of the RUC	19	69
15	The Equality Commission	19	47
16	Changes to British constitutional law	18	52
17	The early release of prisoners	17	80
18	The Civic Forum	15	52
19	North/South implementation bodies	13	56
20	The British/Irish Council	13	55
21	The North/South Ministerial Council	13	52
22	Cultural and language rights	13	50

13	North/South implementation bodies	36	49
14	A Bill of Rights for Northern Ireland	34	52
15	The North/South Ministerial Council	34	48
16	The Principle of Consent of the people of Northern Ireland to decide their status	33	40
17	The British/Irish Council	26	49
18	The early release of prisoners	26	41
19	The Civic Forum	23	47
20	Changes to British constitutional law	17	49
21	Changes to Articles 2 and 3 of the Irish Constitution	13	42
22	The present status of Northern Ireland as part of the UK	13	42

* 'Not satisfied' or 'Not satisfied at all'.

Table 11.8   Do you believe the Belfast Agreement requires...?

Per cent who said 'Yes'	UUP	Sinn Féin
All parties to co-operate with the Independent Commission and use any influence they may have to achieve the decommissioning of all paramilitary arms by May 2000 in the context of the implementation of the overall settlement	90	86
No Executive including Sinn Féin without an end to all IRA violence and intimidation	80	28
No Executive including Sinn Féin without a simultaneous start on decommissioning by the IRA	80	ᶜ 28
No Executive including Sinn Féin without a guarantee that IRA decommissioning will be completed by May 2000	78	34

Table 11.9   Do you believe IRA decommissioning can be completed without...?

Per cent who said 'Yes'	UUP	Sinn Féin
Sinn Féin in the Executive	18	3
An end to Loyalist violence	18	15
Implementation of the Patten Report on police reform	45	20
Full implementation of all of the other parts of the Belfast Agreement	43	28

per cent of Ulster Unionists also believe that there should be 'No Executive' without an end to IRA violence and a start on decommissioning. However only 28 per cent of Sinn Féin voters share this view.

But in a different question only 3 per cent of Sinn Féin voters and 18 per cent of Ulster Unionists said they believed decommissioning can be completed without Sinn Féin being in the Executive (Table 11.9). So a clear majority of both Ulster Unionists and Sinn Féin supporters believe the formation of an inclusive Executive is a necessary part of the decommissioning process. Perhaps that, at least, is something that can be built upon in the search for a resolution of this problem.

A lack of trust

It might be convenient to think that places like Northern Ireland can be governed without trust. But some trust, just a little, is probably a necessary part of doing business and running a government.

In the poll, people were asked to indicate which of the governments and parties who agreed to the terms of the Belfast Agreement they: 'Trust a lot', 'Trust a little', are 'Not sure about', 'Do not trust' or 'Do not trust at all' (Table 11.10).

Table 11.10 Who people trust

Per cent 'Trust a lot' or 'Trust a little'	Protestant	Catholic	UUP	Sinn Féin
The British government	48	48	56	25
The Irish government	35	48	38	55
The Ulster Unionist Party	60	29	72	10
The Progressive Unionist Party	49	27	48	25
The Ulster Democratic Party	51	14	41	10
The Alliance Party	40	46	41	26
The Women's Coalition	30	55	35	39
The SDLP	30	77	36	71
Sinn Féin	5	51	5	99

Ninety-nine per cent of Sinn Féin supporters said they trust their party but only 10 per cent of them trust the Ulster Unionist Party 'a lot' or 'a little'. Conversely 72 per cent of Ulster Unionists trust their party but only 5 per cent of them trust Sinn Féin 'a lot' or 'a little'. This amount of trust just may not be quite enough. This is something that probably has to be worked on. The peace process needs time – what Americans call 'quality time' – as demonstrated by the progress made in the Ambassador's residence this past week.

The fear of failure

The Executive is an essential part of the workings of all the new institutions of government created under the terms of the Belfast Agreement. From a range of possibilities everyone interviewed for the poll was asked what they thought would happen if the Executive is not established or if Sinn Féin are excluded from it. Specifically what options did they consider to be 'Very probable', 'Probable', 'Not sure' about, 'Improbable' or 'Very improbable' (Table 11.11).

The results tell a depressing story. More than 70 per cent of the people of Northern Ireland, across both communities and the different political parties, believe the economy will suffer, community relations will deteriorate and more young people will leave the Province. Similarly the dangers of increased paramilitary activity remain central to people's fears. But the picture is a little more complex here. While 85 per cent of Protestants believe Republican paramilitaries will become more active, only 43 per cent of Catholics share this view, and while 73 per cent of Protestants believe Loyalist paramilitaries will become more active, 67 per cent of Catholics would agree. Catholics, particularly Sinn Féin supporters, seem to have more confidence in the IRA ceasefire. Only 27 per cent of them think it will be broken. But that is still 27 per cent too much.

When these questions were asked last March Ulster Unionists were not nearly so concerned about these affairs (Table 11.12). At that time only

Table 11.11   If the Executive is not established or if Sinn Féin are excluded …

Per cent 'Very Probable' or 'Probable'	All of NI	Protestant	Catholic	UUP	Sinn Féin
The Belfast Agreement and peace process will collapse because Unionists will not work the Agreement in good faith	62	55	73	59	88
The Belfast Agreement and peace process will collapse because Republicans will not work the Agreement in good faith	67	72	45	78	19
The Belfast Agreement and peace process will collapse because the SDLP and UUP will not work together to implement it	44	52	33	56	27
The Belfast Agreement and peace process will collapse because of the lack of co-operation and determined commitment by the two governments	47	55	36	50	50
Dissident Republican paramilitary groups will become more active	72	85	43	85	40
The IRA and other Republican groups will break their ceasefires and return to war	66	82	43	84	27
Dissident Loyalist paramilitary groups will become more active	70	73	67	79	76
The UVF, UFF and other Loyalist groups will break their ceasefires and return to war	61	66	52	71	64
The Northern Ireland economy will suffer and unemployment will rise	71	82	72	75	76
More young people will leave Northern Ireland	71	69	76	73	76
Divisions in Northern Ireland society will deepen and community relations will continue to deteriorate	72	73	73	77	75

23 per cent of them thought Unionists would not work the Agreement and collapse the peace process. Now 59 per cent of them take this view. Similarly 78 per cent of UUP voters now think Republicans will bring the peace process down, up from 49 per cent in March. And 84 per cent of Ulster Unionist supporters believe the IRA will return to war, up from 66 per cent in March.

As for Sinn Féin voters 88 per cent of them would now blame Unionists for the failure of the peace process, up from 83 per cent in March. But only 19 per cent of Sinn Féin supporters would blame Republicans for such a failure, down from 44 per cent in March. The Sinn Féin electorate, it would seem, believe their party did the best that they could this past summer to move the peace process forward. Their concerns about dissident Republican paramilitaries returning to violence are also down from 72 per cent in

Table 11.12   Increases in the 'fear of failure'

Per cent 'Very Probable' or 'Probable'	UUP March	UUP October	Sinn Féin March	Sinn Féin October
The Belfast Agreement and peace process will collapse because Unionists will not work the Agreement in good faith	23	59	83	88
The Belfast Agreement and peace process will collapse because Republicans will not work the Agreement in good faith	49	78	44	19
Dissident Republican paramilitary groups will become more active	69	85	72	40
The IRA and other Republican groups will break their ceasefires and return to war	66	84	39	27
Dissident Loyalist paramilitary groups will become more active	65	79	81	76
The UVF, UFF and other Loyalist groups will break their ceasefires and return to war	57	71	61	64

March to 40 per cent now. But, of course, another Omagh bomb could change all that in literally seconds.

Belfast Telegraph, Wednesday 27 October 1999

Breaking the rock

Senator Mitchell has likened the problem of decommissioning to a rock that must be broken or the peace process will founder upon it. There are many different ways to deal with the problems of setting up the Executive, devolution and 'taking the guns out of Irish politics for ever'. Today's poll reports on your views of all the options at hand to break the rock and move the peace process forward.

Exclusive: day two of the poll on the Mitchell Review

First of all it should be emphasised that as far as the people of Northern Ireland are concerned failure is not an option (Table 11.13). When asked 'Do you want the review of the Belfast Agreement to be successful?' 85 per cent said Yes. Ninety-eight per cent of Alliance voters said Yes followed by the SDLP at 96 per cent, Sinn Féin at 94 per cent, the UUP and PUP at 91 per cent and the DUP at 58 per cent.

But the people of Northern Ireland never like to get their hopes up too much. When asked 'Do you think the review of the Belfast Agreement will be successful?' only 44 per cent said Yes (Table 11.14). The most optimistic were the Alliance voters at 72 per cent followed by the SDLP at 63 per cent,

Table 11.13   Do you want the review of the Belfast Agreement to be successful?

Per cent	All of NI	Protestant	Catholic	DUP	UUP	PUP	Alliance	SDLP	Sinn Féin
Yes	85	80	93	58	91	91	98	96	94
No	15	20	7	42	9	9	2	4	6

Table 11.14   Do you think the review of the Belfast Agreement will be successful?

Per cent	All of NI	Protestant	Catholic	DUP	UUP	PUP	Alliance	SDLP	Sinn Féin
Yes	44	36	58	21	45	41	72	63	45
No	56	64	42	79	55	59	28	37	55

then Sinn Féin and the UUP both at 45 per cent, PUP at 41 per cent and DUP at 21 per cent. The people of Northern Ireland are notoriously sceptical about peace processes – they have every reason to be. Yet 85 per cent of them want the Mitchell Review to be the second exception to prove that rule. But how?

Decommissioning under the terms of the Belfast Agreement

In accordance with the terms of the Belfast Agreement, General de Chastelain has published his programme for the decommissioning of all paramilitary weapons by his Independent International Commission. This programme includes commitments to undertake decommissioning by May 2000; the appointment of paramilitary representatives to co-operate with the Commission; confirmation of how decommissioning will take place; and finally decommissioning with reports made to the two governments. In the poll people were asked if they considered all the parts of this decommissioning programme to be 'Essential', 'Desirable', 'Acceptable', 'Tolerable' or 'Unacceptable' as part of a successful peace process (Table 11.15).

Table 11.15   Support for General de Chastelain's decommissioning programme

Per cent	Essential	Desirable	Acceptable	Tolerable	Unacceptable
All of NI	42	31	19	5	3
Protestant	53	26	18	2	1
Catholic	27	38	20	9	6
DUP	58	21	17	3	1
UUP	53	26	15	4	2
PUP	39	36	20	5	0
Alliance	52	26	18	2	2
SDLP	35	44	14	6	1
Sinn Féin	8	30	27	16	19

Clearly there is broad acceptance for this programme across both communities and all the major Northern Ireland political parties with the exception of Sinn Féin, of whom 19 per cent find it 'Unacceptable'. But, fortunately, this picture changes when decommissioning is combined with setting up an inclusive Executive. If this is done then only 1 per cent of Sinn Féin supporters consider the decommissioning programme to be 'Unacceptable'.

Decommissioning and devolution

The Belfast Agreement is presently under review in an effort to resolve problems of implementation and at the centre of this, rightly or wrongly, is the question of decommissioning and setting up the Executive. Again people were asked to indicate which options for dealing with this problem they considered to be 'Essential', 'Desirable', 'Acceptable', 'Tolerable' or 'Unacceptable' as part of a successful peace process. It is not possible to publish all the results in the *Belfast Telegraph* but all the parties elected to the Assembly will receive detailed reports. To keep things simple the results for the options that are 'Unacceptable' are published here so that the proposals that a strong leader cannot 'sell' to their electorate can be eliminated (Table 11.16).

In today's poll 37 per cent of Ulster Unionists will not accept setting up an Executive including Sinn Féin without any preconditions at all, down from 58 per cent when the same question was asked in March, so although all Sinn Féin supporters would prefer this option it still seems to be a 'non-starter'. Ulster Unionist resistance drops to only 13 per cent when setting up the Executive is combined with de Chastelain's decommissioning programme. It was 31 per cent last March.

This result is interesting for two reasons. Sinn Féin's resistance to decommissioning has now dropped from 19 per cent 'Unacceptable' when viewed in isolation to only 1 per cent 'Unacceptable', while UUP resistance for undertaking decommissioning in this way has risen from 2 per cent to 13 per cent 'Unacceptable'. Having Sinn Féin in government seems to make all the difference for both Sinn Féin and the UUP.

Predictably Ulster Unionist resistance drops as more conditions are brought into play along the lines of the Hillsborough proposal (6 per cent 'Unacceptable') and Way Forward proposal (10 per cent 'Unacceptable'), going down to only 3 per cent 'Unacceptable' for a 'step-by-step' approach. Again, predictably, Sinn Féin resistance rises up to 15 per cent, 27 per cent and 22 per cent 'Unacceptable' respectively (52 per cent considered the SDLP proposals 'Unacceptable' in March).

Clearly, if Unionist confidence could be increased in the de Chastelain programme as the best vehicle to accomplish decommissioning then the second option of setting up an inclusive Executive in combination with

Table 11.16   Support for options to implement the Belfast Agreement

Percentages for 'Unacceptable'	All of NI	UUP	Sinn Féin
The Executive of the New Northern Ireland Assembly should be established, including Sinn Féin, without any preconditions and without any further delay	28	37	0
An inclusive Executive of the New Northern Ireland Assembly should be established and the decommissioning process should be dealt with by General de Chastelain in accordance with his programme	14	13	1
An inclusive Executive, the de Chastelain programme for decommissioning and a day of reconciliation when arms are placed beyond use	11	6	15
An inclusive Executive, the de Chastelain programme for decommissioning and an end to devolution if these requirements are not met	14	10	27
A step-by-step implementation of the Belfast Agreement in parallel with the de Chastelain programme for decommissioning	10	3	22
A combination of the best features of these different proposals that can be agreed to by the parties in the Review	11	6	21
Given the delays in establishing an inclusive Executive and starting the decommissioning process General de Chastelain should be given a little more time to complete his programme of work beyond the Belfast Agreement deadline of May 2000	18	19	9

that programme might be 'do-able'. Perhaps some confidence-building measures could help at this point as part of a Mitchell Review 'package'.

Confidence-building measures

In this question people were asked to consider various options for building trust and confidence between the two communities by indicating which ones they considered to be 'Essential', 'Desirable', 'Acceptable', 'Tolerable' or 'Unacceptable' as part of a successful peace process. Again just the 'Unacceptable' results are considered here. Many of the options are 'do-able' and could end up in a Review 'package' (Table 11.17). (*Author's comments are in italics.*)

What can be done if the Review fails

Eighty-four per cent of the people of Northern Ireland want the Review to succeed. It should, but it might not, and even if a deal is cut that will

Table 11.17 Confidence-building measures

Percentages for 'Unacceptable'	All of NI	UUP	Sinn Féin
The Review should establish a relationship building process between all the parties, in particular Sinn Féin and the Ulster Unionist Party, with a collective public act which marks the beginning of the process of reconciliation. – *'Do-able'*	11	3	0
The 'Yes parties' should establish a special committee to co-ordinate the implementation of the Belfast Agreement in full. – *'Do-able'*	12	6	0
All the parties should accept some responsibility for the conflict and state their determination not to repeat the mistakes of the past. – *'Do-able'*	7	3	0
All the parties should state their absolute commitment to all the provisions in the Good Friday Agreement. – *'Do-able'*	7	2	0
Temporary arrangements should be put in place to get the Assembly working providing they lead to the implementation of the Belfast Agreement in full. – *'Do-able' with leadership support*	12	9	2
All the parties should state their recommitment to the Mitchell Principles of Democracy and Non-violence. – *'Do-able'*	4	1	1
The two governments should clearly say what is meant by a 'Complete and Unequivocal Ceasefire'. – *'Do-able' depending on what is said*	2	0	8
Both the IRA and Loyalist paramilitary groups should say 'The war is over'. – *Difficult at this time*	3	0	17
Both Loyalist and Republican paramilitary groups should indicate their willingness to disarm as part of the peace process. – *'Do-able' as part of the de Chastelain programme*	2	0	12
Both Loyalist and Republican paramilitary groups should end all so-called 'punishment attacks'. – *Difficult without implementation of Patten*	2	0	16
Both Loyalist and Republican paramilitary groups should co-operate with the new Northern Ireland police service to bring an end to all beatings and violence. – *Difficult without implementation of Patten*	6	2	29
Ex-prisoners should be encouraged to make a positive contribution to the establishment of a lasting peace through community work. – *'Do-able' where their efforts are appreciated*	14	19	9
Decommissioning should include all privately held weapons. – *At last the UUP and Sinn Féin agree on decommissioning!*	16	17	15
The British government should publish their paper on the demilitarisation of Northern Ireland. – *'Do-able'*	2	3	1

probably not be the end of the matter. Northern Ireland politics just are not like that. The 'No Parties' could try to bring the Assembly down or block the re-election of Trimble and Mallon. And then there is Patten.

The government say they do not have a plan 'B' but what are the options and what do the people of Northern Ireland think of them? Again people were asked to say which ones they considered to be 'Essential', 'Desirable', 'Acceptable', 'Tolerable' or 'Unacceptable' as part of a successful peace

Table 11.18   'Plan B' options if the Review fails

Percentages for 'Unacceptable'	Protestant	Catholic	UUP	Sinn Féin
The two governments should move quickly and decisively to fill the political vacuum	13	2	4	4
The Ulster Unionists and Sinn Féin should try and reach an agreement through intense negotiations away from Northern Ireland	26	1	13	0
The Civic Forum should be established as a consultative body to government	13	3	6	9
A Shadow Executive should be established to advise the government	15	5	8	9
Assembly Committees should be established to advise each government department	14	4	7	9
Continuation of Direct Rule from London with no Northern Ireland Assembly	15	23	9	52
A new Anglo-Irish Agreement	51	31	42	47
Joint Authority by Direct Rule from both London and Dublin	52	9	47	13
Joint Authority in combination with a Northern Ireland Assembly	24	8	18	22
Scrap the Belfast Agreement and negotiate a new agreement	15	46	18	64

process, and as before the 'Unacceptable' results have been presented here to eliminate those options with the greatest resistance (Table 11.18).

Over 50 per cent of Protestants definitely do not want a new Anglo-Irish Agreement or Joint Authority between London and Dublin, and over 50 per cent of Sinn Féin voters definitely do not want a continuation of Direct Rule from London. Forty-six per cent of Catholics and 64 per cent of Sinn Féin supporters do not want to negotiate a new agreement. So radical solutions or just a continuation of the status quo are probably out of the question.

The course of least resistance seems to be to establish a Civic Forum, Shadow Executive and Assembly Committees to advise government. Resistance to these options averages at only 7 per cent 'Unacceptable' for the UUP and at 9 per cent 'Unacceptable' for Sinn Féin. If all else fails these are potential first steps or fall-back positions. They could even be elements of a creative Mitchell Review 'package' if so required.

In practice the two governments' plan 'B' is to implement as much of the Agreement as they possibly can. Of course they can move ahead with the new independent institutions such as the Northern Ireland Human Rights

Table 11.19 Alternative proposals for the implementation of the Belfast Agreement

Percentages for 'Unacceptable'	DUP	UUP	PUP	Alliance	SDLP	Sinn Féin
The British and Irish governments should implement the Belfast Agreement but only devolve powers to the new institutions of government when this is possible	42	9	5	5	3	8
Temporary arrangements should be put in place to get the Assembly working providing they lead to the implementation of the Belfast Agreement in full	46	7	18	5	2	10
The Assembly should be responsible for the administration of Northern Ireland but should not have powers to make laws until the parties can form an Executive	27	6	2	0	4	19
The Assembly should be run by departmental committees until the parties can form an Executive	30	9	7	7	6	23
All parts of the Belfast Agreement should be worked by the Assembly under any temporary arrangements agreed for its operation	38	11	14	5	6	17
A new referendum should be held to approve any new or partial arrangements made for the implementation of the Agreement	9	8	16	26	14	35

Commission and Equality Commission without reference to an Assembly. But, at some point, the devolution of powers will become an issue.

For the most part UUP, PUP, Alliance and SDLP voters have few problems with the gradual devolution of powers prior to setting up an Executive, with resistance running at between 0 per cent and 11 per cent 'Unacceptable' (Table 11.19). These options are more difficult for Sinn Féin. About 20 per cent of their electorate find this kind of staged devolution 'Unacceptable' at this time.

But only 10 per cent of Sinn Féin voters strongly oppose the idea that 'Temporary arrangements should be put in place to get the Assembly working providing they lead to the implementation of the Belfast Agreement in full', and herein lies the heart of this particular problem. Sinn Féin supporters do not trust the UUP to set up an Executive once they get devolved powers by some other means.

The recent statements by Trimble and the new Secretary of State that they fully support the full implementation of the Belfast Agreement are welcome. But they were too little and too late to affect the results of this poll. Trust must be built and once it is established much that is impossible now may be possible then. Under better conditions the options for gradual devolution of powers could be used as part of a structured peace process. But it is going to take the goodwill of everyone, parties and governments, to make it work, so establishing the Executive now and taking the prize of changes to Articles 2 and 3 and the de Chastelain programme for decommissioning may be the best option.

We have come to learn that the Belfast Agreement is not enough. An Agreement alone cannot bring peace. A degree of trust and confidence is also required and as much co-operation and mutual support as can possibly be mustered. But that may not be enough either. Implementation seems to demand yet one more ingredient – Courage.

12
The Future of the Peace Process

The Mitchell Review concluded with a carefully choreographed programme of events in which the parties recommitted themselves to the full implementation of the Belfast Agreement, the Independent International Commission on Decommissioning (IICD) issued a report detailing how they would now carry out their mandate and the Republicans, as well as Loyalists, undertook to appoint representatives to work with the IICD. In his statement of 18 November 1999 Senator George Mitchell affirmed that 'a basis now exists for the institutions to be established' and that, 'Devolution should take effect, then the executive should meet, and then the paramilitary groups should appoint their authorised representatives, all on the same day, in that order.'

On 27 November the Ulster Unionist Council accepted these proposals and on 2 December 1999 all of this was done in accordance with the stated schedule. But only just. When the Unionists accepted the deal they also added in that their acceptance was conditional on IRA decommissioning starting before their Council met again in February. In effect a post-dated precondition that had all the appearance of an act of surrender. Needless to say decommissioning did not happen and on 11 February 2000 the Secretary of State for Northern Ireland had to suspend all the new institutions of government in order to prevent the Ulster Unionists from bringing them down and with it the collapse of the Belfast Agreement.

Everyone was very angry with everybody else, all blaming each other for the mess they now found themselves in. After a few weeks, when tempers had cooled, what amounted to an informal review got underway with a series of bilateral meetings between representatives of the IRA and Irish government, Ulster Unionists and British government, the two governments and variously all the pro-agreement parties at 10 Downing Street, Chequers, Dublin, Belfast and so on. At the end of the day the IRA agreed to initiate a process that would 'completely and verifiably put IRA arms beyond use' as well as allowing a number of its dumps to be inspected by third parties as a confidence-building measure. But unlike the deal proposed at Hillsborough a year earlier this would only happen after the Executive had been re-established. These new arrangements, for the full implementation of the Belfast Agreement, were announced by the two governments on 5 May 2000 and the IRA formally accepted them on 6 May 2000.

Plans were now made to test these new proposals against public opinion. But the roll of the peace polls had changed once again. The first poll, Chapter 5, had been undertaken as a purely academic exercise without party political input; the next four polls, Chapters 6 through 9, were undertaken with all the parties elected to the negotiations on the future of Northern Ireland; the sixth poll, Chapter 10, was a strictly Sinn Féin/PUP initiative and the most recent poll, Chapter 11, was restricted to the remaining seven pro-agreement parties, Sinn Féin the PUP, UDP, UUP, SDLP, Alliance and Women's Coalition. It was intended that this new poll should be no different but most of the pro-agreement parties did not want to run another poll. However, some did and the Rowntree Trust agreed that the effort and expense were worthwhile. Critically the fieldwork for this final poll was conducted between 12–15 May, a week after the new arrangements for decommissioning, setting up the Executive and fully implementing the Belfast Agreement were announced by the two governments and IRA.

Belfast Telegraph, Wednesday 25 May 2000

Unionism at the crossroads: what the people say – exclusive poll

In the referendum of two years ago 71 per cent of the people of Northern Ireland voted Yes for the Belfast Agreement. In the Queen's University/ Rowntree Trust poll run in October of last year 74 per cent said they voted Yes (Table 12.1). Similarly in the BBC poll run between 3 and 5 May this year 74.6 per cent said they voted Yes. However, in the latest Queen's University/Rowntree Trust poll, run between 12 and 15 May *after* the Hillsborough agreement was struck and new IRA statement made, this result rose to 78 per cent claiming they had voted Yes (Table 12.2).

Similarly those who said they would now vote Yes if the referendum was held today was 65 per cent last October (Table 12.3); 67.2 per cent in the BBC poll run before the recent Hillsborough deal was struck and 74 per cent in the new poll run after Hillsborough and the IRA statement (Table 12.4). Clearly the new arrangements for re-establishing devolved government in Northern Ireland and decommissioning paramilitary weapons have significantly strengthened support for the Belfast Agreement. A majority of Protestants, 55 per cent, now say they would vote Yes.

Rightly or wrongly the future of the Northern Ireland peace process is in the hands of the Ulster Unionist Council and the decision they will make this coming Saturday. But what do rank-and-file Ulster Unionists think? What path would the peace process take if the decision was theirs?

Table 12.1 How did you vote in the referendum for the Belfast Agreement? October 1999

Per cent	All of NI	Protestant	Catholic	DUP	UUP	PUP	Alliance	SDLP	Sinn Féin
Yes	74	64	89	32	82	85	90	96	89
No	26	36	11	68	18	15	10	4	11

Table 12.2 How did you vote in the referendum for the Belfast Agreement? 12/15 May 2000

Per cent	All of NI	Protestant	Catholic	DUP	UUP	PUP	Alliance	SDLP	Sinn Féin
Yes	78	66	91	35	79	86	90	99	90
No	22	34	9	65	21	14	10	1	10

Table 12.3 And if the referendum was held today how would you vote? October 1999

Per cent	All of NI	Protestant	Catholic	DUP	UUP	PUP	Alliance	SDLP	Sinn Féin
Yes	65	49	88	31	56	56	79	95	90
No	35	51	12	69	44	44	21	5	10

Table 12.4 And if the referendum was held today how would you vote? 12/15 May 2000

Per cent	All of NI	Protestant	Catholic	DUP	UUP	PUP	Alliance	SDLP	Sinn Féin
Yes	74	55	94	32	64	70	86	100	94
No	26	45	6	68	36	30	14	0	6

In the second poll conducted for the BBC on 9 May, 66 per cent of Ulster Unionists responded positively to the question: 'In the light of the IRA statement about putting its arms "completely and verifiably beyond use", should David Trimble and the UUP go back into the Executive on 22 May?'

In the latest Queen's University/Rowntree Trust poll, with interviews conducted between 12 May and 15 May, 72 per cent of Ulster Unionist supporters believed their party should go back into the Executive (Table 12.5). The results ranged from a high of 100 per cent for Sinn Féin supporters to 98 per cent for the SDLP, 92 per cent for Alliance, 78 per cent for the PUP, 72 per cent for the UUP and 38 per cent for the DUP.

This is the question that was asked with the results: 'Given the new proposals from the two governments and IRA should the Ulster Unionists now go back into the Executive including Sinn Féin?'

Table 12.5   Support for UUP going back into the Executive with Sinn Féin

Per cent	All of NI	Protestant	Catholic	DUP	UUP	PUP	Alliance	SDLP	Sinn Féin
Yes	79	63	98	38	72	78	92	98	100
No	21	37	2	62	28	22	8	2	0

Some commentators predicted a decline in Unionist support for the current Hillsborough deal after the initial impact of the latest IRA statement had worn off. But this has not happened. Rank-and-file Ulster Unionist support for David Trimble to lead his party back into the Executive has held firm or even slightly increased. Seventy-four per cent of the people of Northern Ireland would also like the DUP to take their seats in the Executive ranging from a high of 89 per cent for SDLP and Alliance supporters to 83 per cent for Sinn Féin, 78 per cent for the PUP, 71 per cent for the UUP and 38 per cent of the DUP electorate (Table 12.6).

This is the question that was asked and the results: 'Should the DUP now take their seats in the Executive along with the UUP, SDLP and Sinn Féin?'

Table 12.6   Support for the DUP going into the Executive

Per cent	All of NI	Protestant	Catholic	DUP	UUP	PUP	Alliance	SDLP	Sinn Féin
Yes	74	63	87	38	71	78	89	89	83
No	26	37	13	62	29	22	11	11	17

Critically, in the Queen's University/Rowntree Trust poll, everyone interviewed was asked twenty-five detailed questions about the new arrangements for implementing the Belfast Agreement before they were asked if they supported the deal as a whole. As well as the IRA statement, which has been the focus of so much attention, there was also a joint statement from the two governments and a letter from the two prime ministers to the parties.

Consequently everyone interviewed was asked to indicate which parts of these various proposals and statements they considered to be 'Essential', 'Desirable', 'Acceptable', 'Tolerable' or 'Unacceptable' as part of a successful peace process. The large table (Table 12.7) lists the 'Essential' items in order of preference for both Ulster Unionist and Sinn Féin supporters.

It is now possible to see, in some detail, who wants what to make the Belfast Agreement work for them. As would be expected, the most important elements of the new Hillsborough deal for Ulster Unionists are those concerned with decommissioning. Policing and equality issues remain at the top of the Republican agenda.

Table 12.7 UUP and Sinn Féin support for new implementation arrangements

	Ulster Unionist Party *Per cent 'Essential'*		*Sinn Féin* *Per cent 'Essential'*	
1st	The IRA leadership have agreed to initiate a process that will completely and verifiably put IRA arms beyond use	56	Legislation will be enacted to implement the Patten report on policing	73
2nd	Paramilitary organisations will state clearly that they will put their arms completely and verifiably beyond use	54	Legislation and a detailed timetable for implementation of the review of the criminal justice system will be published	68
3rd	The third parties will include the diplomats Cyril Ramaphosa from South Africa and Martti Ahtisaari from Finland	53	The new policing board and independent recruitment agency for the Police Service of Northern Ireland will be established	65
4th	The IRA leadership have stated that there is no threat to the peace process from the IRA	48	The establishment of equality schemes for public authorities in Northern Ireland	63
5th	Measures will continue to be taken to reintegrate prisoners into the community	48	In accordance with the terms of the Good Friday Agreement all prisoners qualifying for early release will be released	62
6th	In consultation with representatives from the paramilitary organisations the Commission will develop more effective ways to carry out their mandate	47	Continued support for the victims of violence	59
7th	The IRA dumps will be re-inspected regularly	44	Co-operation between the new Human Rights Commissions in both Northern Ireland and in the Republic of Ireland	58
8th	Continued support for the victims of violence	41	The incorporation of the European Convention on Human Rights into British and Irish domestic law	54

Table 12.7 Continued

	Ulster Unionist Party Per cent 'Essential'	Sinn Féin Per cent 'Essential'
9th	The third parties will report to the Independent International Commission on Decommissioning – the IICD (41)	As early a return as possible to normal security arrangements in Northern Ireland consistent with the level of threat (52)
10th	Both governments will take resolute action against any group that threatens or uses violence against the peace process (40)	Subject to a positive response to all of these commitments from the pro-agreement parties the restoration of the Northern Ireland Assembly and Executive on 22 May 2000 (45)
11th	As a confidence-building measure a number of IRA arms dumps will be inspected by agreed third parties (37)	British support for minority languages in accordance with European standards including new television programmes (42)
12th	If any difficulties arise with any aspect of implementation, in consultation with the Assembly and Executive, the governments will carry out an immediate review (34)	Both governments will take resolute action against any group that threatens or uses violence against the peace process (40)
13th	As early a return as possible to normal security arrangements in Northern Ireland consistent with the level of threat (29)	A commitment to achieve full implementation of all of the remaining aspects of the Good Friday Agreement by June 2001 (36)
14th	The Commission will report to the two governments and these reports will be promptly published (28)	Measures will continue to be taken to reintegrate prisoners into the community (32)
15th	Progress to full implementation of the Agreement will be periodically assessed by the governments and parties (28)	The IRA leadership have agreed to initiate a process that will completely and verifiably put IRA arms beyond use (32)
16th	Subject to a positive response to all of these commitments from the pro-agreement parties (24)	The IRA leadership have stated that there is no threat to the peace process from the IRA (32)

the restoration of the Northern Ireland Assembly and Executive on 22 May 2000

17th	20	A commitment to achieve full implementation of all of the remaining aspects of the Good Friday Agreement by June 2001
18th	17	The incorporation of the European Convention on Human Rights into British and Irish domestic law
19th	16	The establishment of equality schemes for public authorities in Northern Ireland
20th	16	Legislation and a detailed timetable for implementation of the review of the criminal justice system will be published
21st	13	Legislation will be enacted to implement the Patten report on policing
22nd	11	British support for minority languages in accordance with European standards including new television programmes
23rd	10	Co-operation between the new Human Rights Commissions in both Northern Ireland and in the Republic of Ireland
24th	10	The new policing board and independent recruitment agency for the Police Service of Northern Ireland will be established
25th	9	In accordance with the terms of the Good Friday Agreement all prisoners qualifying for early release will be released

32	The third parties will include the diplomats Martti Cyril Ramaphosa from South Africa and Ahtisaari from Finland
30	Paramilitary organisations will state clearly that they will put their arms completely and verifiably beyond use
29	The IRA dumps will be re-inspected regularly
29	The Commission will report to the two governments and these reports will be promptly published
29	Progress to full implementation of the Agreement will be periodically assessed by the governments and parties
26	As a confidence-building measure a number of IRA arms dumps will be inspected by agreed third parties
25	If any difficulties arise with any aspect of implementation, in consultation with the Assembly and Executive, the governments will carry out an immediate review
23	The third parties will report to the Independent International Commission on Decommissioning – the IICD
23	In consultation with representatives from the paramilitary organisations the Commission will develop more effective ways to carry out their mandate

Table 12.8   UUP support for reformed Police Service of Northern Ireland

Per cent for Ulster Unionist Party	Essential	Desirable	Acceptable	Tolerable	Unacceptable
Legislation will be enacted to implement the Patten report on policing	13	16	25	20	26
The new policing board and independent recruitment agency for the Police Service of Northern Ireland will be established	10	10	32	25	23

However, it is interesting to note that when the top policing priorities for Sinn Féin supporters are viewed from an Ulster Unionist point of view only 26 per cent of them consider the governments' commitment that 'Legislation will be enacted to implement the Patten report on policing' to be 'Unacceptable' and a majority of 55 per cent consider this option to be 'Essential', 'Desirable' or 'Acceptable' – 20 per cent consider it 'Tolerable' (Table 12.8).

Similarly only 23 per cent consider the government commitment that 'The new policing board and independent recruitment agency for the Police Service of Northern Ireland will be established' to be 'Unacceptable' and again a majority of 52 per cent view this option as 'Essential', 'Desirable' or 'Acceptable' – 25 per cent consider it 'Tolerable'.

The latest Hillsborough deal is a delicate balance between Unionist and Republican concerns. Inevitably each party think they have given more than the other but 72 per cent of rank-and-file Ulster Unionists want David Trimble to take his party back into the Executive. They clearly have misgivings about the Patten report, and no doubt many other things as well. Sinn Féin supporters have their reservations too. But, on balance, the results of this poll suggest that rank-and-file Ulster Unionists would prefer to have these problems resolved with their party in government rather than out of government.

* * *

The poll had the desired effect and two days after it was published the Ulster Unionist Council voted to accept the new arrangements for decommissioning by the narrow margin of 459 votes to 403, that is 53 per cent to 47 per cent. On 30 May 2000 devolved powers were restored to the Northern Ireland Assembly and the Executive met on 1 June. But the anti-agreement lobby in the Ulster Unionist Party brought matters to a head again when they called another meeting of the Ulster Unionist Council for Saturday, 28 October 2000. Again a narrow majority voted for their party to stay in the Executive and again this decision was supported by a majority of Ulster Unionist Party supporters. In a poll published in the *Belfast Telegraph* on Friday, 27 October 2000, the day before the meeting was to be held and vote was to be taken, only 28 per cent of UUP voters wanted their party to withdraw, 5 per cent were not sure and 69 per cent wanted them to stay in.[1] They did and again there was general relief at the outcome but this poll had been a *Belfast Telegraph* initiative. On this particular occasion there had been no need to test a comprehensive set of new proposals against public opinion, only Ulster Unionist support for their continued participation in government and the newspaper was quite capable of doing that. But the Belfast Agreement and its full implementation continued to be the focus of almost every possible political contention. It sometimes seemed to be the case that all that had not yet been done had to be fought and argued over simply for the sake of doing so. The UUP anti-agreement lobby threatened to call yet another meeting of their Council after the third visit of President Clinton to Northern Ireland in December 2000 failed to break the then current deadlock over progress on police reform, demilitarisation and decommissioning.

With both a Westminster general election and local government council elections scheduled for the spring of 2001 the peace process was now falling victim to the necessity for each party to outperform their competitors at the ballot box. Although all the recent public opinion polls continued to indicate Protestants fairly evenly split on their support for the Belfast Agreement they still, overwhelmingly, wanted it to work. But the DUP and their anti-agreement allies did not. They still wanted to bring the Belfast Agreement down and said they would use the forthcoming elections as 'a referendum' to test Unionist support for it.

If the pro-agreement parties could not be persuaded to co-operate in their drive for votes they could lose out to the anti-agreement forces rallied against them, further polarise the political landscape of Northern Ireland and do harm to the peace process and integrity of the Belfast Agreement. By way of a review of all that had been accomplished these dangers were highlighted in a series of articles published in the *Belfast Telegraph*[2] and *Irish Times*[3] on 21 and 23 February 2001.

Belfast Telegraph, Thursday 21 February 2001

The people's peace process

Eight surveys of public opinion were conducted in support of the Northern Ireland peace process between April 1996 and May 2000. With an average of over 100 questions or options in each poll and 1000 people being interviewed a total of nearly one million answers were given. One answer for almost every person with a right to vote in Northern Ireland. The results of these polls should not be dismissed lightly. They represent the views of the people on their peace process, the people's peace process, and perhaps the time has come to try and take stock of what, collectively, the people have said.

Support for the Belfast Agreement

Public support for an agreement (any agreement) was first tested in March 1997 (Table 12.9) when 94 per cent (93 per cent Protestant and 97 per cent Catholic) said they did 'support the principle of a negotiated settlement for the political future of Northern Ireland.' But when the outline of a real agreement was tested a year later in March 1998 only 77 per cent said they would vote 'Yes' (74 per cent Protestant and 81 per cent Catholic) and just two months later, in the referendum of May 1998, the 'Yes' vote fell to 71 per cent of an 81 per cent turnout. But support for the Belfast Agreement was higher in the Republic at 94 per cent and when, in February 1999, the people of Northern Ireland were asked 'Do you want the Belfast Agreement to work?' 93 per cent said 'Yes' (89 per cent Protestant and 97 per cent Catholic). But by October of 1999, at the time of the Mitchell Review, support started to fall again with only 83 per cent saying they wanted the Agreement to work (72 per cent Protestant and 98 per cent Catholic). On this occasion people were also asked how they would vote if the referendum was held again. Of those who said they would vote only 65 per cent said 'Yes' (49 per cent Protestant and 88 per cent Catholic). But in May 2000, shortly after the IRA said they would 'put their arms beyond use', support for the Agreement rose to a high of 74 per cent 'Yes' (55 per cent Protestant and 94 per cent Catholic) although it fell back again in the most recent *Belfast Telegraph* poll of October 2000 to 69 per cent 'Yes' (47 per cent Protestant and again 94 per cent Catholic).

People do want the Agreement to work but when the Executive was not up and running Catholic support was only 88 per cent (down from 94 per cent) and when decommissioning did not happen Protestant support fell to 47 per cent (down from 55 per cent). Conversely when all appears to be

Table 12.9 Support for Belfast Agreement

Per cent 'Yes'	Date	All of NI	Protestant	Catholic
Support for any agreement	March 1997	94	93	97
Support for Belfast Agreement	March 1998	77	74	81
Referendum for Belfast Agreement	May 1998	71	–	–
Want Belfast Agreement to work	February 1999	93	89	97
Want Belfast Agreement to work	October 1999	83	72	98
Would still vote for Belfast Agreement	October 1999	65	49	88
Want Belfast Agreement to work	May 2000	85	74	98
Would still vote for Belfast Agreement	May 2000	74	55	94
Would still vote for Belfast Agreement	October 2000	69	47	94

going well with the Agreement support for it has risen, for a brief few weeks, above the referendum level of 71 per cent to as much as 74 per cent and has the potential to go as high as 93 per cent for those who, in spite of their doubts, want to see it work. Clearly, come the elections, any pro-agreement party or parties who can be seen to make the Agreement work will receive the thanks of their electorate while playing the 'blame game' may not prove to be the best of winning strategies.

* * *

Unfortunately the 'blame game' was the easiest of all strategies to play. Everyone did it:

• The Democratic Unionists blamed the British for selling them out, the Americans and Irish for interfering in Northern Ireland affairs, the Ulster Unionist for treachery, Sinn Féin for acts of terrorism and the SDLP for conspiring with Sinn Féin and the Irish as part of the 'Pan-Nationalist Front'.

• The Ulster Unionists blamed the British, Irish and Americans for not putting sufficient pressure on Sinn Féin/IRA to decommission, the Democratic Unionists for trying to wreck the Belfast Agreement while enjoying all the benefits of it and the SDLP for not supporting the RUC in their fight against terrorism.

• The SDLP blamed Sinn Féin, the Loyalists, the RUC and the British establishment for the continued violence, the Ulster Unionists for not working the Belfast Agreement in good faith, the Democratic Unionists for continually saying 'no', but they didn't blame the Irish for very much at all.

• Sinn Féin blamed the Irish and SDLP for not standing up to the British, the British for almost everything, the Ulster Unionists for not working the Belfast Agreement in good faith and the Democratic Unionists for not wanting a Catholic 'about the place' in government.

• The British and Irish governments blamed all the Northern Ireland parties for not doing enough to make the Belfast Agreement work while they, themselves, were blameless.

In this context the prospects of using the forthcoming elections as an opportunity to develop new party policies to improve the quality of life for the people of Northern Ireland was little more than wishful thinking. Elections were fought, for the most part, on the simple strategy of how a party could best protect the interests of their own community against their enemies and the political parties that represented them. With resignation a seasoned journalist at the *Belfast Telegraph* explained that, 'It was always thus'. But did it have to be, could these elections be different?

Belfast Telegraph, Thursday 21 February 2001

Party political support and elections

How people will vote for a given candidate, on a given day, in a given constituency is a very complex question depending on whether, for example, the candidate is anti-agreement or pro-agreement, how they feel about that particular candidate, if they wish to register some sort of protest vote by abstaining and last, but by no means least, the voting system used on the day (which varies a lot in Northern Ireland) and the chances of any particular candidate actually getting elected. So who someone votes for, particularly in Northern Ireland, can often be very different to the party and policies a voter may support. As a consequence the 'which one of these Northern Ireland political parties do you support?' question from the polls tells a sometimes very different story to the results of the various elections covering the same period (Table 12.10).

The trends in the polls are quite revealing. For example, although people have tended to slightly inflate their support for the Alliance party for the four polls conducted between March 1997 and March 1998 at 10 per cent, this support has dropped to only 6 or 7 per cent for the three polls

Table 12.10   Political party support in Northern Ireland

Question: Which ONE of these Northern Ireland political parties do you support?

Per cent support on date of poll interviews	March 1997	September 1997	December 1997	March 1998	February 1999	October 1999	May 2000
UUP/Ulster Unionist Party	21	24	26	26	26	26	24
SDLP/Social Democratic Labour Party	25	22	23	21	23	20	21
DUP/Democratic Unionist Party	15	16	11	14	14	18	17
Sinn Féin	9	12	17	16	15	12	15
Alliance	10	10	10	10	7	7	6
UKUP/United Kingdom Unionist Party	4	4	1	1	*	1	*
PUP/Progressive Unionist Party	3	3	5	2	5	4	4
UDP/Ulster Democratic Party	3	2	1	2	*	1	*
Northern Ireland Women's Coalition	1	2	1	1	2	1	1
Other	8	4	5	7	8	9	11

* Less than one per cent.

conducted between February 99 and May 2000 after Lord Alderdice gave up his party's leadership. Although Sinn Féin support tends to be a little underreported it increased from 9 to 17 per cent in 1997 when they went into the Stormont talks while DUP support fell from 16 to 11 per cent when they withdrew from the talks. But DUP support has been restored to as much as 17 or 18 per cent as implementation of the Belfast Agreement has gone through its various difficulties. Support for the major pro-agreement Unionist and Nationalist parties seems to be far more steady with the SDLP averaging about 22 per cent and the UUP 25 per cent. As for the smaller parties the UKUP dropped from 4 to 1 per cent when their leader, Bob McCartney, broke ranks with his other Assembly members. The Loyalist PUP and UDP have consistently held on to about 5 per cent of the voters' support with the PUP outperforming the UDP when the UDA/UFF have been associated with increases in sectarian violence. Support for the Women's Coalition holds firm at about 1 or 2 per cent.

These trends in party support are significant for a number of reasons. Firstly, in the upcoming general elections, with its 'first past the post' system of voting, it is strategic voting and electoral pacts that will most likely win the day – not simple party support. For example, the UUP could strike a deal with the DUP, as they have done in the past, or with Alliance by running pro-agreement candidates. Perhaps the PUP should also be factored into such calculations. Additionally the SDLP and Sinn Féin might also start to enter into pacts. The possibilities and their implications for the future of the Belfast Agreement and peace process seem to be almost endless. But perhaps they should not be. If, as is the case in some other countries, the electoral system returned candidates that reflected simple party support then, like the polls, the political landscape of Northern Ireland would be both far more predictable and stable.[4] The smaller centre parties and Loyalists would be assured of their influence, however limited, and the larger pro-agreement parties would be assured of their political power, albeit slightly restrained. The people of Northern Ireland want the Belfast Agreement to work and, in the absence of effective pro-agreement pacts, this may yet require a reformed electoral system that will better support the peace process – not undermine it.[5]

* * *

Following the publication of this article the parties entered into a flurry of negotiations on various forms of electoral pacts. But the pro-agreement parties were unable to agree on a co-ordinated strategy. Although the Alliance party were willing not to put up candidates in some constituencies and ask their members, instead, to support other pro-agreement parties, notably the UUP, the DUP countered this proposal by saying they would vigorously oppose all pro-agreement UUP candidates. Additionally the DUP said they would not run against UUP candidates if they were anti-agreement.

The Ulster Unionist Party had some impossible decisions to make and given their fragmented organisational structure different constituencies went different ways. Some were pro-agreement while others were anti-agreement.

Sinn Féin and the SDLP could have entered into pacts and won significant gains at the expense of the Unionists by only putting forward one Nationalist candidate in each constituency. Sinn Féin supported such a strategy but the SDLP did not. They said they wanted to give all Nationalist voters a real choice but a Province wide pro-agreement Nationalist pact would have forced the UUP and DUP into a similar anti-agreement Unionist pact. This would have only served to further polarise the Northern Ireland political scene and strengthen community divisions.

In an effort to monopolise the pro-agreement Unionist vote for themselves the Ulster Unionist Party leadership tried to persuade the Alliance Party and Progressive Unionist Party not to put up any candidates in the Westminster general elections at all. They also wanted this to be done without entering into reciprocal arrangements that might have benefited the Alliance Party and PUP in some way. As for UUP co-operation with Nationalists, that was an idea that got no further than the newspaper columns of a few of the most imaginative political commentators. Northern Ireland was not yet ready for cross-community co-operation when it came to contesting political elections. In fact they did not seem to be ready for very much in the way of co-operation at all.

Come the day of the elections the PUP did not contest the Westminster seat of North Belfast where their vote might have made a difference. But the UUP lost the seat anyway because they ran a very weak candidate. The Alliance Party also did not run candidates in a number of constituencies and in so doing helped the Ulster Unionists hold on to several seats as well as winning one that was previously held by the leader of the ant-agreement UK Unionist Party, Robert McCartney. But the bitter disputes over who should or should not stand for election had divided the pro-agreement camp against itself. As a consequence the centre parties lost support to the DUP and Sinn Féin who made significant gains in both seats and votes at the expense of the UUP, SDLP and Alliance.

Post-election calculations undertaken by Alliance and the SDLP suggested that this political polarisation of the Province could have been avoided if systems of proportional representation had been used.[6] Subsequently the Northern Ireland Human Rights Commission recommended such changes to the voting system in their draft Bill of Rights published later that year.[7] But the damage had been done and difficult decisions still had to be taken on the full implementation of the Belfast Agreement. The third and final article in this pre-election series reviewed what the people of Northern Ireland had really expected out of the Belfast Agreement, stressed the political costs of promises delayed and emphasised the political benefits of promises, however difficult, kept and made.

Irish Times, Friday 23 February 2001

Full implementation key to NI success

In four of the eight polls undertaken in support of the peace process (December 1997, February 1999, October 1999 and May 2000) the people of Northern Ireland were asked what their priorities were for success. Some of these issues remain at the top of each community's 'to do' lists while others are now far less important than they once were. Why? Perhaps the people's priorities deserve closer inspection in the hope that their agenda can now be met and their peace process moved forward.

The first poll that asked the people of Northern Ireland to say what they thought was most 'essential' or 'important' for a successful peace process was run four months before the Belfast Agreement was struck in December of 1997 (Table 8.1). Significantly, problems of community peace building, such as segregation in housing and education, were ranked higher in the people's priorities than, for example, 'reformed and shared government'. These social problems were only dealt with in aspirational terms in the Belfast Agreement and still remain substantially unaddressed as has been the case throughout the period of the Troubles. Hopefully the New Northern Ireland Assembly, Civic Forum and Human Rights Commission will give more attention to these omissions than the Northern Ireland Office has done over the past thirty years. If this is not done then the culture of violence that now permeates many sections of Northern Ireland society will probably continue to undermine the efforts made to find a political solution to the ills of the Province.

In a more positive vein it is interesting to note how problems cease to become problems as they are properly dealt with (Table 12.11). For example, for Protestants, the Irish Constitutional issue was second only to problems of paramilitary violence in the poll undertaken before the Belfast Agreement was made but dropped in the post-agreement polls to ninth on their list by October 1999. Similarly 'A Bill of Rights that guarantees equality for all' was the number one priority for Catholics in the first poll but when the 'Equality Commission' was established under the terms of the Belfast Agreement it fell from second in their list of February 1999 to tenth in October 1999.

Resistance to North–South bodies has also diminished amongst the Protestant population as the relatively benign nature of these new institutions has become apparent with the reality of the implementation of this part of the Agreement. In February 1999 a majority of Protestants considered nearly all these new institutions of government to be 'Very Important' or 'Important' ranging from a high of 84 per cent for co-operation on 'Transport' to a low of 54 per cent for implementation of 'Aquaculture and Marine Matters'. The only exception was the implementation body for Language (Irish and Ulster Scots) at 36 per cent 'Very Important' or 'Important'.

Table 12.11   Protestant and Catholic changing priorities

	Date of poll	*Priority*	*Per cent importance*
Protestant changing priorities			
The Republic ends their claim on Northern Ireland	December 1997	3rd	62 Essential
Changes to the Irish Constitution	February 1999	6th	36 Very Important
Changes to Articles 2 and 3 of the Irish Constitution	October 1999	9th	29 Very Important
Changes to Articles 2 and 3 of the Irish Constitution	May 2000	7th	28 Very Important
Catholic changing priorities			
A Bill of Rights that guarantees equality for all	December 1997	1st	78 Essential
The Equality Commission	February 1999	2nd	52 Very Important
The Equality Commission	October 1999	10th	39 Very Important
The Equality Commission	May 2000	9th	49 Very Important

Implementation seems to be the key to success. Success breeds success and things never seem to be as quite as bad as many thought they might be once they are done. Conversely political gridlock appears to present the Agreement with one of its greatest dangers as it opens up more opportunities for the enemies of the Agreement to bring their forces to bear. The Belfast Agreement has, at various times, been compared to a train leaving a station that everyone should be on or to the *Titanic* about to founder. But perhaps a more apt vehicle of analogy would be a bike. Political momentum needs to be maintained if the people of Northern Ireland and two governments are to avoid falling off.

The clear number one priority for the whole community of Northern Ireland is security. Disbanding paramilitary groups, the Mitchell Principles of non-violence, decommissioning, the observation of human rights and police reform remain the top issues through all the polls. Of course the two communities do see these security issues in slightly different terms, and that is a real difficulty, but the people of Northern Ireland voted for the Belfast Agreement in the hope and aspiration that it would deliver peace. When it has not delivered peace there is disenchantment with the Agreement and it is under its greatest threat. There can be little doubt that the Loyalist feud, punishment shootings and murders attributed to Republican groups contributed significantly to the failure of the Ulster Unionist Party to win the South Antrim by-election last year. Conversely if the people of Northern Ireland can be persuaded that police reform could, eventually, lead to the end of paramilitarism then police reform would be more acceptable across the whole community than it presently is. The full engagement of all sections of Northern Ireland society in an acceptable police service is arguably as important as the decommissioning of weapons that can easily be replaced.

But the present debate on this issue is being driven by the politics of the forthcoming elections and what was agreed at Hillsborough Castle last May. The results of the poll taken after that deal was cut clearly illustrate where the electorate stand on these key issues (Tables 12.12 and 12.13). Democratic Unionists, Ulster Unionists, Progressive Unionists, Alliance supporters and SDLP voters all give the highest priority to 'commitments

Table 12.12 'Top five' voter priorities in May 2000

DUP per cent	Essential	Alliance per cent	Essential
Paramilitary decommissioning	71	Commitments to non-violence	42
Commitments to non-violence	66	Support for victims of the 'Troubles'	42
The Principle of Consent	56	The New Northern Ireland Assembly	41
The present status of Northern Ireland	54	The Northern Ireland Executive	41
Support for victims of the 'Troubles'	50	The new Human Rights Commission	40

UUP per cent	Essential	SDLP per cent	Essential
Paramilitary decommissioning	63	Commitments to non-violence	58
Commitments to non-violence	49	The New Northern Ireland Assembly	50
The Principle of Consent	42	The Northern Ireland Executive	49
The present status of Northern Ireland	39	Paramilitary decommissioning	49
Support for victims of the 'Troubles'	35	Support for victims of the 'Troubles'	46

PUP per cent	Essential	Sinn Féin per cent	Essential
The Principle of Consent	76	The reform of the RUC	91
Commitments to non-violence	67	The early release of prisoners	86
Support for victims of the 'Troubles'	67	NI demilitarisation	75
The present status of Northern Ireland	63	The reform of the criminal justice system	74
Changes to Articles 2 and 3	60	Support for victims of the 'Troubles'	70

Table 12.13   Protestant and Catholic priorities in May 2000

	Protestant per cent	Essential	Catholic per cent	Essential
1st	Paramilitary decommissioning	63	The reform of the RUC	62
2nd	Commitments to non-violence	57	Commitments to non-violence	55
3rd	The Principle of Consent	49	NI demilitarisation	55
4th	Support for victims of the 'Troubles'	44	Support for victims of the 'Troubles'	54
5th	The present status of Northern Ireland	44	The reform of the criminal justice system	52
6th	NI demilitarisation	35	The new Human Rights Commission	52
7th	Changes to Articles 2 and 3	28	The New Northern Ireland Assembly	51
8th	The full implementation of the Agreement	24	The Northern Ireland Executive	50
9th	The New Northern Ireland Assembly	22	The Equality Commission	49
10th	The reform of the RUC	21	The early release of prisoners	47
11th	Changes to British constitutional law	21	North/South implementation bodies	43
12th	The Northern Ireland Executive	20	The Principle of Consent	42
13th	The reform of the criminal justice system	20	Cultural and language rights	42
14th	A Bill of Rights for Northern Ireland	19	The North/South Ministerial Council	42
15th	The early release of prisoners	18	The full implementation of the Agreement	41
16th	The new Human Rights Commission	16	Paramilitary decommissioning	39
17th	Cultural and language rights	14	The British/Irish Council	38
18th	The Equality Commission	13	A Bill of Rights for Northern Ireland	37
19th	The Civic Forum	13	The Civic Forum	35
20th	North/South implementation bodies	7	Changes to British constitutional law	29
21st	The North/South Ministerial Council	7	The present status of Northern Ireland	20
22nd	The British/Irish Council	7	Changes to Articles 2 and 3	13

to non-violence' and 'paramilitary decommissioning' listing them in the 'top five' of their priorities out of list of 22 items taken from the Belfast Agreement. The Sinn Féin electorate have a somewhat different agenda, listing 'reform of the RUC', 'the early release of prisoners', 'Northern Ireland demilitarisation' and 'the reform of the criminal justice system' as their top four. The only item that everyone puts in their 'top five' is 'support for victims of the Troubles'. 'The Principle of Consent' makes it into the 'top five' for all the Unionist party supporters (DUP, UUP and PUP). Alliance and SDLP voters both have 'the New Northern Ireland Assembly' and 'the Northern Ireland Executive' high on their list but 'the reform of the RUC' is now just out of the SDLP 'top five' at number six with 'Northern Ireland demilitarisation' at number seven.

The leadership of the pro-agreement parties, and the two governments, have some very difficult decisions to make but, with regards to the future of the peace process, the implementation of the Belfast Agreement and public opinion in general one clear message seems to come through. All of the Agreement needs to be implemented more completely and less slowly than is presently the case and implementation must deliver peace. If peace and stability can be delivered then the pro-agreement parties and two governments might find they have far more licence with regards to the full implementation of the Belfast Agreement than they may presently believe to be the case. When it comes to making peace there is no need to be faint-hearted.

Conclusion

The Northern Ireland roller-coaster

The two governments made real efforts to get the difficult issues of decommissioning, demilitarisation and police reform resolved before the election campaigns got into full swing but negotiations seemed to have entered a state of near paralysis. The peace polls review articles had been written and published in the hope that progress could have been made. But the dynamics of electoral competition and playing the 'blame game' combined to make the political culture of Northern Ireland quite impervious to such advances.

All the parties wanted to appear to be strong in the eyes of their electorate. Sinn Féin would not accept British proposals for reform of the RUC, so the SDLP would not accept them either. Sinn Féin would not make a start on decommissioning, so David Trimble said he would resign after the elections if decommissioning did not happen. Predictably the IRA did not respond to this threat and David Trimble did keep his promise, placing the Northern Ireland Assembly on a six-week 'suspended sentence' effective from the end of June 2001. If decommissioning still did not happen and if the First and Deputy First Minister could not be re-elected the Secretary of State would have to call for new elections or suspend the Northern Ireland Assembly by Friday 10 August 2001.

In an effort to avoid all of these difficulties the two governments arranged for a new round of negotiations to be undertaken away from Northern Ireland at Westland Park, England, in early July. Quite a lot had changed. The elections were past which should have made matters easier. But the centre parties had lost support to the DUP and Sinn Féin. If negotiations failed yet again new Assembly elections might very well lead to more successes for the DUP and Sinn Féin and then they might be required to share the top ministerial posts. But the prospects of the DUP and Sinn Féin successfully sharing power together were remote in the extreme and the collapse of the Belfast Agreement followed by a review seemed to be the more likely outcome. At some point the negotiations would have to be successful and it would be better if this were done sooner rather than later.

There was no reason, in principle, why all of the outstanding problems of implementation should not have been the subject of a new public opinion poll. But the political culture of the negotiations, which had been inclusive of the smaller Loyalist and centre parties during the Stormont talks and Mitchell Review, were now substantially limited to the two governments, Sinn Féin, the Ulster Unionists and SDLP, what the media were calling the 'Big Battalions'. A collective and inclusive approach to decision-making had been replaced with the political culture of executive power. The creative thinking of the centre parties, which had been so indispensable to the success of the peace polls, was being ignored and the Loyalists were increasingly returning to violence when politics did not work for them. These matters were brought to a head when, for the first time, the Alliance party, Women's Coalition, PUP and UDP were sent home from the negotiations because, they were told, their presence was not required. The negotiations at Westland Park failed to produce the hoped-for breakthrough, but perhaps some lessons had been learnt.

The level of engagement with the peace polls depended on a party's interest in using them to find solutions to problems rather than party strength. For similar reasons many of the smaller pro-agreement parties had frequently proposed the establishment of a committee or commission to address problems of implementation as they arose.[1] At the very least it was an idea worth trying as an alternative to the strategy of crisis management by presidential visit, ministerial resignation, institutional suspension and agreement review. So following the failure of Westland Park, when the two governments published a new 'take it or leave it' package on 1 August 2001, aimed at resolving all the outstanding issues, it came as a pleasant surprise that it now included the formation of an 'Implementation Group'.

With a little more work the SDLP accepted the revised policing plan that was part of these new proposals. This was an important step, for without Nationalist backing it was difficult to see how the new Police Service of Northern Ireland would be able to attract sufficient numbers of Catholics into its ranks. No one seriously expected Sinn Féin to join the new Policing Board until the changes, promised in the plan, saw their way into law, but, with much disappointment, the IRA did not make the hoped-for start to decommissioning by the 10 August deadline. Many Republicans still had serious doubts about David Trimble's ability to control the anti-agreement wing of the Ulster Unionist Council and maintain support for an inclusive Executive. So the Secretary of State called a token one-day suspension which gave the Assembly and parties an additional six weeks to try and resolve their differences.

The prospects of success seemed very poor indeed. In the continued uncertainty created by threats of suspension, and in the absence of the formation of an Implementation Group to work with, it proved to be impossible to use the medium of public opinion polling to any worthwhile effect. A little more stability was required and this point was brought to the attention of the parties. But if, as many anticipated, the new deadline passed without decommissioning or the re-election of the First and Deputy First Minister then new Assembly elections and/or an indefinite period of suspension and review would follow. In these unfortunate circumstances it would be possible to collectively work on a new survey of public opinion if that is what the parties wished to do. Preparations were made for this eventuality but then the whole world changed.

On 11 September 2001 two hijacked passenger planes were flown into the twin towers of the World Trade Centre in New York killing almost 3000 people from over 100 nations. The United States and her allies around the world declared a war on terrorism which, many Unionists were quick to argue, should include the IRA who had also recently been found to have links with terrorist groups in Columbia heavily involved in the US drugs trade. Sinn Féin needed to retain the goodwill of the American people and the funding they received from US supporters and they now found themselves the subject of growing political attention and pressure. At the end of September, in these very new circumstances, the Secretary of State decided to give Sinn Féin and the IRA another six weeks to make a start on decommissioning. If it did not happen this time he would have to call fresh Assembly elections or a suspension and review.

It is interesting to note that just before the then current deadline expired the BBC in Northern Ireland broadcast the results of a public opinion poll that gave support to the UUP joining the Police Board in partnership with the SDLP.[2] This they did and one more indispensable element of the peace process was put in place. In another survey published on 4 October the *Daily Telegraph* reported the findings of a poll in which 89 per cent of United Kingdom respondents said they considered the IRA to be terrorists and 79 per cent believed Sinn Féin should be excluded from the Executive if the IRA did not decommission.[3] Under mounting pressure from the US administration the IRA made their move and on 23 October General de Chastelain of the IICD was able to report that he had witnessed 'an event in which the IRA has put a quantity of arms completely beyond use. The material includes arms, ammunition and explosives.'

Decommissioning had happened and a poll published in the *Belfast Telegraph* on Thursday 1 November recorded 54 per cent of Protestants as wanting David Trimble to go back into government as First Minister. Only 27 per cent did not and 19 per cent didn't know.[4] But on Friday 2 November he failed to get re-elected when two of his own party members failed to give him their votes. The PUP and Women's Coalition had supported David Trimble on this occasion but it was only with the additional backing of the Alliance on Monday 5 November that he got his job back and the Assembly was able to get up and running. Perhaps the small centre and Loyalist parties would not be ignored again and told their presence was no longer required.

On this occasion a further suspension and review had been avoided, though only just and then with a considerable degree of luck. But all the polls indicated strong support for local representation and devolution across all parties including Sinn Féin. So hopefully now the desire of the people and interests of those in power will combine to produce a period of relative political stability and progress. However, if the luck runs out and the two governments ever do find they have to take a more proactive approach to implementation then it might be best if this were done in combination with the new institutions created under the terms of the Belfast Agreement. With the notable exception of those very few who actively seek a return to war, everyone fears and no one wants a political vacuum.

The future of the peace polls

During these roller-coaster weeks and months public opinion polls had continued to play a critical role in the Northern Ireland peace process. But they had not been 'peace polls' as such – surveys of public opinion undertaken with the collective participation of the parties to the negotiations. Perhaps now, with all the benefits of hindsight, it may be possible to look back over the years of polling and say what kinds of polls were most effective for what reasons.

The first poll was undertaken by a group of academics as a research exercise to test various policy options for peace building. What was special about it was the effort made to include policies from across the political spectrum so that they would be tested against each other as a series of public preferences. In hindsight this *Public Preference Poll* could have been significantly improved with the inclusion of the 'Essential', 'Desirable', 'Acceptable', 'Tolerable' and 'Unacceptable' scale used in later polls as well as questions that rank ordered problems and solutions. These Public Preference Polls can be undertaken by almost anybody at any time and perhaps should always be encouraged as one of many steps in a peace process and/or tool for conflict analysis.

What are being called *Peace Polls* here are technically no different to the Public Preference Polls except, critically, they are designed with and run for the politicians who must negotiate a peace agreement. In hindsight the success of these polls was very much dependent on the willingness of the parties to become involved. In Northern Ireland the stage was set for this participation with the creation of the Forum for Peace and Reconciliation. If a series of Peace Polls cannot, at some point, lead to real negotiations then politicians will inevitably come to question their practical relevance. Little may be lost by running one Peace Poll, but the credibility of the work would undoubtedly suffer if subsequent polls were not supported by some kind of formal peace initiative.

The last poll run in the Northern Ireland series was undertaken to help the peace process through a critical decision that had to be taken by the Ulster Unionist Council. Similar polls were subsequently run by the BBC and *Belfast Telegraph*. These *Save the Day Polls* require impeccable timing that in turn requires the assistance of a very able market research company that can do both quick and accurate work. Save the Day Polls may be absolutely essential when they are needed but they are arguably partisan and are probably best left to the appropriate party to arrange if they are able to do so.

Partisan Polls are to be avoided by Peace Poll researchers. Although the poll published in the *Daily Telegraph*, on 4 October 2001, underlined how people then felt about terrorism and the IRA it probably did little to advance the Northern Ireland peace process. Sinn Féin dismissed the poll as the work of a right-wing, conservative, British establishment newspaper and, in Irish Republican circles, confirmed their views of that establishment by ignoring the problems of Nationalists. Peace Polls can and should deal with difficult and controversial issues but must do so in a balanced way.

So when it comes to analysing conflicts and promoting peace in other parts of the world running a *Public Preference Poll* would seem to be a very good thing to do indeed. Running a Peace Poll with the co-operation of willing politicians would also seem to be a good thing to do. But the work must become part of a wider political process aimed at conflict resolution if it is to be continued. Save the Day Polls may be indispensable on occasions but are more problematic and should be done under advisement while Partisan Polls should be avoided.

As far as Northern Ireland is concerned there will undoubtedly be more Partisan Polls run from time to time and probably a few more Save the Day Polls undertaken by various media interests. Academics may run more Public Preference Polls in Northern Ireland but once progress has been made to involve politicians in their design it would seem to be an unfortunate step backwards to leave them 'out of the loop'. If the parties require another Peace Poll the resources will almost certainly be made available to them. The choice is theirs and the people's peace process – one way or another – will eventually reach a successful conclusion because, as all the polls show, that is what the people want.

Appendix: Sample Questionnaire (With results for Northern Ireland as a whole)

For more questionnaires and results see www.peacepolls.org

MRNI Ltd
46 Elmwood Avenue
Belfast
BT9 6AW

Tel (01232) 661037

Interviewer   ....

Date   ....

Quest No: 1–4

In search of a settlement

Good morning/afternoon/evening. My name is .... from MRNI Ltd. We are currently undertaking a survey aimed at discovering what the people of Northern Ireland would find acceptable as part of a settlement.

The questions deal with the most important issues and include:

> The principal causes of the conflict and possible solutions
> Human rights
> Reforming the police service
> A regional assembly
> North/South bodies
> Constitutional issues
> Relations between Britain and Ireland
> Implementing and agreeing a settlement

The results of the survey will be analysed and widely published in the local press and in reports that will be sent to *all* ten parties who have been elected to take part in the Stormont Talks.

The research is independently funded by the Joseph Rowntree Trust and is being undertaken by Dr Colin Irwin at the Queen's University of Belfast.

All your answers will be kept completely confidential.

The survey involves interviewing one thousand people from across Northern Ireland to complete a representative sample in terms of age, gender, social class, political and religious affiliation and geographical area.

If you would like to take part in the survey I will start by asking you a few questions about your background to see where you fit into our sample. We can then work on a few questions together and then I will let you finish the questionnaire yourself and arrange to collect it when you have completed it.

Postcode   _____

County   _____

District Council   _____

Parliamentary Constituency   _____

Telephone Number   _____

FOR OFFICE USE ONLY	
DATE RECEIVED	
DATE BACKCHECKED	

Background questions

It is very important that we answer all the questions in this section to ensure that we have given every section of the community a chance to participate in the survey. Please remember that all responses are totally CONFIDENTIAL.

A   Age

Please indicate into which of the following age ranges you may be placed.

18–24	16
25–34	21
35–44	18
45–54	15
55–64	12
65 and over	18

B   Gender (Interviewer to code)

Male	49
Female	51

C   Occupation: What is or was the occupation of the chief wage earner in your household?

AB	15
C1	28
C2	23
DE	34

D Religion

Could you please tell me which of the following best describes your religion? (Please remember that all responses are totally CONFIDENTIAL.)

SHOWCARD 1

Protestant	50
Catholic	40
Other	2
Refused	8

E Political support

Which ONE of these Northern Ireland political parties do you support?

SHOWCARD 2

UUP/Ulster Unionist Party/OUP/Official Unionist Party	23
SDLP/Social Democratic Labour Party	20
DUP/Democratic Unionist Party	10
Sinn Féin	15
Alliance	9
UK Unionist Party	1
PUP/Progressive Unionist Party	4
UDP/Ulster Democratic Party	1
Woman's Coalition Party of Northern Ireland	1
Labour Party of Northern Ireland	*
Other (Write in) _____	3
Refused	13

F   Identity

(Ask for each option in turn)

Do you feel you are 'Strongly', 'Moderately', 'Slightly' or 'Not at all'...?

SHOWCARD 3

	Strongly	Moderately	Slightly	Not at all
Loyalist	17	13	10	60
Republican	8	8	9	75
Unionist	25	15	10	50
Nationalist	17	12	8	63
'The Centre Ground'	13	20	19	48

	Strongly	Moderately	Slightly	Not at all
European	3	18	31	48
Northern Irish	20	27	20	33
British	40	13	9	38
Irish	31	12	12	45
Both British and Irish	8	15	19	58

1. Reasons for the Northern Ireland conflict

People from different communities often hold very different views about the causes of the conflict in Northern Ireland. Please indicate which ones you consider to be 'Very Significant' 'Significant', 'Of Some Significance', 'Of Little Significance' or 'Of No Significance' at all.

SHOWCARD 4

	Very Significant	Significant	Of Some Significance	Of Little Significance	Of No Significance
The continued British presence on the island of Ireland	32	15	19	13	21
The Republic of Ireland's involvement in Northern Ireland	29	18	23	16	14
The British government's pursuit of a political settlement	22	17	33	17	11
The Republic's territorial claim on Northern Ireland	38	19	17	12	14

Contd.

The failures of Northern Ireland politicians	46	22	24	5	3
Unaccountable and secretive government	40	21	22	10	7
The lack of equality and continued discrimination	43	18	18	10	11
Segregated education	30	18	22	15	15
Segregated public housing	28	22	24	13	13
A lack of respect for the people of the 'other' tradition	43	26	20	7	4
The sectarian division of Northern Ireland politics	47	24	16	5	8
The prominent role of the Roman Catholic Church	21	22	22	19	16
The 'Established Church' in Britain and the Orange Order	18	22	27	19	14
The Irish Republican Army and their use of violence	68	11	9	4	8
The Loyalist paramilitaries and their use of violence	55	17	15	7	6
All paramilitary groups and their use of violence	61	18	14	4	3
The British Army and their use of violence	24	16	21	14	25
The failure to provide a police service acceptable to all	32	15	19	15	19
The failure of government and the security forces to deal with terrorism	48	21	17	8	6

Choosing your options for a lasting settlement

Most of the remainder of this questionnaire will present you with various options on what could be the different parts of a settlement.

For each option you will be asked to indicate which ones you consider to be 'Essential', 'Desirable', 'Acceptable', 'Tolerable' or 'Unacceptable'.

For the purposes of this poll 'Essential', 'Desirable', 'Acceptable', 'Tolerable' and 'Unacceptable' mean:

SHOWCARD 5

'Essential' – You believe this option is a necessary part of a lasting settlement and should be implemented under any circumstances.

'Desirable' – This option is not what you would consider to be 'Essential', but you think this option, or something very similar to it, is a good idea and should be put into practice.

'Acceptable' – This option is not what you would consider to be 'Desirable', if you were given a choice, but you could certainly 'live with it'.

'Tolerable' – This option is not what you want. But, as part of a lasting settlement for Northern Ireland, you would be willing to put up with it.

'Unacceptable' – This option is completely unacceptable under any circumstances. You would not accept it, even as part of a lasting settlement.

You may use each of the terms 'Essential', 'Desirable', 'Acceptable', 'Tolerable' and 'Unacceptable' as many times as you wish in each question.

2. Steps towards a lasting peace in Northern Ireland

As steps needed to help secure a lasting peace please indicate which of the following options you consider to be 'Essential', 'Desirable', 'Acceptable', 'Tolerable' or 'Unacceptable'.

SHOWCARD 6

	Essential	Desirable	Acceptable	Tolerable	Unacceptable
British withdrawal from Northern Ireland	20	14	13	10	43
End the Anglo-Irish Agreement	24	17	21	19	19
Integrate Northern Ireland into the UK	20	14	20	12	34
The Republic ends their claim on Northern Ireland	38	13	12	10	27
Reformed and shared government	21	14	28	18	19

Contd.

Open government and Freedom of Information Act	33	25	25	11	6
A Bill of Rights that guarantees equality for all	54	22	17	6	1
A right to choose integrated education	43	24	26	4	3
A right to choose integrated housing	39	24	28	6	3
A Bill of Rights that protects the culture of each community	49	22	23	4	2
Politics without a sectarian division	43	29	19	6	3
Separate politics and religion in the Republic	24	23	27	13	13
Separate politics and religion in Northern Ireland	27	26	26	10	11
Disband all paramilitary groups	70	12	10	4	4
Return the army to their barracks	31	14	20	11	24
Completely reform the police service	34	10	14	11	31
Stronger and effective anti-terrorist measures	57	18	13	5	7

3. Protecting the rights of the people of Northern Ireland

The European Convention on Human Rights

The European Convention on Human Rights protects individuals by guaranteeing each person:

the right...
To life.
Not to be tortured or subjected to inhuman or degrading treatment.
To protection from slavery or forced work.
Not to be unlawfully arrested or detained.
To a fair trial.
To freedom of belief and expression.
To free association.
To privacy and family life.
Not to be discriminated against.
To a remedy for breaches of human rights.

The new Labour government plan to introduce this Convention into the domestic law of the United Kingdom of Great Britain and Northern Ireland. This will allow any complaints regarding failures to meet these minimum standards to be heard by courts in the UK and Northern Ireland. Do you think this is 'Essential', 'Desirable', 'Acceptable', 'Tolerable' or 'Unacceptable'.

	Essential	Desirable	Acceptable	Tolerable	Unacceptable
The European Convention on Human Rights should be part of the domestic law of Northern Ireland	51	23	17	7	2

An additional Bill of Rights for Northern Ireland

Some recent negotiated settlements have included a Bill of Rights to deal with many of the special political, social and cultural problems that lay at the heart of their conflict. Please indicate which of these options you consider to be 'Essential', 'Desirable', 'Acceptable', 'Tolerable' or 'Unacceptable'.

	Essential	Desirable	Acceptable	Tolerable	Unacceptable
An additional Bill of Rights to address the special problems of Northern Ireland	38	29	20	8	5
No additional Bill of Rights, just new laws to address the special problems of Northern Ireland	12	17	35	17	19

Human rights courts and commissions

How should Human Rights complaints be dealt with? Please indicate which of these options you consider to be 'Essential', 'Desirable', 'Acceptable', 'Tolerable' or 'Unacceptable'.

	Essential	Desirable	Acceptable	Tolerable	Unacceptable
A special Court to hear Human Rights complaints	31	25	31	8	5
A Commission to monitor, investigate and promote Human Rights	24	28	31	11	6
A Commission with powers to bring Human Rights complaints to court	32	26	28	8	6

Economic, social and cultural rights

In addition to the European Convention on Human Rights other international conventions include:

the right to:
Food, clothing and shelter
Health
Education
Work
Safe and fair conditions of work
Social security
Cultural expression

These economic, social and cultural rights could be included in a Northern Ireland Bill of Rights. Do you think this is 'Essential', 'Desirable', 'Acceptable', 'Tolerable' or 'Unacceptable'.

	Essential	Desirable	Acceptable	Tolerable	Unacceptable
Economic, social and cultural Rights should be part of a Northern Ireland Bill	52	24	20	3	1

Collective rights of peoples and members of minorities

Some international conventions also include collective rights. Please indicate which ones you consider to be 'Essential', 'Desirable', 'Acceptable', 'Tolerable' or 'Unacceptable' for Northern Ireland.

The right...	Essential	Desirable	Acceptable	Tolerable	Unacceptable
To self-determination	46	26	19	5	4
To practise their religion, use their language and enjoy their culture	52	17	17	10	4
To be taught or educated in their distinctive language	29	18	26	16	11
To participate effectively in government on matters affecting them	39	23	25	8	5
To parity of treatment and esteem	44	24	19	9	4
Not to be treated as members of a distinct community against their will	50	21	17	6	6

Collective and minority rights in Northern Ireland

Collective rights can be introduced into Northern Ireland law in a number of different ways. Please indicate which options you consider to be 'Essential', 'Desirable', 'Acceptable', 'Tolerable' or 'Unacceptable'.

	Essential	Desirable	Acceptable	Tolerable	Unacceptable
A Bill of Rights that includes collective and minority rights	35	23	25	10	7
A British and Irish Treaty to protect minority rights	25	16	23	15	21
No Bill of Rights or Treaty to protect minorities, just new policies and laws	12	12	27	18	31

Some special rights for Northern Ireland

It may also be necessary to include some rights that deal specifically with some of the political, social and cultural problems that are distinctive features of the Northern Ireland conflict. Please indicate which ones you consider to be 'Essential', 'Desirable', 'Acceptable', 'Tolerable' or 'Unacceptable'.

The right to ...	Essential	Desirable	Acceptable	Tolerable	Unacceptable
Freedom of political expression	57	22	19	2	0
Freedom of religious expression	61	20	16	3	0
Freedom from incitement to hatred	67	17	12	1	3
Freedom of worship	73	17	10	0	0
Freedom from intimidation	78	11	9	1	1
Peaceful demonstrations and parades	53	22	15	8	2
The right to use the Irish language	31	17	22	19	11
Education in Irish language schools	28	16	23	20	13
Education in Integrated schools	37	27	21	12	3
Education in Catholic schools	32	19	28	15	6
Education in Protestant schools	35	23	31	9	2
Choose single religion public housing	21	12	25	19	23
Choose mixed religion public housing	32	26	25	11	6

4. Reforming the police service

Reforming the police services in Northern Ireland can be divided up into several issues.

Police complaints procedures

At the present time complaints against the RUC are investigated by the police and supervised by an independent commission. Please indicate which of the following options you consider to be 'Essential', 'Desirable', 'Acceptable', 'Tolerable' or 'Unacceptable' with regards to this procedure.

	Essential	Desirable	Acceptable	Tolerable	Unacceptable
Give the existing commission more scope to initiate and supervise complaints but maintain the role of the RUC in the investigation	18	17	27	14	24
Establish a completely independent agency to deal with all aspects of investigations into complaints against the RUC	40	20	19	10	11

The character of the police force

Please indicate which of the following options you consider to be 'Essential', 'Desirable', 'Acceptable', 'Tolerable' or 'Unacceptable' with regards to the future character of the police service.

	Essential	Desirable	Acceptable	Tolerable	Unacceptable
Special training in community relations and human rights	44	30	23	2	1
A policing charter to set duties and responsibilities in law	36	30	26	6	2
Monitor policing standards and publish reports	39	31	21	7	2
Recruit more Catholics	42	19	22	12	5
A new name for the RUC more acceptable across the whole community	25	12	17	13	33

Contd.

New emblems and symbols more acceptable across the whole community	26	12	15	12	35
Require police to declare their membership of Loyal Orders	36	11	9	12	32
Do not allow police to be members of Loyal Orders	31	10	9	8	42
Make the Oath of Allegiance more acceptable across the whole community	29	16	15	10	30
The police should not normally be armed	17	20	15	8	40
Leave the police service as it is	16	15	15	15	39

The structure of the police force

At the present time the Royal Ulster Constabulary is a single force that has responsibility for providing all policing duties throughout the whole of Northern Ireland. Please indicate which of the following options you consider to be 'Essential', 'Desirable', 'Acceptable', 'Tolerable' or 'Unacceptable' regarding the structure of the police force.

	Essential	Desirable	Acceptable	Tolerable	Unacceptable
Create new community policing units as part of the RUC	16	28	27	11	18
Create new community policing units separate to the RUC	11	13	24	16	36
Disband the RUC and create a new single police force	20	10	12	10	48
Disband the RUC and create a number of regional and city forces	11	12	16	10	51
Leave current policing structures as they are	18	14	19	13	36

Responsibility for policing services

Present responsibility for policing in Northern Ireland is divided between the Secretary of State, the Chief Constable and the Police Authority of Northern Ireland. Community Police Liaison Committees, established by District Councils, also have a consultation role. Please indicate which of the following options you consider to be 'Essential', 'Desirable', 'Acceptable', 'Tolerable' or 'Unacceptable' regarding future responsibility for policing services.

Give more responsibility for the management of the police services to:	Essential	Desirable	Acceptable	Tolerable	Unacceptable
The Secretary of State	9	10	25	23	33
A new Department of Justice and Northern Ireland Assembly	13	22	26	18	21
The Chief Constable	14	17	29	16	24
The Police Authority of Northern Ireland	12	15	32	16	25
A number of regional and city Police Authorities	6	12	29	25	28
Community Liaison Committees	12	17	27	18	26
Or no change – leave the responsibility for the police service as it is	14	16	19	14	37

Political reform and the Stormont talks

The Stormont talks have been divided into three parts called Strands.

Strand One covers relationships in Northern Ireland and deals with questions of regional government.

Strand Two covers relationships within the island of Ireland and deals with North/South bodies.

Strand Three covers relationships between the British and Irish governments and deals with a replacement for the Anglo-Irish Agreement.

Negotiations also include constitutional issues.

5. Strand One: political reform in Northern Ireland

At the present time Northern Ireland is governed under Direct Rule from Westminster with most important decisions being made by the Northern Ireland Office. Please indicate which reforms you consider to be 'Essential', 'Desirable', 'Acceptable', 'Tolerable' or 'Unacceptable'.

The structure and powers of a Regional Assembly

Establish a Northern Ireland Regional Assembly with:	Essential	Desirable	Acceptable	Tolerable	Unacceptable
An elected assembly	25	26	33	8	8
An appointed second chamber or senate	5	8	37	20	20
Committees that shadow and monitor the departments of the Northern Ireland Office	20	20	33	15	12
Powers of administration	17	23	38	14	8
Powers to initiate and develop new policies	19	25	34	13	9
Powers to make new laws	18	23	29	15	15
Powers to alter taxes	12	16	33	17	22
Or no assembly – Northern Ireland should *not* have a regional assembly	6	10	15	23	46

Appointments in a Regional Assembly

Chairpersons and the membership of committees are assigned:	Essential	Desirable	Acceptable	Tolerable	Unacceptable
In proportion to the representation of each party in the assembly	23	22	27	16	12
Equally between the two main traditions	30	17	14	18	21

Voting in a Regional Assembly

Voting in the Assembly is by:	Essential	Desirable	Acceptable	Tolerable	Unacceptable
Simple majority for all business	18	21	29	12	20
'Weighted' majority to ensure the support of both of the main traditions for *all* business	16	18	28	18	20
'Weighted' maority for *contentious* business only	5	12	29	26	28
'Sufficient Consensus' which requires a majority from *both* of the main traditions for all business	15	22	27	18	18
'Sufficient Consensus' for *contentious* business only	7	11	31	26	25

The Executive in a Regional Government

Members of the Executive are appointed:	Essential	Desirable	Acceptable	Tolerable	Unacceptable
Equally between the two main traditions	32	16	17	15	20
In proportion to the representation of each party in the assembly	20	22	28	19	11
From the party or coalition that can form a majority	6	13	26	23	32
Only from parties committed to principles of democracy and non-violence	51	21	12	7	9

The Executive in a Regional Government

And the Executive in the Assembly is:	Essential	Desirable	Acceptable	Tolerable	Unacceptable
Appointed by the Secretary of State	6	9	26	23	36
Nominated by the Secretary of State for approval by the assembly	6	17	32	24	21
Voted in by the members of the assembly	18	25	35	14	8
Made up from the Chairpersons of each committee in the assembly	7	16	41	22	14
Or no executive – All the business of government is conducted by the various committees	2	9	25	29	35

The leadership in a Regional Government

The Assembly should have:	Essential	Desirable	Acceptable	Tolerable	Unacceptable
A leader and deputy leader representing the two main traditions	20	28	25	14	13
A 'panel' of three prominent politicians sharing power	10	13	35	20	22

And they should be:	Essential	Desirable	Acceptable	Tolerable	Unacceptable
Appointed by the Secretary of State	7	8	24	22	39
Nominated by the Secretary of State for approval by the assembly	9	12	29	26	24
Voted in by the members of the assembly	16	19	38	16	11
Voted for directly by the people of Northern Ireland	46	20	21	8	5

Or no leader, deputy leader or 'panel':	Essential	Desirable	Acceptable	Tolerable	Unacceptable
All the business of government is conducted by the executive and/or committees	7	11	33	27	22

Local government

More powers and responsibilities should be given to local government:	Essential	Desirable	Acceptable	Tolerable	Unacceptable
Even if there is no Northern Ireland Assembly	15	22	35	15	13
But a new Northern Ireland Assembly should decide how this is done	13	22	43	11	11
To replace the work presently undertaken by various boards	8	24	41	16	11
And combine some of the smaller 26 District Councils to create larger units of local government	8	20	35	20	17

Safeguards and protections

All levels of government in Northern Ireland should be protected by laws that ensure:	Essential	Desirable	Acceptable	Tolerable	Unacceptable
The views of representatives from the whole community are taken into account	52	25	16	3	4
Political and administrative responsibilities are shared	36	26	24	7	7
Power can not be abused by one group over another	60	19	17	2	2
And independent committees or courts of arbitrators should be established to resolve problems that become intractable	40	24	23	7	6

6. Strand Two: reforming the relationship between Northern Ireland and the Republic of Ireland

The Foyle Fisheries Commission has been established as a 'North/South Body' between the former Northern Ireland parliament at Stormont and the Republic of Ireland to jointly manage the waters of the Foyle estuary. Similar bodies, or a single body, could be established to deal with other matters of mutual concern.

The responsibilities of North/South bodies

These bodies could be set up to deal with various aspects of government policy with different powers or functions. Please indicate which powers or functions you consider to be 'Essential', 'Desirable', 'Acceptable', 'Tolerable' or 'Unacceptable'.

On matters of mutual interest North/South bodies should:	Essential	Desirable	Acceptable	Tolerable	Unacceptable
Be required to consult	33	21	20	10	16
Be required to co-operate	34	22	17	9	18
Have powers to administer laws made by the separate government in the North and the South of Ireland	17	21	19	12	31
Have powers to develop and execute forward planning for the island of Ireland as a whole	21	19	14	10	36
Have powers to make laws which would apply to the island of Ireland as a whole	20	13	16	9	42
Or there should not be any North/South bodies with any powers or functions	16	10	11	18	45

And what areas of government policy should North/South bodies deal with:

	Essential	Desirable	Acceptable	Tolerable	Unacceptable
The environment	39	21	19	10	11
Agriculture	39	21	17	9	14
Fisheries	38	22	19	9	12
Tourism	44	21	15	8	12
Medical care and research	37	19	18	8	18
Roads and public transport	34	19	20	9	18

Contd.

	Essential	Desirable	Acceptable	Tolerable	Unacceptable
Water, gas and electric	29	22	19	10	20
Communications	33	21	20	8	18
Industrial development boards	30	19	20	11	20
Financial institutions	25	18	22	12	23
Economic development in general	31	20	18	12	19
Training and employment	29	21	18	9	23
Joint representation in Europe	31	19	17	11	22
Trade	34	18	19	10	19
Taxation	21	14	18	14	33
Broadcasting and film	22	19	23	16	20
Minority languages	24	16	20	18	22
Culture and sport	30	19	23	11	17
Local government and planning	25	14	18	11	32
Social services	26	14	18	13	29
Human rights	43	14	11	10	22
Education	32	13	16	12	27
Policing and security	34	13	12	7	34
Defence	31	13	14	8	34
Foreign policy	27	15	15	12	31

The structure and control of North/South bodies

Please indicate which options you consider to be 'Essential', 'Desirable', 'Acceptable', 'Tolerable' or 'Unacceptable' with regard to the structure and powers of North/South bodies.

Matters of mutual interest should be dealt with by:	Essential	Desirable	Acceptable	Tolerable	Unacceptable
One North/South body for everything	16	16	21	16	31
A separate North/South body for each issue	10	18	29	16	27
Powers to establish and dissolve North/ South bodies should be given to:	Essential	Desirable	Acceptable	Tolerable	Unacceptable
A Northern Ireland Assembly and the Irish Dail (Parliament)	14	15	22	15	34
Westminster and Dublin	3	11	20	18	48

Contd.

Westminster, Dublin and a Northern Ireland Assembly	13	18	25	16	28
North/South bodies should:	Essential	Desirable	Acceptable	Tolerable	Unacceptable
Able to act independently	12	18	24	14	32
Controlled by and responsible to the respective governments parliamentary bodies and NI Assembly who establish them	17	20	26	17	20
The management of North/South bodies should be undertaken by:	Essential	Desirable	Acceptable	Tolerable	Unacceptable
Elected politicians	18	16	32	16	18
civil servants	4	8	24	24	40
Both elected politicians and civil servants	6	15	32	21	26
Representatives of business, trade unions, local government etc. as and when required	15	21	26	18	20
North/South bodies should:	Essential	Desirable	Acceptable	Tolerable	Unacceptable
Only deal with specific projects agreed to by the politicians who set up the bodies	11	12	32	23	22
Only deal with policies agreed to by the politicians who set up the bodies	7	11	33	24	25
'Harmonise' their actions, policies and laws in the areas of policy they are responsible for	11	18	34	18	19
Only deal with policies the European Union is responsible for	2	8	29	27	34

Contd.

Only do business with the European Union	2	7	24	25	42
Deal with all aspects of government business	15	14	23	17	31
Appointments to a North/South body should be made:	Essential	Desirable	Acceptable	Tolerable	Unacceptable
In proportion to the representation of each party in the Northern Ireland Assembly	15	19	27	19	20
Equally between the two main traditions in the North	20	18	22	17	23
Equally between Northern Ireland and the Republic of Ireland	20	14	20	14	32
Voting on business in a North/South body requires:	Essential	Desirable	Acceptable	Tolerable	Unacceptable
A simple majority only	8	15	25	19	33
A weighted majority	8	15	28	20	29
A majority from *both* of the main traditions in the North	18	17	27	17	21
A majority from *both* Northern Ireland and the Republic of Ireland	18	17	20	15	30
Unanimity – Everyone has to agree	22	20	19	13	26

7. Constitutional issues

The Constitution of the Republic of Ireland makes both legal claims on the territory of Northern Ireland and a claim of jurisdiction.

In an effort to meet the concerns of the different communities in Northern Ireland several possibilities are available for the modification of the Republic's Constitution. Please indicate which reforms you consider to be 'Essential', 'Desirable', 'Acceptable', 'Tolerable' or 'Unacceptable'.

The Republic of Ireland's constitutional claim over Northern Ireland should:	Essential	Desirable	Acceptable	Tolerable	Unacceptable
Be completely deleted	37	13	9	8	33
Be modified to only allow for a united Ireland with the consent of a majority of the people of Northern Ireland	22	16	21	17	24
Be replaced with an 'aspiration' for a united Ireland	4	11	20	20	45
Be replaced with a responsibility for the well-being of the Nationalist community in Northern Ireland	7	8	23	23	39
Be amended to reflect any new agreements reached at the Stormont talks	6	15	27	25	27
Be replaced with full and guaranteed rights of Irish citizenship for all members of the Nationalist community in Northern Ireland	14	10	20	20	36
Or the Republic of Ireland's Constitution should not be changed at all	12	7	13	17	51

The Constitutional Status of Northern Ireland as part of the United Kingdom has been established through the Acts of Union and other Acts of Parliament passed in Westminster.

In an effort to meet the concerns of the different communities in Northern Ireland several possibilities are available for the modification of the constitutional status of Northern Ireland. Please indicate which reforms you consider to be 'Essential', 'Desirable', 'Acceptable', 'Tolerable' or 'Unacceptable'.

The constitutional status of Northern Ireland as part of the United Kingdom should:	Essential	Desirable	Acceptable	Tolerable	Unacceptable
Be completely removed	19	11	8	9	53
Only allow for a united Ireland with the consent of a majority of the people of Northern Ireland (No change)	29	17	18	16	20
Be replaced with an 'aspiration' for a single state comprised of the whole of the British Isles and Ireland	2	10	18	20	50
Be replaced with a responsibility for the well-being of the Unionist Community in Northern Ireland	8	10	24	23	35
Be amended to reflect any new agreements reached at the Stormont Talks	8	13	29	22	28
Be replaced with full and guaranteed rights of British citizenship for all members of the Unionist community on the island of Ireland	16	14	24	15	31
Or the constitutional status and boundaries of Northern Ireland should not be changed at all	31	11	15	12	31
Alternatively both governments could provide for Joint Authority, or Repartition:	Essential	Desirable	Acceptable	Tolerable	Unacceptable
Shared authority and sovereignty of Northern Ireland with the Republic of Ireland	9	13	19	11	48

Contd.

Redefine the boundaries of Northern Ireland so that a maximum of Unionists are in the 'North' and a maximum of Nationalists are in the 'South'	2	6	12	14	66

8. Strand Three: reforming the relationship between the Republic of Ireland and the United Kingdom

Principles of co-operation

The British and Irish governments intend to negotiate a new treaty to replace the Anglo-Irish Agreement. Such an agreement can be based on a number of principles. Please indicate which principles you consider to be 'Essential', 'Desirable', 'Acceptable', 'Tolerable' or 'Unacceptable'.

	Essential	Desirable	Acceptable	Tolerable	Unacceptable
Co-operation in Europe	27	28	28	12	5
Peace and stability in Northern Ireland	65	19	12	2	2
Equal rights of the two major traditions	50	19	19	7	5
Rejection of violence for political objectives	66	16	14	2	2
Reconciliation between unionists and nationalists	44	25	19	5	7
Respecting the identities of the two communities	51	22	16	5	6
A society free from discrimination and intolerance	65	21	11	1	2
Both communities to participate fully in the structures and processes of government	48	22	16	7	7
The consent of *a majority* of the people of Northern Ireland is required for any change in it's status	51	17	17	6	9
The recognition of the present status and wishes of the majority of the people of Northern Ireland	47	19	16	9	9

Contd.

The right of *a majority* of the people of Northern Ireland to establish a united Ireland in the future	35	14	20	14	17

Structures for co-operation

Additionally agreement could also to be reached on the kinds of 'bodies' or institutions that should be established to facilitate co-operation. Please indicate which 'bodies' or institutions you consider to be 'Essential', 'Desirable', 'Acceptable', 'Tolerable' or 'Unacceptable'.

As part of a new treaty that replaces the Anglo-Irish Agreement the British and Irish governments should establish:	Essential	Desirable	Acceptable	Tolerable	Unacceptable
A special organisation for consultation between the two governments on Northern Ireland issues only	11	20	29	16	24
Offices in Belfast for consultation between the two governments on Northern Ireland issues only	10	17	33	16	24
A special organisation for consultation between the two governments on any issues of mutual interest	11	20	31	18	20
Offices in London, Dublin and Belfast for consultation between the two governments on any issues of mutual interest	13	22	27	19	19
An inter-parliamentary body to promote good relations between Dublin and Westminster	12	20	28	23	17
An inter-parliamentary body responsible for all agreements made between London and Dublin	11	14	29	20	26
A regional 'Council of the Islands' that facilitates co-operation between Scotland, Wales, England, Northern Ireland and the Republic of Ireland	10	20	31	20	19

Contd.

Or the Anglo-Irish Agreement should be brought to an end and should not be replaced	19	11	18	16	36
However, the Republic of Ireland should rejoin the Commonwealth	8	8	28	22	34

9. Agreeing a settlement

Who should vote in a referendum

The terms of a settlement will have to be voted on in a referendum. In practice most of the issues covered in this questionnaire will probably have to be dealt with together as parts of a settlement 'package'. Please indicate which options for a referendum you consider to be 'Essential', 'Desirable', 'Acceptable', 'Tolerable' or 'Unacceptable'.

	Essential	Desirable	Acceptable	Tolerable	Unacceptable
A referendum in Northern Ireland only	33	19	19	11	18
Separate but concurrent referenda in both Northern Ireland and the Republic of Ireland	10	17	20	15	38
A single referendum in the island of Ireland as a whole	14	11	16	10	49
A single referendum in the United Kingdom of Great Britain and Northern Ireland as a whole	8	7	22	17	46
A single referendum in the United Kingdom of Great Britain plus the island of Ireland as a whole	7	8	15	17	53

How votes should be counted in Northern Ireland

Agreement at the Stormont Talks requires the consent of the political parties who represent a majority from both the Unionist and Nationalist communities in Northern Ireland. How should this principle of 'Sufficient Consent' be applied in a referendum? Please indicate which methods you consider to be 'Essential', 'Desirable', 'Acceptable', 'Tolerable' or 'Unacceptable'.

	Essential	Desirable	Acceptable	Tolerable	Unacceptable
A simple majority – more than 50%	19	19	27	16	19
A 'weighted' majority – about 60%	3	18	36	23	20
A large 'weighted' majority – about 70%	9	16	27	19	29
Everyone living in Unionist and Nationalist areas having their votes counted separately (District Councils, parliamentary constituencies or Counties could be used)	7	9	21	21	42
Everyone in Northern Ireland registering as a Unionist or Nationalist and having their votes counted separately	10	8	17	14	51
Everyone in Northern Ireland being obliged to vote by law and being fined if they don't	17	13	11	12	47

Registration

If a method of voter registration were to be used would you be willing to register as either a Unionist or Nationalist?

Yes	63
No	37

10. The implementation of a settlement

The introduction of political reforms

A comprehensive settlement will have to deal with many changes to political life. This could be done all at once, or gradually over a period of time, perhaps subject to periodic review. How do you think a settlement should be implemented? Please indicate which options you consider to be 'Essential', 'Desirable', 'Acceptable', 'Tolerable' or 'Unacceptable'.

	Essential	Desirable	Acceptable	Tolerable	Unacceptable
The settlement should be final with no more changes allowed	12	16	19	15	38
The settlement should be final but changes could be introduced over an agreed transitional period	7	17	37	22	17
Allow for an interim agreement that can be reviewed after a set period of time	9	17	38	22	14
Introduce reforms slowly subject to periodic assessment and review	11	19	29	24	17

Mechanisms for reviewing a settlement

Even if an overall settlement can be agreed and does receive consent intractable disputes may arise or parts of the settlement may need to be radically reformed at some time in the future. Please indicate which of the following options you consider to be 'Essential', 'Desirable', 'Acceptable', 'Tolerable' or 'Unacceptable'.

As part of a settlement:	Essential	Desirable	Acceptable	Tolerable	Unacceptable
An international court should be established with the responsibility of ruling on disputes	19	19	31	13	18
A mechanism should be put in place that will allow voters to change the terms of the settlement after a minimum period of 10 years	10	17	30	23	20

11. In search of a settlement

The views of the 'other' community

How important do you think it is for people in Northern Ireland to recognise the views and aspirations of the other community as part of a settlement? Do you think it is 'Essential', 'Desirable', 'Acceptable', 'Tolerable' or 'Unacceptable'?

	Essential	Desirable	Acceptable	Tolerable	Unacceptable
The views and aspirations of the 'other' community should be part of a settlement	42	19	20	13	6

A settlement 'package'

A comprehensive Northern Ireland settlement will probably have to deal with all of the issues covered in this questionnaire. Such a 'package' will be placed before the people of Northern Ireland in a referendum. Please indicate which of the following settlement 'packages' you consider to be 'Essential', 'Desirable', 'Acceptable', 'Tolerable' or 'Unacceptable'.

	Essential	Desirable	Acceptable	Tolerable	Unacceptable
Separate Northern Irish state – The complete separation of Northern Ireland from both the United Kingdom and the Republic of Ireland and the establishment of a separate state within the European Union	3	8	17	15	57
Full incorporation into the British state – Direct rule from Westminster and local government similar to the rest of the United Kingdom with no Northern Ireland Assembly or separate laws for Northern Ireland and no Anglo-Irish Agreement	13	14	18	16	39
Continued direct rule (No change) – The continuation of direct rule from London in consultation with the Irish government under the terms of the Anglo-Irish Agreement	2	8	21	25	44
Power sharing and the Anglo-Irish Agreement – Government by a Northern Ireland Assembly and power sharing Executive under the authority of the British government but in consultation with the Irish government under the terms of the Anglo-Irish Agreement	3	8	24	23	42

Contd.

Power sharing with North–South institutions but no joint authority – Government by a Northern Ireland Assembly, power sharing Executive and a number of joint institutions established with the Republic of Ireland to deal with matters of mutual interest. (But these arrangements will not include joint authority between the British and Irish governments.)	3	11	23	23	40
Joint authority and power sharing – Government by joint authority between the British and Irish governments in association with an elected power sharing Executive and Assembly	4	13	20	14	49
Separate institutions for the two main communities – Creation of separate structures for the government of each of the two main communities in Northern Ireland, subject to joint authority by the British and Irish governments	3	5	17	20	55
Full incorporation into the Irish state – Full incorporation of Northern Ireland into the Republic of Ireland to create a single state within the European Union	14	12	9	9	56

12. Your views and comments

A settlement has to deal with a lot of difficult and sometimes complex issues. Do you think more should be done to explain these issues to the general public:

By:	Essential	Desirable	Acceptable	Tolerable	Unacceptable
The political party you support	42	26	19	7	6
The television, radio and press	42	28	22	6	2
The British government and Northern Ireland Office	50	24	18	6	2
The Irish government	29	16	18	11	26

Finally if you have any views and comments on any of the issues dealt with here please feel free to add them below:

Notes and References

Preface

1 C. J. Irwin, 'Half-way Mark for a Mighty Endeavour', *Geographical Magazine*, April 1972. C. J. Irwin, 'Alone through the Northwest Passage', *Geographical Magazine*, July 1971.

2 C. J. Irwin, 'The Inuit and the Evolution of Limited Group Conflict', in *Sociobiology and Conflict*, ed. J. van der Dennen and V. Falger (London: Chapman and Hall, 1990) pp. 189–226.

3 C. J. Irwin, 'How Many Sleeps to Thom Bay'. Made in co-operation with *Southern Independent Television*. A one-hour documentary film that investigated the problems and implications of social and cultural change amongst the Inuit of Spence Bay, Northwest Territories, Canada (1974).

4 C. J. Irwin, 'Trek Across Arctic America', *National Geographic Magazine*, March (1974). For an account of the navigation techniques used see C. J. Irwin, 'Inuit Navigation, Empirical Reasoning and Survival', *Journal of the Royal Institute of Navigation*, Vol. 38, No. 2 (1985) pp. 178–90.

5 C. J. Irwin, 'Chesterfield Inlet: a Discussion Paper on Some Demographic, Social and Economic Problems Facing the New Generation', *84th Annual Meeting of the American Anthropological Association*, Washington, D.C., December 1985.

6 C. J. Irwin, 'Lords of the Arctic: Wards of the State, a Postscript', *Northern Perspectives*. pp. 19–20, Vol. 17, No. 1, January–March 1989. C. J. Irwin, 'Lords of the Arctic: Wards of the State, a Summary Report', *Northern Perspectives*, pp. 2–12, Vol. 17, No. 1, January–March (1989). C. J. Irwin, 'Lords of the Arctic: Wards of the State', *Demographic Review Secretariat, Ministry of Health and Welfare*, pp. 1–88, Ottawa, October (1988). C. J. Irwin, 'Lords of the Arctic: Wards of the State, the Growing Inuit Population, Arctic Resettlement and their Effects on Social and Economic Change', in *Update Number Five, the Review of Demography and its Implications for Economic and Social Policy, Ministry of Health and Welfare*, Ottawa (1988).

7 The setting up of a Royal Commission to investigate the plight of all Canada's 'first nation' peoples was first proposed in the editorial 'To Confront a Crisis', after an unpublished draft of 'Lords of the Arctic: Wards of the State' was leaked to the press, *Globe and Mail*, Toronto, Saturday 15 October 1988.

8 For a discussion of interdisciplinary approaches to social science and the sociology of science see: D. T. Campbell, 'Ethnocentrism of Disciplines and the Fish-Scale Model of Omniscience', in *Interdisciplinary Relationships in the Social Sciences*, ed. M. Sherif and C. W. Sherif (Chicago: Aldine, 1969).

9 C. J. Irwin, *Inuit Ethics and the Priority of the Future Generation*, MA Interdisciplinary Thesis (Anthropology, Religion and Philosophy), University of Manitoba (1981).

10 C. J. Irwin, *Sociocultural Biology: Studies in the Evolution of some Netsilingmiut and other Sociocultural Behaviors*, PhD Dissertation, Social Science, Syracuse University (1985).

11 C. J. Irwin, 'A Study in the Evolution of Ethnocentrism', in *The Sociobiology of Ethnocentrism*, ed. V. Reynolds and V. Falger (London: Croom Helm, 1986) pp. 131–56.

12 C. J. Irwin, 'Les éthiques naturalists et le contrôle du conflict de groupe, dans *Fondements Natureles de L'Éthique*, Sous la direction de Jean-Pierre Changeux, (Paris: Editions Odile Jacob, 1993) pp. 227–65. C. J. Irwin, 'A Study in the Evolution of Ethnocentrism', in *The Sociobiology of Ethnocentrism*, ed. V. Reynolds and V. Falger (London: Croom Helm, 1986) pp. 131–56.

13 C. J. Irwin, 'A Study in the Evolution of Ethnocentrism', in *The Sociobiology of Ethnocentrism*, ed. V. Reynolds and V. Falger (London: Croom Helm, 1986) pp. 131–56.

14 C. J. Irwin, 'Social Conflict and the Failure of Education Policies in Two Deeply Divided Societies: Israel and Northern Ireland', in *Culture and Policy in Northern Ireland*, ed. D. Hastings and G. McFarlane (Belfast: Institute of Irish Studies, Queen's University Belfast, 1997) pp. 97–116. C. J. Irwin, 'Integrated Education: From Theory to Practice in Divided Societies', *Prospects, UNESCO Quarterly Review of Education*, Vol. 22, No. 1 (1992) pp. 67–79.

15 C. J. Irwin, *Peace Making, Discrimination and the Rights of Children to Attend Integrated Schools in Northern Ireland*. A brief on Human Rights violations submitted to the Committee on Conventions and Recommendations of the United Nations Education Scientific and Cultural Organisation, Paris, 31 August 1993.

16 C. J. Irwin, *Education, Peace Building and the Rights of Children to Attend Integrated Schools in Northern Ireland*. A brief on Human Rights violations submitted to the UN Committee on Economic Social and Cultural Rights, Geneva, 21 October 1994. C. J. Irwin, *Peace Making, Discrimination and the Rights of Children to Attend Integrated Schools in Northern Ireland*. A brief on Human Rights violations submitted to the UN Committee on the Rights of the Child, Geneva, 29 July 1994.

17 UN Economic and Social Council; Committee on Economic, Social and Cultural Rights; Consideration of Reports Submitted by States Parties under Articles 16 and 17 of the Covenant, Concluding observations of the Committee on Economic, Social and Cultural Rights, United Kingdom of Great Britain and Northern Ireland. E/C.12/1/Add.19, Geneva, 12 December 1997. UN Committee on the Rights of the Child, Committee on the Rights of the Child, Eighth Session, Consideration of Reports Submitted by States Parties Under Article 44 of the Convention, Concluding observations of the Committee on the Rights of the Child: United Kingdom of Great Britain and Northern Ireland, CRC/C/15/Add.34, Geneva, 12 January 1995.

18 A. Rosenberg, *Sociobiology and the Pre-emption of Social Science* (Baltimore, Maryland: Johns Hopkins University Press, 1980).

19 C. J. Irwin, The Sociocultural Biology of Netsilingmiut Female Infanticide, in *Sociobiology of Sexual and Reproductive Strategies*, ed. A. Rassa, C. Vogel and E. Voland (London: Croom Helm, 1989).

20 D. T. Campbell, 'The Two Distinct Routs Beyond Kin Selection to Ultrasociality: Implications for the Humanities and Social Sciences', in *The Nature of Pro-social Development: Interdisciplinary Theories and Strategies*, ed. D. L. Bridgeman (New York: Academic Press, 1983). D. T. Campbell, 'On the Conflicts Between Biological and Social Evolution and Between Psychology and Moral Tradition', *American Psychologist*, December 1975.

21 D. T. Campbell, 'Systems Theory and Social Experimentation', in *A Science of Goal Formation: American and Soviet Discussions of Cybernetics and Systems Theory*, ed. S. A. Umpleby and V. N. Sadovsky (New York: Hemisphere, 1991).

22 *Agreement Between the Inuit of the Nunavut Settlement Area and Her Majesty the Queen in Right of Canada* (Ottawa: The Minister of Indian Affairs and Northern Development and the Tungavik, 1993).

23 Belfast Agreement (Good Friday Agreement), *Agreement reached in the multi-party negotiations* (Belfast, 10 April 1998). A copy can be found in Appendix 2 of M. Cox, A. Guelke and F. Stephen (eds), *A Farewell to Arms? From 'long war' to long peace in Northern Ireland* (Manchester University Press, 2000).

Introduction

1 For a review of this period of the Northern Ireland peace process see M. Cox, A. Guelke and F. Stephen (eds), *A Farewell to Arms? From 'long war' to long peace in Northern Ireland* (Manchester University Press, 2000).

2 Although, for the most part, the public opinion polls helped the parties to make well-informed political decisions it was still possible for them to lose voter support through errors of judgement in other matters or through the actions or inactions of other parties. For example, it has been suggested that the UUP lost votes in the 2001 general election not only because the IRA failed to decommission but because David Trimble mismanaged the affairs of his party (Leader, 'The poverty of Trimbleism', *Fortnight*, 397, Belfast, July/August, 2001).

3 This is a revised version of two papers that reviewed the role of the polls in the Northern Ireland peace process. I am grateful for the many useful suggestions of both the editor and referees of *Security Dialogue*. C. J. Irwin, 'The People's Peace Process: Northern Ireland and the Role of Public Opinion Polls in Political Negotiations', *Security Dialogue*, Vol. 30, No. 3, September (1999), pp. 105–17. C. J. Irwin, 'Public Opinion During the Peace Process', *Northern Ireland: Paths to Peace, Conference in University College Cork*, 20th and 21st October 2000.

4 I am grateful for the suggestions made by the referee who reviewed an earlier draft of this chapter as a paper for the *Journal of Conflict Resolution*.

5 I am grateful for the many useful suggestions made by the referees and the editor of *International Negotiation* who made many useful suggestions on an earlier draft of this chapter as a paper.

6 I am grateful for the many useful suggestions made by the referees and the editor of the *Journal of Peace Research* who made many useful suggestions on an earlier draft of this chapter as a paper.

7 In addition to M. Cox, A. Guelke and F. Stephen (eds), *A Farewell to Arms? From 'long war' to long peace in Northern Ireland* (Manchester University Press, 2000), see, J. Bowyer Bell, *The Irish Troubles: a Generation of Violence 1967–1992* (Dublin: Gill & Macmillan, 1993) for a comprehensive history of this period in the Northern Ireland conflict.

8 For a review of this period of the Northern Ireland peace process see, M. Cox, A. Guelke and F. Stephen (eds), *A Farewell to Arms? From 'long war' to long peace in Northern Ireland* (Manchester University Press, 2000).

1 Political Negotiations and Public Opinion Polls

1 C. J. Irwin, 'Ulster People Could Decide Way Forward', *Belfast Telegraph*, Tuesday 3 December 1996. C. J. Irwin, 'The FEC. Fair To Meddling?' *Belfast Telegraph*, Wednesday 20 November 1996. C. J. Irwin, 'Hitting a Brick Wall', *Belfast Telegraph*, Tuesday 22 October 1996. C. J. Irwin, 'Ulster Amnesty Rejected', *Belfast Telegraph*, Monday 30 September 1996. C. J. Irwin, 'The Battle for the Middle Ground, *Belfast Telegraph*, Thursday 12 September 1996. C. J. Irwin,

'Changing the Force of Habit', *Belfast Telegraph*, Friday 2 August 1996. C. J. Irwin, 'The Parade Question', *Belfast Telegraph*, Thursday 4 July 1996.

2   T. Hadden, C. Irwin and F. Boal, 'Separation or sharing? the people's choice', Supplement with *Fortnight* 356, Belfast, December 1996.

3   See note 1 above for references.

4   T. Hadden, C. Irwin and F. Boal, 'Separation or sharing? the people's choice', Supplement with *Fortnight* 356, Belfast, December 1996.

5   C. J. Irwin, 'STILL POLLS APART, People longing for real talks to start', *Belfast Telegraph*, Wednesday 9 April 1997. C. J. Irwin, 'Referendums could bypass politicians', *Belfast Telegraph*, Wednesday 9 April 1997. C. J. Irwin, 'DRUMCREE THREE, Rule of law is what people of Northern Ireland want', *Belfast Telegraph*, Tuesday 8 April 1997. C. J. Irwin, 'Wide support for Bill of Rights', *Belfast Telegraph*, Tuesday 8 April 1997. C. J. Irwin, 'TRUCE HOLDS KEY, Sharp divisions on how talks replace the guns', *Belfast Telegraph*, Monday 7 April 1997. C. J. Irwin, 'Voter's query parties' push', *Belfast Telegraph*, Monday 7 April 1997. C. J. Irwin, 'Few believe peace is at hand', *Belfast Telegraph*, Monday 7 April 1997.

6   C. J. Irwin, 'The people's vote', *Belfast Telegraph*, Friday 12 September 1997. C. J. Irwin, '*YES* vote for talks', *Belfast Telegraph*, Thursday, 11 September 1997.

7   C. J. Irwin, 'The Search for a Settlement: the People's Choice', Supplement with *Fortnight* 368, Belfast, February 1998. C. J. Irwin, 'A Comprehensive Settlement', *Belfast Telegraph*, Wednesday 14 January 1998. C. J. Irwin, 'Constitutional Issues', *Belfast Telegraph*, Wednesday 14 January 1998. C. J. Irwin, 'What hope for Council of the Isles?', *Belfast Telegraph*, Wednesday, 14 January 1998. C. J. Irwin, 'Feasibility and reality of north-south bodies', *Belfast Telegraph*, Tuesday 13 January 1998. C. J. Irwin, 'Why Ulster now wants to have new assembly', *Belfast Telegraph*, Monday 12 January 1998. C. J. Irwin, 'Reforming RUC quite 'acceptable', *Belfast Telegraph*, Saturday 10 January 1998. C. J. Irwin, 'Protecting the rights of the people', *Belfast Telegraph*, Saturday 10 January 1998. C. J. Irwin, 'Steps we need to take to win peace', *Belfast Telegraph*, Saturday 10 January 1998.

8   C. J. Irwin, 'Little support for SF agenda', *Belfast Telegraph*, Wednesday 1 April 1998. C. J. Irwin, 'Majority say yes to the search for settlement', *Belfast Telegraph*, Tuesday 31 March 1998. C. J. Irwin, 'Compromise or common ground?', *Belfast Telegraph*, Tuesday 31 March 1998. C. J. Irwin, 'Alternatives to a comprehensive settlement', *Belfast Telegraph*, Tuesday 31 March 1998.

9   C. J. Irwin, 'Implementation of the Belfast Agreement', *Belfast Telegraph*, Thursday 4 March 1999. C. J. Irwin, 'What are the fears of failure?' *Belfast Telegraph*, Thursday 4 March 1999. C. J. Irwin, 'Why the peace package is important', *Belfast Telegraph*, Thursday 4 March 1999. C. J. Irwin, 'Ceasefires, paramilitary activity and decommissioning', *Belfast Telegraph*, Wednesday 3 March 1999. C. J. Irwin, 'Education, Health and Jobs', *Belfast Telegraph*, Wednesday 3 March 1999. C. J. Irwin, '93 per cent say: MAKE THE AGREEMENT WORK', *Belfast Telegraph*, Wednesday 3 March 1999.

10   C. J. Irwin, 'A better way to implement the Belfast Agreement', *Belfast Telegraph*, Monday 17 May 1999.

11   C. J. Irwin, 'Breaking the Rock', *Belfast Telegraph*, Wednesday 27 October 1999. C. J. Irwin, 'Guns, trust and the Agreement', *Belfast Telegraph*, Tuesday 26 October 1999.

12   C. J. Irwin, 'Unionism at the Crossroads: What the people say', *Belfast Telegraph*, Thursday 25 May 2000.

13 N. McAdam and C. Thornton, 'VOTE OF CONFIDENCE FOR TRIMBLE', *Belfast Telegraph*, Friday 27 October 2000.

14 C. J. Irwin, 'The PEOPLE'S peace process', *Belfast Telegraph*, Wednesday 21 February 2001.

15 C. J. Irwin, 'Full implementation key to NI success', *Irish Times*, Friday 23 February 2001. C. J. Irwin, 'It's the Agreement, stupid', *Irish Times*, Friday 23 February 2001.

16 BBC Northern Ireland, *Hearts and Minds*, Thursday 20 September 2001.

17 C. Thornton, 'TRIMBLE BACKED', *Belfast Telegraph*, Thursday 1 November 2001.

18 C. J. Irwin, 'Lords of the Arctic: Wards of the State, a Postscript', *Northern Perspectives*, pp. 19–20, Vol. 17, No. 1, January–March 1989. C. J. Irwin, 'Lords of the Arctic: Wards of the State, a Summary Report', *Northern Perspectives*, pp. 2–12, Vol. 17, No. 1, January–March 1989. C. J. Irwin, 'Lords of the Arctic: Wards of the State', *Demographic Review Secretariat, Ministry of Health and Welfare*, pp. 1–88, Ottawa, October 1988. C. J. Irwin, 'Lords of the Arctic: Wards of the State, the Growing Inuit Population, Arctic Resettlement and their Effects on Social and Economic Change', in *Update Number Five, the Review of Demography and its Implications for Economic and Social Policy, Ministry of Health and Welfare*, Ottawa (1988).

19 The setting up of a Royal Commission to investigate the plight of all Canada's 'first nation' peoples was first proposed in the editorial 'To Confront a Crisis', after an unpublished draft of 'Lords of the Arctic: Wards of the State' was leaked to the press, *Globe and Mail*, Toronto, Saturday 15 October 1988.

2 The Calculus of Agreement

1 G. Mitchell, *Making Peace: the Inside Story of the Making of the Good Friday Agreement* (London: William Heinemann, 1999).

2 P. J. Emerson, *The Politics of Consensus* (Peter Emerson, Rhubarb Cottage, 36 Ballysillan Road, Belfast, 1994). P. J. Emerson (ed.), 'Where Lies the Compromise', *Fortnight Educational Trust*, 7 Lower Crescent, Belfast (1995).

3 Peter Emerson's refinement of the de Borda method involves discounting points awarded to partial votes. In this way a voter is penalised (and certainly not rewarded) for only making their preferred selection of preferences known.

4 T. Hadden, C. Irwin and F. Boal, 'Separation or sharing? The people's choice', Supplement with *Fortnight* 356, Belfast, December 1996.

5 Emerson also got an inconclusive result when he independently tested his methods in a separate piece of research. P. J. Emerson (ed.), 'Preferendum Social Survey', *The de Borda Institute*, 36 Ballysillan Road, Belfast (1998).

6 It should be noted that this particular questionnaire 'In Search of a Settlement', which was the most complex run, was not undertaken as a 'face-to-face' interview. It was given to the informant as a booklet which they could fill out in their home, over a period of several days, if they so wished.

7 *Belfast Telegraph*, Tuesday 31 March 1998.

3 The Drafting of Consensus and the Decommissioning Story

1 C. J. Irwin, 'TRUCE HOLDS KEY, Sharp divisions on how talks replace the guns', *Belfast Telegraph*, Monday 7 April 1997.

2   During the negotiation, drafting and publishing of the questions the convention was observed that options would not be attributed to specified political parties. Consequently only broad political categories will be used here as most parties could guess what the general attribution was. The Unionist parties elected to take part in the talks included the Ulster Unionist Party (UUP), Democratic Unionist Party (DUP) and United Kingdom Unionist Party (UKUP) who would generally hold the views attributed to 'Unionists'. The Loyalist parties, the Progressive Unionist Party (PUP) and Ulster Democratic Party (UDP), who also supported the maintenance of the 'Union' between Northern Ireland and the rest of the United Kingdom, would hold similar views to the other Unionist parties on constitutional issues but would take a more pragmatic approach to issues relating to decommissioning and would therefore often appear to side with centre, Nationalist or Republican parties on such matters.

3   Republicans have traditionally supported the armed struggle for a united Ireland and include Sinn Féin, who were elected to take part in the talks and were affiliated with the Irish Republican Army (IRA), as well as those who supported the Irish National Liberation Army (INLA).

4   The centre parties elected to take part in the talks included the Alliance Party of Northern Ireland, Northern Ireland Women's Coalition and Labour Party of Northern Ireland. The Nationalist, Social Democratic and Labour Party (SDLP), which strove for a united Ireland by peaceful means, would generally line up, in principle, with centre party views on issues relating to decommissioning although, like Loyalists, they would sometimes be more pragmatic and more closely ally themselves with Republican views.

5   C. J. Irwin, '*YES* vote for talks', *Belfast Telegraph*, Thursday 11 September 1997.

6   C. J. Irwin, 'Steps we need to take to win peace', *Belfast Telegraph*, Saturday 10 January 1998.

7   C. J. Irwin, 'Little support for SF agenda', *Belfast Telegraph*, Wednesday 1 April 1998.

8   Nationalists were dominantly represented by the Social Democratic and Labour Party (SDLP) in the 'talks' although 'Nationalists' who wanted a united Ireland by peaceful means could also be found in the Women's Coalition and Labour Party of Northern Ireland as well as Sinn Féin – after they had declared their ceasefire.

9   C. J. Irwin, '93% SAY: MAKE THE AGREEMENT WORK', *Belfast Telegraph*, Wednesday 3 March 1999. C. J. Irwin, 'Cease-fires, Paramilitary Activity and Decommissioning', *Belfast Telegraph*, Wednesday 3 March 1999. C. J. Irwin, Why the peace package is important, *Belfast Telegraph*, Thursday 4 March 1999. C. J. Irwin, 'What are the fears of failure?' *Belfast Telegraph*, Thursday 4 March 1999. C. J. Irwin, 'Implementation of the Belfast Agreement', *Belfast Telegraph*, Thursday 4 March 1999.

10   C. J. Irwin, 'Guns, trust and the Agreement', *Belfast Telegraph*, Tuesday 26 October 1999. C. J. Irwin, 'Breaking the Rock', *Belfast Telegraph*, Wednesday 27 October 1999.

4   Polling as Peace Building

1   D. L. Horowitz, *Ethnic Groups in Conflict* (Berkeley: University of California Press, 1985).

2   T. Hadden, C. Irwin and F. Boal, 'Separation or sharing? The people's choice', Supplement with *Fortnight* 356, Belfast, December 1996.

3 C. J. Irwin, 'STILL POLLS APART', People longing for real talks to start', *Belfast Telegraph*, Wednesday 9 April 1997. C. J. Irwin, 'Referendums could bypass politicians', *Belfast Telegraph*, Wednesday 9 April 1997. C. J. Irwin, 'DRUMCREE THREE', Rule of law is what people of Northern Ireland want', *Belfast Telegraph*, Tuesday 8 April 1997. C. J. Irwin, 'Wide support for Bill of Rights', *Belfast Telegraph*, Tuesday 8 April 1997. C. J. Irwin, 'TRUCE HOLDS KEY', Sharp divisions on how talks replace the guns', *Belfast Telegraph*, Monday 7 April 1997. C. J. Irwin, 'Voters query parties' push', *Belfast Telegraph*, Monday 7 April 1997. C. J. Irwin, 'Few believe peace is at hand', *Belfast Telegraph*, Monday 7 April 1997.

4 T. Hadden, C. Irwin and F. Boal, 'Separation or sharing? the people's choice', Supplement with *Fortnight* 356, Belfast, December 1996.

5 M. Simpson, 'YOUR VERDICT', *Belfast Telegraph*, Monday 7 April 1997.

6 M. Simpson, '92% SAY YES', *Belfast Telegraph*, Thursday 11 September 1998.

7 M. Simpson, 'Put talks package to vote', *Belfast Telegraph*, Friday 12 September 1998.

8 Political Staff, 'Poll signals backing for new assembly', *Belfast Telegraph*, Monday 12 January 1998.

9 M. Purdy, 'NORTH–SOUTH LINKS VERDICT', *Belfast Telegraph*, Tuesday 13 January 1998.

10 N. McAdam, 'Poll reveals Ulster yes for islands council', *Belfast Telegraph*, Wednesday 14 January 1998.

11 P. Connolly, '77% SAY YES', *Belfast Telegraph*, Tuesday 31 March 1998.

12 M. Purdy, 'DUP voters want deal to work: poll', *Belfast Telegraph*, Wednesday 3 March 1999.

13 N. McAdam, '65% STILL FOR DEAL', *Belfast Telegraph*, Tuesday 26 October 1999.

14 C. J. Irwin, '*YES* vote for talks', *Belfast Telegraph*, Thursday 11 September 1997.

15 C. J. Irwin, 'Steps we need to take to win peace', *Belfast Telegraph*, Saturday 10 January 1998.

16 C. J. Irwin, 'The people's vote', *Belfast Telegraph*, Friday 12 September 1997.

17 C. J. Irwin, 'Reforming RUC quite "acceptable"', *Belfast Telegraph*, Saturday 10 January 1998. C. J. Irwin, 'Protecting the rights of the people', *Belfast Telegraph*, Saturday 10 January 1998. C. J. Irwin, 'Steps we need to take to win peace', *Belfast Telegraph*, Saturday 10 January 1998.

18 C. J. Irwin, 'Why Ulster now wants to have new assembly', *Belfast Telegraph*, Monday 12 January 1998.

19 C. J. Irwin, 'Feasibility and reality of north–south bodies', *Belfast Telegraph*, Tuesday 13 January 1998.

20 C. J. Irwin, 'A Comprehensive Settlement', *Belfast Telegraph*, Wednesday 14 January 1998. C. J. Irwin, 'Constitutional Issues', *Belfast Telegraph*, Wednesday 14 January 1998. C. J. Irwin, 'What hope for Council of the Isles?', *Belfast Telegraph*, Wednesday 14 January 1998.

21 C. J. Irwin, *In Search of a Settlement, Summary Tables of Principal Statistical Results*, Institute of Irish Studies, The Queen's University of Belfast, January 1998, pp. 1–100.

22 C. J. Irwin, 'Feasibility and reality of north–south bodies', *Belfast Telegraph*, Tuesday 13 January 1998.

23 C. J. Irwin, 'Alternatives to a comprehensive settlement', *Belfast Telegraph*, Tuesday 31 March 1998.

24 C. J. Irwin, 'Little support for SF agenda', *Belfast Telegraph*, Wednesday 1 April 1998.

25 P. Connolly, '77% SAY YES', *Belfast Telegraph*, Tuesday 31 March 1998.

26 C. J. Irwin, 'Guns, trust and the Agreement', *Belfast Telegraph*, Tuesday 26 October 1999.

27 C. J. Irwin, 'Ulster People Could Decide Way Forward', *Belfast Telegraph*, Tuesday 3 December 1996. C. J. Irwin, 'The FEC...Fair To Meddling?' *Belfast Telegraph*, Wednesday 20 November 1996. C. J. Irwin, 'Hitting a Brick Wall', *Belfast Telegraph*, Tuesday 22 October 1996. C. J. Irwin, 'Ulster Amnesty Rejected', *Belfast Telegraph*, Monday 30 September 1996. C. J. Irwin, 'The Battle for the Middle Ground', *Belfast Telegraph*, Thursday 12 September 1996. C. J. Irwin, 'Changing the Force of Habit', *Belfast Telegraph*, Friday 2 August 1996. C. J. Irwin, 'The Parade Question', *Belfast Telegraph*, Thursday 4 July 1996.

28 T. Hadden, C. Irwin and F. Boal, 'Separation or sharing? the people's choice', Supplement with *Fortnight* 356, Belfast, December 1996.

29 G. Mitchell, *Making Peace: the Inside Story of the Making of the Good Friday Agreement* (London: William Heinemann, 1999).

30 For reviews of violent conflicts around the world see: A. P. Schmid, 'Early Warning of Violent Conflicts: Causal Approaches', in *Violent Crime and Conflicts*, ed. P. Alex Schmid, International Scientific and Professional Advisory Council of the United Nations Crime Prevention and Criminal Justice Program, Milan (1997). B. Harff, and T. R. Gurr, 'Systematic Early Warning of Humanitarian Emergencies', *Journal of Peace Research*, Vol. 35, No. 5 (1998), pp. 551–79.

31 For a review of group conflicts in general see: Minority Rights Group (ed.), *World Directory of Minorities* (London: Minority Rights Group International, 1997).

5   Peace Building and Public Policy

1 For a review of the parades issue see: D. Bryan, *Ritual, Tradition and Control: the Politics of Orange Parades* (London: Pluto Press, 2000).

2 For example see: F. W. Boal, 'Territoriality on the Shankill-Falls divide, Belfast', *Irish Geography*, Vol. 6, No. 1 (1969), pp. 30–50. P. Doherty and M. A. Poole, *Ethnic Residential Segregation in Belfast* (Coleraine: University of Ulster, Centre for the Study of Conflict, 1995).

3 M. C. Keane, 'Segregation Processes in Public Sector Housing', in P. Doherty (ed.), *Geographical Perspectives on the Belfast Region, Geographical Society of Ireland Special Publications No. 5* (Jordanstown: University of Ulster, 1990).

4 For a review of the policing issue see: M. O'Rawe and L. Moore, *Human Rights on Duty – Principles for Better Policing: International Lessons for Northern Ireland* (Belfast: Committee on the Administration of Justice, 1997).

5 SACHR, 'Chapter 6 Police Matters', in the *Twenty-First Report of the Standing Advisory Commission on Human Rights*, Report for 1995–96 (London: HMSO, 1996).

6 C. J. Irwin, 'Social Conflict and the Failure of Education Policies in Two Deeply Divided Societies: Israel and Northern Ireland', in *Culture and Policy in Northern Ireland*, ed. D. Hastings and G. McFarlane (Belfast: Institute of Irish Studies, Queen's University Belfast, 1997) pp. 97–116. C. J. Irwin, 'Integrated Education: From Theory to Practice in Divided Societies', *Prospects, UNESCO Quarterly Review of Education*, Vol. 22, No. 1 (1992) pp. 67–79.

7 The primary focus of my research had been an empirical study in the social psychology of integrated education. For social values see, M. G. Montgomery, *Integration by Chance or Design?* (Queen's University of Belfast: unpublished Master of Education Dissertation, 1993) and for a general review see C. Moffat (ed.), *Education Together for a Change: Integrated Education and Community Relations in Northern Ireland* (Belfast: Fortnight Educational Trust, 1993).

8 C. J. Irwin, *Peace Making, Discrimination and the Rights of Children to Attend Integrated Schools in Northern Ireland*. A brief on Human Rights violations submitted to the Committee on Conventions and Recommendations of the United Nations Education Scientific and Cultural Organisation, Paris, 31 August 1993.

9 C. J. Irwin, *Education, Peace Building and the Rights of Children to Attend Integrated Schools in Northern Ireland*. A brief on Human Rights violations submitted to the UN Committee on Economic Social and Cultural Rights, Geneva, 21 October 1994. C. J. Irwin, *Peace Making, Discrimination and the Rights of Children to Attend Integrated Schools in Northern Ireland*. A brief on Human Rights violations submitted to the UN Committee on the Rights of the Child, Geneva, 29 July 1994.

10 UN Economic and Social Council, 'Committee on Economic, Social and Cultural Rights, Consideration of Reports Submitted by States Parties under Articles 16 and 17 of the Covenant, Concluding observations of the Committee on Economic, Social and Cultural Rights, United Kingdom of Great Britain and Northern Ireland', E/C.12/1/Add.19, Geneva, 12 December 1997.

11 D. Magill and S. Rose (eds), *Fair Employment Law in Northern Ireland: Debates and Issues*, Employment Equality in Northern Ireland, Vol. I (Belfast: Standing Advisory Commission on Human Rights, 1996). E. McLaughlin and P. Quirk (eds), *Policy Aspects of Employment Equality in Northern Ireland*, Employment Equality in Northern Ireland, Vol. II (Belfast: Standing Advisory Commission on Human Rights, 1996). J. McVey and N. Hutson, *Public Views and Experiences of Fair Employment and Equality Issues in Northern Ireland*, Employment Equality in Northern Ireland, Vol. III (Belfast: Standing Advisory Commission on Human Rights, 1996).

12 For a review of the Irish language issue see: G. McCoy, 'Rhetoric and Realpolitik: the Irish Language Movement and the British Government', in *Culture and Policy in Northern Ireland*, ed. D. Hastings and G. McFarlane (Institute of Irish Studies, Queen's University Belfast, 1997), pp. 117–38.

12 The Future of the Peace Process

1 N. McAdam and C. Thornton, 'VOTE OF CONFIDENCE FOR TRIMBLE', *Belfast Telegraph*, Friday 27 October 2000.

2 C. J. Irwin, 'The PEOPLE'S peace process', *Belfast Telegraph*, Wednesday 21 February 2001.

3 C. J. Irwin, 'Full implementation key to NI success', *Irish Times*, Friday 23 February 2001. C. J. Irwin, 'It's the Agreement, stupid', *Irish Times*, Friday 23 February 2001.

4 For a general discussion of the failures of different systems of voting in deeply divided societies see D. L. Horowitz, *Ethnic Groups in Conflict* (Los Angeles: University of California Press, 1985).

5 D. L. Horowitz, *Paths to Conciliation: Northern Ireland and the World of Severely Divided Societies*, The Opsahl Memorial Lecture, The Queen's University of Belfast, 12 December 2000.

6   Leader, 'The poverty of Trimbleism', *Fortnight* 397, Belfast, July/August 2001.
7   Northern Ireland Human Rights Commission, *Making a Bill of Rights for Northern Ireland* (Belfast: Northern Ireland Human Rights Commission, 2001).

Conclusion

1   D. Ervine, 'Why we need help on the Good Friday Agreement', *Belfast Telegraph*, Wednesday 29 November 2000.
2   BBC Northern Ireland, *Hearts and Minds*, Thursday 20 September 2001.
3   A. King and G. Jones, 'Treat the IRA like bin Laden', *The Daily Telegraph*, Thursday 4 October 2001.
4   C. Thornton, 'TRIMBLE BACKED', *Belfast Telegraph*, Thursday 1 November 2001.

Select Bibliography

Bell, J. Bowyer, *The Irish Troubles: a Generation of Violence 1967–1992* (Dublin: Gill & Macmillan, 1993).

Boal, F. W., 'Territoriality on the Shankill-Falls divide, Belfast', *Irish Geography*, Vol. 6, No. 1 (1969).

Bryan, D., *Ritual, Tradition and Control: the Politics of Orange Parades* (London: Pluto Press, 2000).

Campbell, D. T., 'Ethnocentrism of Disciplines and the Fish-Scale Model of Omniscience', in *Interdisciplinary Relationships in the Social Sciences*, ed. M. Sherif and C. W. Sherif (Chicago: Aldine, 1969).

Campbell, D. T., 'On the Conflicts between Biological and Social Evolution and between Psychology and Moral Tradition', *American Psychologist*, December (1975).

Campbell, D. T., 'The Two Distinct Routs Beyond Kin Selection to Ultrasociality: Implications for the Humanities and Social Sciences', in *The Nature of Pro-social Development: Interdisciplinary Theories and Strategies*, ed. D. L. Bridgeman (New York: Academic Press, 1983).

Campbell, D. T., 'Systems Theory and Social Experimentation', in *A Science of Goal Formation: American and Soviet Discussions of Cybernetics and Systems Theory*, ed. S. A. Umpleby and V. N. Sadovsky (New York: Hemisphere, 1991).

Cox, M., Guelke, A. and Stephen, F. (eds), *A Farewell to Arms? From 'Long War' to Long Peace in Northern Ireland* (Manchester University Press, 2000).

Doherty, P. and Poole, M. A., *Ethnic Residential Segregation in Belfast* (Coleraine: University of Ulster, Centre for the Study of Conflict, 1995).

Emerson, P. J., *The Politics of Consensus* (Peter Emerson, Rhubarb Cottage, 36 Ballysillan Road, Belfast, 1994).

Emerson, P. J. (ed.), 'Where Lies the Compromise', *Fortnight Educational Trust*, 7 Lower Crescent, Belfast (1995).

Emerson, P. J. (ed.), 'Preferendum Social Survey', *The de Borda Institute*, 36 Ballysillan Road, Belfast (1998).

Hadden, T., Irwin, C. and Boal, F., *Separation or Sharing? The People's Choice.* Supplement with *Fortnight* 356. Belfast, December (1996).

Harff, B. and Gurr, T. R., 'Systematic Early Warning of Humanitarian Emergencies', *Journal of Peace Research*, Vol. 35, No. 5 (1998).

Horowitz, D. L., *Ethnic Groups in Conflict* (Berkeley: University of California Press, 1985).

Irwin, C. J., 'Alone through the Northwest Passage', *Geographical Magazine*, July (1971).

Irwin, C. J., 'Half-way Mark for a Mighty Endeavour', *Geographical Magazine*, April (1972).

Irwin, C. J., 'Trek Across Arctic America', *National Geographic Magazine*, March (1974).

Irwin, C. J., 'Inuit Navigation, Empirical Reasoning and Survival', *Journal of the Royal Institute of Navigation*, Vol. 38, No. 2 (1985).

Irwin, C. J., 'A Study in the Evolution of Ethnocentrism', in *The Sociobiology of Ethnocentrism*, ed. V. Reynolds and V. Falger (London: Croom Helm, 1986).

Irwin, C. J., 'Lords of the Arctic: Wards of the State, a Postscript', *Northern Perspectives*, Vol. 17, No. 1, January–March (1989).

Irwin, C. J., 'Lords of the Arctic: Wards of the State, a Summary Report', *Northern Perspectives*, Vol. 17, No. 1, January–March (1989).

Irwin, C. J., 'The Sociocultural Biology of Netsilingmiut Female Infanticide', in *Sociobiology of Sexual and Reproductive Strategies*, ed. A. Rassa, C. Vogel and E. Voland (London: Croom Helm, 1989).

Irwin, C. J., 'The Inuit and the Evolution of Limited Group Conflict', in *Sociobiology and Conflict*, ed. J. van der Dennen and V. Falger (London: Chapman and Hall, 1990).

Irwin, C. J., 'Integrated Education: From Theory to Practice in Divided Societies', *Prospects, UNESCO Quarterly Review of Education*, Vol. 22, No. 1 (1992).

Irwin, C. J., 'Les éthiques naturalists et le contrôle du conflict de groupe', dans *Fondements Natureles de L'Éthique*, Sous la direction de Jean-Pierre Changeux (Paris: Editions Odile Jacob, 1993).

Irwin, C. J., 'Social Conflict and the Failure of Education Policies in Two Deeply Divided Societies: Israel and Northern Ireland', in *Culture and Policy in Northern Ireland*, ed. D. Hastings and G. McFarlane (Belfast: Institute of Irish Studies, Queen's University Belfast, 1997).

Irwin, C. J., *The Search for a Settlement: the People's Choice*. Supplement with *Fortnight* 368. Belfast, February (1998).

Irwin, C. J., 'The People's Peace Process: Northern Ireland and the Role of Public Opinion Polls in Political Negotiations', *Security Dialogue*, Vol. 30, No. 3, September (1999).

Keane, M. C., 'Segregation Processes in Public Sector Housing', in P. Doherty (ed.), *Geographical Perspectives on the Belfast Region, Geographical Society of Ireland Special Publications No. 5* (Jordanstown: University of Ulster, 1990).

Magill, D. and Rose, S. (eds), *Fair Employment Law in Northern Ireland: Debates and Issues*, Employment Equality in Northern Ireland, Vol. I (Belfast: Standing Advisory Commission on Human Rights, 1996).

McCoy, G., 'Rhetoric and Realpolitik: the Irish Language Movement and the British Government', in *Culture and Policy in Northern Ireland*, ed. D. Hastings and G. McFarlane (Institute of Irish Studies, Queen's University Belfast, 1997).

McLaughlin, E. and Quirk, P. (eds), *Policy Aspects of Employment Equality in Northern Ireland*, Employment Equality in Northern Ireland, Vol. II (Belfast: Standing Advisory Commission on Human Rights, 1996).

McVey, J. and Hutson, N., *Public Views and Experiences of Fair Employment and Equality Issues in Northern Ireland*, Employment Equality in Northern Ireland, Vol. III (Belfast: Standing Advisory Commission on Human Rights, 1996).

Minority Rights Group (eds), *World Directory of Minorities*, Minority Rights Group International (London, 1997).

Mitchell, G., *Making Peace: the Inside Story of the Making of the Good Friday Agreement*, (London: William Heinemann, 1999).

Moffat, C. (ed.), *Education Together for a Change: Integrated Education and Community Relations in Northern Ireland* (Belfast: Fortnight Educational Trust, 1993).

Northern Ireland Human Rights Commission, *Making a Bill of Rights for Northern Ireland* (Belfast: Northern Ireland Human Rights Commission, 2001).

O'Rawe, M. and Moore, L., *Human Rights on Duty – Principles for Better Policing: International Lessons for Northern Ireland* (Belfast: Committee on the Administration of Justice, 1997).

Rosenberg, A., *Sociobiology and the Pre-emption of Social Science* (Baltimore, Maryland: Johns Hopkins University Press, 1980).

SACHR, 'Chapter 6 Police Matters', in the *Twenty-First Report of the Standing Advisory Commission on Human Rights*, Report for 1995–96 (London: HMSO, 1996).

Schmid, A. P., 'Early Warning of Violent Conflicts: Causal Approaches', in *Violent Crime and Conflicts*, ed. Alex P. Schmid, International Scientific and Professional Advisory Council of the United Nations Crime Prevention and Criminal Justice Programme, Milan (1997).

UN Economic and Social Council, Committee on Economic, Social and Cultural Rights; Consideration of Reports Submitted be States Parties under Articles 16 and 17 of the Covenant, Concluding Observations of the Committee on Economic, Social and Cultural Rights, United Kingdom of Great Britain and Northern Ireland, E/C.12/1/Add.19, Geneva, 12 December (1997).

Index